CW01084252

THE SHAPING OF ULSTER PRESBYTERIAN BELIEF AND PRACTICE, 1770–1840

The Shaping of Ulster Presbyterian Belief and Practice, 1770–1840

ANDREW R. HOLMES

OXFORD

UNIVERSITY PRESS

OXFORD
UNIVERSITY PRESS

Great Clarendon Street, Oxford OX2 6DP

Oxford University Press is a department of the University of Oxford.
It furthers the University's objective of excellence in research, scholarship,
and education by publishing worldwide in

Oxford New York

Auckland Cape Town Dar es Salaam Hong Kong Karachi
Kuala Lumpur Madrid Melbourne Mexico City Nairobi
New Delhi Shanghai Taipei Toronto

With offices in

Argentina Austria Brazil Chile Czech Republic France Greece
Guatemala Hungary Italy Japan Poland Portugal Singapore
South Korea Switzerland Thailand Turkey Ukraine Vietnam

Oxford is a registered trade mark of Oxford University Press
in the UK and in certain other countries

Published in the United States
by Oxford University Press Inc., New York

© Andrew R. Holmes 2006

The moral rights of the author have been asserted
Database right Oxford University Press (maker)

First published 2006

British Library Cataloguing in Publication Data
Data available

Library of Congress Cataloging in Publication Data
Holmes, Andrew R., 1977–
The shaping of Ulster Presbyterian belief and practice, 1770–1840
Andrew R. Holmes.
Includes bibliographical references amd index.
ISBN-13: 978-0-19-928865-6 (alk. paper)
ISBN-10: 0-19-928865-8 (alk. paper)
1. General Synod of Ulster—Customs and practices.
2. General Synod of Ulster—Doctrines.
3. Presbyterian Church in Ireland—History.
4. Ulster (Northern Ireland and Ireland)—Church history—18th century.
5. Ulster (Northern Ireland and Ireland)—Church history—19th century.
I. Title.
BX9060.H58 2006
285'.241609033—dc22   2006021300

Typeset by
SPI Publisher Services, Pondicherry, India
Printed in Great Britain on acid-free paper by
Biddles Ltd., King's Lynn, Norfolk
ISBN   978-0-19-928865-6

To Mum and Dad

Acknowledgements

This book began as a Ph.D. thesis submitted to Queen's University, Belfast, in 2002. For financial assistance during that time I wish to thank the Arts and Humanities Research Board. I was able to carry out additional research and revise the text for publication while a Research Associate at the Academy for Irish Cultural Heritages, University of Ulster, Magee. I wish to record my thanks to Brian Graham, formerly Director of the Academy, for giving me the space to do so and for his encouragement and wise counsel. I would also like to thank my colleagues at the Institute of Irish Studies at Queens, especially the Director, Dominic Bryan, for providing a stimulating environment in which to finalize the text for publication.

I offer my sincere thanks for all their courtesy and assistance to the staff and librarians of the Belfast Central Library, the Linenhall Library, the Presbyterian Historical Society of Ireland, the Public Record Office of Northern Ireland, and the library of Queen's University, Belfast. In particular I would like to thank the following individuals: Alan McMillan, assistant secretary of the Presbyterian Historical Society, for his unfailing help during time spent consulting materials held by the Society in Church House, Belfast; Ian McElhinny of the Board of Finance and Personnel in Church House who graciously facilitated access to the various records located in the strong room; Deirdre Wildy and Michael Smallman at Queens who took an interest in my research and offered assistance above and beyond the call of duty; and Stephen Gregory, librarian of the Gamble Library in Union Theological College, who granted me unprecedented access to the manuscript and pamphlet material under his care. His encouragement and friendship are especially acknowledged.

For permission to quote from manuscript collections I would like to thank the Deputy Keeper of the Records, Public Record Office of Northern Ireland; Patricia Walker, Belfast Public Libraries; the Revd Dr Donald J. Watts, Clerk of the General Assembly and General Secretary of the Presbyterian Church in Ireland; the Presbyterian Historical Society of Ireland; and the Faculty of Union Theological

College, especially Professor L. S. Kirkpatrick. Parts of this book originally appeared in *Studies in Church History* and I gratefully acknowledge the permission of the Editors to reproduce material from the following essays: 'Community and discipline in Ulster Presbyterianism, 1770–1840', in Kate Cooper and Jeremy Gregory (eds.), *Retribution, repentance, and reconciliation*, Studies in Church History, 40 (Woodbridge, 2004) and 'Ulster Presbyterianism as a popular religious culture, 1750–1860', in Kate Cooper and Jeremy Gregory (eds.), *Elite and Popular Religion*, Studies in Church History, 42 (Woodbridge, 2006).

For their practical assistance I am indebted to Kilian McDade, who drew the maps; the staff at Oxford University Press who have been remarkably helpful and gracious, particularly Lucy Qureshi, Jenny Wagstaffe, Dorothy McCarthy, Enid Barker, Elizabeth Robottom, and David Sanders; and to my colleagues at Queen's, Diarmuid Kennedy and Elaine Yeates (Centre for Data Digitization and Analysis) for supplying the digital image for the book cover.

I have incurred many intellectual and personal debts to a variety of scholars. I am grateful to the examiners of my thesis, Sean Connolly and David Bebbington, for their continued support and for questioning my ideas with rigour and good humour. My supervisor, David Hayton, deserves special thanks. His ready wit, encouragement, and friendship have made me a better historian. David W. Miller kindly read parts of this book and his invaluable comments have saved me from numerous errors. I wish to record my thanks to others who have helped in a variety of ways; Allan Blackstock, Stewart J. Brown, Frank Ferguson, Neal Garnham, Crawford Gribben, Myrtle Hill, Finlay Holmes, David Livingstone, Ian McBride, Mark Noll, Mark Smith, Norman Vance, and Stephen Williams. Needless to say, none of these are responsible for any errors of fact or interpretation contained in this book. The author alone is responsible.

Numerous friends and family members, especially my sister Deborah, have encouraged me throughout my university career. I want to thank my wife, Jillian, for her love and support and for dragging me away from work when it needed to be done. My next book will be dedicated to her. It is fitting that my first book should be dedicated to my Mum and Dad, both typically untypical Presbyterians, who have shown me constant love and support throughout my time at university and beyond.

Andrew R. Holmes

Belfast
July 2006

Contents

List of Table and Maps

Abbreviations and Editorial Note

AB	Antiburgher
B	Burgher
BCL, Bigger Collection	Bigger Collection, Belfast Central Library
Church House, strong room	Strong room, Presbyterian Church House, Fisherwick Place, Belfast
Code (1825) and (1841)	*The constitution and discipline of the Presbyterian Church; with a directory for the celebration of ordinances, and the performance of ministerial duties* (Belfast, 1825). A revised edition produced in 1841.
Confession	*The Confession of Faith; agreed upon by the assembly of divines at Westminster, with the assistance of the commissioners of the Church of Scotland ... Approved by the General Assembly 1647.* Contained in, *The Confession of Faith; the Larger and Shorter Catechisms, with the Scripture proofs at large* ... ([1835] Inverness, 1976)
Directory	*The directory for the public worship of God; agreed upon by the assembly of divines at Westminster, with the assistance of commissioners from the Church of Scotland* [1645] [Included with *Confession*]
GSU	General Synod of Ulster
Larger Catechism	*The Larger Catechism; agreed upon by the assembly of divines at Westminster, with the assistance of commissioners from the Church of Scotland* [1648] [Included with *Confession*]
MASAB	Minutes of the Associate Synod, Antiburgher [1788–1818] (held in UTC)
MASB	Minutes of the Associate Synod, Burgher [1779–1818] (held in UTC)
MGA i–ii	*Minutes of the General Assembly*

MPSI	*Minutes and proceedings of the Presbyterian Synod of Ireland, distinguished by the name Seceders* (1822–40)
MRSU	*Minutes of the Remonstrant Synod of Ireland* (1828–40)
OSMI	*Ordnance Survey Memoirs of Ireland*, 40 vols., eds. Angélique Day, Patrick McWilliams, Nóirín Dobson, Lisa English (Belfast, 1990–8)
PA	Presbytery of Antrim
Pby	Presbytery
PHS	Presbyterian Historical Society of Ireland, Presbyterian Church House, Fisherwick Place, Belfast
PRONI	Public Record Office of Northern Ireland
QUB	Queen's University, Belfast
Rem.	Remonstrant
RGSU i–iii (1691–1820)	*Records of the General Synod of Ulster from 1691–1820*, 3 vols. (Belfast, 1897–8)
RGSU (1821–40)	*Minutes of the General Synod of Ulster* (Belfast, 1821–40)
RP	Reformed Presbyterian
Sec.	Seceder
Shorter Catechism	*The Shorter Catechism; agreed upon by the assembly of divines at Westminster, with the assistance of commissioners from the Church of Scotland* [1648] [Contained in *Confession*]
UTC	Union Theological College, Belfast

EDITORIAL NOTE

Quotations from manuscript sources have been modernized throughout the text. Footnote references to contemporary material published before 1870 have been given in short title form. Full title and authorial details are given in the bibliography. The author and title details of articles in periodicals have been given where possible.

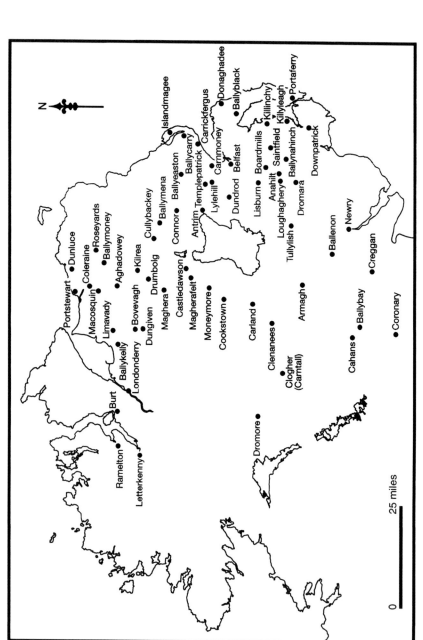

Map. 1. Principal places mentioned in the text

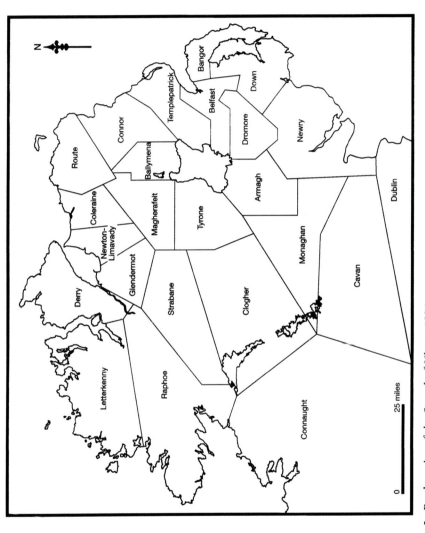

Map. 2. Presbyteries of the Synod of Ulster, 1834

Introduction

This book considers the religious beliefs and practices of Presbyterians in the north-eastern part of Ireland and how they developed over time in a period of religious, economic, social, and political upheaval. The historians who have written about Ulster Presbyterianism, the largest Protestant denomination in the north of Ireland, see the decades between 1770 and 1840 as crucial to the modern development of the denomination and of Ulster society in general. Hitherto the focus of academic historians in particular has been upon the political implications of Presbyterian theology as a way to explain the origins of the United Irish movement, the involvement of Presbyterians in the 1798 rebellion, and their swift conversion to support for the Union with Great Britain thereafter. Yet the changes associated with this period also provide a stimulating context in which to assess the changing character of Presbyterian religious life. The year 1770 marks the high point of New Light or moderate theological opinion within the Synod of Ulster, the largest Presbyterian grouping in Ireland. For once nineteenth-century conservative and liberal commentators were agreed in their assessment of the spiritual state of the Synod. According to the evangelical Thomas Witherow, Professor of Church History at Magee College, Derry, between 1865 and 1890, the spiritual temperature of Presbyterianism in the late eighteenth century approached freezing-point; 'There was ice in the pulpit—there was snow in the pew.'[1] The most prominent Irish Unitarian of the period, Henry Montgomery, agreed that by 1780 there was 'a nominal orthodoxy amidst a real indifference to all doctrinal opinions, or

---

[1] T. Witherow, *Three prophets of our own* (Belfast, 1855), 19.

a positive dislike to the recognised standards of the church'. Consequently few congregations were established and older ones 'were unable to maintain their ground'.[2] By the end of the century over two-thirds of the presbyteries belonging to the Synod of Ulster did not require from licentiates and ministers formal adherence to the *Westminster Confession of Faith*, the doctrinal standard of the church.[3] However, by 1840, the entire outlook of the Synod had been transformed. Presbyterian evangelicalism had been rising to prominence within the Synod from the early 1800s, resulting in greater religious devotion and the reform of church structures. These developments paved the way for the unification of the Synod of Ulster and the Secession Synod in 1840 to form the present-day General Assembly of the Presbyterian Church in Ireland and, more spectacularly, to the revival of 1859.

Informed by the work of recent historians of religion, this study breaks new ground by examining the religious beliefs and practices of Ulster Presbyterians in all their variety. In order to do so, two interrelated questions are addressed: how should historians characterize Ulster Presbyterianism, and, what made a Presbyterian a Presbyterian? By attempting to answer these questions, I hope to illuminate four key themes. The first concerns the symbiotic relationship between the beliefs and practices prescribed by the church and those held by the laity, in particular, the connection between lay practice and the changes promoted by the rise to cultural and ecclesiastical prominence of evangelicalism from the 1790s. Second, there will be an emphasis upon the variety of Presbyterianism in terms of theological belief, religious commitment, social standing, gender, and regional location. The third theme is that of the interaction between various Presbyterian groupings and between ministers, the laity, and neighbours. Finally, the integrity and importance of personal religious belief will be stressed, which allows for a more satisfactory assessment of personal motivation and how people understood their relationship with God, the world, the church, and

---

[2] H. Montgomery, 'Outlines of the history of Presbyterianism in Ireland', *Irish Unitarian Magazine, and Bible Christian*, 2 (1847), 233–4.

[3] J. M. Barkley, *The Westminster formularies in Irish Presbyterianism* (Belfast, 1956), 13.

with each other. This does not entail a lack of rigour when assessing the motivations of historical figures or the divorcing of ideas from the cultural context by which they are shaped. It does mean that the symbiotic relationship between religious beliefs and their environment will be stressed rather than attempting to explain religious change solely by reference to factors apart from religious beliefs.

This book considers the three principal influences that shaped Presbyterian belief and practice in this period, namely, tradition, reform, and revival. Tradition has a dual meaning. On the one hand it refers to the Presbyterian theological tradition as enshrined in the Westminster standards, adopted by the General Assembly of the Church of Scotland between 1645 and 1648 and subsequently accepted by Presbyterians in Ireland. These comprised the *Westminster Confession of Faith*, the *Larger* and *Shorter Catechisms*, the *Directories for Public* and *Family Worship*, and the *Form of presbyterial church government*. On the other, tradition indicates those beliefs and practices of long continuance held by the laity that combined theological orthodoxy, social utility, and customary belief. The second term, reform, refers to the forces of reform that attempted to overhaul the structures and beliefs of the church and remove the popular, or traditional, accretions upon official Presbyterian belief and practice. These forces were a product of economic developments, the commercialization of the economy, the Enlightenment imperative to improve the morals of society, and the rise to social prominence of evangelicalism. Finally, for Presbyterian evangelicals, the programme of reform they embarked upon from the 1820s was stimulated by a broader revival of religion from the 1790s, entailed a revival of traditional Presbyterian practice as laid down in the Westminster standards, and would act as a stimulus to a further revival of religion within the denomination. The reforms that were initiated by evangelicals in the 1820s and 1830s laid the foundation for the Reformed and evangelical ethos of Presbyterianism for the rest of the nineteenth century. Presbyterian evangelicalism was not an exotic import from Methodism or the Church of Ireland. Certainly, it was shaped by the same social and cultural context as those denominations, but the origins of the movement within Presbyterianism may be traced to the Presbyterian theological tradition itself and how that was articulated and shaped by Old Light and Seceder Presbyterians in the eighteenth century. Rather than seeing evangelicalism as a byword for religious enthusiasm and unbridled individualism, this book defines it as a movement for reformation and revival within Presbyterianism that ultimately created the conditions for the 1859 revival.

Presbyterianism came to Ireland with the arrival of Scottish settlers to Ulster in the early years of the seventeenth century.[4] Over the following century they consolidated a separate ecclesiastical and political identity in the north-eastern counties of Ireland, particularly Antrim, Down, and Londonderry, through the establishment of congregations, presbyteries, and a General Synod in 1690. In the eighteenth century, the coherence of the community was disrupted as Presbyterianism fractured along doctrinal and social lines. In the 1720s the General Synod of Ulster experienced internal controversy over subscription to the *Westminster Confession of Faith*, which led to the formation of the numerically small non-subscribing Presbytery of Antrim. The members of this presbytery cultivated links with those non-subscribers who, for a variety of reasons, had remained within the Synod and who would facilitate the rise to prominence of moderate theological views known as New Light. This tendency was fitfully opposed within the Synod by a large yet inchoate Old Light party who comprised the majority of ministers but who did not possess the social and cultural clout of their opponents. From the 1790s onwards, the dominance of New Light refinement was eroded gradually by the reawakening of conservative and evangelical Presbyterianism. Led by Henry Cooke, the most prominent Presbyterian of the nineteenth century and figurehead of the evangelical movement, the conservative majority in 1829 forced out of the Synod a non-subscribing and, in the majority of cases, Arian minority who were direct descendants of the New Light party and who subsequently formed their own Remonstrant Synod of Ulster. For the rest of the nineteenth century, evangelicalism was the dominant voice within Ulster Presbyterianism.

Two other groups criticized the laxity of the Synod of Ulster in the eighteenth century, the Seceders and the Covenanters. The Secession

---

[4] R. F. G. Holmes, *Our Irish Presbyterian heritage* (Belfast, 1985); R. Gillespie, 'The Presbyterian revolution in Ulster, 1600–1690', in W. J. Sheils and D. Wood (eds.), *The churches, Ireland, and the Irish*, Studies in Church History, 25 (Oxford, 1989), 159–70.

was formed after a series of conflicts in the Scottish General Assembly in the early eighteenth century over the issues of lay patronage of church livings and the doctrines of grace.[5] For Seceders, these doctrines were Calvinist and stressed human sinfulness, the need for divine grace mediated through the person and work of Christ, the particular redemption of the elect, the free offer of the gospel to all, faith as an affectionate commitment to Christ, and the possibility of obtaining assurance of salvation. In 1746 Seceders established their first Irish congregation at Lylehill in County Antrim and, despite division into Antiburgher and Burgher synods the following year over the issue of whether or not it was appropriate to take the Burgess Oath (1744) in some Scottish burghs, became the growth sector of Presbyterianism before 1820, appointing forty-six ministers between 1746 and 1792.[6] The Burgher Synod tended to be more moderate and accommodating than the Antiburghers, largely because it had gained its independence from their parent body in Scotland at an earlier date. Compared with their Scottish co-religionists, the Irish Secession remained more conservative and unified, though over time the Irish synods did relax adherence to the Scottish covenants of the seventeenth century. There was no wholesale shift to the theological and political left on the issues of the power of the civil magistrate in enforcing religious conformity, as defined in chapter 23 of the *Confession*, or over the rise of evangelicalism. Both issues had split the Scottish Secession synods in the late eighteenth and early nineteenth centuries leading to the formation of the 'Neu' and 'Old Licht' parties. In 1818 both Irish Secession synods, comprising eighty-three Burgher and thirty-one Antiburgher congregations, united to form the 'Presbyterian Synod of Ireland, distinguished by the name Seceders'. The reunification of the Seceders reinforced their commitment to the doctrines of grace and along with the growing dominance of evangelicalism within the Synod of Ulster paved the way for the union of both bodies in 1840 to form the General Assembly.

The theological outlook of the Seceders was virtually identical to that of the Reformed Presbyterians or Covenanters. The two groups

---

[5] J. McKerrow, *History of the Secession church*, rev. edn. (Edinburgh, 1847); D. Stewart, *The Seceders in Ireland with annals of their congregations* (Belfast, 1950).

[6] J. S. Reid, *History of the Presbyterian Church in Ireland*, ed. W. D. Killen, 3 vols., 2nd edn. (Belfast, 1867), iii. 373.

disagreed, however, over the power and role of the civil magistracy and the attitude that should be adopted towards the existing state.[7] The Covenanters adhered to the seventeenth-century National Covenant (1638) and Solemn League and Covenant (1643) and could not in good conscience give their support to the British constitution as established in the aftermath of the Glorious Revolution. Their principles entailed the non-recognition of the authorities in matters such as exercising the franchise, registering leases, and paying various dues. During the eighteenth century the Covenanters had a significant, yet numerically small, presence in Ulster sustained by a handful of itinerant ministers and a system of local societies for fellowship and public worship. Their first presbytery was formed in 1763 but had collapsed by 1779 due to emigration to America, though it was reorganized in 1792 with six ministers and twelve congregations. Over subsequent years, the number of members and congregations grew and by 1810 four presbyteries were formed and the first meeting of synod was held in the following year. Though in many cases they remained aloof from politics and membership of evangelical associations, Reformed Presbyterians were sympathetic to evangelicalism. In the 1830s, however, the synod was shaken by an internal debate over the interpretation of chapter 23 of the *Confession* that ultimately led to the formation in 1842 of the breakaway Eastern Reformed Presbyterian Synod.

A note on the terminology used in this book may be necessary. New Light Presbyterians and their nineteenth-century successors will be referred to by their official titles or as non-subscribers, theological moderates, or liberals. Old Light Presbyterians will be variously described as subscribers, theological conservatives, or the orthodox, without any judgement as to the relative theological merits of either tradition. Note that the use of liberal and conservative in the text refers to theological outlook and not political persuasion, unless directly specified. Seceders were both subscribing and orthodox, though they were divided into conservative and moderate camps

---

[7] M. Hutchinson, *The Reformed Presbyterian Church in Scotland: its origin and history 1680–1876* (Paisley, 1893), 206–12. A. Loughridge, *The Covenanters in Ireland* (Belfast, 1984); C. Kidd, 'Conditional Britons: the Scots covenanting tradition and the eighteenth-century British state', *English Historical Review*, 117 (2002), 1147–76.

over a number of issues, including involvement in evangelical societies. The term evangelical refers to any individual or group who adhered to the distinctive doctrines outlined in section 3 below or who were involved in distinctively evangelical societies.

This introductory chapter provides the necessary historiographical and contextual background for the chapters that follow. The historiography of Ulster Presbyterianism is critically examined before an alternative interpretative framework is outlined, suggested by current trends in the historical study of religion and culture. The two following sections will provide an overview of the relevant economic and social developments in the period from 1770 to 1840 and their impact upon religious structures before establishing a broad interpretation of the changes within Ulster Presbyterianism and especially the origins and rise of evangelicalism.

1. HISTORIOGRAPHY

Hitherto, the historiography of Ulster Presbyterianism has largely been institutional in focus. Intellectual or theological developments have been examined either in their own right or in an attempt to explain the involvement of thousands of Presbyterians, especially ministers, in late eighteenth-century Irish republicanism and the 1798 rebellion. In many respects, eighteenth-century Presbyterianism seems to be an inviting subject for study, as the union of Catholic, Protestant, and Dissenter in the United Irish movement provides a corrective to the sectarian politics of the nineteenth and twentieth centuries.[8] As with so much writing about Ulster religion, the religious beliefs and practices of Presbyterians have rarely been examined outside an analytical framework that seeks to explain subsequent developments in Ulster politics. An example of this is the use of covenant theology and culture as an explanation for

---

[8] The best example of this tendency is K. Whelan, *The tree of liberty: radicalism, Catholicism and the construction of Irish identity 1760–1830* (Cork, 1996). For a critique of this interpretation, I. R. McBride, 'Reclaiming the rebellion: 1798 in 1998', *Irish Historical Studies*, 31 (1999), 395–410.

contemporary Ulster loyalism.[9] In order to explain these political changes, historians have been forced to comment on the internal dynamics of Ulster Presbyterianism. Two areas are of particular importance, namely, How should the Presbyterian community be characterized and what were the factors that made a Presbyterian a Presbyterian?

During the nineteenth century, the ascendancy of evangelicalism within Ulster Presbyterianism gave rise to a distinct evangelical view of Presbyterian history that has provided the chronological framework for subsequent historians. The standard periodization was given succinct expression by Thomas Witherow who divided Irish Presbyterian history into three periods: the hard yet providentially fruitful origins in the seventeenth century; the eighteenth century, a 'time of religious declension—declension in doctrinal purity, in zeal and in usefulness'; and the nineteenth century, 'a period of revival and recovery, characterised by growth in orthodoxy, in activity, and in every symptom of spiritual life'.[10] In a similar vein, W. D. Killen observed in his continuation of James Seaton Reid's magisterial *History of the Presbyterian Church in Ireland* that the prospects of Irish Presbyterianism in 1770 were 'never more discouraging' and blamed New Light theology for the spiritual lethargy of the church and the involvement of Presbyterian ministers in the United Irish movement.[11] Presbyterian historians did offer two important qualifications to this gloomy analysis of the eighteenth-century church, namely, the continued orthodoxy of the laity and the role of the Seceders in upholding Presbyterian structures and evangelical theology.[12] It is no surprise that these historians saw the expulsion of the Remonstrants in 1829 as the beginning of a period of religious renewal that would culminate in the 1859 revival.

Twentieth-century denominational historians have largely written about theology, prominent church leaders, or the history of

---

[9] D. H. Akenson, *God's peoples: covenant and land in South Africa, Israel, and Ulster* (Ithaca, N. Y., 1992), ch. 4.

[10] T. Witherow, *Historical and literary memorials of Presbyterianism in Ireland*, 2 vols. (Belfast, 1879–80), ii. 341.

[11] Reid, *History*, iii. 333, 397–8.

[12] W. T. Latimer, *A history of the Irish Presbyterians*, 2nd edn. (Belfast, 1902), 445; Reid, *History*, iii. 326; Witherow, *Memorials*, ii. 345–6.

individual congregations, though there are two notable exceptions to these trends. First, J. M. Barkley wrote extensively about Presbyterian practice, particularly the eldership and public worship, which represents the first serious attempt in modern times to examine how Presbyterians both practised their religion and interacted as a church community.[13] Nevertheless, his approach was influenced by his involvement in the ecumenical movement, which led him to emphasize the radicalism of his Presbyterian heritage and the liturgical and theological foundations of Presbyterian worship. Barkley was deeply impressed by the efforts of reformers in the second half of the nineteenth century to raise the standard of Presbyterian public worship in Scotland and Ireland and consequently showed little patience for both the standard of public praise and efforts to reform public worship in previous centuries. Furthermore, his analysis of church discipline was formed by the official standards of the church and seventeenth- and early eighteenth-century source material. As a result, there is little sense of development over time, a marked disregard for Seceder practice, and slight concern with the interrelationship between various types of Presbyterianism. The second major denominational historian of the twentieth century is Finlay Holmes. Unlike Barkley, Holmes has been more concerned with nineteenth-century Presbyterianism, particularly the nature and extent of political change within the denomination between 1798 and the First Home Rule Bill in 1886.[14] He has also been the best expositor of Presbyterian evangelicalism and the centralizing tendencies of the denomination, particularly in his superb biography of Henry Cooke.[15] As with other historians, however, Holmes has focused upon political developments and though he has ably delineated the importance of religious motivation, his main focus has not been

---

[13] For a full list of his writings, see, J. M. Barkley, *Blackmouth and dissenter* (Dundonald, 1991), 184–8.

[14] John Erskine, 'Finlay Holmes: a checklist of his writings, 1965–2002', in W. D. Patton (ed.), *Ebb and flow: essays in church history in honour of R. Finlay G. Holmes* (Belfast, 2002), 162–73.

[15] *Henry Cooke* (Belfast, 1981); 'The 1859 revival reconsidered', intro. to J. T. Carson, *God's river in spate: the story of the religious awakening in Ulster in 1859*, 2nd edn. (Belfast, 1994), pp. i–xvii; 'The triumph of evangelicalism in the Synod of Ulster in the early nineteenth century', in Patton, *Ebb and flow*, 9–19.

upon the beliefs and practices of the laity nor the impact of evangelicalism upon grass-roots Presbyterian church life.

Turning to the mainstream historical examination of Ulster Presbyterianism, the spectre of 1798 looms large on subsequent developments, although valuable work has been done on late seventeenth-century Presbyterian religious life and a series of collected essays on smaller dissenting groups in the eighteenth century has been published, though Presbyterianism is not well served.[16] The first modern analysis of Presbyterian political radicalism was by A. T. Q. Stewart in an MA thesis completed in 1956.[17] In a memorable passage Stewart later wrote that a Presbyterian 'is happiest when he is being a radical'. This he attributed to the 'austere doctrines of Calvinism, the simplicity of his worship, the democratic government of his church, the memory of the martyred Covenanters, and the Scottish refusal to yield or to dissemble—all these incline him to that difficult and cantankerous disposition which is characteristic of a certain kind of political radicalism'.[18] Stewart's characterization of the Presbyterian community in order to explain subsequent behaviour is both obvious and compelling. His concern with the Presbyterian origins of the United Irish movement established a subject for research that has dominated the scholarly agenda since. In some respects, the recent work of Ian McBride in explaining more fully the emergence of political radicalism may be seen as a culmination of the insights of both Stewart and denominational historians. McBride's wider historiographical frame of reference does set his *Scripture politics* (1998) apart from previous writings on the subject and is an exemplary

---

[16] R. M. Browne, 'Kirk and community: Ulster Presbyterian society, 1640–1740' (QUB M.Phil., 1998); Gillespie, 'The Presbyterian revolution in Ulster', in Sheils and Wood, *The churches, Ireland, and the Irish*; R. L. Greaves, *God's other children: Protestant nonconformists and the emergence of denominational churches in Ireland, 1660–1700* (Stanford, 1997), chs. 4 and 5; P. Kilroy, *Protestant dissent and controversy in Ireland 1660–1714* (Cork, 1994), chs. 1, 2 and 5; M. J. Westerkamp, *Triumph of the laity: Scots-Irish piety and the Great Awakening 1625–1760* (New York, 1988). Kevin Herlihy has edited a series of collections on Irish dissent: *The Irish dissenting tradition 1650–1750* (Dublin, 1995); *The religion of Irish dissent 1650–1800* (Dublin, 1996); *The politics of Irish dissent 1650–1800* (Dublin 1997); *Propagating the word of Irish dissent 1650–1800* (Dublin, 1998).

[17] 'The transformation of Presbyterianism radicalism in the north of Ireland, 1792–1825' (QUB MA, 1956).

[18] *The narrow ground: aspects of Ulster 1609–1969* (London, 1977), 83.

analysis of the complex interactions between different types of Presbyterian theology and political discourse, and the emergence of political radicalism from denominational principles and Enlightenment thought.[19]

As with other historians, McBride sees a development within Ulster Presbyterianism in the eighteenth and nineteenth centuries from religion as 'public testimony' to religion as 'private spirituality', in other words from traditional Presbyterianism to evangelicalism. In that regard, the work of David Hempton and Myrtle Hill in delineating the spread and influence of evangelicalism in Ulster Protestantism is of particular importance to the present study.[20] Their work has consolidated nearly forty years of disparate research on the various Protestant denominations and demonstrated the interdenominational character of the movement by placing it in a broader social and political context. The interdenominational focus of their work and its concentration upon Methodism does, however, reduce its value when considering changes within mainstream Protestantism and the individual characteristics of evangelicalism as this developed within a denominational context. This is particularly the case for Presbyterianism which, unlike Methodism, was Calvinist or Reformed in theology. The concentration upon Methodist Arminianism means that evangelicalism is seen in terms which are alien to Presbyterian theology and which postpones the emergence of an evangelical tradition until after the 1740s.

A stimulating attempt to characterize Ulster Presbyterianism as a distinct political and intellectual community has been offered by Peter Brooke.[21] Brooke argues that the period before 1825 was characterized by doctrinal indifference and apathy that inhibited the development of both theological radicalism and evangelicalism. Consequently, he argues, Henry Cooke had considerable difficulty in rousing the Synod of Ulster against Arianism in the late 1820s and he sees the Remonstrant exodus in 1829 not as the product of

---

[19] *Scripture politics: Ulster Presbyterians and Irish radicalism in the late eighteenth century* (Oxford, 1998).

[20] *Evangelical Protestantism in Ulster society 1740–1890* (London, 1992).

[21] 'Controversies in Ulster Presbyterianism, 1790–1836' (University of Cambridge Ph.D., 1980); *Ulster Presbyterianism: the historical perspective, 1610–1970*, 2nd edn. (Belfast, 1994).

evangelicalism but as a stimulus to it. More generally, Brooke characterizes eighteenth-century Presbyterianism as a coherent intellectual and political community, membership of which depended upon ethnic and political factors rather than religious commitment, circumstances that held in check the growth of evangelicalism. Yet, for a variety of economic and political reasons, this cohesion was fatally weakened in the nineteenth century and Presbyterianism was only saved by the 1859 revival, which he characterizes in part as a reassertion of community discipline. 'In the eighteenth century to be a Presbyterian was to be a member of a self-organising community. By the 1850s to be a Presbyterian was to be a person with particular religious views.'[22] Presbyterianism, in other words, had become distinctly religious.

The most ambitious effort to describe and explain the character of Presbyterians as a community and Presbyterianism as a religious system has been advanced by the American historian David W. Miller. Miller's work, which first appeared in the 1970s, is indebted to methodology and models derived from sociological and political science. In a 'speculative essay' published in 1978, Miller attempted to explain change within Ulster Presbyterianism in the eighteenth and nineteenth centuries by reference to the process of modernization.[23] He argued that traditional eighteenth-century Presbyterianism may be characterized as having a 'prophetic' emphasis, a world-view indelibly marked by seventeenth-century Scottish Calvinism and an eschatological vision in which the Kirk was God's chosen instrument to transform the entire social order in accordance with Scripture. God's activity in the world was therefore obvious and had important implications as a mode of social criticism. Consequently, commitment to the structures of Presbyterianism and confessional orthodoxy mattered a great deal and the fidelity of the Seceders to these principles ensured their popularity amongst the Presbyterian laity of Ulster. Though this concern with community and social transformation remained, it was constrained by the quasi-established character of Ulster Presbyterianism and the fixed geographical limits of Scottish settlement in the north-east. This

---

[22] *Ulster Presbyterianism*, 157.

[23] 'Presbyterianism and "modernization" in Ulster', *Past and Present*, 80 (1978), 66–90.

situation fits well into Miller's general observation that in eighteenth-century Ireland, the three main religious denominations (Presbyterian, Anglican, and Catholic) rarely attempted to proselytize, focusing instead on providing for the religious needs of their own distinct ethnic communities.

According to Miller, 'prophetic' Presbyterianism was swept away by the process of 'modernization' in Ulster society, associated with the growth of the linen industry and the industrialization of Belfast. This process involved a reorientation of attitudes towards 'a disposition to view the world as calculable and problems as amenable to solution'.[24] The failure of the 1798 rebellion and the excitement generated amongst the Presbyterian laity by the expectation of the imminent return of Christ and the commencement of the millennium effectively marked the end of an apocalyptic world-view. To meet the exigencies of the brave new world of industrialization and rationalism, Presbyterians adopted conversionist evangelicalism in place of prophetic orthodoxy, as the experience of personal conversion accorded well with the need to demonstrate empirically that an individual was a true believer. Miller argued that this change was inevitable. 'In order to meet people's real needs for the alleviation of stress, prophetic orthodoxy requires a capacity to believe in the possibility of supernatural intervention in the external world. By the early nineteenth century modernization had proceeded far enough to eliminate that capacity in most Presbyterians. Conversionist evangelicalism, which confined the "magic" to the internal world of the individual's psyche, moved into the gap.'[25] God's activity in the world was now internalized. The impact of this shift upon Presbyterianism was far-reaching as doctrinal disputation was set aside in favour of 'vital godliness' and a broader evangelical outlook. Hence, in Miller's view, 1829 and the imposition of full subscription (which, incidentally, only occurred in 1836) freed ministers from the need to express their theological views in a detailed manner.

Miller has since developed these ideas in a number of articles. His recent work is much less schematic and eschews the functionalist interpretation of religious belief he employed in 1978. A key theme remains the failure of Presbyterianism in the nineteenth century to

[24] Ibid., 69.   [25] Ibid., 85.

cope with social and economic changes. In 1999 he suggested that the predominant change in the nineteenth century was from a community that encompassed all Scottish settlers in Ulster to one that increasingly catered for middle-class respectability.[26] He reaffirms his opinion that the miraculous and providential activity of God had been internalized by evangelicalism but that the impact of evangelical reforms upon the belief and practice of the laity was limited before 1859. In an essay published a year later, Miller attempted to conceptualize the three Irish denominations as belonging to the same religious system comprised of four major components that should be examined comparatively, namely, creed, code, cultus, and community.[27] In that essay he clarifies what he means by divine intervention, maintaining that it was limited in Calvinist theology to one of 'the mighty acts of God', such as the Irish Famine, and did not extend to the minute occurrences of daily life. In a couple of recent articles, Miller has modified his understanding of religious change and, instead of claiming the decisive influence of modernization, argues that it is a result of the interaction between official and popular religion.[28] He identifies two types of official religion, Old Light and New Light, and two types of popular religion, old leaven and new leaven. Old leaven again refers to the politicized forms of Presbyterianism that emerged in the 1640s and includes Covenanters, Seceders, and members of the Popular Party in the Church of Scotland. In character, it is essentially intellectual and 'logocentric' and salvation is gained by having the right answers to doctrinal and ecclesiological questions. These characteristics were expressed through a ritual of inversion, which took the form of haggling between laity and ministers over doctrine, and a ritual of integration, namely open-air communions. On the other hand, new leaven

---

[26] 'Irish Presbyterians and the great famine', in J. Hill and C. Lennon (eds.), *Luxury and austerity*, Historical Studies, 21 (Dublin, 1999), ch. 10.

[27] 'Irish Christianity and revolution', in J. Smyth (ed.), *Revolution, counter-revolution and Union: Ireland in the 1790s* (Cambridge, 2000), ch. 11.

[28] 'Did Ulster Presbyterians have a devotional revolution?', in J. H. Murphy (ed.), *Evangelicals and Catholics in nineteenth-century Ireland* (Dublin, 2005), 38–54; 'Religious commotions in the Scottish diaspora: a transatlantic perspective on "evangelicalism" in a mainline denomination', in M. G. Spencer and D. A. Wilson (eds.), *Ulster Presbyterians in the Atlantic World: religion, politics and identity* (Dublin, 2006), ch. 1.

religion was emotional, conversionist, and expressed through revivals. This version of popular religion posed a serious threat to the older variety which was, once again, driven out of mainstream Presbyterianism in the early nineteenth century as Cooke reintroduced subscription and 'took all the fun out of being a Presbyterian' by thus reducing the opportunities for haggling. It ought to be pointed out that Miller is more aware of the continuing influence of old leaven ideas on Presbyterian evangelicalism than in his previous works.

Miller's arguments have many strengths, not least his bold attempt to relate changes within Presbyterianism to social and economic developments. Moreover, he also correctly identified the important relationship between evangelicalism and the Enlightenment, a topic that has recently received much-needed attention.[29] Yet, three observations about his work and that of McBride and Brooke are in order. First, Miller's earlier work and that of Brooke is hampered by a limited view of religious belief. In this view, religion emerges as a functional means of reaffirming community, providing a discourse for the transmission of political ideas, or alleviating stress in a changing society. Though these are important outcomes of religious beliefs they are by no means the only or, indeed, the central 'function' of belief. Church historians in particular are reticent about the implications of any type of economic or social determinism upon the content, validity, and integrity of personal belief. It is important to examine any ideas, whether religious or otherwise, within the social and cultural context from which they emerge, without regarding them as being wholly determined by that context or blindly accepting an unsatisfactory relativism.[30] Indeed, recent studies of the growth of evangelicalism in this period have shown that religious and economic changes are not epiphenomenal and that the precise

---

[29] For example, D. W. Bebbington, 'Revival and Enlightenment in eighteenth-century England', in A. Walker and K. Aune (eds.), *On revival: a critical examination* (Carlisle, 2003), ch. 5; B. Stanley (ed.), *Christian missions and the Enlightenment* (Grand Rapids, Mich., 2001).

[30] J. E. Bradley and R. E. Muller, *Church history: an introduction to research, reference works and methods* (Grand Rapids, Mich., 1995), 3. The model is Mark Noll's monumental, *America's God: from Jonathan Edwards to Abraham Lincoln* (New York, 2002).

linkages between the two were highly complex and must be considered at various levels of analysis.[31] The relationship between Christianity and culture has always been multi-layered and symbiotic, and though Christianity is undoubtedly shaped by culture, it in turn provokes responses from culture.[32] Certainly Miller's contention of 1978 that modernization led to a decline in a propensity to believe in divine intervention, however conceived, is suspect given the continued importance of popular supernaturalism in twentieth-century rural Ulster and the prevalence of eschatological interest amongst educated Presbyterians until the 1890s.[33]

Second, the distinction made by historians such as McBride between religion as 'public testimony' and religion as 'private spirituality', while helpful in elucidating long-term changes, tends to obscure the continuity of religious experiences of Presbyterians in the period up to 1860.[34] A personal relationship with Christ, though rarely involving a stereotypical conversion experience, was as much a part of Presbyterian piety in the eighteenth century as it would be in the nineteenth. The debates between Synod of Ulster and Seceder ministers in the eighteenth century over correct doctrine were not only

[31] D. Hempton, *The religion of the people: Methodism and popular religion in Britain, c. 1750–1900* (London, 1996). For a broader consideration see, S. Connolly, ' "The moving statue and the turtle dove": approaches to the history of Irish religion', *Irish Economic and Social History*, 31 (2004), 1–22.

[32] My understanding of the relationship between Christianity and culture is indebted to the work of the missiologist Andrew Walls, especially *The missionary movement in Christian history: studies in the transmission of the faith* (Edinburgh, 1996). See also, D. Meek, 'God and Gaelic: the Highland churches and Gaelic cultural identity', in G. McCoy and M. Scott (eds.), *Gaelic identities: aithne na nGael* (Belfast, 2000), 28–47.

[33] A. D. Buckley, 'Beliefs in County Down folklore', in L. Proudfoot (ed.), *Down: history and society. Interdisciplinary essays on the history of an Irish county* (Dublin, 1997), ch. 20; A. Holmes, 'Millennialism and the interpretation of prophecy in Ulster Presbyterianism, 1790–1850', in C. Gribben and T. C. F. Stunt (eds.), *Prisoners of hope? Aspects of evangelical millennialism in Scotland and Ireland, 1800–1880* (Carlisle, 2005), ch. 7; idem, 'The uses and interpretation of prophecy in Irish Presbyterianism, 1850–1930', in Crawford Gribben and A. R. Holmes (eds.), *Protestant millennialism, evangelicalism, and Irish society, 1790–2005* (Basingstoke, 2006), ch. 7.

[34] These criticisms are fleshed out in more detail in, A. Holmes, 'Tradition and enlightenment: conversion and assurance of salvation in Ulster Presbyterianism, 1700–1859', in M. Brown, C. I. McGrath, and T. P. Power (eds.), *Converts and conversions in Ireland, 1650–1850* (Dublin, 2005), ch. 6.

intellectual exercises to discover the correct answers but had profound implications for how Presbyterians understood their spiritual and emotional relationship to God through Christ. Ministers argued about these matters because they were first of all pastors and only after trained theologians. Furthermore, as Miller acknowledges in his most recent work and as this book demonstrates, Presbyterian evangelicals were committed to the importance of correct doctrine, which was reinforced in the 1830s by strengthening synodical supervision of licentiates, the reintroduction of full subscription, and the restoration of presbytery visitations. This is not to deny that there were shifts of emphasis, but the changes should not be unnecessarily simplified. In that regard, the Presbyterian laity were not upset that Cooke had reduced the opportunities for haggling, because he was bringing the church back to the traditional Presbyterian beliefs and practices of the Westminster standards. Indeed, middle-class Presbyterian evangelicals such as Cooke and James Seaton Reid defined revival in precisely those terms. Moreover, as Part II of this book demonstrates, the type of public worship that dominated Presbyterian evangelicalism in the nineteenth century was not emotional and owed much to the Presbyterian theological tradition for its form and content.

Third, scholars, in an effort to explain political developments, have tended to describe the religion of the Presbyterian laity in blanket terms. Miller has been the welcome exception to this trend by demonstrating through cartography the geography of Presbyterianism in Ulster and dealing in broad terms with issues such as non-practising Presbyterians, differences in social class, and gender. Most other analyses of change within Presbyterianism fail to distinguish between variations of religious commitment, traditions of Presbyterian theology, and elementary differences regarding class, gender, and geographical location. For example, as shown in Chapter 1, a substantial number of Presbyterians did not submit themselves to the oversight and discipline of the local Kirk and could not be compelled to do so. As Chapter 6 indicates, the failure of discipline to operate in many Presbyterian areas previous to the 1830s depended to an extent upon the refusal of the laity to submit. Though Presbyterianism became more respectable and middle class in the nineteenth century, social distinctions existed in the previous century in the form of pew rents, and a very substantial number of working-class Presbyterians continued to attend Belfast meeting-houses on a regular basis in the decades after 1870.[35]

This critique of previous scholarship is informed both by the findings of this book and recent developments in the historical study of religion and culture. Though it is almost impossible to define in a satisfactory manner what religious history is, it is clear that the focus of study has moved from traditional ecclesiastical history towards a greater concentration upon the social context and import of religious ideas, especially amongst the laity.[36] This movement was in part inspired by the turn to 'history from below' in the 1970s represented by scholars such as Keith Thomas and, particularly germane to this period, James Obelkevich.[37] Avoiding the excessive determinism of some of these accounts, the pioneering work of Sean Connolly on Catholic belief and practice, first published in 1982, may be seen as an Irish expression of this wider historiographical mood alongside D. W. Miller's earlier work.[38] Two prominent characteristics of this broader trend are worth noting. First, a rigid dualism often emerged, or was imposed upon, the religious beliefs and cultures of the past, separating religion into elite and popular forms, and beliefs into official and unofficial varieties. The latter was often expressed as a dualism between orthodox religion and superstitious magic. Furthermore, nineteenth-century religious and social reformers were often characterized in implacable opposition to the traditional culture they wanted to reform. The second characteristic was that popular belief and culture declined over time as the components of modernization inevitably secularized society by making individuals more sensible than to believe in

---

[35] D. Huddleston, 'Religion and social class: church membership in Belfast, *c.* 1870–1930' (QUB M.Phil., 1998), 60–8.

[36] C. Brooke *et al.*, 'What is religious history?', in J. Gardiner (ed.), *What is history today?* (Basingstoke, 1988), ch. 5.

[37] For an overview see, J. Sharpe, 'Popular culture in the early modern West', in M. Bentley (ed.), *Companion to historiography* (London, 1997), ch. 17. K. Thomas, *Religion and the decline of magic* (London, 1971); J. Obelkevich, *Religion and rural society: South Lindsey 1825–1875* (Oxford, 1976).

[38] *Priests and people in pre-Famine Ireland 1780–1845*, 2nd edn. (Dublin, 2001).

old-fashioned religion and more respectable than to take part in customary activity.

The numerous criticisms of this model have concentrated upon two themes, the variety of popular culture and religion and the variable chronology of decline. Though Niall Ó Cíosáin agrees that considerable economic and social changes were under way in this period, he has criticized historians of Irish popular culture for imposing a rigid model of social change from 'traditional' to 'modern' societies that 'misses much of the complexity of cultural practice at any given time'.[39] Ó Cíosáin and others, especially those who debate secularization, also criticize the rather mechanical and inevitable manner in which change and the decline of popular culture or institutional religion are portrayed, particularly as research has demonstrated time and again that this model does not explain the complex interaction between various factors and different social contexts.[40] Moreover, change was not always enforced from above and, in many cases, it was, to use a pejorative term, the common people who ensured the success of the changes by consciously stimulating change in the first place, sharing the values that were being presented by reformers, or adapting them to meet their own needs. Instead of a dualistic model, historians increasingly see both eighteenth- and nineteenth-century popular culture as an ambiguous phenomenon, complicated by class, gender, geographical, and religious factors, and cultural change as complex in origin and chronology. One historian has argued that popular culture should not be seen as a thing but as a process, constantly adapting to both internal and external pressures.[41]

With a few notable exceptions, the study of popular religion in the modern period lags well behind the advances made by historians both of religion in early modern Europe and of nineteenth-century

---

[39] N. Ó Cíosáin, *Print and popular culture in Ireland, 1750–1850* (Basingstoke, 1997), 200.

[40] Ibid., 197–203; T. Harris (ed.), *Popular culture in England, c. 1500–1850* (Basingstoke, 1995); C. G. Brown, *The death of Christian Britain: understanding secularisation 1800–2000* (London, 2001).

[41] T. Harris, 'Problematising popular culture', in idem, *Popular culture*, 20–5.

popular culture.[42] This is attributable to the tendency to adopt unconsciously or otherwise a secularizing and modernizing worldview that automatically assumes the subservience of religion to culture in the modern world. Yet it is clear that the insights of early modern historians of religion have much to offer their modern counterparts. In particular, both groups confront similar problems of evidence. The difficulties for this book are many, including the relative lack of materials before 1830, the absence of references to routine activities, and the bias introduced by a reformist perspective.[43] However, early modern historians have demonstrated that such constraints do not negate the usefulness of the surviving sources but rather focus attention upon the interaction between lay practice and the expectations of reformers. Protestant Reformers in the early modern period, including Scottish Calvinists, acted as important intermediaries between official and popular cultures, softening the impact of change by retaining much customary practice while imparting the essential theological principles. In terms of the actual texture of lay belief, it has been demonstrated that the religious beliefs and practices of the laity were often syncretistic and that individuals did not necessarily perceive any conflict between official and popular religion or culture. Far from being at the mercy of processes beyond their control, the laity were active in the adoption and adaptation of official religious beliefs and practices for their own ends. As the eminent historian of New England Puritanism D. David Hall writes, 'popular religion designates the ways in which ordinary people understood, appropriated and put to use the customary

---

[42] J. Dawson, 'Calvinism and the Gaidheatachd in Scotland', in A. D. M. Pettegree, A. Duke, and G. Lewis (eds.) *Calvinism in Europe 1540–1620* (Cambridge, 1994), ch. 12; R. Gillespie, *A devoted people: belief and religion in early-modern Ireland* (Manchester, 1997); R. Hutton, 'The English Reformation and the evidence of folklore', *Past and Present*, 148 (1995), 89–116; M. Todd, *The culture of Protestantism in early modern Scotland* (New Haven, Conn., 2002); R. W. Scribner and T. Johnson (eds.), *Popular religion in Germany and Central Europe, 1400–1800* (London, 1996). For a review of the current historiography of nineteenth-century popular culture see, E. Griffin, 'Popular culture in industrialising England', *Historical Journal*, 45 (2002), 619–35. A significant exception to this characterization of the study of popular religion in the modern period is S. C. Williams, *Religious belief and popular culture in Southwark c. 1880–1939* (Oxford, 1999).

[43] For a discussion of similar problems elsewhere see, Harris, 'Problematising popular culture', in idem, *Popular culture*, 6–10.

motifs of the Christian tradition'.[44] The keyword is interaction, interaction between the laity and their ministers and between beliefs and their social and cultural contexts. Leigh Eric Schmidt, in his excellent study of Scottish communion seasons, stated that his work had 'tried to disclose continuities and discontinuities between elite and popular religion. It has sought to explore the dynamic, interactive relationship between ministers and congregants, between clerical expectations and lay experiences.' Instead of uncovering a structuralist *mentalité*, Schmidt emphasizes the variety of lay experience and the relationships between different groups of people.[45] Popular religion, therefore, no longer refers to unorthodox or superstitious beliefs, as implied by the analysis of an older generation of historians, but those beliefs held by the laity in all their variety.

Three other historiographical trends should be highlighted at this stage. The first is the growing awareness of the ritual character of Protestant practice. As the explicit rituals of Catholicism were abolished, Protestant reformers, often unconsciously, replaced them with other informal ritual practices such as communion seasons, rites of passage, love feasts, and the rhythms of daily and weekly devotion.[46] In this context ritual could embrace both orthodox and alternative beliefs as it 'was a formalised procedure, a patterned means of connecting the natural and the social worlds to the supernatural power'.[47] It will become clear in the chapters that follow that such patterned behaviour was a significant feature of public and private Presbyterian piety and provided both comfort and meaning for the laity and ministers. The second theme is the recent upsurge in interest shown by historians in the private spiritual devotions and

[44] D. D. Hall, 'The literary practices of dissent', in Herlihy, *Propagating the word of Irish dissent*, 13.

[45] L. E. Schmidt, *Holy fairs: Scotland and the making of American revivalism*, 2nd edn. (Grand Rapids, Mich., 2001), 7.

[46] E. Muir, *Ritual in early modern Europe* (Cambridge, 1997); L. E. Schmidt, 'Time, celebration, and the Christian year in eighteenth-century evangelicalism', in M. A. Noll, D. W. Bebbington, and G. A. Rawlyk (eds.), *Evangelicalism: comparative studies in popular Protestantism in North America, the British Isles, and beyond 1700–1900* (Oxford, 1994), 90–109; C. Hambrick-Stowe, *The practice of piety: Puritan devotional disciplines in seventeenth-century New England* (Chapel Hill, N. C., 1982).

[47] D. D. Hall, *Worlds of wonder, days of judgement: popular religious belief in early New England* (Cambridge, Mass., 1989), 168.

orthodox religious practices of believers. The preoccupation of the *fin de siècle* western world with all things spiritual has undoubtedly provided an important context for this development. Yet, the work of nineteenth-century historians of religion such as David Bebbington and Charles Cashdollar displays a genuine desire to understand the personal experiences and concerns of lay believers who have too often been ignored in accounts of nineteenth-century society.[48]

The increased attention of historians to the religious roles and experiences of women is the third historiographical theme of importance. Some historians have argued that middle-class women in the nineteenth century suffered from the separation of 'the spheres of public power and private domesticity'.[49] The argument goes that women were increasingly relegated to the domestic sphere of raising a family and running the home while men cemented their position in the public sphere of politics and business. The differentiation of gender roles was facilitated by evangelicalism and was intimately related to the formation of middle-class and Victorian respectability. Though gender stereotyping and separate spheres certainly existed, there are a number of problems with this view, particularly as it simplifies gender relations and draws too stark a distinction between the apparent golden age of women's involvement in the public sphere before 1800 and their enslavement in the following century. According to Amanda Vickery, if evangelicalism 'took some women's public lives with one hand, it undoubtedly gave with the other in the burgeoning of religious associations, moral campaigns and organized charity'.[50] The idea of separate spheres within Presbyterianism did not refer to women solely as wives and mothers but also in terms of the type of activity women could do outside of the home. Women were given an opportunity to be involved in the public witness of

---

[48] D. W. Bebbington, 'Evangelical conversion, c. 1740–1850', *Scottish Bulletin of Evangelical Theology*, 18 (2000), 102–27; idem, *Holiness in nineteenth-century England* (Carlisle, 2000); C. D. Cashdollar, *A spiritual home: life in British and American Reformed congregations, 1830–1915* (University Park, Pa., 2000).

[49] The relevant literature is surveyed in A. Vickery, 'Golden age to separate spheres? A review of the categories and chronology of English women's history', *Historical Journal*, 36 (1993), 383–414.

[50] Ibid., 399. Hempton, *Religion of the people*, ch. 10; L. Wilson, *Constrained by zeal: female spirituality amongst Nonconformists 1825–1875* (Carlisle, 2000).

Presbyterianism to an unprecedented degree through Sunday schools, clothing societies, house-to-house visitation, and poor relief agencies. Gender is obviously of central importance to a study of this kind. Unfortunately, there is a chronic lack of information about female involvement in church life in the eighteenth century, and the nineteenth-century evidence is mediated through sources written by men. Throughout the text, mention will be made where possible about gender differences in religious belief or distinctively female practices. The comparative neglect of a gender dimension to this study is a result of the constraints of evidence rather than myopia.

2. THE ECONOMIC AND SOCIAL BACKGROUND

The period from 1770 to 1840 was one of upheaval for western society. The American, French, and Industrial Revolutions, urbanization, and the shift from Enlightenment to Romanticism had far-reaching implications for every European country and the relationship between institutional religion and the people.[51] In Ireland, the granting of legislative independence in 1782, the upheavals of the 1790s, the Union of 1801, the rise of Catholic nationalism under Daniel O'Connell, and the resurgence of sectarian conflict in the 1820s and 1830s, provide the important political context for the chapters that follow. During the eighteenth century, Ireland was essentially a type of confessional state in which the members of the minority established Anglican Church of Ireland had a substantial hold upon the political and economic structures of the island owing to their domination of land ownership. This meant that Catholics and Presbyterians suffered from the imposition of discriminatory legislation, which in the case of the latter affected such matters as marriage and political representation, and led both groups to find common cause in movements for political reform

---

[51] N. Aston, *Christianity and revolutionary Europe c. 1750–1830* (Cambridge, 2002); H. McLeod, *Religion and the people of western Europe 1789–1989*, 2nd edn. (Oxford, 1997).

in the late eighteenth century.[52] Yet Presbyterians had an anomalous position, for they also received a state grant towards the payment of their ministers, known as the *regium donum*, first granted in 1672 by Charles II, augmented by William III and the Hanovarians, and continued until the abolition of all Irish church endowments in 1869–71.

Presbyterians in Ulster were also deeply involved in, and affected by, the rapid economic and social transformation of the north-east.[53] Within the context of the general expansion of the western European economy in the second half of the eighteenth century, Ulster's economy developed rapidly through the increasing market orientation of tillage farming, improved communications, and the rise of an urban middle class in Belfast. The main engine of Ulster's economic growth, however, was the domestic linen industry. The production of linen yarn and cloth complemented the pattern of rural life and the household economy. It provided employment in periods when farming was slack and allowed women and children to spin yarn while men did the heavier work of weaving. In general terms, linen provided the foundation for the region's industrial pre-eminence in Ireland by attracting British capital and allowing Ulster merchants to invest in other sectors of the economy. In 1750, 11 million yards of linen cloth were exported from Ireland. That figure had risen to 43 million by 1815 and to over 50 million by the mid-1830s.[54] The industry grew initially in the linen triangle of south Ulster (comprising the towns of Lurgan, Armagh, and Dungannon), where a proto-capitalist system of production developed, but soon production spread into other parts of Ulster including counties Antrim and Down. Supplemented by the increase of agricultural exports, the

---

[52] I. McBride, 'Presbyterians in the penal era', *Bullán*, 1 (1994), 73–86; D. W. Hayton, 'Exclusion, conformity and parliamentary representation: the impact of the Sacramental Test on Irish dissenting politics', in Herlihy, *The politics of Irish dissent*, 52–73.

[53] The following summary of economic developments is indebted to: J. Bardon, *A history of Ulster*, new edn. (Belfast, 2001), chs. 7 and 8; W. H. Crawford, 'Economy and society in eighteenth-century Ulster' (QUB Ph.D., 1982); L. Kennedy 'The rural economy, 1820–1914' and P. Ollerenshaw, 'Industry, 1820–1914', in eidem (eds.) *An economic history of Ulster 1820–1939* (Manchester, 1985).

[54] Kennedy, 'Rural economy', 2.

growth of the linen industry led to unprecedented wealth and population growth in late eighteenth-century Ulster. The province became the most prosperous in Ireland though prosperity also produced tensions that manifested themselves in agrarian unrest, sectarian conflict in the linen triangle, and movements for political reform such as the Volunteers and the United Irishmen.

The Napoleonic Wars boosted the economy of Ulster but the end of hostilities in 1815 ushered in a period of deflation that affected badly many sections of society and caused a series of food shortages in the province between 1816 and 1817 and in 1821. The economic circumstances were exacerbated by changes in the linen industry and the growth of Belfast as an industrial centre. The main stimulus to change was the growth of the cotton industry in the Belfast–Lagan valley area in the 1770s, which had been fostered by tariff protection and cheap imports of raw materials. Two consequences are particularly important. First, it helped develop a workable 'putting out' system that entailed a loss of independence on the part of handloom weavers who no longer could obtain yarn for themselves and instead became dependent on linen merchants who distributed, or 'put out', the yarn to them. Second, the cotton industry promoted the development of the factory system. The construction in Belfast of Andrew Mulholland's linen-spinning mill in 1828 marked a decisive shift in the fortunes of the domestic industry. Those weavers working in the hinterland of Belfast saw their standard of living tumble as linen prices fell owing to an excess of labour and competition from cheap English cotton. To meet the ever-increasing demand, weavers had to work anything from fourteen to eighteen hours a day for a pittance while facing the spectre of underemployment.[55] Despite the social cost, Belfast benefited from these changes and the position of the town itself was transformed. From a prosperous commercial centre in the late eighteenth century, Belfast emerged as the industrial capital of Ireland in the first half of the nineteenth century.

The population history of Ulster in the 1750 to 1850 period was governed by the above economic changes. Between 1750 and 1841

---

[55] *Report from select committee on handloom weavers' petitions*, HC (1835), xiii. 88.

the population of Ulster quadrupled from 500,000 to 2.4 million.[56] Despite the large-scale emigration of around 100,000 persons to America by 1778, the annual growth rates peaked at a remarkable 1.9 per cent in the period from 1753 to 1791 and fell to between 1.3 and 1.4 per cent in 1791 to 1821, making Ulster one of the fastest growing regions in Europe. This growth resulted from a combination of a decrease in mortality linked with the prosperity of the linen industry and a higher than average fertility rate that had been held in check before 1750 by high mortality. The lower growth levels in the nineteenth century were caused by an increase in both the age of marriage and emigration rates. Indeed, migration from Ulster comprised 40 per cent of the Irish total between 1815 and 1845.[57] The most significant aspect of this increase of population was the growth of Belfast from around 20,000 persons in 1800 to 349,000 in 1901. Between 1821 and 1841 in particular the population grew from 37,277 to 75,308.[58] Throughout the century the annual growth rate was around 3 per cent, sustained by a massive influx of workers from rural areas, attracted by the prospect of employment in linen mills and later the shipyards. Urbanization on this scale was an unprecedented development for a region that had until 1770 only a very poorly developed urban network. In 1800 only a tenth of the population of Ulster lived in settlements of over a thousand persons. Though by 1851 there had been an increase, the situation remained broadly similar, as only one person in eight lived in settlements of 2,000 or more.[59] Whereas the commercial expansion of Belfast allowed New Light Presbyterianism to exert its influence over the town in the eighteenth century, industrialization in the nineteenth was more conducive to evangelicalism, which thrived in the environment of economic and sectarian competition.[60]

[56] W. Macafee, 'The demographic history of Ulster, 1750–1841', in H. T. Blethen and C. W. Wood, Jr (eds.), *Ulster and North America: transatlantic perspectives on the Scotch-Irish* (Tuscaloosa, Ala., 1997), ch. 4.

[57] T. Parkhill, 'Between revolution and famine: patterns of emigration from Ulster 1776–1845', in J. Gray and W. McCann (eds.), *An uncommon bookman: essays in memory of J. R. R. Adams* (Belfast, 1996), 59–73.

[58] L. Clarkson, 'The city and the country', in J. C. Beckett *et al.*, *Belfast: the making of a city 1800–1914* (Belfast, 1988), 153; Hempton and Hill, *Evangelical Protestantism*, 106.

[59] Crawford, 'Economy and society', ch. 6.

[60] J. W. Nelson, 'The Belfast Presbyterians, 1670–1830: an analysis of their political and social interests' (QUB Ph.D., 1985); Hempton and Hill, *Evangelical Protestantism*, ch. 6.

As Belfast increasingly became the centre of Presbyterianism, an overture was brought before the Synod of Ulster in 1836 calling for the establishment of a synod house in Belfast. Though the resolution was passed two years later it was not acted upon and it met with determined opposition from some rural ministers.[61] Tensions between rural and urban Presbyterianism were further intensified in the mid-nineteenth century over the issues of tenant right and the foundation of Magee College, Derry.[62] Though Belfast gradually became the epicentre of Presbyterianism, its spiritual and numerical heartland in this period remained in the Ulster countryside. The sense of place in a small community, of rootedness in the Ulster soil, is a significant aspect of the Ulster Presbyterian experience and is reflected in the works of the weaver poets, a significant source for lay belief and practice.[63] The framework of the individual Presbyterian was the local community and often that meant the community as assembled in the meeting-house. As David Hall suggests, the meeting-house was not just a place to receive religious teaching but 'made visible the fellowship of Christians; it symbolised a set of rules or ethics that defined the meaning of community'.[64] This phenomenon may be easily comprehended in the seemingly unique obsession of Ulster Presbyterians with writing and reading congregational histories.[65] Moreover, in these small communities, the importance of good neighbourliness was critical and, as will be shown, certain communal values often determined, amongst other things, the exercise of church discipline and popular understandings of the rites of passage.[66] The emphasis upon good conduct, of doing right by your

---

[61] *RGSU* (1836), 70–1; (1838), 16, 50–1.

[62] R. Dill, *Prelatico Presbyterianism: or, curious chapters in the recent history of the Irish Presbyterian Church* (Dublin, 1856).

[63] Akenson, *God's peoples*, 137–43; I. Herbison, 'A sense of place: landscape and locality in the work of the rhyming weavers', in G. Dawe and J. W. Foster (eds.), *The poet's place: Ulster literature and society. Essays in honour of John Hewitt, 1907–1987* (Belfast, 1991), ch. 5.

[64] Hall, *Worlds of wonder*, 165.

[65] Good examples include, T. H. Mullin, *Aghadowey: a parish and its linen industry* (Belfast, 1972); J. E. Mullin, *New Row: the history of New Row Presbyterian Church, Coleraine 1727–1977* (Antrim, 1976); D. Nesbitt, *Full circle: a story of Ballybay Presbyterians* (Monaghan, 1999).

[66] D. B. Rutman, 'Assessing the little communities of early America', *William and Mary Quarterly*, 3rd ser., 43 (1986), 163–78.

neighbour, was often in conflict with the expectations of ministers and with confessional standards that demanded more than a simple equation between goodly and godly living.

In social terms, Presbyterians tended to occupy the middling ranks of Ulster society and were certainly better off than their Catholic neighbours, though in terms of land ownership they fell far behind members of the Church of Ireland. According to Sean Connolly, the Presbyterians of counties Antrim, Down, and Londonderry in the eighteenth century continued a pattern of mixed farming on comparatively large holdings, while linen weavers retained their independence by producing directly for the market. In south Ulster where the Seceders were particularly prominent, weavers did not have the same independence and were obliged to act as waged labour.[67] The social profile of Presbyterian congregations tended to mirror the economic structure of the surrounding area. Of the 160 persons between 1752 and 1759 who brought their children to be baptized in Cahans Secession congregation, situated in the linen heartland of County Monaghan, 66 were farmers, 72 were weavers, and 15 were involved in various service occupations.[68] Samuel Elder, minister of Ballyeaston Synod of Ulster congregation in south Antrim, conducted a census of his congregation in 1813. He recorded the occupations of 388 heads of families; 219 were farmers, 68 were weavers, and 37 employed in the service sector.[69] Presbyterians continued to be extensively involved in agriculture during the nineteenth century and it is noteworthy that a large majority of ministers came from this section of society.[70] Though the period of deflation from 1813 to the 1840s did pose problems for Ulster farmers, the living standards 'among the minority of middling and larger farmers' improved in the decades prior to the Famine and Presbyterians continued to be

[67] S. J. Connolly, 'Ulster Presbyterians: religion, culture and politics, 1660–1850', in Blethen and Wood, *Ulster and North America*, 30.

[68] Cahans (B/Sec.) session book, 1752–8 (PRONI, CR/3/25B/1 & 2), 100–37.

[69] The Revd S. Elder, 'Population of Ballyeaston congregation in 1813' (PRONI, T/1013/1).

[70] J. M. Barkley, 'The Presbyterian minister in eighteenth-century Ireland', in J. L. M. Haire *et al.*, *Challenge and conflict: essays in Irish Presbyterian history and doctrine* (Belfast, 1981), 49; K. D. Brown, 'Life after death? A preliminary survey of the Irish Presbyterian ministry in the nineteenth century', *Irish Economic and Social History*, 22 (1995), 55–6.

well represented amongst the ranks of linen drapers and merchants, shopkeepers, and grocers.[71] They were also the main beneficiaries of the commercial development of Belfast and came to dominate the town's merchant and industrial elite in both the eighteenth and the nineteenth centuries.[72] Presbyterians tended to have more disposable income than other sectors of the Irish population and possessed sufficient wealth to be able to deal with economic difficulties. The economic and social position of Presbyterians allowed them to initiate and benefit from changes within Ulster society. A desire for improvement or reform developed in response to economic growth and commercialization, which led to the formation of book clubs, mechanics institutes, farming improvement societies, and various educational schemes. In the wake of the French Revolution a variety of groups across Europe from political radicals to evangelicals began to challenge the traditional practices of society 'which they regarded as crude and degrading' and instead stressed 'the virtues of knowledge, industry, and a rational, calculating mentality'.[73] This desire to reform perceived social failings was shared by a variety of groups in Ireland including the government, landlords, Catholic priests, social reformers, conservative churchmen, Arians, and Presbyterian evangelicals.

There are important distinctions to be made between, on the one hand, middling farmers and upper working-class weavers and, on the other, lower working-class cottiers and labourers. This distinction is important, as better-off Presbyterians were more likely to be involved in the various schemes for social and religious improvement. There was a sizeable group of poor Presbyterian cottiers and linen employees who were badly affected by the adverse economic conditions of the first half of the nineteenth century. Many left their rural homes and came to Belfast seeking employment but were soon

---

[71] Kennedy, 'Rural economy', in Kennedy and Ollerenshaw, *Economic History of Ulster*, 36; K. J. James, 'Aspects of Protestant culture and society in Mid-Antrim, 1857–67' (University of Edinburgh Ph.D., 2000), 52–4.

[72] McBride, *Scripture politics*, 34–5; Nelson, 'Belfast Presbyterians, 1670–1830'; J. R. B. McMinn, 'Presbyterianism and politics in Ulster, 1871–1906', *Studia Hibernica*, 21 (1981), 127–46.

[73] McLeod, *Religion and the people*, 41. B. Bushaway, *By rite: custom, ceremony and community in England 1700–1880* (London, 1982), ch. 7.

disillusioned when confronted with the harsh conditions of an expanding industrial town. Other poor Presbyterians became victims of the Famine in the 1840s. Along with social and political develop-ments, the economic difficulties of the domestic linen industry had a direct impact upon participation in customary activities such as cockfighting, wakes, and other social gatherings. In the 1830s, it was reported that the inhabitants of the overwhelmingly Presbyterian parish of Templecoran in east Antrim had largely abandoned their traditional amusements except for a few idle days at Christmas and Easter 'from want of time and means'.[74]

3. REFORM, REVIVAL, AND THE DEVELOPMENT OF EVANGELICALISM IN ULSTER PRESBYTERIANISM, 1770–1840

Eighteenth-century Presbyterianism was a complex phenomenon. By 1800, it was divided into no less than six separate groupings, five of which were concentrated in Ulster and form the basis of this book; the Synod of Ulster, the two Secession Synods, the Reformed Pres-bytery, the Presbytery of Antrim, and the Southern Association. It was generally the case that other than occasional local disputes in the 1770 to 1800 period, the various Presbyterian bodies either related in a business-like manner or ignored each other. Each group embodied different understandings of Presbyterianism that reflected their dis-tinctive social, ethnic, and historical backgrounds. They defined themselves against the others by reference to the standards of Pres-byterianism, to the cultural and intellectual fashions of the day, or to both simultaneously. Despite their differences, Presbyterians shared a similar theological language and certain ideas about the church, which they attempted to relate to the needs of the times with varying degrees of success. This shared vocabulary included God's love,

---

[74] *OSMI* (Templecoran), xxvi. 106. For broader comments see, S. J. Connolly, '"Ag déanamh *commanding*": elite responses to popular culture, 1660–1850', in J. S. Donnelly and K. A. Miller (eds.), *Irish popular culture 1650–1850* (Dublin, 1998), 21–4.

sovereignty, providence, grace, salvation, love to others, liberty of conscience, and the sole headship of Christ over the Church. However, this vocabulary was at best ambivalent. On the one hand, to say they had a similar language does not mean they meant the same thing when they talked about, for example, Christ's death on the cross. On the other, a shared understanding of the content of certain key doctrinal issues provided Presbyterians with the ability to transcend the boundaries of their groups. This was particularly the case in the nineteenth century when a shared concern with spreading and upholding the doctrines of grace brought ministers from the Synod of Ulster and Secession synods together in missionary societies and ultimately led to the unification of the synods in 1840. Though evangelicalism derived its theological weight from the Presbyterian theological tradition, conservative Presbyterians could adopt a variety of positions. An important strand was a conservative confessional view of Presbyterianism that often exhibited itself through the defence of confessional principles against the disruption caused by evangelical preaching and interdenominational missionary societies. Another was the tendency of some ministers to settle for a less than zealous orthodox position that entailed an emphasis upon good conduct and apathy towards theological controversy, which, in some cases, led to Arminianism.

The religious life of the Presbyterian laity in the eighteenth century was just as complex. The relative shortage of source material for the late eighteenth century means that it is easy to adopt the critical perspectives of nineteenth-century commentators with their high expectations of the level of religious practice. Their criticisms are confirmed to some degree by presbytery visitations from before 1800 which show that Seceders who criticized the laxity of the Synod of Ulster were themselves guilty of moral and procedural lapses and that sections of their laity were lukewarm in their religious observance. However, this did not mean that the laity were ignorant of the distinctive features of Presbyterianism, unorthodox in their beliefs, or indifferent to certain forms of religious practice. The mechanisms by which congregations were organized, as will be shown in Chapter 1, militated against full attendance at public worship. Many believers did the best they could and there were significant differences between godly and less committed Presbyterians. Nineteenth-century evangelicals also glossed over both the attachment of the laity to a traditional understanding of Presbyterianism, which they had attempted to reform in the 1830s, and their own accommodation of lay practices. The laity had their own definitions of what Presbyterianism should be and were willing to defend them in a variety of ways, including the use of official disciplinary procedures. Moreover, many lay Presbyterians mixed their commitment to orthodox Presbyterianism with an implicit belief in the efficacy of various alternative or 'superstitious' beliefs and indulged in often rowdy customary activities. The complexity of the structure of Presbyterianism was matched by the variety of lay belief and practice.

The origins of change within a religious culture are difficult to determine, and the nature of local and intensely conservative communities often means that a long-term perspective is required. Change in the present study includes the influence of the Enlightenment, which stimulated a desire for the reform of church practice across the Presbyterian theological spectrum. During the eighteenth century, New Light ministers and Scottish Moderates were at the vanguard of Enlightenment refinement and taste, which led them to advocate the reform of preaching, psalmody, and the communion season.[75] Yet theological liberals were not the only group shaped by the Enlightenment. Recent studies of the eighteenth-century Church of Scotland have noted the considerable influence of Enlightenment thought upon the theology of the evangelical or Popular Party. In the context of the supreme authority of biblical revelation, evangelicals emphasized the importance of natural religion in defence of the faith, the necessity of the ethical import of Christian ideas, and a more positive view of human potential.[76] A general desire for reform stimulated by the Enlightenment was expressed by the publication in 1825 of the Synod of Ulster's *The constitution and discipline of the Presbyterian Church*, known as the *Code*. Though prominent liberals

[75] Schmidt, *Holy fairs*, 170–83.

[76] N. Landsman, 'Presbyterians and provincial society: the evangelical enlightenment in the west of Scotland, 1740–1775', in J. Dwyer and R. B. Sher (eds.), *Sociability and society in eighteenth-century Scotland* (Edinburgh, 1991), 194–209; J. R. McIntosh, *Church and theology in enlightenment Scotland: the Popular Party, 1740–1800* (East Linton, 1998); K. B. E. Roxborough, *Thomas Gillespie and the origins of the Relief Church in 18th century Scotland* (Berne, 1999).

like A. G. Malcolm of Newry were on the drafting committee, conservative evangelicals such as James Horner of Dublin, Samuel Hanna of Belfast, and Henry Cooke were the leading figures and it was evangelicalism that gave reform its dynamism.[77] The interaction between traditional belief and practice as defined by the laity and the reforming efforts of Presbyterian evangelicals provide the main evidence for, and thrust of, this study.

The term evangelicalism is often used in a loose way to label a phenomenon that has assumed so many guises since the eighteenth century. Evangelicalism is a movement of renewal and reform within transatlantic Protestantism that traces its origins back to British Puritanism and German Pietism. It emerged in the early eighteenth century and is often associated with Moravian missionaries, English Methodists, and various revivals of religion in America and Scotland.[78] In a widely adopted definition, David Bebbington has argued that evangelicalism may be defined by a fourfold theological emphasis upon personal conversion, the final authority of the Bible, the cross of Christ, and religious and social activism.[79] Bebbington's typology has proved a useful framework for assessing the doctrinal characteristics of the movement, especially as he relates changes within the movement to the predominant cultural mood. Nevertheless, this fourfold definition may lead to the impression that evangelicalism was a homogeneous movement solely defined by religious principles. More problematically, though Bebbington does acknowledge that the movement had antecedents, he does stress the novelty of evangelicalism. When applied to the Irish and Scottish contexts this analysis does not wholly satisfy. Though the Enlightenment certainly modified orthodox Presbyterian understandings of the Christian faith for many, the process was anything but radical or unambiguous in its outcomes. There were strong elements of spiritual and doctrinal continuity with traditional forms of Presbyterianism that should not be dismissed as being un-evangelical. There was

---

[77] For details of the compilation of the *Code* and its antecedents, see, Reid *History*, iii. 440–3.

[78] Noll, Bebbington, and Rawlyk, *Evangelicalism*; W. R. Ward, *The Protestant evangelical awakening* (Cambridge, 1992).

[79] D. W. Bebbington, *Evangelicalism in modern Britain: a history from the 1730s to the 1980s*, rev. edn. (London, 1995), 2–17.

an evangelical Presbyterian tradition that comprised a significant section of the Old Light party and the Seceders. Within this tradition were the theological and pastoral emphases of nineteenth-century evangelicalism.

The type of evangelicalism that existed within Ulster Presbyterianism during this period was conservative in character and content. It was indebted to the doctrinal, ecclesiological, and eschatological priorities of the Presbyterian theological tradition as enshrined in the various Westminster standards.[80] In terms of doctrine, the standards provided an understanding of salvation predicated upon God's grace and achieved through the life, death, and resurrection of Christ. As a consequence of Adam's disobedience in Eden, humans needed to be saved from their inherent rebellion against God. Until the coming of Christ, humanity was under the covenant of works, bound to obey God's law but unable to do so because of their initial disobedience. At the heart of God's plan of salvation was the person and work of Christ. It was argued that God the Father entered into a covenant with his Son, who undertook to make atonement for the sins of those elected to eternal life. Old Light and Seceder Presbyterians held that Christ's death on the cross atoned for the sins of the elect, allowing them to come to Christ in repentance and faith. Sincerity, obedience, or mere profession of faith were wholly inadequate to gain God's favour, as salvation was by grace through faith alone. Salvation was not earned but was a gift of God, solely based upon Christ's sacrifice. True faith was not meritorious and ought to manifest itself in evangelical holiness. In this context, the Presbyterian understanding of conversion was distinguished from regeneration. Conversion was the human response to the regeneration of the individual by the Holy Spirit. This response consisted of two elements, namely, faith and repentance, each of which were described as 'a saving grace' involving the affective self and a conscious turning away from sin. God had ordained 'means of grace' consisting of the sacraments, prayer, Bible reading, and, pre-eminently, preaching to call the elect to himself by the influence of the Holy Spirit. Throughout this process, it was the Holy Spirit that convicted individuals of sin and enabled them to

---

[80] For further details of how Presbyterian evangelicalism was indebted to the Presbyterian theological tradition see, Holmes, 'Tradition and enlightenment'.

respond positively to the gospel. The Reformed or Calvinist understanding of salvation outlined above was common to both Seceders and the majority of Old Light Presbyterians and laid the basis for the Presbyterian evangelical consensus of the nineteenth century. However, from the 1770s, some Old Light and Burgher Presbyterians began to downplay the language of an explicit covenant or federal theology and to articulate this Reformed soteriology in more general terms. The robust language of a systematic covenant theology would not be as noticeable a component of Presbyterian evangelicalism in the following century.

In terms of ecclesiology, Presbyterianism is organized around a hierarchical series of church courts. At the base, each congregation has a Kirk session made up of the minister and elected lay elders. The second tier is the presbytery, which comprises all the ministers and a representative elder from each congregation in its jurisdiction. Finally, there is the synod or general assembly which meets once a year and contains the ministers and a representative elder from all the congregations under its care. During the eighteenth century, the Synod of Ulster also set up sub synods between presbyteries and itself, but these proved cumbersome and ineffectual. Like Anglicanism, Presbyterianism is not a gathered church of individuals who demonstrate a conversion experience as proof of membership. Instead, the standards of the church admitted individuals to membership of the visible church through baptism and excluded the ignorant, scandalous, and ungodly from communion.[81] Nineteenth-century Presbyterian evangelicals remained committed to this view of church membership, purity of communion, and church government.

Finally, the Westminster standards gave to Presbyterian evangelicalism the expectation and means of bringing the world to Christ.[82] In accordance with the second petition of the Lord's Prayer, 'Thy kingdom come', ministers were invited by the *Directory for Public Worship* to pray before their sermon 'for the propagation of the gospel and

---

[81] Barkley, *Westminster formularies*, 61–72; *Confession* 29: 8; *Larger Catechism*, Q. 173.

[82] Holmes, 'Millennialism and the interpretation of prophecy'. For a broader perspective, J. A. De Jong, *As the waters cover the sea: millennial expectations and the rise of Anglo-American missions 1640–1810* (Kampen, 1970).

kingdom of Christ to all nations; for the conversion of the Jews, the
fullness of the Gentiles, the fall of Antichrist, and the hastening of
the second coming of our Lord'.[83] The gospel would be spread by the
diligent use of the means of grace, animated by the power of the Holy
Spirit. On the basis of this understanding of God's action in the end
times, Presbyterian evangelicals in this period were postmillennial-
ists. According to this scheme, missionary activity and religious
revival would usher in the millennial reign of Christ, which would
be consummated by the Second Coming.

Two strands of evangelicalism may be identified within eighteenth-century Ulster Presbyterianism.[84] The Seceders represented
the first strand. Miller's appellation of them as purveyors of 'ink
divinity', having confessionally correct answers to theological questions, is a central component of their world-view, though it is not the
only one. The Seceders represent a populist form of Presbyterianism
that had a complex, often contradictory, relationship with popular
culture.[85] They also brought to Ulster distinctive theological preoccupations that had been debated at length during the Marrow
Controversy that rocked the Scottish General Assembly in the
1720s.[86] The defenders of Edward Fisher's *The Marrow of Modern
Divinity*, originally published in the seventeenth century, included
many of the founders of the Associate Presbytery, including the
Erskine brothers, Ebenezer and Ralph. The 'Marrowmen' stood in
the mainstream of the Reformed tradition by reacting against the
European-wide legalizing tendencies within Reformed theology that
stressed both the human preparations necessary for salvation and a
strong cognitive description of faith. They emphasized instead that
salvation was by grace alone through the person and work of
Christ. Consequently, an earnest and earthy type of Seceder preaching developed as the gospel of grace was to be offered to everyone as

---

[83] *Directory*, 377. Also, *Larger Catechism*, Q. 191.

[84] Holmes, 'Tradition and enlightenment', 135–46.

[85] McBride, *Scripture politics*, 73–5.

[86] The following is based upon, P. G. Ryken, *Thomas Boston as preacher of the
fourfold state* (Carlisle, 1999) and D. C. Lachman, *The Marrow controversy 1718–1723:
an historical and theological analysis* (Edinburgh, 1988). A convenient summary of the
Marrow Controversy may be found in D. C. Lachman, 'Marrow controversy', in
N. M. de S. Cameron (org. ed.), *Dictionary of Scottish church history and theology*
(Edinburgh, 1993), 546–8.

individuals and without distinction. Contrary to their critics, this reflected an orthodox understanding of preaching as a means of grace animated by the Holy Spirit rather than a rejection of the Reformed understanding of limited atonement.

The Seceders' understanding of the Christian faith in experiential and individualistic terms was nurtured within a strongly regulated church community with well-defined confessional principles that set them apart from other Presbyterians. As their formula for ordination made clear, Seceders were scrupulous in their defence and exposition of Presbyterian orthodoxy as found in the Westminster standards and their own *Testimony*.[87] It should be noted that Seceders initially subscribed to the Solemn League and Covenant though their fidelity was not unconditional and by the end of the eighteenth century the Burghers especially had quietly relaxed their adherence.[88] The Seceders were also committed to correct church order and the prosecution of discipline through presbytery visitations, privy censures for ministers and elders, and the maintenance of Kirk session discipline. Their defence of confessional and ecclesiological orthodoxy led in the 1740s to a repudiation of the revivalism associated with George Whitefield. The problem for Seceders was that the revival was affecting the apostate Church of Scotland, from which they had recently separated, rather than any difficulties with the concept of revival or indeed with Whitefield's commitment to the doctrines of grace.[89] The rigour of Secession discipline ensured that holiness and personal morality were realities in the lives of church members. Predating the spectacular growth of Methodism in south Ulster, the Seceders made this area a heartland, giving handloom weavers and small farmers a sense of importance and identity in a rapidly changing society increasingly marked by sectarian conflict. In many respects, the Secession was similar to Methodism in that it grew in areas where the number of Synod of Ulster congregations was inadequate to meet the demand for gospel preaching and where economic and political upheaval provided a context for the adoption of their world-view.

---

[87] Stewart, *Seceders*, 406–9.

[88] McKerrow, *History*, 195–6, 530–3.

[89] M. J. Crawford, *Seasons of grace: Colonial New England's revival tradition in its British context* (New York, 1991), 167–70; McKerrow, *History*, 150–71.

David Hempton's characterization of Irish evangelicalism more generally may be applied with equal validity to the Seceders as encouraging 'a sturdy sobriety and sense of responsibility, which attracted
those with a small stake in the world, but who were anxious to
increase it'.[90]

The second strand of Presbyterian evangelicalism contained sections of the Old Light party in the Synod of Ulster and displayed a
number of characteristics similar to the Popular Party in Scotland.
Two points are worth emphasizing.[91] First, the Popular Party wanted
to promote correct views of the person and work of Christ rather
than a certain conversion experience. Second, they desired to maintain the unity of the Kirk and sought to deal with heresy by reaffirming the doctrinal standards of the church rather than 'a vigorous
policy of ecclesiastical censure'. A number of prominent ministers in
the Synod of Ulster in the late eighteenth century, such as Benjamin
McDowell, minister of Ballykelly and later Mary's Abbey in Dublin,
and Sinclare Kelburn, minister of the Third Congregation in Belfast
and a prominent political radical, shared a similar approach and may
legitimately be described as enlightenment evangelicals. As with the
Popular Party, evangelicalism for these men was not contained in a
conversion experience but with 'the exaltation of scriptural doctrines
and right perceptions of the atonement and of man's consequent
relationship with God'.[92] McDowell upheld subscription in print and
Old Lights collectively took decisive action only in exceptional circumstances, as with the largely amicable formation of the subscribing
Presbytery of Belfast in 1772.[93] Significantly, McDowell and Kelburn,
along with Robert Rogers and William Wilson, were appointed by
the Synod of Ulster in 1788 and 1789 to visit the scattered Presbyterian congregations in the south and west of Ireland to determine
their condition, an indication of a concern with planting new
churches beyond their traditional heartland.[94] In the early nineteenth
century, Presbyterian evangelicals such as these were to be found at
the forefront of interdenominational missionary societies. During

[90] Hempton, *Religion of the people*, 34.
[91] McIntosh, *Popular Party*, 234, 236.
[92] Ibid., 236.
[93] Witherow, *Memorials*, ii. ch. 72; Reid, *History*, iii. 335–8.
[94] *RGSU* iii. (1788), 100; (1789), 111.

the 1820s, the prominent evangelical ministers Samuel Hanna and James Seaton Reid testified to the moderate nature of Old Light evangelicalism by questioning Cooke's belligerent policy against theological liberals, while a handful of others, such as James Carlile, were impeccably orthodox yet non-subscribers.[95]

Until the nineteenth century, evangelicalism in general was seen by many in church and state, both in Britain and Ireland, as deeply disruptive, owing to itinerant preaching, seemingly bizarre religious practices, and continuous flouting of ecclesiastical, and sometimes political, control by Methodists in particular. The dislocation of the 1790s and the new economic and political dispensation provided the context for a truly remarkable transatlantic growth in both the numerical power and the social influence of evangelicalism.[96] Across the transatlantic world in this period, evangelicalism thrived in areas of conflict and upheaval, providing different sections of society with ways of dealing with the stresses of change. Ulster experienced these changes and also had a higher percentage of respectable and relatively wealthy supporters who could provide the numbers, social networks, and finances needed to ensure the successful spread of evangelicalism.[97] The failure of the 1798 rebellion was undoubtedly an important stimulus, as evangelicalism seemed to provide a ready-made antidote to the religious and social ills of the day by promoting a delicate blend of religious earnestness, social sobriety, and political loyalty to the recently established United Kingdom. In addition, the transformation of evangelicalism in the nineteenth century from a movement of religious renewal to public pre-eminence accorded well with contemporary socio-economic changes and the social composition of Protestant society in Ulster.

As Hempton and Hill have demonstrated, it would be unwise to divorce the development of Presbyterian evangelicalism from the broader evangelical movement.[98] The growth of Methodism certainly

---

[95] Holmes, *Henry Cooke*, 49, 55–6; R. J. Rodgers, 'James Carlile, 1784–1854' (QUB Ph.D., 1973).

[96] For a helpful discussion that places the 1790s in a wider perspective see, M. A. Noll, 'Revolution and the rise of evangelical social influence in North Atlantic societies', in idem, Bebbington, and Rawlyk, *Evangelicalism*, ch. 6.

[97] Hempton and Hill, *Evangelical Protestantism*, ch. 2.

[98] Ibid., chs. 3–5.

encouraged evangelical sentiment within Presbyterianism, though its Arminian theology caused considerable unease amongst Calvinists. More important was the influence of Anglican evangelicalism and the personal friendships that developed between leaders of the evangelical party, particularly Henry Cooke, and Anglican clergymen and landlords. Cooke was in no doubt that reform within the Established Church of Ireland 'may serve as a beacon' to those seeking reform in the Synod of Ulster.[99] It is important to point out that the majority of Presbyterian ministers were politically liberal and did not agree with Cooke's positive view of the Church of Ireland or his political conservatism. Attempts to challenge the ecclesiastical integrity and independence of Presbyterianism were vigorously rebutted. Despite the efforts of Cooke, relations with the Established Church of Ireland deteriorated quickly in the 1830s and 1840s owing to the rise of Puseyism, the outlawing of marriages performed by Presbyterian ministers, the Disruption of the Church of Scotland in 1843, and the campaign to legalize tenant right in Ireland.[100] Cooke's evangelicalism was much more belligerent and politically conservative than the moderate evangelicalism represented by Samuel Hanna and James Carlile.

Cooke's difficulties were in part caused by the paradox of evangelicalism that, on the one hand, broke down denominational barriers through voluntary societies while, on the other, it encouraged denominational self-confidence.[101] In that regard, evangelicalism was part of a broader trend amongst churches across Europe to tighten discipline and increase religious fervour, often drawing together individuals from different theological and social backgrounds. Stewart J. Brown has recently outlined how this reformist agenda influenced the Established Churches of Britain and Ireland.[102] For instance, the diocesan revival of the Church of England in the early nineteenth century included visitations, the establishment of rural deaneries, and the formation of various missionary and

---

[99] *Christian Enquirer*, 1 (1828), 74–5.

[100] Holmes, *Henry Cooke*, chs. 7–8.

[101] D. M. Thompson, *Denominationalism and dissent, 1795–1835: a question of identity* (London, 1985).

[102] S. J. Brown, *The national churches of England, Ireland, and Scotland 1801–46* (Oxford, 2001).

philanthropic organizations. Under the influence of evangelicalism, the Church of Scotland in the 1830s implemented a series of measures to reform its ecclesiastical machinery, including a renewed eldership, church extension, presbytery visitations from 1835, home and foreign missions, education schemes, the publication of newspapers and periodicals, a renewed sense of their past, and the cultivation of links with other Presbyterian churches.

In the case of Ulster Presbyterians, the events of 1798 led to a rejection of New Light hegemony as evangelicals portrayed it as a spiritually mortifying and politically dangerous creed, overlooking the fact that half of the ministers implicated in the rising were Old Light in theology.[103] More importantly, 1798 also brought to cultural prominence the two strands of evangelicalism latent within Ulster Presbyterianism. The events of the final decade of the eighteenth century encouraged Presbyterian involvement in the formation of evangelical missionary societies, most notably the General Evangelical Society, founded in Dublin in 1787, and the Evangelical Society of Ulster, founded in Armagh in 1798. In the first decades of the nineteenth century, Presbyterian interest in home and foreign mission was channelled through the great voluntary evangelical societies of the day such as the London Missionary Society (LMS) and the Hibernian Bible Society (HBS).[104] These societies were motivated to spread the gospel throughout the world by an eschatological belief that entailed 'nothing less than the realisation of the biblical vision of a world transformed by being filled with the knowledge of the Lord as the waters cover the sea'.[105] The Seceders initially exhibited the most interest in mission as they were committed to confessional orthodoxy, avidly marked the signs of the times, and had established a large number of congregations in North America during the previous

---

[103] A. Holmes, 'Nineteenth-century Ulster Presbyterian perspectives on the 1798 rebellion', in J. Augusteijn, Mary Ann Lyons, and D. McMahon (eds.), *Irish history: a research yearbook, 2* (Dublin, 2003), 43–52.

[104] For the development of the Presbyterian interest and involvement in mission see, idem, 'The shaping of Irish Presbyterian attitudes to mission, 1790–1840', *Journal of Ecclesiastical History* (forthcoming, 2006); W. P. Addley, 'A study of the birth and development of the overseas missions of the Presbyterian Church in Ireland up to 1910' (QUB Ph.D., 1994), chs. 1–4.

[105] B. Stanley, 'The future in the past: eschatological vision in British and American Protestant missionary history', *Tyndale Bulletin*, 51 (2000), 103.

century. However, all nineteenth-century Presbyterian evangelicals believed missionary activity would help to bring about the millennium. The HBS received official support from the Synod of Ulster in 1811, and, in the following year, the main Presbyterian bodies in Ulster received a deputation on behalf of the LMS from the Revd Alexander Waugh, a Scottish Seceder. In 1824 the Scottish Missionary Society sent representatives to Ulster and it was under its auspices that Hope Waddell and Thomas Leslie became the first missionaries of Irish Presbyterian origin to go overseas. Cooke and his evangelical supporters in the Synod of Ulster recognized the importance of these Bible and missionary societies in placing orthodox sentiments into the public consciousness and popularizing evangelical religion amongst the upper echelons of society.[106] The mood of evangelical activism led to the erection of thirty-nine Synod of Ulster congregations between 1814 and 1830 and to the formation of denominational missionary societies, beginning in 1820 with the Presbyterian Society of Ireland, a joint venture between the Synods of Ulster and Munster, and the home mission of the Seceders.[107] In 1826 the Synod of Ulster Home Mission Society was established, in 1828 the Reformed Presbyterian Synod reorganised their home and foreign missionary society (originally formed in 1823), and in 1830 the Home Mission and the Presbyterian Society for Ireland were combined to form the Synod of Ulster's Presbyterian Missionary Society to promote 'the revival and extension of vital religion, especially among Presbyterians in Ireland, by disseminating the pure principles of the Gospel'.[108] The Presbyterian support for missionary societies demonstrates both the influence of the theological priorities of the Presbyterian tradition and the vibrancy of evangelical sentiment amongst ministers and the laity outside the official structures of the church.

The rise of Presbyterian evangelicalism was encouraged by the foundation of the Belfast Academical Institution or 'Inst' in 1815.[109] As outlined in Chapter 5 below, ministers before that date

---

[106] *Fourth report of the commissioners of Irish education inquiry*, HC (1826–7) xiii.157, 128, 149.

[107] 'Increase of congregations under the care of the Synod of Ulster', *Orthodox Presbyterian*, 1 (1830), 194.

[108] *RGSU* (1830), 35.

[109] R. Allen, *The Presbyterian College Belfast 1853–1953* (Belfast, 1954), ch. 1.

had received their liberal arts education at Glasgow University and their theological training under a presbytery, both of which encouraged the growth of theological moderatism. The foundation of a college in Belfast provided the opportunity for the appointment of divinity professors by the Synod of Ulster and the Seceders. Both chose Calvinists who were actively involved in evangelical missionary societies. The Seceder concern with the doctrines of grace was upheld by Samuel Edgar of Ballynahinch and his son and successor John Edgar, the prominent advocate of evangelical and philanthropic causes. Samuel Hanna gave Synod of Ulster students a thoroughly Calvinist theological education and encouraged the formation of prayer meetings amongst his students. Hanna believed that 'more Calvinists have gone into the ministry in the Synod of Ulster, since the commencement of my lectures' than from previous universities.[110] Both the Arian Henry Montgomery and John Paul, Covenanter minister and scourge of the non-subscribers, agreed that the appointment of Hanna was a significant indication of the growth of evangelical sentiment more generally in Ulster and would encourage the revival of conservative theological views within the Synod.[111] Orthodox and liberal authorities were sure that ministers were more inclined to orthodoxy if educated at Belfast rather than in Glasgow.[112]

The reform movement within Presbyterianism increased momentum in the 1820s. Since 1810 a committee of the Synod of Ulster had been attempting to compile an official constitution and discipline for the Synod and some presbyteries, such as Ballymena and Route, renewed the practice of visiting each congregation under their care. The *Code*, finally published in 1825, had a variety of functions, including confirming procedure, controlling the excesses of popular evangelicalism, and reforming traditional beliefs and practices amongst the laity. It was Cooke who eagerly supervised its completion and it was evangelicalism that gave reform its crusading zeal and

---

[110] *Fourth report of the commissioners of Irish education inquiry*, 61.

[111] Ibid., 49; R. L. W. McCollum, 'John Paul and his contribution to the shaping of Presbyterianism in the 19th century' (QUB Ph.D., 1992), 45.

[112] *Fourth report of the commissioners of Irish education inquiry*, 49, 61–2, 93, 131, 136–7.

social influence.[113] In a sermon preached at the Synod in 1825, Cooke called for the thorough reform of Presbyterian church life. His main concern was to ensure that the structures and procedures of the church were directed towards religious ends. 'In the Presbyterian church, a revival of religion may fairly be expected, when presbyteries divest themselves of the character of mere routine meetings attending to literary examinations, or the secularities of the Church, and make the business of vital religion the chief object of their enquiry, their solicitude, and their discipline.'[114] He urged ministers to be more assiduous visitors, recommended the revival of family worship, and advocated the collection of religious statistics for the number of families, Bibles, communicants, frequency and pattern of family worship, catechizing, and public worship. The publication of the *Code* and the increasing prominence of evangelicalism led to the reorganization of some presbyteries and provided the template for the evangelical reforms of the 1830s.[115] An open letter to the Synod published just before the momentous meeting of the Synod in June 1828 and signed by Cooke, John Johnston of Tullylish, William Craig of Dromara, and W. D. Stewart of Downpatrick, invited all Presbyterians to support their calls for a reformation of the church. They demanded reform of the ministry, eldership, and visitation presbyteries, as well as the restoration of the religious character of church courts and the revival of family worship.[116] Overall, the defeat of Montgomery in 1828 and the withdrawal of the Remonstrants in 1829 were a product of, and accelerator to, the growth of Presbyterian evangelicalism.

Mirroring developments in the Church of Scotland, the tempo of change within Ulster Presbyterianism increased dramatically in the 1830s, especially within the Synod of Ulster. At an institutional level, doctrinal and moral discipline was tightened through the establishment of the Theological Examination Committee in 1828, the reorganization of Kirk sessions, and the reimposition of subscription to the *Confession* in 1836. When subscription was renewed it was

---

[113] For Cooke's role see, Reid, *History*, iii. 441–2.

[114] H. Cooke, *A sermon, preached at the opening of the General Synod of Ulster* (Belfast, 1825), 38–9.

[115] Armagh Pby (GSU), 1825–32 (PHS); Derry Pby (GSU), 7 Sept. 1825 (UTC); Letterkenny, 20 Apr. 1825 (Church House, strong room), 73–5.

[116] *Belfast News-Letter*, 17 June 1828.

supported by ninety-one ministers and thirty-one elders and opposed by twenty ministers and eight elders.[117] It is important to note that what mattered to some Presbyterian evangelicals were the doctrines contained in the *Confession* rather than full conformity as an end in itself. In the late eighteenth century, the subscribing Presbytery of Belfast had sixteen different formulas of subscription and in the nineteenth century a number of notable evangelicals, including James Carlile, Samuel Dill, and John Johnston, did not agree that full subscription to the *Confession* was necessary to maintain theological integrity.[118] In 1826 Cooke admitted that the Old Light party included Arminians and that there was 'a kind of compromise' on subscription in presbyteries to allow their peaceful coexistence with Calvinists. He suggested that a less rigid form of subscription to all the key evangelical doctrines could be introduced into the Synod, though he did believe that Arminianism conceded the essential points of Calvinism and claimed that the main point of controversy was over the *Confession*'s teaching on the power of the civil magistrate in enforcing religious conformity.[119] Yet it was precisely this uneasy coexistence between Calvinists, Arminians, and Arians that proved an insurmountable barrier to union with the Seceders. Full subscription, therefore, was crucial for closer relations with both the Secession Synod and the Church of Scotland.[120]

The reorganization of presbyteries and the renewal of regular visitations were seen as a key means of reasserting discipline, renewing spiritual commitment, and ensuring that any reforms were implemented. Seceders had regular visitation presbyteries before the 1820s though at this time they and the Covenanters also sought to revitalize their presbyteries and to standardize practice.[121] By 1830 the Synod of Ulster had fifteen presbyteries of varying sizes and

[117] *RGSU* (1836), 45.

[118] Barkley, *Westminster formularies*, 13–14; T. Croskery 'Memoir of the Rev. Samuel Dill, of Donoughmore, Co. Donegal', *Evangelical Witness*, 8 (1870), 12.

[119] *Fourth report of the commissioners of Irish education inquiry*, 146–8, 155.

[120] Ibid., 112, 120; R. Allen, *James Seaton Reid: a centenary biography* (Belfast, 1951), 91–6.

[121] A draft of questions for visitation presbyteries was presented to the Secession Synod in 1837 (*MPSI* (1837), 36–9). Questions for Covenanter visitation presbyteries were drawn up in 1823 (Minutes of the Synod of the Reformed Presbyterian Church in Ireland, 1821–35 (PRONI CR/5/5A/1/4), 20).

lacking geographical cohesion.[122] Proposed by Seaton Reid as early as 1830 and enacted in 1834, the 230 congregations belonging to the Synod of Ulster were reorganized into twenty-four presbyteries in order to increase the efficiency of business, scrutinize the records of Kirk sessions, mobilize the laity, and encourage the formation of Sunday schools (see Map 2). In addition, each presbytery was to become an auxiliary to the Presbyterian Missionary Society and each Kirk ses-sion was to act as a local sub-committee.[123] The type of business transacted by presbyteries was also to be transformed. Before the 1820s the remaining presbytery records show that pro-cedural and financial matters dominated meetings with little or no attention devoted to the religious state of the congregations under their jurisdiction. During the first half of the 1830s the Committee of Books, which supervised the records of the various church courts, uncovered evidence of negligence in various presbyteries including poor record-keeping, infrequent or no visitations, and the lack of questions directed towards ascertaining the theological beliefs of ministers at existing visitations. In 1832 they recommended a stricter enquiry into congregational discipline and the drafting of a common set of questions that elicited full statements on matters of discipline and doctrine.[124] Despite the efforts of the Committee, the need for a common set of visitation questions was only finally satisfied in the 1841 revision of the *Code*, though by that stage most presbyteries had already adopted a more thorough visitation programme.[125]

This reimposition of doctrine and discipline demonstrates that theological and denominational principles were as important for nineteenth-century evangelicals as they had been for 'prophetic' Calvinists. The dominant evangelical party targeted for reform cold orthodoxy and traditional lay understandings of Presbyterian-ism, while also asserting denominational self-confidence against Arianism, Catholicism, and, later, Anglicanism. The overall tone of

---

[122] 'The General Synod of Ulster and its presbyteries', *Orthodox Presbyterian*, 1 (1830), 117–23.
[123] *RGSU* (1834), 19–20, 47; 'Approaching meeting of the General Synod of Ulster' and 'The General Synod of Ulster', *Orthodox Presbyterian*, 5 (1834), 292–3, 341–4.
[124] *RGSU* (1832), 30–1.
[125] *RGSU* (1834), 36–7; (1838), 37; *Code* (1841), 39–45.

Presbyterianism in the Synod of Ulster became much more assertive. In 1809 the Synod urged their members to 'hold fast to the profession of your faith, but at the same time endeavour as much as is in you lies, to preserve the unity of the spirit, in the bond of peace'.[126] The address from which this was extracted was composed by the Dublin Presbytery, which contained a number of prominent evangelicals, and appointed by a synod over which Samuel Hanna was moderator. By 1833 the tone was markedly different though the address published that year had been composed by the Presbytery of Belfast and the moderator had been John Brown, a prominent evangelical and political liberal; 'Hold fast, although you should incur the charge of bigotry—attempt no conciliation with error—yield not one jot or tittle of the truth.'[127] In practical terms, the efforts to reform practice were to have a far-reaching impact upon the laity. They would have noticed changes in the preaching they heard, the books they read, the new religious societies they attended, the style of psalmody they joined in, and the ways in which rites of passage were administered. In general, expectations of both lay and ministerial behaviour increased dramatically. Traditional duties such as church attendance and family worship were enjoined with renewed fervour along with new areas of service that included missionary societies, Sunday schools, and various moral reform campaigns, particularly temperance societies.

The aim of reformers was to increase the moral and religious character of Presbyterianism and to promote religious revival.[128] In so doing, they drew upon the eschatological priorities of the Presbyterian theological tradition. Presbyterian evangelicals believed that the growth of interest in vital religion and the formation of various voluntary missionary and philanthropic agencies signalled a revival of religion.[129] Interest in revival was stimulated by accounts in Presbyterian periodicals of revivals of religion in Europe and

---

[126] *A pastoral address from the ministers of the Synod of Ulster* (n.p., 1809), 6.

[127] *Annual address of the General Synod of Ulster* (Belfast, 1833), 6.

[128] For further details, A. Holmes, 'The experience and understanding of religious revival in Ulster Presbyterianism, c. 1800 to 1930', *Irish Historical Studies* 34 (2005), 361–85.

[129] *MGA* i. (1840), 23.

America during the eighteenth century and in their own time.[130] More importantly, Presbyterians were made aware of their own revival heritage through Reid's moderatorial sermon of 1828 and the publication in 1834 of the first volume of his *History*, both of which recounted the Six Mile Water revival of 1625.[131] Furthermore, Presbyterian evangelicals saw the expulsion of the Remonstrants in 1829 in terms of the rediscovery of seventeenth-century Presbyterian beliefs and practices. According to a writer in the *Orthodox Presbyterian*, mouthpiece of Presbyterian evangelicals, 'a day of refreshing from above has visited us; the doctrines in which our fathers gloried are, *once more*, the doctrines that are acknowledged and maintained by our church'. He continued, 'in humble dependence on the Eternal Spirit of Truth, we are confidently anticipating a revival of truth and righteousness to result from our return to the "good old days" of our ancestors, and our determination to entrust the gospel amongst us to those only who maintain those precious truths, on which the preaching and professing of which, our Scriptural and Apostolic Church was originally founded'.[132]

Evangelicals believed that the reforms of the 1830s were evidence of a revival of religion and that this should be encouraged for at least three reasons. First, they wanted make up for the laxity of discipline that had characterized the eighteenth-century church under New Light influence. During the 1830s and 1840s discipline was seen as both a stimulus to, and a feature of, genuine revival.[133] Second, building upon the growing enthusiasm for mission in the early

---

[130] 'Revival of religion', *Christian Freeman*, 1 (1833), 171–4; *Orthodox Presbyterian*, new ser., 2 (1839), 361–71; *Presbyterian Penny Magazine*, 2 (1835), 6–8, 45–6, 147–8; R. S. Jennings, 'The origins of Ulster Presbyterian revivalism in the mid-nineteenth century' (QUB M.Th., 1985), 84–9.

[131] J. S. Reid, *The history of the Presbyterian Church in Ireland, briefly reviewed and practically improved* (Belfast, 1828); *History of the Presbyterian Church in Ireland* (Edinburgh, 1834), 106–27.

[132] [J. S. Reid], 'On the doctrinal principles held by the founders of the Presbyterian Church in Ireland', *Orthodox Presbyterian*, 1 (1829), 97.

[133] *Annual address of the General Synod of Ulster* (1833), 10–11; 'Presbytery of Magherafelt', *Orthodox Presbyterian*, 6 (1834), 69; 'Purity of communion', *Christian Freeman*, 1 (1833), 333–8; J. Brown, *The Christian ambassador* (Belfast, 1833); J. Morgan, *The foundation, character, and security of the Christian Church* (Belfast, 1832).

decades of the century, Presbyterians wanted revival to stimulate their efforts at evangelism both at home and overseas. Presbyterians continued to support interdenominational missionary societies but they also believed they had been negligent of their gospel calling and ought to use the structures and finances of their church to spread the gospel. A special meeting of the Synod of Ulster was held in Dublin in September 1833 to heighten awareness of mission within the church and plan for the expansion of its evangelistic activity. The published account of the meeting explicitly linked missionary activism with revival.[134] Third, Presbyterians desired a revival to strengthen the public witness of the church in response to urban and industrial expansion and the growing political and religious belligerence of Irish Catholicism. For these and other reasons the 1833 pastoral address of the Synod of Ulster declared, 'Revival, brethren, is what we want. Let it be sought by every scriptural means.'[135]

Presbyterians in the decades before 1859 saw revival in terms of the reformation of the structures and spiritual life of the church. They believed that a revival was prayed down rather than worked up. Consequently, they were lukewarm in their attitude towards the 'new measures' revivalism associated with the American preacher Charles Finney.[136] The sober definition propounded by Presbyterian writers allowed them to characterize as a true revival of religion the renewed interest in mission, the campaign against Arianism, and the reimposition of discipline and correct doctrine. The Synod in 1834 set aside a day of prayer in August to ask God for an outpouring of the Holy Spirit 'and at the same time to express gratitude to Almighty God for the manifestation of that spirit in the revival of religion in our church, in the peace and harmony which happily pervade our meetings, and in the gradual improvement of discipline which appears in the congregations under our care'.[137] Furthermore, the ongoing revival of religion was identified as a means of bringing

---

[134] *Missionary sermons and speeches delivered at a special meeting of the General Synod of Ulster* (Belfast, 1834), pp. x–xii.

[135] *Annual address of the General Synod of Ulster* (1833), 9.

[136] R. Carwardine, *Transatlantic revivalism: popular evangelicalism in Britain and America, 1790–1865* (Westport, Conn., 1978) and C. Hambrick-Stowe, *Charles G. Finney and the spirit of American evangelicalism* (Grand Rapids, Mich., 1996).

[137] *RGSU* (1834), 40.

about the millennium. In language reminiscent of the Westminster standards, the Synod in 1836 once more directed the people under their care 'earnestly to pray that God, by the gracious outpourings of His Spirit, will carry on His own work among us, and cause the kingdoms of this world soon to become the kingdoms of our Lord and His Christ'.[138] It is no surprise that the union of 1840 was interpreted as the product of a revival of religion and as a stimulus to it. Not only had Presbyterians witnessed a renewal of religious zeal, they had also, they believed, revived the true spirit of primitive Christianity in Ireland.[139]

   Evangelical or religious 'enthusiasm' would not become dominant in Ulster Presbyterianism because of its conservative Reformed heritage and geographical concentration in the north-east. The quasi-established status of the Presbyterian churches bred a sense of distinctiveness and a certain amount of provincial chauvinism that was given increasing prominence by the economic and political developments of the nineteenth century. Presbyterian evangelicalism had more to do with discipline, the creation of a godly community, and biblical spirituality than with promoting a stereotypical religious experience. The godly community, was to be created by the reassertion of church discipline and pastoral visitation, and the formation of missionary auxiliaries, prayer meetings, and Sunday schools. W. T. Latimer's view that the revival of Presbyterianism in the 1830s 'was produced by instructing the understandings rather than exciting the emotions of Ulster Presbyterians' was largely correct.[140] Personal conversion may be one of the hallmarks of evangelicalism, but it is by no means the only one.

This book describes the religious beliefs and practices of Presbyterians and how these were shaped by the influence of tradition, reform, and revival. The following chapters in turn examine the prescribed components of corporate and individual devotion and the various ways in which the laity adapted aspects of these practices for their own ends. Variety and interaction will be key themes throughout this

---

[138] *RGSU* (1836), 58.
[139] *MGA* i. (1840), 22–5.
[140] Latimer, *History,* 449.

study. The very meaning of Presbyterianism itself was contested as New Light and Old Light, evangelicals and orthodox, ministers and the laity attempted to articulate their own understanding of what it was. Variety was also expressed in the different levels of adherence to institutional Presbyterianism, along with variations in social class, gender, and regional location. Interaction occurred at different levels, from the relationship between religious reform and social change, to the dynamics of local congregational communities, and the connection between confessional orthodoxy and popular religious practice. By examining these themes, it will be easier to characterize the Presbyterian community and enumerate those factors that made a Presbyterian a Presbyterian.

Part I

Time

The Lord's Day, or the Sabbath, was the only holy day recognized by the Puritans and the Westminster divines as having biblical warrant. Consequently, the pre-Reformation religious calendar of patrons' days, feast days, saints' days, and popular calendrical customs, was assailed in the interests of true religion. The debate over the calendar in the sixteenth and seventeenth centuries reflected concerns that were to remain central to Reformed Protestants in subsequent centuries. These included the authority and role of the Bible and tradition, the place of the Sabbath, anti-Catholicism, liberty of conscience, and the reform of popular customs and the alternative beliefs associated with them.[1] Yet these developments did not mean that Protestants no longer had special days of religious observance or that they abandoned popular holidays. A new set of dates was now observed that recorded Protestant victories over Catholicism,[2] while Puritans and other Reformed Protestants observed the Sabbath, fast days, and the ceremonies that surrounded the Lord's Supper. In the eighteenth and nineteenth centuries, evangelicals set apart special days for love feasts, prayer meetings, revival events, and other religious activities. Furthermore, despite the efforts of English and Scottish Puritans, popular calendrical customs associated with prominent

[1] L. E. Schmidt, 'Time, celebration, and the Christian year in eighteenth-century evangelicalism', in M. A. Noll, D. W. Bebbington, and G. A. Rawlyk (eds.), *Evangelicalism: comparative studies in popular Protestantism in North America, the British Isles, and beyond 1700–1900* (Oxford, 1994), 94.

[2] D. Cressy, *Bonfires and bells: national memory and the Protestant calendar in Elizabethan and Stuart England* (London, 1989).

days in the agricultural calendar, for example May Day or Halloween, continued to be observed. It has been suggested that this survival reflected well upon both the robustness of the customs and the sensitivity of the reformers. They realized that a secularized calendar, divested of its popish elements, would retain the support of the people while the more important imposition of doctrinal and liturgical change was carried out and alternatives to boisterous activities were put in place.[3]

The Presbyterians of Ulster had their own ways of marking the passage of time; from the rhythm of their communion seasons and the week-in, week-out observance of the Sabbath, to a calendar of holidays and festivities that were, theoretically at least, prohibited by the standards of the church. In the nineteenth century, this yearly cycle was coming under increasing pressure from economic and social changes, particularly the slump in domestic industries, the growth of Belfast, and the coalition of social and religious reformers. There had always been tensions in the religious use of time amongst eighteenth-century evangelicals and these were exacerbated by broader changes within society: the redeeming of time versus lengthy worship and communion seasons; the improvement of time versus 'idle days' and the waste of time; corporate versus individual time.[4] As will be shown, each of these tensions was played out in Presbyterian Ulster during this period. There was little attempt by reformers to dismantle the traditional calendar, but an intensive effort to make sure the Sabbath was better observed and to eradicate the anti-social elements of popular culture, particularly intemperance.

The next three chapters outline the means by which Ulster Presbyterians marked the passage of time and how they responded to, and prompted, changes in the way it was observed. Chapter 1 will examine attitudes to the Lord's Day, particularly the issues of attendance and observance within the context of economic and social change. Chapter 2 will describe how Presbyterians observed days of special religious activity, in particular focusing upon what the observance of

[3] R. Hutton, 'The English Reformation and the evidence of folklore', *Past and Present*, 148 (1995), 89–116; M. Todd, 'Profane pastimes and Reformed community: the persistence of popular festivities in early modern Scotland', *Journal of British Studies*, 39 (2000), 123–56.

[4] Schmidt, 'Christian year', in Noll *et al.*, *Evangelicalism*, 102–4.

fast days tells us about how Presbyterians thought about God and his activity in the world. The third chapter will look at calendrical customs not officially sanctioned by the church and the alternative beliefs associated with them, especially those surrounding spring-time, harvest home and Halloween, and Christmas. A discussion of public worship, the Lord's Supper, and family devotions will be covered in later chapters.

1

The Lord's Day

The observance of the Lord's Day, as laid out in the *Directory*, entailed not merely attendance at meeting, but the setting aside of the whole day as holy to God.[1] In order to do so, necessary preparations had to be made, all worldly business postponed, and servants were to be allowed a day of rest to attend meeting. The Christian Sabbath was to begin with private and family devotions before the family assembled at the meeting-house, the head of the household ensuring that all under his care attended punctually and remained until the benediction was given. During the intermission in the middle of the service, and for the remainder of the day, time was to 'be spent in reading, meditation, religious conversation, catechising, repeating of sermons, private and family prayer, visiting the sick, relieving the poor, and in performing any other duties of piety, charity, and mercy'.[2] The Puritan use of the Sabbath as the focal point of piety was a significant innovation in the life of the church as it inaugurated a weekly rather than a yearly cycle of piety.[3] The Sabbath was a time when the people of God were to meet, irrespective of social rank or wealth, to worship God and encourage one another in the faith. This chapter outlines the attitude of Ulster Presbyterians to Sabbath attendance and observance, along with the efforts of religious reformers in the nineteenth century to improve lay practice and deal with the problems caused by population and urban growth.

[1] *Directory*, 375, 386.
[2] *Code* (1825), 87.
[3] C. Hambrick-Stowe, *The practice of piety: Puritan devotional practice in seventeenth-century New England* (Chapel Hill, N. C., 1982), 96.

I

The use of church attendance statistics is fraught with difficulties concerning the collection, presentation, and interpretation of data. The debates that have surrounded the timing and character of secularization and the significance of the 1851 religious census as an indicator of working-class non-attendance are cases in point.[4] Attendance or membership figures tell us little about the intensity with which religious beliefs were held, but they are a useful indicator in determining the 'social significance' of religion.[5] In Ulster there were different degrees of attachment to organized religion and various factors often militated against a deeper commitment to the local congregation. Bare statistics therefore need to be placed and interpreted within the complicated context from which they have been extracted. The following section is not meant to be an in-depth examination of all the variables surrounding Presbyterian church attendance in Ulster, but a broad description of the main issues.

In the 1780s, the minister of Armagh, William Campbell, calculated that if the average number of families attending each of the 180 congregations of the Synod of Ulster was 400, and if there were six persons in each family, then the estimated population belonging to the Synod would be 432,000. To that number, he added approximately 82,800 Seceders to give 514,800 persons attached to mainstream Irish Presbyterianism.[6] Campbell's figures did not include either Reformed Presbyterians or members of the Southern Association, and his estimated totals seem to be somewhat inflated. The publication in 1835 of average church attendance figures in the *First report of the commissioners of public instruction* were similar to his estimates but were taken after several decades of net population growth. If the 1835 figures are compared with the *regium donum* returns of 1834, which gave the total number of individuals

    [4] For a stimulating, though not entirely convincing, reading of these themes see, C. G. Brown, *The death of Christian Britain: understanding secularisation 1800–2000* (London, 2001).

    [5] Idem, *Religion and society in Scotland since 1707* (Edinburgh, 1997), 42–4.

    [6] I. R. McBride, *Scripture politics: Ulster Presbyterians and Irish radicalism in the late eighteenth century* (Oxford, 1998), 27–8.

Table 1. Size and average attendance of the principal Presbyterian groupings in Ulster, 1835

Body	Number of congregations	Adherents	Average attendance	Ratio of adherents to attendees
Synod of Ulster	229	379,622	87,980	23.2
Seceders	123	83,549	32,198	38.5
Remonstrants	17	17,859	3,625	20.3
Presbytery of Antrim	9	9,075	3,720	41
Totals	378	490,105	127,523	26

Sources: *First report of the commissioners of public instruction, Ireland,* HC (1835), xxxiii; *An account, in detail, of the application of the sums voted to defray the expense of non-conforming, Seceding, and Protestant dissenting ministers in Ireland in 1833,* HC (1834), xlii. 523–6. For the calculation of these figures, see A. R. Holmes, 'Ulster Presbyterian belief and practice, 1770–1840' (QUB Ph.D., 2002), 340–51.

connected with a congregation and who are referred to in Table 1 as adherents, it is possible to calculate ratios between the total number of people who could attend meeting (adherents) and the average number who actually did.

In addition to these figures were 1,831 persons who belonged to the Synod of Munster and an estimated 20,000 belonging to other Presbyterian groupings, including 16,000 Reformed Presbyterians.[7] An examination of the figures indicates variations in attendance based upon geographical location, the type of Presbyterianism of the congregation, and the time of the year, with attendance increasing during the summer months. In addition, there were problems associated with the collection of the original data. Presbyterian congregations did not correspond with the Church of Ireland parishes upon which the census was based, which may have led to either the under- or over-reporting of Presbyterian strength in certain areas. The Synod of Ulster established a committee in 1835 to correspond with the government as many of the returns appeared to underestimate the number of Presbyterians in Ulster, while the Remonstrants alleged that some orthodox Presbyterians had deliberately inflated their attendance figures in order to receive a higher *regium donum* grant.[8]

[7] G. Mathews, *An account of the regium donum* (Dublin, 1836), 27.

[8] *RGSU* (1835), 59, 72–3; 'Presbyterian statistics', *Bible Christian*, 5 (1834), 527–30.

In congregations belonging to the Synod of Ulster and the Remonstrant Synod, between one-fifth and one-quarter of those who could attend meeting on a regular basis did so. Perhaps owing to its size and geographical concentration, the small Presbytery of Antrim had a high level of adherence, while the more scrupulous and committed attitude of the Seceders may account for their higher attendance ratio. In fact, the situation was even more complicated. On the basis of the 1835 figures, George Mathews, a Presbyterian who worked as a government official in Dublin Castle, reckoned there were 130,898 Presbyterians in 1836 'who are not under the charge of any clergyman of their own'.[9] Matthew observed that 'after making every allowance for aged, sick, juvenile, and those otherwise absent, the attendance is (particularly throughout the Synod of Ulster) far below what it ought to be, whatever are the geographical obstructions in mountainous or sea coast districts'.[10] The existence of a large group of people who were called Presbyterian but who had no formal connection with the church has significant implications for the present study. It highlights variations in the level of lay attachment to the structures and beliefs of Presbyterianism. Being a Presbyterian for some people had little to do with attendance at meeting. Their identity signified attachment to certain cultural, ethnic, and political ideals that were informed but not necessarily beholden to the peculiar doctrines of Presbyterianism. The Presbyterian laity was not homogeneous but varied according to the religious, social, and cultural outlook of the individual or group concerned.

The question still remains, why did so many not attend meeting on a regular basis? A variety of factors contributed, including a lack of suitable clothing, tiredness after working all week, dislike of a preacher's style, and want of inclination.[11] The above figures must also be placed within the context of rapid population growth between 1750 and 1841. Some Presbyterians recognized the implications of this for church accommodation and pastoral provision. In 1807 the Synod of Ulster in its pastoral address noted that the number of communicants had not kept pace with population

⁹ Mathews, *Account*, 27.
¹⁰ Ibid., 25.
¹¹ 'Public worship', *Bible Christian*, 3 (1832), 393–9.

growth.[12] Yet, it was only in the late 1820s and 1830s that serious concerns were raised. The prominent evangelical minister of Aghadowey, the Revd John Brown, stated the problem in stark terms to the Synod of Ulster in 1833. While presbyteries and ministers reported that attendance was good and communicant members were as numerous as ever, he believed that such statements failed to take into account that the population in some areas had doubled in the past thirty years and that a comparable increase of ministers was needed to meet this new need. He claimed that, 'dense masses of heathenism exist in our large towns and in country parishes, while no adequate exertions are being made to enlighten and reclaim them'.[13]

The problems caused by population growth were exacerbated by the organization of local congregations, particularly the pew rent system. Pews or 'sittings' were let to individuals and families in return for a fixed sum payable at set times during the year, the bulk of which made up the minister's stipend.[14] Pews were accorded different monetary values depending on their location in the meeting-house. Ostensibly, this system ensured that anyone who wanted a pew, irrespective of wealth, had access to public worship, but it also meant that social differences were reflected in congregational seating plans. In 1834 the stipend of £80 paid to the Revd William Montieth of Glendermott was made up by three classes of pew-sitter, ranging from 'gentlemen' at £1.10s., to farmers at £1, and artisans/cottiers at 15s.[15] The congregations of Lisburn and Cahans, County Monaghan, were more elaborately arranged with eight and nine classes respectively.[16] In Synod of Ulster congregations, this social differentiation based on ability to pay was carried further in a 1733 resolution that a two-thirds majority of both church-members and money had to be achieved when voting for a new minister.[17] The pew rent system did exclude poorer Presbyterians from attending public worship as they

[12] *A pastoral address from the ministers of the Synod of Ulster* (n.p., 1807), 7.

[13] J. Brown, *The Christian ambassador* (Belfast, 1833), 34–6.

[14] For information regarding stipend see, C. Porter, *Irish regium donum and ministerial maintenance* (Belfast, 1884).

[15] *OSMI* (Clondermot), xxxiv. 24.

[16] W. I. Craig, *Presbyterianism in Lisburn from the seventeenth century. First Lisburn Presbyterian church* (Belfast, [1961]), 52; Cahans (B/Sec.) session book, Feb. 1846 (PHS).

[17] *RGSU* ii. (1733), 187.

could simply not afford the seat rent for themselves and their families. Owing to demand for seating, it was usually the case that not all members of a family attended meeting. The Presbytery of Route in 1836 found that generally seatholders were 'not disposed ... to take sufficient accommodation for their families' and that on average 'the sittings taken by seatholders do not amount to two sittings for each family'.[18] In some areas the economic difficulties of the 1820s and 1830s also inhibited the ability of individuals to pay pew rents.

Though the provision of church accommodation remained inadequate, a number of points are worth noting. First, the brisk growth in the number of Seceder congregations in the second half of the eighteenth century provided a safety valve for an increasing population by providing extra ministers and congregations without the procedural and financial constraints of the Synod of Ulster. They had no such rule as that passed by the Synod of Ulster in 1733 and often stressed the lack of wealth or gender differentiation between church members in their congregations.[19] Second, until the early 1770s, around 100,000 individuals, mostly Presbyterians, had left Ulster and migrated to America. This led directly to the collapse of the first Reformed Presbyterian presbytery and more generally to a reduced demand for church accommodation. Third, non-attendance at worship did not suddenly become a problem in the nineteenth century, and synodical pronouncements, presbytery records, and Kirk session books demonstrate the concern of eighteenth-century Presbyterians with this issue.[20] By the nineteenth century, the desire to collect data and the rhetoric of evangelicals drew greater attention to the scale and possible moral consequences of non-attendance. Indeed, the almost excessive expectations of evangelicals concerning appropriate levels of churchgoing have done much to distort our appreciation of working-class attendance in this period.[21]

---

[18] Route Pby (GSU), 20 Dec. 1836 (Church House, strong room). Templepatrick Pby (GSU), congregational census, 1832 (PRONI, MIC/1P/85).

[19] For example, *MPSI* (1834), 39.

[20] Down Pby (B/Sec.), 10 Dec. 1788 (PHS); Anahilt (GSU) session book, 23 Nov. 1771, 13 Apr. 1778 (J. M. Barkley, 'A history of the ruling eldership in Irish Presbyterianism', 2 vols. (QUB MA, 1952), ii. 274); C. Porter, 'Congregational memoirs: Glenarm', *Christian Unitarian*, 5 (1866), 223.

[21] Brown, *Death of Christian Britain*, 18–30.

It is not self-evident that Presbyterians were automatically excluded by pew rents or a lack of suitable clothing as this presupposes that every Presbyterian had a similar desire to attend public worship. Some Kirk sessions expressed concern that presumably well-to-do seatholders and those who took church privileges were not attending public worship.[22] Conversely, Henry Cooke observed in 1825 that the 'poor are generally as forward to pay according to their means as the rich'.[23] Nor does it necessarily follow that the poor resented the social differentiation implied by the different classes of pew rent or indeed the suitability of their clothing.[24] In his evidence to a House of Commons Select Committee in 1835, Alexander Moncrieff, a Belfast muslin manufacturer, took issue with the view that a lack of decent clothing deterred the poor from attending church and reiterated the point that it was personal inclination that determined whether an individual attended or not. He continued, 'If they are very religiously inclined they are generally economical in their habits; and the desire they have to attend a place of worship induces them to strain every point to do so; and, of course, they generally manage to attend.'[25] Likewise, the Revd William Moore of Moneymore, County Londonderry, commented in the 1830s that Presbyterians in the area were so proud they 'actually live on scanty meals and work hard all week in order to appear well dressed on Sunday'.[26] Where possible, congregations also ensured that provision was made for those who could not afford to pay pew rent but who wanted to attend public worship. Cheap or free seating was often provided at the back or in the balcony of the meeting-house and in other cases the pew rent of the less well-off was paid out of the poor fund or a special collection.[27]

---

[22] Ballykelly (GSU) session book, 7 Feb. 1809 (PHS); Cahans (B/Sec.) session book, 1 Mar. 1825 (PRONI, CR/3/25B/2), 122; Loughaghery (B/Sec.) session book, 5 Feb. 1819 (PRONI, CR/3/8/1).

[23] *First report of the commission of Irish education inquiry*, HC (1825), xii. 824.

[24] C. D. Cashdollar, *A spiritual home: life in British and American Reformed congregations, 1830–1915* (University Park, Pa., 2000), 169.

[25] *Report from select committee on handloom weavers' petitions*, HC (1835), xiii. 104–5.

[26] *OSMI* (Lissan), xxxi. 105–6.

[27] Down Pby (B/Sec.), 15 Oct. 1788; Roseyards (AB/Sec.) committee minutes, 4 June 1790 (PRONI, Tennent papers, D/1748/A/2/3/10); T. Kilpatrick, *Millisle and Ballycopeland Presbyterian church: a short history* (Newtownards, 1934), 27; 'Rules of the First Presbyterian church, Ray' (Barkley, 'Eldership', ii. 292–3); Ballybay (GSU) session minutes, 16 Nov. 1811 (PHS).

The alarm caused by the growth of population led the Synod of Ulster to attempt a number of initiatives to increase the opportunities for attendance. The Synod recommended in 1828 that evening services should be held in the summer months in all their congregations and, though initially the adoption of a second service was slow, it soon became the norm.[28] More important, a remarkable church building programme was undertaken in the 1830s. In a resolution passed in 1833 and repeated the following year, the Synod recognized that 'very many of the members of this church are totally destitute of accommodation for public worship' and recommended presbyteries to 'take immediate steps for the erection of new congregations wherever they may appear necessary'.[29] During the 1830s, the Synod erected eighty-three congregations (at least fifteen of which where located in the five presbyteries with the lowest attendance ratios) compared with only seventy-three established between 1729 and 1829. Congregations also spent £107,000 on rebuilding and repairs. The home mission of the Seceders organized a further thirty-three congregations between 1820 and 1840.[30]

Establishing a congregation was financially more viable in the nineteenth century due to the new terms upon which the government endowment of Presbyterianism, the *regium donum*, was granted. Until 1803 it was given as a fixed sum to both the Synod of Ulster and the Secession synods who then divided that sum equally between their ministers. After that date, each congregation belonging to the Synod of Ulster was placed into one of three classes, each receiving a fixed sum of £100, £75, or £50. The Seceders received their augmentation in 1809, classified at £70, £50, and £40. Therefore, establishing a new congregation after 1803 meant that the overall share a minister received from the government would remain the same. Despite this, the importance of religious principle in church growth should not be ignored. The terms of the *regium donum* were altered in 1803 and though thirty-four congregations were erected by the synod in the 1820s, eighty-two were formed in the 1830s. It was

---

[28] *RGSU* (1828), 61; (1831), 32.

[29] *RGSU* (1834), 43–4.

[30] J. S. Reid, *History of the Presbyterian Church in Ireland*, ed. W. D. Killen, 3 vols., 2nd edn. (Belfast, 1867), iii. 465; D. Stewart, *The Seceders in Ireland with annals of their congregations* (Belfast, 1950), 207–8.

only after the triumph of Cooke and evangelicalism in 1829 that the Synod embarked wholeheartedly upon its church-building programme. Any previous official mention of providing extra accommodation was through committees dominated by evangelicals.[31] Furthermore, until the 1780s, the Seceders significantly increased the number of congregations under their care without any government grant.

II

Recent studies of the nature and chronology of secularization have claimed that social and cultural changes from the 1960s have had a greater impact upon levels of churchgoing than industrialization and urbanization in the nineteenth century.[32] Consequently, Victorian cities may no longer be seen as the graveyards of organized religion and churches as middle-class institutions. This view is echoed by work on church membership and social class in Belfast between 1870 and 1930, which has shown that, though Belfast Presbyterianism became predominantly middle-class in character, working-class membership continued to increase and by 1901 36.4 per cent of the total church membership belonged to the upper working class.[33] Despite this re-evaluation, it is important to consider the impact of the growth of Belfast in particular upon Sabbath attendance and the provision of church accommodation. Owing to immigration from rural areas, the population of Belfast grew from 37,277 in 1821 to 75,308 in 1841.[34] As noted in the Introduction, the rate of growth was impressive in itself, but its concentration in one area was unprecedented and qualitatively different to anything that had occurred

[31] For example, *An address to the public, by the committee of the Synod of Ulster Home Mission Society* (Belfast, 1827), 7–9.

[32] Brown, *Death of Christian Britain*; P. L. M. Hillis, 'Church and society in Aberdeen and Glasgow, c. 1800–c. 2000', *Journal of Ecclesiastical History*, 53 (2002), 707–34.

[33] D. Huddleston, 'Religion and social class: church membership in Belfast, c. 1870–1930' (QUB M.Phil., 1998), 63.

[34] D. Hempton and M. Hill, *Evangelical Protestantism in Ulster society 1740–1890* (London, 1992), 106.

previously, since Ulster did not have an extensive urban network until the middle of the nineteenth century.

At first glance, the census returns for the Synod of Ulster in 1834 would seem to contradict the view that urban centres were inimical to organized religion.[35] The two presbyteries with the highest attendance ratios were Belfast and Dublin, with figures of 33 and 37.9 per cent respectively. Five rural Synod of Ulster presbyteries had ratios below 20 per cent, namely, Cavan (18.5%), Clogher (19.5%), Down (18.7%), Monaghan (19.3%), and Templepatrick (17.9%). The first four were situated in the heartland of the Seceders, which explains in part the low attendance figures for the Synod of Ulster in those areas. In only one case did Seceders have an attendance ratio below 30 per cent (Tyrone, 29.8%). Templepatrick Presbytery had experienced deep divisions and upheavals after the Remonstrants' exodus and it may be the case that there was considerable confusion in the area as to membership. Nonetheless, it is clear that non-attendance was not a solely urban phenomenon and that the churches' concentration of resources upon Belfast may have increased attendance there by providing extra church accommodation and activities for urban dwellers to the detriment of Presbyterians in rural areas.

On closer examination, the figures for Belfast are misleading. The census returns for 1834 gave the Presbyterian population of Belfast (Shankill Parish) as 25,939 (the Anglican and Catholic populations were 17,942 and 22,078).[36] Yet when the total numbers of adherents of each of the twelve Presbyterian congregations given in the report are added together, the total comes to 12,661 persons; the total average attendance each Sunday was 5,900. In other words, over one half of those termed Presbyterian in the 1834 returns were not connected with the Presbyterian churches in the parish. A significant number of the non-affiliated 13,278 persons may have been children, those unable to attend for a variety of reasons, and some may have gone to congregations in neighbouring parishes, though given the lack of accommodation across the board that is unlikely.

---

[35] The figures given below are taken from, A. R. Holmes, 'Ulster Presbyterian belief and practice, 1770 to 1840' (QUB Ph.D., 2002), 342, 349.

[36] *First report of the commissioners of public instruction*, 216–17a.

Callum Brown has shown that the economic and industrial expansion of Glasgow between 1780 and 1820 caused a massive escalation in pew rents and the subsequent alienation of many working-class people from Church of Scotland congregations.[37] As early as 1812, Samuel Hanna, minister of Third Belfast, discovered during his visitation work 'that there were many families residing in Belfast, who have not connected themselves with any place of public worship. They are generally poor.'[38] An author of a pamphlet published in the same year, and written in response to the formation of an interdenominational Sunday school, claimed, 'It has long been matter of infinite concern to many, to observe the gross ignorance on the subject of religion which prevails among the lower class of Presbyterians in this town and neighbourhood.'[39] The author outlined a number of reasons for this level of religious ignorance. One of the main causes was the pew rent system and the inability of the poor to contribute anything towards a minister's stipend. Another was the lack of zeal for visiting displayed by Presbyterian ministers compared with that of the Catholic clergy, who did so without the promise of financial reward. Owing to this, the author claimed that Presbyterians were deserting their own church for 'Methodists, evangelicals, or other enthusiasts'.[40] The final reason he noted was the false pride of the Presbyterian laity who would not attend meeting unless they had respectable clothing.

Anxiety about urban growth intensified amongst Presbyterians as the population of Belfast increased rapidly during the 1820s and 1830s. In his role as chaplain of the county jail, James Seaton Reid observed that newly arrived migrants 'saw themselves completely overlooked and lost in the great mass of the neglected population'. He continued, 'in the course of time, [they] sunk into indifference about religion and religious duties, and thus passed from one stage of

---

[37] C. Brown, 'The costs of pew-renting: church management, church-going and social class in nineteenth-century Glasgow', *Journal of Ecclesiastical History*, 38 (1987), 347–61. More generally, idem, *Religion and society*, ch. 5.

[38] E. Wakefield, *An account of Ireland*, 2 vols. (London, 1812), ii. 593.

[39] A Poor Old Light Presbyterian, *An address to the most reverend the Synod of Ulster, in behalf of the poor of the Presbyterian body of the town of Belfast* (Belfast, 1812), 5. A. McClelland, 'The early history of Brown Street primary school', *Ulster Folklife*, 17 (1971), 52–60.

[40] Poor Old Light, *Address*, 18.

evil to another, till they committed the crime for which they were suffering when they came under his notice'.[41] Once they had been transplanted to urban areas, Presbyterians did not have access to the traditional framework of pastoral visitation and communal identity that existed in their rural communities. In response, the Seceder Presbytery of Down in 1837 attempted to make sure that rural and urban ministers liaised with one another to ensure that no one would be without church provision.[42] Concern was also expressed that the growth of Belfast would have an adverse effect upon the morals of its hinterland. James Morgan, the prominent evangelical minister of Fisherwick Place congregation and tireless advocate of missionary and philanthropic societies, stated in 1837 that Belfast was 'a stagnant pool, emitting an atmosphere hurtful to the morals and religion of the people, while it might, and ought to be, a living fountain, pouring out streams of purity and peace over the face of the land'.[43] John Dill, minister of Carnmoney congregation just to the north of Belfast, was worried that being situated 'near the contagion of a large town' encouraged breaches of the Sabbath in his congregation.[44]

Commentators believed, and the statistical evidence confirms their fears, that there was a growing pool of nominal Presbyterians in Belfast who had little or no formal link with the church. Morgan estimated in 1837 that there were 18,000 persons in Belfast without connection with the churches whose plight was made all the worse by the density, increase, baneful influence, and obscurity of the population.[45] Some recommended that Scripture readers be appointed to visit and catechize those who had no links with established congregations.[46] Yet as the presbyteries of Bangor and Belfast realized in 1833, the pressing need was to provide extra accommodation for nominal Presbyterians.[47] Initially the ecclesiastical machinery was

[41] *Belfast News-Letter*, 15 Feb. 1828. For a similar view, R. M. Sibbett, *For Christ and Crown: the story of a mission* (Belfast, 1926), 26.

[42] *MPSI* (1837), 9–10.

[43] J. Morgan, *Reflections on the death of Mr William Cochrane, one of the agents of the Belfast Town Mission* (Belfast, 1837), 5.

[44] Belfast Pby (GSU), 7 Mar. 1837 (Church House, strong room).

[45] Morgan, *Reflections*, 6. For a similar view, 'Home and heart heathenism', *Christian Freeman*, 4 (1836), 324.

[46] 'Scripture readers', *Orthodox Presbyterian*, 4 (1833), 301–5. For further information about Scripture readers, see Chapter 10.

[47] *Belfast News-Letter*, 21 May 1833.

cumbersome. For example, the initiative for Townshend Street congregation came, not from the General Synod, but from the exertions of Cooke and Morgan who initiated and oversaw the completion of the project. The congregation was fitted with free pews and a number of very cheap seats for the poor.[48] Once the initial obstacles had been overcome, the church could move quickly. The Presbytery of Belfast recorded in 1837 that over £45,300 had been spent on erecting new or repairing old congregations in the previous decade.[49] By 1842 the General Assembly had fifteen congregations in Belfast compared with only two Synod of Ulster charges in 1800.[50] Valiant attempts were also made by evangelicals in general to provide for the religious and social needs of a growing urban population through the formation of voluntary organizations. For instance, the object of the Belfast Town Mission, founded in 1827, was to address the problems associated with urban growth by distributing Bibles, encouraging church attendance, 'and contributing, in every possible way, to the promotion of religious knowledge, feeling, and practice'.[51]

Theologically liberal Presbyterians also voiced their concern about the absence of poorer Presbyterians in their Belfast congregations. They recognized that it was difficult to attract the poor as Unitarianism was associated with wealth and social respectability. One writer even suggested that 'while avoiding their unworthy artifices, [they] imbibe something of [the] proselytising spirit' of the Synod of Ulster.[52] Overall, the Unitarian response to urban growth was piecemeal. After the success of an evening lecture series for the working class in Second Belfast in 1834, the congregational committee decided to reserve seats in the west gallery, and later in the east gallery also, for the working class at 1s. 3d. per month.[53] Previously, in 1833, they decided that a new Unitarian meeting-house should be

---

[48] Hempton and Hill, *Evangelical Protestantism*, 111; 'New meeting-house in Belfast', *Orthodox Presbyterian*, 5 (1833), 35.

[49] Belfast Pby (GSU), 7 Feb. 1837.

[50] Figures from Hempton and Hill, *Evangelical protestantism*, 111.

[51] 'Statement of the objects of the Belfast Town Mission', in J. Morgan, *Growth in grace* (Belfast, 1831), 29. A general overview of evangelical activism in Belfast may be found in, Hempton and Hill, *Evangelical Protestantism*, ch. 6.

[52] 'To the Unitarians of Belfast', *Bible Christian*, 3 (1833), 539–42.

[53] S. S. Millin, *History of the Second Congregation of Protestant dissenters in Belfast 1708–1896* (Belfast, 1900), 54.

established in Belfast, though First Congregation 'did not deem such an object to be then expedient'. Undaunted, Second Congregation eventually bought a derelict meeting-house in York Street for £250, which was officially opened in January 1840.[54] The problem was that the commercial and bourgeois Belfast of the late eighteenth century in which liberal Presbyterianism had thrived had disappeared and the harsh industrial centre of the nineteenth century was not congenial to their refined ways and liberal beliefs.

III

Attendance at meeting is only one indicator of how well the Lord's Day was observed as the whole day was to be set aside for religious devotions and activities. It was a common opinion that Ulster Presbyterians strictly observed the Sabbath. Samuel Walker's poem, 'The cotter's Sabbath day', gives a somewhat idealized, yet not wholly misleading, glimpse into the devotional observance and educational interests of lay Presbyterians.

> Then some to readin' verse-about commence,
>   And some the alphabet to wee anes tell;
> The father taks some beuk o' sober sense,
>   Or godly sermon, which he reads himsel'.
> Syne at the question-beuk they tak a spell—
>   The father spiers, the bairns their answers gie;
> Some say them pat, and ithers no sae weel,
>   Accorin' as their size is big or wee,
> And some can say them a'—some but twa sides, or three.[55]

Henry Cooke observed in 1825 that 'the Presbyterians in the north are generally speaking excessively puritanical in their observance of Sunday', adding that when he was a boy 'I dare not go bird's nesting, or after any other boyish amusement ... or I should receive a severe chastisement'.[56] Presbyterian respect for the Sabbath may be gauged

---

[54] Ibid., 54–5.
[55] S. Walker, 'The cotter's Sabbath day', *Belfast Penny Journal*, 1 (1845), 94.
[56] *First report of the commission of Irish education inquiry*, 811.

by their sartorial habits. One observer of Presbyterians in Balteagh, County Londonderry, stated that 'On Sunday they all endeavour to display as much of their finery as possible.'[57] Similarly in Aghadowey, 'The men appear at meetings in skirted dress coats and the females in shoes, stockings and bonnets.'[58] In some cases, the style and colour of Presbyterian dress marked them as distinct from their non-Presbyterian neighbours. Some males had a penchant for wearing black and those in Glendermot were called 'Rooks'.[59] The importance of Sabbath observance was also enshrined in local legends of retribution. Sometime in the late eighteenth century in the Larne and Kilwaughter district, the harvest was delayed due to bad weather and, as a consequence, the grain was in danger of rotting in the fields. A dry day came along, but happened to be a Sabbath. William Agnew, the local squire, convinced the minister, Robert Sinclair, to let the congregation gather the corn. Many refused to do so and they always remembered that the first man to yoke his horse that day lost it before the year's end.[60]

Those who did not observe the Sabbath correctly could be disciplined by the Kirk session. According to the synodical address of the Burgher Synod in 1781, not observing the Lord's Day would harden the heart and dull the conscience of the individual thus leading to greater sins and, in some cases, to the gallows.[61] In a study of Sabbath breach in Scotland, Leah Leneman found that between 1740 and 1780 there was a general decline in the prosecution before Kirk sessions of those who broke the Sabbath. She also suggested, but did not demonstrate, that Seceders tended to be more severe in their discipline of such offenders.[62] Even before 1740, the situation in Ulster as regards the prosecution of Sabbath breach seems never to have been as severe as in Scotland. It has been calculated from the nine remaining pre-1740 session books that out of the 1,275 cases

---

[57] *OSMI* (Balteagh), ix. 15.

[58] *OSMI* (Aghadowey), xxii. 14.

[59] *OSMI* (Clondermot), xxxiv. 28. See also *OSMI* (Balteagh), ix. 16 and (Aghnanloo), xi. 10.

[60] C. Porter, *Congregational memoirs. Old Presbyterian congregation of Larne and Kilwaughter* (Larne, 1929), 65–6.

[61] MASB (1781), 12–13.

[62] L. Leneman, ' "Prophaning" the Lord's Day: Sabbath breach in early modern Scotland', *History*, 74 (1989), 217–31.

recorded only seventy-eight were for breach of the Sabbath (sixty-two were from one congregation alone).[63] During our period, congregations belonging to the Synod of Ulster and the Presbytery of Antrim prosecuted few, if any, such cases. The failure of Synod of Ulster Kirk sessions to impose discipline in this area did not mean they were not alarmed by open profanation of the Sabbath. However, when a dispute arose over the propriety of Volunteer parading on the Sabbath, it is significant that those ministers with New Light sympathies actively encouraged it while Sinclare Kelburn and the Seceders emphatically did not.[64]

Seceder and Covenanter Kirk sessions prosecuted more cases of Sabbath profanation than the Synod of Ulster, but even then such cases did not comprise a major proportion of their caseload. The scrupulous session of Cahans prosecuted only one such instance out of a total of fifty-six in the period from 1751 to 1758; between 1767 and 1836, only four out of 188.[65] Other Seceder and Covenanter session books record discipline for unlawful travelling, intoxication, and farm work on the Sabbath.[66] The Eastern Presbytery in 1815 referred two cases to the Reformed Synod, one involving a man who had to distribute milk on the Sabbath evening, the other involving a baker who had to set his sponge. Despite the risk to their livelihoods, the Synod agreed that both activities were a breach of the Sabbath.[67] An example of Seceder discipline from 1840 involved a postmaster who was prevented from becoming an elder in Sandholes congregation, County Tyrone, as his employment entailed working on the Sabbath.[68] For liberal Presbyterians, such strictness smacked too much of hypocrisy and legalism. A Remonstrant writer urged his readers 'not to spend it [the Sabbath] in a slavish round of superstitious

    [63] R. M. Browne, 'Kirk and community: Ulster Presbyterian society, 1640–1740' (QUB M.Phil., 1998), 161.

    [64] T. Witherow, *Historical and literary memorials of Presbyterianism in Ireland*, 2 vols. (Belfast, 1879–80), ii. 212–13; S. Kelburn, *The morality of the Sabbath defended* (Belfast, 1781); MASB (1781), 12–13; W. H. Crawford and B. Trainor (eds.), *Aspects of Irish social history 1750–1850* (Belfast, 1969), 99.

    [65] Cahans (B/Sec.) session book, 1767–1836.

    [66] Boardmills (B/Sec.) session book, 22 Apr. 1790, Nov. 1818 (Barkley, 'Eldership', ii. 278–9); Cahans (B/Sec.) session book, 17 May 1772 (Barkley, 'Eldership', ii. 234); Linenhall Street (RP) session book, 3 Oct. 1833, 6 and 20 June 1836 (PRONI, CR/5/4A).

    [67] Minutes of the Reformed Synod of Ireland, 1815 (PRONI, CR/5/5A/1/3), 33.

    [68] Tyrone Pby (Sec.), 4 Aug. 1840 (Church House, strong room).

austerities; but ... to reserve it from the world, and devote it to moral and religious exercises'.[69] Different types of Presbyterians obviously observed the Sabbath in different ways according to their religious and social values.

IV

Seceder and Synod of Ulster Presbyterians in the early nineteenth century showed increasing concern about the profanation of the Sabbath. In 1807 the Synod of Ulster declared, 'This day, which should be devoted to the public and private exercises of religious worship, is in too many instances passed in walking or jaunting abroad for amusement, in visiting and receiving visits, in idleness, vain conversation, or evil company.'[70] According to contemporary opinion, one of the most flagrant examples of Sabbath profanation was the over-consumption of alcohol by sections of the congregation who during the intermission in public worship headed to the local alehouse or dram-shop.[71] Drinking alcohol in the period before the 1820s was neither a socially nor a religiously unacceptable activity for the laity and ministers unless it led to drunkenness or further sin. That is not to say that such behaviour did not constitute a breach of the Sabbath as Kirk sessions did censure some for drinking on that day. In general, Presbyterians could drink ale or spirits when they wanted. This accounts for the paradoxical reports often found in the Ordnance Survey Memoirs of the 1830s. The memoir for Templepatrick noted that Presbyterians were 'rather moral and are very strict in their observance of the Sabbath' by their attendance at meeting, abstinence from work, and devotional exercises. Yet, on the other hand, 'most of all classes, particularly during the "intermission 'tween sermons" in summer, resort to the alehouse for some time'.[72] An earlier commentator writing in 1812 gives us the following account.

---

[69] 'The Lord's Day', *Bible Christian*, 4 (1833), 170–8.
[70] *Pastoral address* (1807), 6. *Reasons for humiliation and thanksgiving ... corrected and approved of by the Associate Synod of Ireland* (n.p., 1811), 3.
[71] *Annual pastoral address of the General Synod of Ulster* (Belfast, 1831), 6.
[72] *OSMI* (Templepatrick), xxxv. 121.

As we entered Broughshane, the people were coming out from worship, between sermons and not a few entering the public-houses; our inn was soon nearly full to the door, old and young merrily sacrificing to the 'jolly god', in a manner which fully evinced, that they were 'o'er all the ills of the life victorious'. This scene left some doubts in our minds, which our short stay did not allow us to solve; namely, what was the chief object of the people coming to Broughshane on Sundays?[73]

The question posed is a pertinent one, for it highlights the importance of the Sabbath to the social life of rural communities. The prevalence of 'tween sermon drinking in south Antrim, an area of dispersed settlement and few villages, was part of the Sabbath's social function in providing 'one of the regular social meeting points in the pattern of rural life'.[74] One contemporary writer observed that Sabbath conversation tended to concentrate on every subject except religion; 'The weather, the crops, the markets, perhaps the common gossip and scandal of the neighbourhood—these are their all-engrossing topics of discourse, with the exception, it may be, of a serious observation occasionally thrown in for the sake of decency.'[75] The prevalence of stalls selling alcohol, food, and other items outside the meeting-house gate offers another indication of the social importance of the Lord's Day. Joseph Kinkead, minister of Killinchy in the 1770s, took drastic action against stalls that sold spirits. Finding that preaching had no effect, 'the following Sunday he took a stick, broke all the liquor bottles, demolished the stalls and thus settled the question of roadside liquor for the time being at any rate'.[76] In the light of the widespread use of alcohol, it is little wonder that the temperance movement specifically linked intemperance with the profanation of the Sabbath. In a letter published in the *Belfast News-Letter* on 14 August 1829, John Edgar, the noted temperance advocate, outlined the extent of Sabbath breach in Ulster and the 'terrific demoralising influence' of treating the Lord's Day 'as a mere holiday'.

[73] [S. McSkimin], 'Ramble in 1810', *Belfast Monthly Magazine*, 8 (1812), 368.

[74] A. Gailey, 'Folk-life study and the Ordnance Survey Memoirs', in idem and D. Ó hÓgáin (eds.), *Gold under furze: studies in folk tradition* (Dublin, 1983), 153.

[75] 'Sabbath-day conversation', *Christian Freeman*, 4 (1836), 119.

[76] C. W. McKinney, *Killinchy: a brief history of Christianity in the district, with special reference to Presbyterianism* (n.p., n.d.), 43. Henry Cooke displayed a similar attitude (A. McCreery, *The Presbyterian ministers of Killyleagh: a notice of their lives and times* (Belfast, 1875), 252).

He argued that if the Sabbath was to be made special once more, the main cause of Sabbath profanation, 'the sale and use of spirituous liquor', must be addressed. 'We can never secure effectual permanent cure for this monster ill on the Sabbath except by putting an end to the customary use of spirits on all days. To have sanctity on the Sabbath, there must be temperance all year round.'[77]

During the nineteenth century a variety of reformers endeavoured to ensure that the Sabbath was well observed for a variety of economic, religious, and social reasons.[78] Ulster Presbyterians attempted to influence public opinion against profanation of the Sabbath through various means such as Sunday Schools and ensuring that church courts disciplined those who breached the fourth commandment as well as the more frequently prosecuted seventh.[79] By the mid-1830s, visitation presbyteries were asking questions about levels of attendance, late arrival, early leaving, and coming in an out of the service.[80] The Presbytery of Tyrone had specific questions regarding the sale of alcohol and attendance at public houses on the Sabbath presumably on account of the prevalence of illicit distillation in west Ulster.[81] The burgeoning Presbyterian periodical press printed the resolutions passed by the various synods and presbyteries in favour of sanctification of the Sabbath and provided advice as to how the Sabbath should be observed, invariably reinforcing the strictness of the *Directory*'s original prescriptions and the spiritual benefits of doing so.[82] Others were astute enough to appreciate that the practical benefits would appeal to those who did not normally observe the Sabbath. For many factory workers and other exploited groups, sabbatarianism offered a means by which they could guarantee a

---

[77] Letter reprinted in W. D. Killen, *Memoir of John Edgar, D.D., LL.D.* (Belfast, 1867), 29–36, quotation from 30.

[78] B. Harrison, 'Religion and recreation in Victorian England', *Past and Present*, 38 (1967), 98–125.

[79] *RGSU* (1833), 46–7.

[80] For example, 'Questions for visitation presbyteries, adopted by the Presbytery of Raphoe', *Orthodox Presbyterian*, 8 (1837), 166–8.

[81] Tyrone Pby (GSU), 1836–41 (Church House, strong room); Gailey, 'Folk-life study', 153.

[82] For example, 'Remember the Sabbath-day to keep it holy', *Orthodox Presbyterian*, 5 (1834), 126–30; 'The Presbytery of Connor to the people under their charge', *Orthodox Presbyterian*, 7 (1836), 424–5; *Covenanter*, 3 (1833), 389–91; new ser., 1 (1834), 191, 237–8.

day's rest. It also chimed well with the working-class desire for self-
improvement, independence, and respectability.[83] These values were
expressed in a petition from 1836 that hoped to 'promote the comfort
and moral improvement of the poor man by protecting him in his
privilege of the Sabbath, and by leading him, after the labours of the
week, away from the haunts of dissipation and profligacy, to spend this
holy day in the bosom of his family and the service of his God'.[84]

Petitioning Parliament was a significant means by which reformers
sought to enforce observance. One of the first synodical petitions was
Henry Cooke's against Sabbath distilling, transmitted through the
Synod of Ulster in 1819.[85] The numbers of petitions increased dramatically during the 1830s in support of, for example, a bill presented
to Parliament in 1833 by the famous Scottish Sabbatarian Sir Andrew
Agnew, Sunday trading, and the running of trains on the Sabbath.[86]
There were dissenting voices against aspects of petitioning. One
Seceder believed that signing petitions on the Lord's Day was itself
a breach of the fourth commandment.[87] Non-subscribers voiced
concerns about any means of attempting to legally enforce observance. Referring to the spate of petitions sent to Parliament in 1833,
one writer, while agreeing with the principle, argued that the existing
laws against Sabbath profanation were already too severe and that
legislation was not the way to commend Christian morality. He
believed that the way to encourage observance was by increasing
public knowledge and promoting the principles of true religion
rather than by further legislation.[88]

For nineteenth-century Presbyterians, non-attendance and Sabbath
profanation became major issues of concern. The growth of Belfast
presented the church authorities with the unprecedented problem of

[83] Harrison, 'Religion and recreation', 105.
[84] 'Petitions to Parliament for preventing intemperance and desecration of the
Sabbath', *Christian Freeman*, 4 (1836), 243.
[85] *RGSU* iii. (1819), 502.
[86] 'Review of the Scottish Sabbath Bill', 'Sabbath profanation', 'The General
Assembly, to the people of Scotland, in the Observance of the Lord's Day', *Orthodox
Presbyterian*, 5 (1833), 20–7, 69–73, 434–40; Bovevagh (GSU) session book, Mar. and
Apr. 1833 (PRONI, MIC/1P/229); 'The Sabbath-day', *Orthodox Presbyterian*, 4
(1833), 139–43; Belfast Pby (GSU), 6 Aug. 1839.
[87] 'Sabbath sanctification', *Christian Freeman*, 4 (1836), 299–303.
[88] 'Laws for the observance of the Sabbath', *Bible Christian*, 4 (1833), 94–6.

how to deal with nominal Presbyterians who had little or no links with urban congregations. Their concern with Belfast overshadowed the problems of non-attendance in rural areas, but it does show how perceptions amongst Presbyterians were significantly altered by the onset of urbanization. Non-attendance and its associated problems were more obvious when concentrated in a small area. For evangelicals, this acted as a spur both to missionary endeavour and to the provision of accommodation for thousands of non-churchgoers. At the same time, the Sabbath had more social rather than religious significance for many Presbyterians. The social side of the Sabbath has been stressed because that is what reformers believed needed to be reformed. Non-attendance and Sabbath breach were widespread in some areas, though how far this was a wilful rejection of the Sabbath or how far it was determined by practical considerations depended upon a variety of factors. The stereotypical view that Presbyterians were scrupulous in their observance of the Sabbath focuses upon only one, albeit a significant, aspect of Presbyterian practice and, to some degree, is itself a product of the rhetoric and reforms of nineteenth-century evangelicals.

2

Days of Fasting and Thanksgiving

Alongside their strict sabbatarianism, the Westminster divines made provision for special days of fasting and thanksgiving.[1] Public fasting was a godly duty and ought to be called when 'some great and notable judgements are either inflicted upon a people, or apparently imminent, or by some extraordinary provocation notoriously deserved; as also when some special blessing is to be sought and obtained', such as the ordination of a minister.[2] Fast days were to be strictly observed through fasting, public worship, and private devotion in order to bring both the community and the individual to a keener sense of what God required of them. Thanksgiving days for God's deliverance and provision were to be marked by public worship, collections for the poor, and solemn, reverential festivity where appropriate. The Irish revisions of the *Directory* were much less detailed than the original, although this did not lessen the importance of fast days for nineteenth-century Presbyterian evangelicals in particular. Fast days were also observed by Presbyterians as part of their communion seasons and will be examined in Chapter 6. The focus of this chapter will be upon special days of fasting and thanksgiving as appointed by synods, presbyteries, or Kirk sessions.

In seventeenth-century Scotland and New England, fast days became embedded in the calendar of Reformed communities, occurring at salient points in the agricultural year.[3] In the same period, the

---

[1] *Directory*, 391–3.

[2] For ordination fast days see, J. M. Barkley, *A short history of the Presbyterian Church in Ireland* (Belfast, 1959), 73–4.

[3] M. Todd, *The culture of Protestantism in early modern Scotland* (New Haven, Conn., 2002), 343–52; C. Hambrick-Stowe, *The practice of piety: Puritan devotional disciplines in seventeenth-century New England* (Chapel Hill, N. C., 1982), 100–3.

Presbyterians of Ulster observed fast days as a means of asserting communal solidarity in the face of political and economic hardships, especially when bad weather threatened the harvest. The large numbers attending on these occasions indicated a need to deal with the corporate sin that had called forth God's judgement.[4] In the following century, fast days formed a central part of the religiosity of Seceders and were also appointed by the government, though more prosaically they provided farm labourers with the opportunity to take a day off work.[5] Nevertheless, the religious significance of fast days is important for they established a link for orthodox Presbyterians, struggling in what they saw as the religiously lax environment of the eighteenth century, to their forefathers of the previous century. This was especially the case for Seceders and Covenanters. From its inception, the Scottish Burgher synod at each meeting appointed individual ministers to 'mark the dispensations of providence' in order to prepare reasons for days of fasting, humiliation, and thanksgiving.[6] The marking of the 'signs of the times' and the appointment of fast days were characteristics of the religious zeal of the seventeenth century and it is in that context that their importance to Ulster Presbyterians in the eighteenth and nineteenth centuries should be assessed. Moreover, the reasons given by Presbyterians for calling these special days reveals how they thought about God and his relationship with the created order.

Days of fasting and thanksgiving were important times for rural congregations and reflected the interaction between the faith of the community and its natural environment. The successful gathering in of the harvest was particularly significant and was often included in reasons for thanksgiving drawn up by presbyteries or Kirk sessions.[7] An excellent example of this may be found in the records of Roseyards Antiburgher congregation situated in rural north Antrim. The

---

[4] A. G. Lecky, *In the days of the Laggan Presbytery* (Belfast, 1908), ch. 9; R. Gillespie, *A devoted people: belief and religion in early-modern Ireland* (Manchester, 1997), 49.

[5] C. G. Brown, *Religion and society in Scotland since 1707* (Edinburgh, 1997), 80. For a general comment about observance of government fast days see, [H. Henry], *An address to the people of Connor* (Belfast, 1794), 19.

[6] J. McKerrow, *History of the Secession church*, rev. edn. (Edinburgh, 1847), 524–5.

[7] Moira and Lisburn Pby (AB), 27 Oct. 1784 (PRONI, Stewart papers, MIC/637/6), 56; Bangor Pby (GSU), 26 Oct. 1831 (Church House, strong room).

reasons given by the Kirk session in August 1797 give us a valuable insight into the world-view of rural Presbyterians.[8] More generally, they also reflect the salient themes of the jeremiad tradition within Reformed communities in this period. Four themes in particular were emphasized in this tradition, 'the absolute sovereignty of God, the sinful nature of man, the intelligibility of Providence and (implicitly, at least) the existence of a covenant between God and his "chosen" people'.[9] The Roseyards example begins by observing the 'very threatening aspect of providence for a long time respecting the unseasonable rains and storms', which endangered the safe gathering in of the harvest. The rough weather indicated the 'displeasure of almighty God' and was only one of 'innumerable other signs of his displeasure gone out against us and this sinning and perverse generation and this congregation in particular'. The only proper response for God's people was to humble themselves in prayer and fasting and to plead God for forgiveness 'and in great mercy remember for us his gracious love respecting seedtime and harvests'. The document concluded by reminding the congregation to give thanks 'for former and present mercies [because] it is of his mercies that we are not consumed'. The reasons given by the Roseyards session are earthy and immediate. They gave the farmer, anxious about his harvest, a way of explaining what was happening, a means of changing the situation through humility and prayer, and, failing that, a conviction that no matter what occurred, God was still sovereign.

The same basic themes may be traced in the reasons given by the Burgher and Secession synods for fasting and thanksgiving. The reasons given in 1823 began with the bold statement, 'Whilst a careless and irreligious world close their eyes against the passing events of Providence, or, perhaps, deny the particular providence of God altogether, and refuse to be thereby instructed; it becomes the duty of the devout Christian, accurately to observe, and wisely to improve the doings of the Lord.'[10] With this principle clearly in

---

[8] Roseyards (AB/Sec.) session book, 6 Aug. 1797 (PRONI, Tennent papers, D/1748/A/2/3/1).

[9] R. B. Sher, 'Witherspoon's *Dominion of providence* and the Scottish jeremiad tradition', in idem and J. R. Smitten (eds.), *Scotland and America in the age of the Enlightenment* (Edinburgh, 1990), ch. 2, quotation, p. 50.

[10] *MPSI* (1823), 22.

mind, the reasons given by the synods may be divided into three main sections. The first section dealt with the various national, individual, and church sins that had called forth God's displeasure in the form of military conflicts, rumours of wars, or stormy weather. These sins included open profanity and licentiousness (usually drunkenness, profanation of the Sabbath, and sexual impropriety), lack of Christian unity, the relaxation of church discipline, promiscuous admission to the sacraments, formality, works righteousness, ignorance of the Gospel, and open infidelity in the form of Deism, Arianism, and Socinianism. Non-recognition of the seventeenth-century covenants was included in the earliest lists of sins, though by 1793 these were described as 'Official engagements to the various relative duties' and thereafter dropped.[11] The second section acknowledged divine blessing in temporal and spiritual terms. Temporally, they gave thanks for general peace and prosperity, especially good harvests; spiritually, they acknowledged that the Gospel and the means of grace were still administered in purity and that a 'godly remnant', clearly themselves, remained. The final section was one of supplication for forgiveness and revival, peace and prosperity, blessing upon the royal family and Parliament, and the maintenance of civil and religious liberty. In particular, the revival theme developed in significant ways during the 1780s and 1790s. It moved from an entreaty to revive 'our covenanted work of Reformation', to a more general spiritual renewal of the body, to asking that God 'would bless the reformed churches at home and abroad'.[12] In 1797 the Burgher Synod passed a resolution redolent with the language of the Westminster standards encouraging ministers and Kirk sessions to promote 'extraordinary prayer' for the 'spreading of the gospel through the heathen world, the revival of true Godliness amongst ourselves, and the hastening of the glory of the latter day according to the scriptures'. The synod also drew up causes for thanksgiving that included a reference to the success of overseas missions 'which affords grounds of hope (amidst threatening judgements) that the Happy days are approaching when his name shall be known through

---

11 MASB (1784), 29; (1790), 64; (1793), 85.
12 MASB (1784), 30; (1790), 64; (1791), 74; (1792), 81; (1795), 101.

all the earth, and that incense and pure offerings shall be offered, where the rising and setting sun surveys'.[13]

As the observance of these special days by Presbyterians indicates a self-conscious assertion of orthodoxy, it is instructive to note the attitude of the Synod of Ulster. Between 1691 and 1777 the Synod appointed forty-three fast days and four for thanksgiving. For the years 1778 to 1820, they held one fast day, in 1801.[14] When the Synod addressed those congregations under their care in the wake of the 1798 rebellion, it is remarkable how little spiritual reflection and advice there is, not to mention the absence of any call to prayer or fasting.[15] This most certainly reflects the influence of liberal theological opinion within the Synod. The Presbytery of Antrim never called a day of special religious observance in this period, testifying to how far removed their modern, optimistic, and benevolent views of God and humanity were from that of the Seceders. Certainly contemporary liberal writers questioned the sincerity with which conservative Presbyterians observed fasts.[16] On the other hand, conservatives such as Samuel Dill, a stalwart of the orthodox party in the Synod of Ulster, assiduously observed fast days and, according to his biographer writing in 1869, 'considered it as evidence of decaying piety that our fast days were not kept according to the original design of their appointment'.[17]

The calling of these days for fasting and thanksgiving ultimately depended upon how Presbyterians conceived of God. A belief in divine providence and resignation to the will of God united liberal and orthodox laity. Mary Ann McCracken remarked that her brother Henry Joy and herself 'had been brought up in a firm conviction of an all wise and overruling providence, and of the duty of entire resignation to the divine will'.[18] The poetry of Hugh Tynan, a poet

[13] MASB (1797), 114.

[14] R. S. Tosh, 'An examination of the origin and development of Irish Presbyterian worship' (QUB Ph.D., 1983), 361.

[15] *RGSU* iii. (1798), 210–12.

[16] 'Thoughts on fasts and thanksgiving days', *Belfast Monthly Magazine*, 13 (1814), 30–1.

[17] T. Croskery, 'Memoir of the Revd Samuel Dill, of Donoughmore, Co. Donegal', *Evangelical Witness*, 8 (1869), 52.

[18] R. R. Madden, *Antrim and Down in 98* (London, n.d.), 76. For similar views see, R. R. Madden, *The United Irishmen, their lives and times*, 4 vols., 2nd edn. (Dublin, 1858–60), iv. 118; L. Lunney, 'Attitudes to life and death in the poetry of James Orr, an eighteenth century Ulster weaver', *Ulster Folklife*, 31 (1985), 5.

of impeccable orthodoxy, is replete with references to God's providential rule and the duty of his creatures to submit to both his mercy and judgement.[19] New and Old Light believers shared the language of providence as a result of their immersion in the concept of God's sovereignty through sermons, psalm singing, catechizing, and other devotional exercises. George Dugall underlined the importance of resignation to the will of God amongst Presbyterian farmers whose worldly existence was not always assured.

> Nor heedless do they heaven's protection share,
>   All rude and simple as their lives appear;
> But piety sincere's their dearest care,
>   When morning's ruddy smiles the vallies cheer,
> Or vespers deigns her silver robe to wear;
>   They labour close with pray'r as it began:
> The[y] calmly trust the encrease of the year
>   To Providence, and own 'tis His alone,
> To bless their needful toil, and work them for His own.[20]

David W. Miller argues that during the early nineteenth century, divine activity in the world was relegated from an all-encompassing influence to the mighty acts of God.[21] However, this was not the view of conservative Presbyterians in particular. It is obvious from reading their sermons and personal papers that God's providence extended, as the Bible taught, 'to the most minute events of life, even to the falling of a sparrow, and the numbering of the hairs of the head'.[22] Consequently, believers took a keen interest in particular providences, that is, specific events seen by individuals as expressly ordained by God for a specific reason. More generally, the Presbyterian laity were urged by their ministers to read the signs of the times and not to remain 'unmoved, unwarned, unimproved' by them.[23] Presbyterians believed that God controlled events and that these could be understood with the aid of the Bible in order to know his will. Divine displeasure could be detected in unfavourable

---

[19] H. Tynan, *Poems* (Belfast, 1803), esp. 10, 47.

[20] G. Dugall, *The Northern cottage* (Londonderry, 1824), 10.

[21] D. W. Miller, 'Irish Christianity and revolution', in J. Smyth (ed.), *Revolution, counter-revolution and Union: Ireland in the 1790s* (Cambridge, 2000), 204.

[22] J. B. Rentoul, *Wesleyan Methodism and Calvinism contrasted* (Belfast, 1836), 6.

[23] *A pastoral address from the ministers of the Synod of Ulster* (n.p., 1807), 8.

weather or diplomatic developments, or in the realm of personal experience. A series of hardships, unexpected struggles, or escape from injury and death, could be interpreted as a judgement from God for wilful sins or as demonstrating God's providential care. Robert Magill, the evangelical minister of Antrim (Millrow) Synod of Ulster congregation, noted in 1823 at least six occasions on which he believed he had been shown God's hand at work for his benefit. These included falling down the stairs aged five years, being nearly shot dead by a cock-eyed yeoman in 1803, and surviving falling upon a shearing hook aged eighteen.[24]

The conviction that God was at work in the grand affairs of the world as well as daily life laid the theological basis for the return to days of fasting and thanksgiving in the 1830s. After the Remonstrants had been ejected in 1829, the Synod of Ulster resumed the practice of composing annual addresses to their people and appointing 'special days for religious exercises', a practice continued by the General Assembly after 1840. In a letter to the General Assembly of the Presbyterian Church in America in 1832, the Synod commented, 'we have ... seen cause to renew the godly practice of recommending to our churches days of public humiliation or thanksgiving, according to the circumstances of our times, and the aspect of Providence'.[25] The language and theology of the reasons given for fasting are almost identical to those of the eighteenth-century Seceders.[26] As with evangelicals in other parts of the United Kingdom, the constitutional, political, and religious upheavals of the 1830s led Irish Presbyterians to view the times as charged with meaning. Some of the key developments included the troubles of the Papacy, various European wars, revolutions and diplomatic tensions, the advent of premillennialism, cholera epidemics, the Irish famine of the 1840s, the threat to church establishments, National Education, Tractarianism, the Maynooth grant, concessions to Catholicism, and, in some cases, political liberalism. In 1832 the *Orthodox Presbyterian* declared, 'We live, perhaps, with one exception, in the most eventful period of the history

---

[24] Diary of the Revd Robert Magill, 27 Mar. 1823 (PRONI, Young papers, D/2930/9/8).

[25] *RGSU* (1832), 40.

[26] For example, *Address from the General Synod of Ulster, assigning reasons for a day of public humiliation* (n.p., 1831).

of man—in an age when mighty moral movements are taking place in our own land, and in the nations around us.'[27] In such a period Presbyterians were required to read the signs of the times to determine what action God required of them. In an address advocating the cause of Irish Protestantism to a Scottish audience in 1838, John Brown observed

Since God often conveys to us lessons of duty, not merely by his revealed word, and by the works of nature, but also by the dispensations of his providence, and as every period of time brings with it a special duty, it becomes us not merely to mark the aspect of the sky, to form conjectures about the revolutions of nature, but also to discern the times and seasons that we may attend to the duties arising from our present circumstances, lest he command his curse upon us, as the angel said 'Curse ye Meroz'.[28]

It would be a mistake to characterize the mood of nineteenth-century Presbyterianism as one of pessimism and gloom. To be sure, the jeremiad tradition remained alive and well with the Covenanters and sections of mainstream orthodox Presbyterianism. The predominant mood, however, was one of optimism that was reflected in the Presbyterian commitment to postmillennialism which lasted for the rest of the century.[29] According to this scheme, missionary activity and religious revival would usher in the millennial reign of Christ, which would be consummated by the Second Coming. The relationship between mission, revival, and the millennium had been made explicit in the formularies of Presbyterianism and was clearly expressed in the pronouncements of Seceders and Old Light evangelicals.[30] Postmillennialism also reflected Enlightenment narratives of progress and improvement as the millennium would be established through missionary exertion, Bible distribution, schools, and philanthropic

---

[27] 'The closing year', *Orthodox Presbyterian*, 4 (1832), 74.

[28] J. Brown, *Meroz: a sermon showing the duty of Scottish Christians to Ireland at the present crisis* (Glasgow, 1838), 7–8.

[29] A. Holmes, 'Millennialism and the interpretation of prophecy in Ulster Presbyterianism, 1790–1850', in C. Gribben and T. C. F. Stunt (eds.), *Prisoners of hope? Aspects of evangelical millennialism in Scotland and Ireland, 1800–1880* (Carlisle, 2005), ch. 7; 'The uses and interpretation of prophecy in Irish Presbyterianism, 1850–1930', in Crawford Gribben and A. R. Holmes (eds.), *Protestant millennialism, evangelicalism, and Irish society, 1790–2005* (Basingstoke, 2006), ch. 7.

[30] *Directory*, 377; *Larger Catechism*, Q. 191.

activities.[31] Days of special religious exercises for prayer were of
central importance to the new mood of mission and revival, as the
'means of grace' enumerated in the *Confession* were useless without
the power of the Holy Spirit. For example, in 1836 the Synod of Ulster
set apart 28 December to thank God for his goodness to them and for
the success of their evangelistic endeavours. They also thanked God
for his promise to overthrow Antichrist and referred to recent conversions amongst Catholics as evidence of the 'shaking which the
Papal power is experiencing in its strongest holds', pointing, they
believed, to the imminent return of Christ. Their reasons end with a
call for congregations to 'earnestly pray that God, by the gracious
outpourings of His Spirit, will carry on His work amongst us, and
cause the kingdoms of the world soon to become the kingdoms of our
Lord and his Christ'.[32] Unfortunately for the Synod, the day was only
partially observed, so they appointed another for 27 December the
following year.[33] Presbytery fast days also reflected the missionary and
revivalistic mood of the times. In 1839, the Secession Presbytery of
Belfast appointed 'the third Wednesday of August to be observed as a
day of fasting and special prayer for a revival of religion, and the
increase of missionary spirit in our churches'.[34]

Congregations not only observed fasts appointed by their synods
and presbyteries, but also those called by the government and their
own Kirk sessions.[35] A fast was called in May 1835 by the Kirk session
of Brigh congregation, County Tyrone, to placate God's wrath after a
number of recent scandals in the congregation.[36] When in the early
1830s cholera appeared in Ireland, Presbyterians perceived God's
judgement and called for fasting and repentance.[37] Magherafelt session in July 1832 saw the disease as an 'awful judgement from God',

---

[31] A. Holmes, 'Tradition and enlightenment: conversion and assurance of salvation
in Ulster Presbyterianism, 1700–1859', in M. Brown, C. I. McGrath, and T. P. Power
(eds.), *Converts and conversions in Ireland, 1650–1850* (Dublin, 2005), 147–8.
[32] *RGSU* (1836), 57–8.
[33] *RGSU* (1837), 31–2.
[34] *MPSI* (1839), 14.
[35] Magherhamlet (Sec.) session book, 28 Dec. 1831, 21 Mar. 1832, 8 Aug. 1832, 7
Jan. 1835 (PRONI, D/2487/1), 9, 10, 13, 27.
[36] Brigh (GSU) session book, 17 and 19 May 1835 (PRONI, MIC/1P/13), 4.
[37] *RGSU* (1832), 35; (1833), 35; 'Eighteen hundred and thirty-two', *Christian
Freeman*, 1 (1833), 76–7.

which presented them with a 'solemn warning and a more than ordinary call to the exercise of humility, repentance and prayer'.[38] In January 1834 cholera made its first appearance in the town. The session immediately directed the congregation 'to humble their souls before him [God], to repent of their sins and flee for refuge to the Lord Jesus Christ, "the hope set before them in the gospel" '. The following Tuesday was set aside as a day of humiliation and prayer, and midweek services were continued for six weeks until the disease had passed, at which time a day of thanksgiving was observed.[39] From reports in the minutes of presbyteries and synods, it seems that attendance was generally good and observance was suitably decorous for those who voluntarily marked days of special religious devotions. Robert Magill recorded in his diary that he preached on Joel 2: 17–20 and collected 8*s*. 11*d*. for the poor when he celebrated a synodical fast in 1831, though he does not mention any actual fasting.[40] The stipulations of the original *Directory* had undoubtedly been tempered by time, yet the observance was still important to many, particularly those at the forefront of Presbyterian evangelicalism in the Synod of Ulster in the 1830s. When, under the moderatorship of James Morgan, the Synod drew up reasons for fasting in 1832, they recommended '*abstinence from all servile work* in their fields, shops, and houses; and, where the state of bodily health permits, *such abstinence from food* as the Scriptures evidently sanction and require'.[41]

The reasons why fast days were held provide an insight into how Presbyterians, particularly the orthodox, saw God at work in the world. They believed that God was sovereign in both judgement and mercy, using a variety of temporal developments to make them aware of their duty. There was a growing awareness in the 1820s and 1830s that God was doing a 'new thing'; revivals were breaking out in America, while foreign missionary agencies were reporting

[38] Magherafelt (GSU) session book, 11 July 1832 (J. M. Barkley, 'A history of the ruling eldership in Irish Presbyterianism', 2 vols. (QUB MA, 1952), ii. 200).

[39] Magherafelt (GSU) session book, 5 Jan. 1834 (PRONI, CR/3/13/C/1), 100; Feb. 1834 (Barkley, 'Eldership', ii. 201–2).

[40] Diary of Revd Robert Magill, 28 Dec. 1831 (PHS).

[41] 'Reasons for a fast-day', *Orthodox Presbyterian*, 3 (1832), 364.

spectacular successes in far-flung corners of the world. The days of special religious exercises called in the years before 1859 were predictably concerned with praying for an outpouring of the Holy Spirit in revival, though the famine of the 1840s reminded Presbyterians that God was also the judge of the world and that their sins called for repentance.[42] The fact that the General Assembly continued to call fast days shows that the sovereign God who controlled and interfered in and through worldly events was still an indispensable component of the Presbyterian world-view in the modern nineteenth century.

[42] *Missionary Herald* (1847), 547.

3

Calendrical Customs and Alternative Beliefs

The *Directory* stated that 'Festival-days, vulgarly called *Holy-days*, having no warrant in the word of God, are not to be continued.'[1] In many instances, the yearly pre-Reformation cycle of religious feasts and holy days was dismantled in the interests of 'true religion'. Recent research has shown, however, that the Reformed assaults upon calendrical customs in the sixteenth and seventeenth centuries were less crudely iconoclastic than once thought. Ronald Hutton and others have suggested that reformers displayed a 'canny sense of priorities' in allowing such customs to be stripped of their popish and pagan associations while retaining them as an integral part of popular culture.[2] As a result of this symbiotic process, calendrical customs and the alternative beliefs attached to them remained widespread throughout the British Isles, including Presbyterian Ulster. This customary world-view remained intact because it was intimately bound up with the needs and the rhythms of rural activity, from the beginnings of new life in spring to the fulfilment of that promise at harvest. The observance of communion in Ulster occurred in May and October and it was known for communion to be moved if harvesting proved difficult. Generally, calendrical customs were important socially as they allowed Presbyterians to mark the passage of the seasons. The days they observed had little or no formal religious connotations but were instead 'idle days' for relaxing and indulging

---

[1] *Directory*, 394.

[2] R. Hutton, 'The English Reformation and the evidence of folklore', *Past and Present*, 148 (1995), 89–116; M. Todd, *The culture of Protestantism in early modern Scotland* (New Haven, Conn., 2002); J. Dawson, 'Calvinism and the Gaidheatachd in Scotland', in A. D. M. Pettegree, A. Duke and G. Lewis (eds.), *Calvinism in Europe 1540–1620* (Cambridge, 1994), ch. 12.

in traditional activities. According to John Caldwell, a New Light Presbyterian from north Antrim, people on these occasions 'were free from all check or restraint, our own masters or mistresses for the time being and enjoying all the pleasures of unrestrained merriment and romping'.[3] This chapter describes and assesses the various customs and beliefs in which Presbyterians indulged at springtime, Halloween, and Christmas. This will not be an exhaustive catalogue of the calendrical customs or the popular alternative beliefs observed in Ulster and can only hint at the variety of activities and their geographical distribution.[4]

I

Ulster Presbyterians did not attach any religious significance to Easter. During the second half of the eighteenth century in Ulster, Easter Monday 'was one of the few "idle" or free days in the year for the mass of the people'. One of the most notable events occurred on the slopes of the Cave Hill, near Belfast, and involved, according to an account in the *Belfast News-Letter* from April 1822, 'Climbing, dancing, racing, tumbling, courting, egg trundling, ... frisking, laughing and jumping, with several other mental and bodily exercises.'[5] Elsewhere, the Ordnance Survey Memoirs recorded other Easter activities in the 1830s including cockfighting, egg-rolling, 'thread the needle', the 'round ring', and 'a kind of kissing gallopade' in the parish of Tamlaght Finlagan.[6] May Day celebrations had their origins in the Celtic festival of Beltaine and in Ireland the day was reckoned to be the beginning of the summer.[7] One of the ways in

---

[3] J. Caldwell, 'Particulars of history of a north county Irish family' (PRONI, Caldwell papers, T/3541/5/3), 30.

[4] R. H. Buchanan, 'Calendar customs, part one: New Year's Day to Michaelmas', *Ulster Folklife*, 8 (1962), 15–34; 'Calendar customs, part two: harvest to Christmas', *Ulster Folklife*, 9 (1963), 61–79.

[5] A. Gailey, 'Sources for the historical study of Easter as a popular holiday in Ulster', *Ulster Folklife*, 26 (1980), 68–9.

[6] *OSMI* (Banagher), xxx. 11; (Raloo), xxxii. 103; (Antrim), xxix. 29; (Ballymoney), xvi. 18; (Connor), xix. 25; (Ahoghill), xxiii. 17; (Tamlaght Finlagan), xxv. 92.

[7] For a list of activities see, Buchanan, 'Calendar customs, part one', 24–30.

which this 'new birth' was symbolized was by adorning dwellings with flowers and other foliage. In some areas, rowan branches were placed above byres and kitchen doors, or tied to the tails of their cows, as a 'charm against witchcraft and fairyism'.[8] The threat of black magic was taken seriously in Cullybackey, a staunchly Presbyterian district, where it was widely believed that witches collected dew on May Day morning to help them steal butter.[9] The yarrow and the snail were also employed by young people to determine their future partner.[10]

The observance of Halloween is a distinguishing cultural characteristic of the Ulster-Scots. Feasting and celebration were considered appropriate at this time, as the harvest had been gathered in, the cattle had returned from summer grazing, and the long nights of winter beckoned.[11] Traditional customs, particularly those relating to the last sheaf, accompanied the gathering in of the harvest. Samuel Walker, in his poem 'The Churn, or the Last Day of the Harvest', described how the last sheaf was plaited and left in the field. The harvesters then took it in turns to throw their sickles at the sheaf and the person who severed it was made the 'harvest king'. He was then paraded to a feast of celebration where he took the seat at the right hand of the master of the harvest and said grace for the meal.[12] More generally, Halloween was 'devoted to merry-making and all kinds of amusement'.[13] The following description of events in Islandmagee in 1817 captures well the range of activities: 'On Holyeve, alias Hallow-e'en, apples and nuts are eaten, with which young boys and girls often play some harmless tricks, for the purposes of prying into futurity about sweethearts; boys also go about and strike the doors of dwelling houses with cabbages, or the like, same time.'[14] The mixture of food treats, magic, especially

---

[8] *OSMI* (Ballymoney), xvi. 19; S. McSkimin, *The history and antiquities of the county of the town of Carrickfergus*, ed. E. J. McCrum (Belfast, 1909), 352–3.

[9] W. Shaw, *Cullybackey: the story of an Ulster village* (Edinburgh, 1913), 54.

[10] E. Sloan, *The bard's offering: a collection of miscellaneous poems* (Belfast, 1854), 58–9.

[11] P. S. Robinson, 'Harvest, Halloween, and Hogmanay: acculturation in some calendar customs of the Ulster Scots', in J. Santino (ed.), *Halloween and other festivals of death and life* (Knoxville, Tenn., 1994), 10–12.

[12] S. Walker, 'A miscellaneous collection of poetry composed and written by Samuel Walker of Shaneshill near Templepatrick' [n.d.] (BCL, Bigger Collection), 26–30.

[13] *OSMI* (Dunboe), xi. 54.

[14] S. McSkimin, 'A statistical account of Islandmagee', *Newry Magazine*, 3 (1817), 435.

prognostication, and amusement mark this as a celebration of life before the darkness of winter set in, though for others it was just another day for drinking whisky. The editorial in the September 1832 issue of the *Orthodox Presbyterian* stated that harvest ought indeed to be a time of celebration and thanksgiving for God's kindness and goodness. Yet, the custom in Ulster had degenerated from the solemn and reverential celebration it was meant to be. 'Is it not deplorable that the harvest-home should be one of the great carnivals of intemperance in our intemperate land—and that such a season and such a circumstance should be abused—profaned by wreathing laurels round the brow of the fell-destroyer.'[15] There is evidence that Presbyterian ministers colluded in the marking of Halloween for religious purposes. In a diary entry dated 31 October 1832, Robert Magill recorded, 'distributed to 130 Sunday school scholars of Millrow 4 bushels of apples and 7 quarts of nuts as gifts for Halloween—the apples cost me 2*s*. 6*d*., the nuts 3*s*.'.[16] This demonstrates the flexible attitude of one minister towards customary practice and his utilization of the occasion for religious ends, in this case the rewarding of diligent Sunday school pupils.

Once more, the Presbyterian celebration of Christmas was marked more by customary amusements and rituals than by any religious activities.[17] Indeed, Presbyterians were the exception for not holding religious services on that day. Yet Christmas remained important for it offered festivity in the depths of winter. The activities began well before 25 December with peripatetic musical performances in some areas known as the 'waits' or, in other parts of Ulster, the visitation of Christmas rhymers. On Christmas Day, Presbyterians sometimes attended the local alehouse or dram-shop and more usually shot at marks or fowl. One ruffled traveller through south Antrim in 1809 said that he could not 'compare the exhibition of *fusiliers*, on that day, to any thing with more propriety, than to an army in disguise'.[18]

Christmas day services were clearly the exception amongst Presbyterians during the period. For twenty years after 1798, Mary's

[15] 'The harvest', *Orthodox Presbyterian*, 3 (1832), 401–6, 406.

[16] Diary of the Revd Robert Magill, 31 Oct. 1832 (PHS).

[17] For an indication of the various Christmas customs see, Buchanan, 'Calendar customs, part two', 71–3; K. Danaher, *The year in Ireland: Irish calendar customs* (Dublin, 1972), 233–64; Robinson, 'Harvest, Halloween, and Hogmanay', 12–13.

[18] 'On national polish of manners', *Belfast Monthly Magazine*, 4 (1810), 95.

Abbey, Dublin, held sermons on 25 December, irrespective of the day.[19] One of the visiting preachers was the Revd James Morell of Ballybay who in his own charge marked Christmas by preaching 'appropriate' sermons on relevant texts such as Isaiah 9: 6.[20] Though Morell preached his sermon in Dublin on a Wednesday, there is no record of him preaching on a weekday in Ballybay, which may indicate that his congregation would not tolerate such an innovation. Again, Magill of Antrim provides more evidence of his flexible attitudes to popular culture. In 1821, and again in 1828, he preached weekday Christmas Day sermons, though he did not do so in 1835.[21] In 1832, he did hold a service on a weekday, this time preaching on Luke 2: 27 and examining a hundred children in their catechism. When he had finished, he gave them 'gingerbread nuts', sugar candy, lemon balls, almonds, and lozenges amounting to £3. 3*s.* 6*d.* He also gave 6*d.* to his daughter 'as a Christmas box'.[22] Reflecting increased sectarian tensions and economic imperatives the Kirk session of Mary's Abbey in 1832 resolved no longer to hold a religious service on 25 December. They stated there was no scriptural warrant for its observance, that it encouraged disrespect for the Sabbath, gave 'an excuse for irreligious feasting, revelry and amusement', and demeaned the name of Christ. It was also their duty as the 'Scots' Church' in Dublin to uphold the strict views of their forefathers regarding Christmas, 'especially in a country such as this'.[23]

A significant feature of these calendrical customs is the superstitious or alternative beliefs that many Presbyterians associated with them. Alternative beliefs to those expounded by preachers and taught through catechisms provided the means by which lay Presbyterians could deal with the uncertainties of life. These beliefs were a complex blend of an individual's experience, basic knowledge of Christian

[19] J. M. Barkley, *A short history of the Presbyterian Church in Ireland* (Belfast, 1959), 97.

[20] Diary of the Revd John Morell, 25 Dec. 1816, 25 Dec. 1814, 24 Dec. 1815 (PHS).

[21] Diary of the Revd Robert Magill, 25 Dec. 1821 (PRONI, Young papers, D/2930/9/6); J. Kenny, *As the crow flies over rough terrain; incorporating the diary 1827/8 and more of a divine* (Newtownabbey, 1988), 397; diary of the Revd Robert Magill, 25 Dec. 1835 (PHS).

[22] Diary of the Revd Robert Magill, 25 Dec. 1832. For 'Christmas boxes' see Buchanan, 'Calendar customs, part two', 71.

[23] R. J. Rodgers, 'James Carlile, 1784–1854' (QUB Ph.D., 1973), 27–8.

doctrine, superstitious belief, and the values and traditions of the community. According to one commentator, 'alternative knowledge and belief was a coping mechanism which could deal with the aspect of chance but was also a source of dignity, self-respect and self-help'.[24] Certain persons could be consulted and practices could be employed to confront a host of scenarios, including the illness of an animal or family member, the tragedy of an unfruitful marriage bed, revenge on an enemy, or the breaking of communal mores. According to a writer in the 1850s, belief in fairies answered a range of felt needs within a community; 'They are with us ... to improve our morals and our habits, to reward and punish, to delight and terrify, to torment and amuse, and even to combat in serried legions for our material interests....'[25] The evidence suggests that those who did attend public worship and submitted to church discipline held these beliefs as well as those who called themselves Presbyterian but rarely attended public worship. Though the surviving session records for the 1770 to 1840 period record only four instances of discipline in which superstitious practices played a part, this does not reflect the depth of Presbyterian attachment to alternative beliefs.[26] The alternative beliefs held by Presbyterians utilized orthodox concepts and symbols, such as the Bible and the names of God and the Devil. The belief in God's sovereignty provided an explanatory framework for lay Presbyterians both to see God's activity in natural phenomena and to use special means and places to exploit his power in an immediate, practical way. Moreover, a clear-cut division between good and evil added to the sense that the world was essentially moral, that wrongdoing would be punished, and correct conduct rewarded. The rational restriction of magic and religion to their proper places had no resonance for many who were called Presbyterians. An antiquarian

---

[24] B. Bushaway, ' "Tacit, unsuspected, but still implicit faith": alternative belief in nineteenth-century rural England', in T. Harris (ed.), *Popular culture in England c. 1500–1850* (London, 1995), 215.

[25] Anon., 'Fairy annals of Ulster—No. 1', *Ulster Journal of Archaeology*, 1st ser., 6 (1858), 355.

[26] W. H. Crawford and B. Trainor (eds.), *Aspects of Irish social history 1750–1850* (Belfast, 1969), 100; Roseyards (AB/Sec.) session book, 17 Oct. 1795 (PRONI, Tennent papers, D/1748/A/2/3/1), 105; Anahilt (GSU) session book, 9 Jan. 1779 (J. M. Barkley, 'A history of the ruling eldership in Irish Presbyterianism', 2 vols. (QUB MA, 1952), ii. 274); Ballymoney (GSU) session book, loose leaf, undated (UTC).

remarked in 1858 that belief in fairies amongst Dunluce Presbyterians 'sufficiently proved that the profession of a stern and gloomy mode of faith was not incompatible with this element, and that the pressure from without had not altogether extinguished it'.[27]

Alternative beliefs coalesced around certain objects, natural phenomena, persons, or places that were said to display supernatural properties, whether for healing, prognostication, or harm.[28] Hawthorn bushes provided the focus for some of the most common superstitious beliefs. It was around these and the remnants of Iron Age forts that fairies were said to gather at night to indulge in merrymaking and various magical rituals. The belief prevailed that to uproot these bushes or to plough out a rath would incur the anger of the fairies.[29] Certain people within communities, or itinerants who visited on an irregular basis, were perceived to hold particular powers that could be used for either good or ill. Positively, spaemen and spaewomen were employed to tell the future and provide advice when making decisions. Others were malevolent, particularly those who possessed the 'evil eye'. It was claimed that such people by merely blinking were able to deprive a cow of the ability to produce milk or to cause personal misfortune and injury. Usually these people tended to be old, single women, though not exclusively.[30] Means could be employed to counteract the influence of fairies, the evil eye, and witches. Once a person or animal had become sick, there were hosts of herbal remedies available along with various charms to protect against evil spirits. Rowan branches and prehistoric flint arrowheads, supposedly made by fairies and known as elfshot, were used as charms to ward off malevolent spirits from animal stalls or human dwellings. The arrowheads were also used in potions to cure

[27] Anon., 'Fairy annals', 354–5.

[28] R. Gillespie, *A devoted people: belief and religion in early-modern Ireland* (Manchester, 1997), chs. 3–5.

[29] G. Benn, *The history of the town of Belfast* (Belfast, 1823), 205–7; McSkimin, *Carrickfergus*, 344; OSMI (Ballylinny), xxxii. 26; (Killead), xxxv. 24; (Grange of Muckamore), xxxv. 68.

[30] E. J. McKean, 'Blinking or ill-wishing', *Report and Proceeding of the Belfast Natural History and Philosophical Society* (1903–4), 70–3; S. McSkimin, 'An essay on witchcraft', *Belfast Monthly Magazine*, 3 (1809), 416; OSMI (Maghera), xviii. 70.

sick animals.[31] Certain people could also be employed to remove illness or misfortune caused by magical means. One of the most infamous white witches was Mary Butters who was consulted by Alexander Montgomery of Carnmoney in 1807 to help increase the butter yield of his cow after a certain individual had bewitched it. During the ritual to reverse the spell, Butters managed to kill three individuals by suffocation, caused by the noxious fumes of her potion. She was eventually acquitted at the Carrickfergus assizes and continued to believe that the three victims had been killed 'by a Black man with a huge club, who also knocked over herself.'[32]

One may argue that there was nothing distinctly Presbyterian about the days they chose to observe or the alternative beliefs and practices they employed. In one sense this is an appropriate conclusion as the seasonal rhythm of life was shared with Anglicans and Catholics. Presbyterians also needed idle days like anyone else. The rector of Maghera parish observed in 1811 that 'we have no controversy here, about regaling ourselves with the juice of the barley on St Patrick's day; eating pancakes on Shrove Tuesday; a goose at Michaelmas, and nuts and apples on Halloween: on Sunday before Easter, palm twigs; on the 17th March, a green shamrock; and on the 12th July, orange lilies are worn'.[33] A shared commitment to alternative beliefs is also evident in areas such as Macosquin, County Londonderry, where it was observed that 'All denominations are superstitious about fairies.'[34] Presbyterians used holy wells and holy water to cure their ills and, in Carrickfergus, poor Protestants applied in secret to the local priest for a 'priest's book' to help cure mentally ill relatives or 'overseen' children for fear of being found out by their own ministers.[35]

If calendrical customs and alternative beliefs were not wholly distinctive, they had distinctive Presbyterian elements, none more

[31] OSMI (Lissan), xxxi. 93; Ulster Journal of Archaeology, 1st ser., 2 (1854), 205.

[32] R. M. Young, Historical notices of old Belfast and its vicinity (Belfast, 1896), 267; OSMI (Carnmoney), ii. 75–6.

[33] W. S. Mason, A statistical account, or parochial survey of Ireland, 3 vols. (Dublin, 1814–19), i. 593.

[34] OSMI (Macosquin), xxii. 90.

[35] McSkimin, Carrickfergus, 349. For an example of the Presbyterian use of holy wells see, OSMI (Faughanvale), xxxvi. 31.

so than the general lack of religious significance attached to holidays.[36] What is more, Presbyterians did not observe patrons' days and nor did they generally attend midsummer bonfires.[37] Presbyterians were also part of a broader Protestant popular culture that was inherently anti-Catholic. This identity was expressed through local stories about the massacre of Protestants in 1641 and the involvement of some Presbyterians in Brunswick Clubs and the Orange Order in the late 1820s and early 1830s.[38] Presbyterians also had their own Scottish-derived beliefs and practices. For example, the 'browney', a giant fairy akin to the banshee, and the use of rowan branches to ward off fairies and the evil eye were of Scottish origin and found in predominantly Presbyterian areas.[39] More generally, John McCloskey, in a statistical account of Banagher parish written in 1821, maintained that the Scottish settlers of the seventeenth century brought with them the 'whole train of witches, the tribe of fairies, the overlooking of horses and cows', and the value of elfshot. He observed that 'there is hardly a single fairy tale in the notes of the *Minstrelsy of the Scottish border* that may not be heard verbatim, as also many of the best ballads in that collection, from many old women in this district'.[40] Above all, Presbyterians observed their own fast days and conducted their Sabbaths in distinctive religious and cultural ways, each embodying their views about God and how he should be worshipped. Presbyterians observed holidays because they marked the passing of the seasons and allowed them the opportunity to relax. They utilized alternative beliefs and practices because they made practical sense and accorded with their belief in God who was omnipresent, omniscient, and omnipotent.

[36] For general comments on the distinctiveness of Presbyterian culture see, A. Gailey, 'The Scots element in north Irish popular culture: some problems in the interpretation of an historical acculturation', *Ethnologia Europa*, 8 (1975), 2–22.

[37] *OSMI* (Islandmagee), x. 75; (Dundermot), xiii. 33; (Donegore), xxix. 113; (Ballywillan), xxxiii. 37.

[38] For some of these local stories see, *OSMI* (Racavan), xiii. 102–3; (Faughanvale), xxxvi. 109–11.

[39] [S. McSkimin], 'On fairies', *Belfast Monthly Magazine*, 4 (1810), 172; *Ulster Journal of Archaeology*, 1st ser., 2 (1854), 205.

[40] *OSMI* (Banagher), xxx. 11. A comparison of Scottish and Ulster beliefs is facilitated by a reading of L. Henderson and E. J. Cowan, *Scottish fairy belief: a history* (East Linton, 2001).

II

For moral and religious reasons, Presbyterian ministers expressed concern about the manner in which calendrical customs were observed and the superstitious beliefs attached to them. In the mid-eighteenth century, the elders of Cahans Secession congregation were directed to ask those in their districts, 'Do they use any charms on certain days as November 1st, or encourage spae-men and the like by consulting and giving heed to them?', 'Do they go to any cockfights, horse races, or dancings?', and 'Do they attend bonfires on Mid-Summer Eve?'[41] The questions proposed for fellowship meetings at Knockbracken Reformed Presbyterian congregation near Belfast in 1832 included whether they abstained from prelatic and popish holy days 'or any of the practices common at these seasons; the use of *charms* of any kind, whether in relation to your children, yourselves, your cattle, or property, knowing that such usages are expressly condemned by God in his word, and that they do aim to set aside his holy and particular providence?'[42] Generally speaking, Presbyterians across the theological spectrum condemned the popish character and immorality of calendrical customs. In a Christmas Day sermon to his congregation in 1792, William Steel Dickson, the prominent United Irishman and New Light minister, argued that the observance of Christ's birth was not a prescribed duty established by either Christ or his apostles. He continued, 'Still ... I am convinced, as the observance is kept up, it is better to apply it to religious services, than spend it in dissipation, drunkenness, and blasphemy—a practice equally injurious to religion, inconsistent with the purpose of the saviour's coming, and dishonourable to men.'[43] Mixing religious and economic concerns, another New Light minister, A. G. Malcolm of Newry, argued that such observances encouraged superstition, damaged the public witness of the church, and often led to the 'criminal neglect of secular business'.[44]

---

[41] Barkley, *Short History*, 99.

[42] [Thomas Houston], *Queries to be proposed to the members in fellowship meetings, at corresponding societies, and at general congregational meetings* (Belfast, 1832), 5.

[43] W. S. Dickson, *Three sermons, on the subject of Scripture politics* (Belfast, 1793), 24.

[44] A. G. Malcolm, *A catechism* (Newry, 1812), 38.

During the nineteenth century, evangelicalism gave such opinions added urgency and social influence. Presbyterian evangelicals condemned the popish nature of holy days, though they were more anxious about the various immoral practices associated with those dates than the marking of the days themselves. The greatest challenge to traditional ways of observing holidays came from the temperance movement, which was itself part of a broader evangelical campaign against various immoral practices, such as animal cruelty, and the opportunities for indecent behaviour afforded by the assembling of large crowds.[45] Early temperance reformers did not advocate total abstinence from all alcohol but only from the drinking of 'ardent spirits', the consumption of which had soared since the 1750s through illicit distilling.[46] The following passage written in 1830 by John Edgar illustrates well the new attitude of Presbyterians towards these aspects of popular culture.

Our holy days are all drinking days; the holy Sabbath of the Lord witnesses more intemperance than half the days of the week; and our Christmas days, and New-years days, and Patrick's days, and Easters and Halloweves, are all the jubilees of drunkenness, sacred to the worship of Moloch, who makes both children and fathers pass through the fire; and all this too before the eyes, and by the connivance of temperate men! In direct opposition to common sense and the word of God, temperate men give their countenance continually to the monstrous fabrication, that the rites of friendship and hospitality could not be properly observed, nor the enjoyments of the social circle maintained, without the assistance of ardent spirits; and for the support of falsehood, they daily heap up expense and labour, and temptation, and trouble on themselves and their families.[47]

Founded in Belfast on 24 September 1829, the Ulster Temperance Society had 3,000 members by March of the following year. By 1833 it was estimated there were over 150 societies and 15,000 members in Ulster.[48] For instance, the Coleraine Temperance Society, established

---

[45] For example, the views of Josias Wilson on horse racing (H. Hastings, *Memoir of the life and labours of the late Rev. Josias Wilson, London* (London, 1850), 112–18).

[46] E. Malcolm, *'Ireland sober, Ireland free': drink and temperance in nineteenth-century Ireland* (Dublin, 1986), 21–55.

[47] J. Edgar, *The evils, cause and cure of drunkenness*, 2nd edn. (Belfast, 1830), 18.

[48] 'Retrospective of temperance societies from the commencement of 1833', *Temperance Advocate*, 1 (1833), 129.

in 1829, had 531 members by 1835, 129 of whom were children. Connected with the society were at least ten auxiliaries whose membership ranged from 180 in Portstewart to sixteen at Islandmore.[49] By the late 1830s, however, the temperance cause had made little impact upon the consumption of spirits as it faced financial problems and internal debates over total abstinence that led to the formation of the Irish Temperance Union in 1839.[50] The movement did, however, provide the means of diffusing the ethos of evangelicalism and allowed individuals and groups to challenge blatant examples of drunkenness and immorality such as the revelry on Cave Hill and local 'punch dances'.[51]

The popularity of these campaigns rested upon their appeal to the respectable within Ulster society and the resonance they had with the prevailing mood of the times. Edgar deliberately cultivated the support of moderate drinkers from respectable society because, if they abandoned the drinking of spirits, 'only then could they expect to have any influence over the heavy-drinking working classes'.[52] He forged links with mill-owners and provision merchants in Belfast, such as Robert Workman, John Herdman, and John and Thomas Sinclair, emphasizing the practical benefits of temperance in increased worker efficiency and public demand.[53] This mood of self-improvement and respectability was the product of an amalgam of social, economic, political, and religious factors. The rationalization of time, the failure of the 1798 rebellion, the industrialization of Belfast, and the difficulties experienced in domestic linen manufacture, all reduced the attractiveness of observing certain days in dissipation and drunkenness.[54] The contribution of religious opinion to this process should not be underestimated. The crusading zeal and organizational capacities of evangelicals were instrumental in

---

[49] *OSMI* (Coleraine), xxxiii. 143.

[50] Malcolm, 'Ireland sober, Ireland free', 85–99.

[51] J. Gray, 'Popular entertainment', in J. C. Beckett *et al., Belfast: the making of a city 1800–1914* (Belfast, 1988), 99–100; T. Hamilton, 'Faithful unto death': a biographical sketch of the Rev. David Hamilton of Belfast (Belfast, 1875), 58–61.

[52] Malcolm, 'Ireland sober, Ireland free', 63.

[53] Ibid., 59, 81.

[54] S. J. Connolly, ' "Ag Déanmah *commanding*": elite responses to popular culture, 1660–1850', in J. S. Donnelly and K. A. Miller (eds.), *Irish popular culture 1650–1850* (Dublin, 1998), 24.

channelling the mood of the times into areas perceived to be in need of reform. A symbiotic process was at work as evangelicalism both promoted and gained from changes within Ulster society. The *Orthodox Presbyterian* in 1830 noted, 'Whether from an increasing depression in their worldly circumstances, or from an increasing elevation in their religious feelings, or rather from both causes conjointly, they [northern Presbyterians] are every year evincing less inclination to engage in those wild and licentious festivities which they formerly pursued with so much eagerness.' Oaths, gambling, intemperance, 'disorder and impurity', had been swapped for 'more rational amusements'.[55]

Early nineteenth-century commentators also observed that alternative beliefs were being laid aside. Such beliefs were ridiculed by reformers of various types, including writers of the Ordnance Survey Memoirs, who believed that modern society with its schools, factories, medicines, new farming techniques, and a more 'sensible' attitude to life and belief had signalled the end of superstition.[56] In addition, contemporary and historical commentators have described Ulster Presbyterians as level-headed, rational types who seldom succumbed to superstition.[57] This impression was strengthened by three developments in the early nineteenth century. First, the increased access to education provided by reformers of various types increased knowledge of the natural world and replaced the old collections of fairy tales often used in teaching with proper spelling and reading primers.[58] Second, economic hardships in the 1830s saw a more general decline in customary activity and it is legitimate to assume that this may have included the jettisoning of alternative beliefs as well. Finally, increased sectarian tensions led to the reassertion of the inherent similarity between Catholicism and superstition. The first issue of the *Christian Freeman* thundered, 'The

---

[55] 'The New Year', *Orthodox Presbyterian*, 1 (1830), 110.

[56] Bushaway, '"Tacit, unsuspected, but still implicit faith"', in Harris, *Popular culture in England*, 190–1; A. Day, ' "Habits of the people": traditional life in Ireland, 1830–1840, as recorded in the Ordnance Survey Memoirs', *Ulster Folklife*, 30 (1984), 26.

[57] For examples, *OSMI* (Cairncastle), x. 5; (Aghanloo), xi. 11; (Kilraughts), xvi. 129.

[58] J. R. R. Adams, *The printed word and the common man: popular culture in Ulster 1700–1900* (Belfast, 1987), ch. 6.

multitude of superstitious practices prevailing amongst many Protestants; their attention to omens—their observance of heathenish
customs—their belief in charms—all prove, not only how congenial
the spirit of Romanism is to corrupt human nature, but how dangerous and infectious is its contact.'[59] To reformers, the upshot was that
alternative beliefs were confined to the old and the lower orders who,
by definition, were badly educated, too old to change, or too popish.[60]

These factors are central to any understanding of the decline of
popular amusements and alternative beliefs, yet a number of caveats
may be offered. First, each generation of observers since the seventeenth century has bemoaned the decline of popular festivities and
traditions.[61] Such views tend to ignore the tenacity of such practices
and the modern interest in the supernaturalism of New Age spirituality or druidism. Second, the concept of decline is clumsy as it
neglects the capacity of popular cultures to adapt to new contexts.
Bob Bushaway has pointed out that English popular culture in the
nineteenth century underwent a process of 'transformation rather
than extinction' as customs became more bourgeois and less rustic.[62]
The same process occurred in Ulster and, by the end of the century,
harvest thanksgiving services were being held in most congregations
as Halloween and harvest time were divested of their superstitious
and intemperate associations and treated as a set time of thanksgiving to God. Though reformers could take pride in the evident
decline of alternative beliefs, significant numbers of Presbyterians, in
supposedly enlightened parishes such as Carnmoney, Ballylinny, and
Antrim, continued quietly to believe in the efficacy of popular beliefs
and practices while at the same time espousing modern ideas.[63] As
one memoirist wrote, the Presbyterians of Dungiven, 'being fond of

---

[59] *Christian Freeman*, 1 (1832), 1.

[60] *OSMI* (Drumachose), ix. 87; (Racavan), xiii. 95; (Donegore), xxix. 113; (Lissan),
xxxi. 93.

[61] Bushaway, ' "Tacit, unsuspected, but still implicit faith" ', in Harris, *Popular
culture in England*, 213; Henderson and Cowan, *Scottish fairy belief*, 24–30.

[62] *By rite: custom, ceremony and community in England 1700–1880* (London,
1982), 260.

[63] *OSMI* (Ballylinny), xxxii. 19; (Antrim), xxix. 29; W. S. Smith, *Historical gleanings in Antrim and neighbourhood* (Belfast, 1888), 135–54. For general comments on
the survival of alternative beliefs see, Bushaway, ' "Tacit, unsuspected, but still
implicit faith" ', in Harris, *Popular culture in England*.

information, gradually acquire a large stock of knowledge. They cannot, however, completely shake off the superstitious belief of fairies.'[64] Finally, the reform of popular culture was not solely from above. On the one hand, lay Presbyterians were active in the process by upholding the new values being advocated, adapting them to meet their own circumstances, or ignoring them altogether. Indeed, the emphasis upon the reform of conduct and anti-Catholicism may have allowed alternative beliefs to survive as Presbyterian reformers and their Catholic counterparts did not consider the eradication of such beliefs as a priority.[65] On the other hand, the persistence of these customs within Ulster Presbyterianism displays the 'canny sense of priorities' of both seventeenth-century reformers and nineteenth-century ministers. Those elements that were either anti-social or popish were dealt with while leaving the customs themselves as secularized social events or the alternative beliefs as harmless rituals. The process of cultural change is a complex and often messy affair.

---

[64] *OSMI* (Dungiven), xv. 21.
[65] For the attitude of Catholic priests to alternative beliefs see, S. J. Connolly, *Priests and people in pre-Famine Ireland 1780–1845*, 2nd edn. (Dublin, 2001), 125–9.

Part II

Public Worship in the Meeting-House

Public worship in the meeting-house each Sunday shaped and defined how Presbyterians viewed God, the created order, and those they lived amongst.[1] The service was usually split into two halves with a morning and afternoon diet of worship separated by a break for refreshment. In the eighteenth century, some ministers took the opportunity to lecture on a passage of Scripture in the morning while preaching a full sermon after lunch. In the following century, there was a move towards having two separate Sunday services, morning and evening, especially during the summer. From the evidence of presbytery visitations, public worship could last anything between two and five hours, usually commencing between 11 a.m. and noon. The *Directory* and its Irish revisions outlined the constituent parts of public worship, but Irish Presbyterians were alarmed by any semblance of a fixed liturgy to such an extent that the Lord's Prayer was seldom used. Those who compiled the 1825 revision of the *Directory* included in the *Code* stated that it was not their intention 'to lay down or enforce a positive rule, but merely to exhibit a model'.[2] Yet, no matter how far Presbyterians tried to distance themselves from popish forms, ritualized patterns of public worship did develop and proved very hard to reform once they had passed into what the Presbyterian laity deemed a traditional form.

---

[1] The best overview of the theory and practice of Presbyterian worship in Ireland is, R. S. Tosh, 'An examination of the origin and development of Irish Presbyterian worship' (QUB Ph.D., 1983).

[2] *Code* (1825), 85.

As Chapter 1 has demonstrated, people attended meeting for both religious and social reasons as the meeting-house was often the main forum for social interaction in the small rural communities that dotted the Ulster countryside. The following three chapters show how the religious and cultural identity of congregations was established and proclaimed by the public worship that occurred within the meeting-house. Though attention has rightly focused upon the importance of preaching in the Reformed tradition, congregational singing and the sacrament of the Lord's Supper were indispensable aspects of the self-identity of Ulster Presbyterians. The way these components of public worship were acted out embodied the distinctiveness of the Presbyterian communities in Ulster as they distinguished themselves from their non-Presbyterian neighbours and from other strands of Presbyterianism. It will be shown that lay definitions of what constituted orthodox Presbyterianism were closely related to how these aspects of public worship were delivered as much as to the doctrinal content they contained. Furthermore, the experience of public worship extended well beyond the confines of the meeting-house, literally in the case of open-air communions, and provided the focus for much interest and debate in the following week. Chapter 4 examines congregational singing by assessing the standard of public praise, lay attitudes to psalm singing, and attempts to reform congregational praise. Chapter 5 outlines the various preaching styles employed by Presbyterian ministers, the response of the laity to that preaching, and the impact of evangelicalism upon the style and content of Presbyterian sermons. Finally in this section, Chapter 6 focuses upon the Lord's Supper, the preparations made for it, the role of church discipline, the structure of the communion season and its various meanings, and the efforts made to reform popular practice.

4

Psalmody

The order of service outlined in the *Directory* allotted only a small portion of time to the singing of psalms in public worship, the main emphasis falling upon the preaching of the word.[1] This situation was exacerbated in Ulster where it was common for ministers to 'explain' a psalm before or after it was sung. The opportunity to sing psalms publicly was further reduced by the late arrival of worshippers to meeting and the tendency of some ministers to drop a few verses of the last psalm if their sermons ran on too long. Yet the attachment of Ulster and Scottish Presbyterians to the psalms remained tenacious as singing them provided spiritual comfort, a sense of identity, and, on occasions, entertainment. Though the cantankerous debates that blighted the General Assembly over hymns and instrumental accompaniment in the second half of the nineteenth century have received some attention, little or nothing has been written about psalmody in this earlier period.[2] This is unfortunate as the public praise of Protestant dissent in the eighteenth century developed significantly on both sides of the Atlantic with the use of scriptural paraphrases and hymns, particularly those of Isaac Watts and the Wesley brothers.[3] During the nineteenth century, evangelicals and other reformers exhibited a desire to increase both lay piety and social respectability

---

[1] *Directory*, 393.

[2] R. S. Tosh, 'One hundred and fifty years of worship: a survey', in R. F. G. Holmes and R. B. Knox (eds.), *The General Assembly of the Presbyterian Church in Ireland 1840–1990: a celebration of Irish Presbyterian witness during a century and a half* (Coleraine, 1990), 141–6.

[3] M. J. Crawford, *Seasons of grace: Colonial New England's revival in its British context* (New York, 1991), 90–7; H. Davies, *Worship and theology in England: from Watts and Wesley to Maurice, 1690–1850* (Princeton, 1961), 99–102, 201–4.

by purging popular expressions of praise of their more unseemly elements.[4] In Ulster reformers in both centuries sought to change popular attitudes to the psalms, the style in which they were sung, and the secular attachments they had attracted. The following chapter begins by examining the place of psalms in public worship, the style and standard of public praise, and attitudes to the psalms amongst the laity. The next section describes the strategies for reform devised by various reformers, the impact these had upon congregational praise, and the tensions within Presbyterianism that were brought to the surface as a result of attempts to change this central component of Presbyterian self-identity.

I

In the opinion of some contemporaries, congregational singing left much to be desired. The Ordnance Survey memoirist for Ballynure, County Antrim, was impressed with the singing voices possessed by the local Presbyterians, 'though in the meeting-houses, in which the entire congregation everywhere join, the nasal and monotonous hum of their psalm tunes would form a contradiction to this statement'.[5] Judging by a comment made by one contemporary 'that a drawling, vulgar nasal style, is no proof of Orthodoxy, either in preaching or singing', the very style of singing was seen by the laity as constituting true Presbyterianism.[6] Furthermore, though reformers lamented the use of twelve tunes or fewer, this low number had great significance for many Presbyterians. It was believed that 'the twelve' had been composed by King David and were the 'true Covenanter tunes' of

---

[4] V. Gammon, '"Babylonian performances": the rise and suppression of popular church music, 1660–1870', in E. Yeo and S. Yeo (eds.), *Popular culture and class conflict 1590–1914: explorations in the history of labour and leisure* (Brighton, 1981), ch. 3; J. Obelkevich, 'Music and religion in the nineteenth century', in idem, L. Roper, and R. Samuel (eds.), *Disciplines of faith: studies in religion, politics and patriarchy* (London, 1987), ch. 35.

[5] *OSMI* (Ballynure), xxxii. 37.

[6] 'Psalmody', *Orthodox Presbyterian*, 7 (1836), 238.

seventeenth-century Presbyterianism.[7] The laity was loath to discard these tunes and sing anything other than the metrical psalms as these declared their identity as God's people and connected them with their ancestors who had secured Presbyterianism. The focus of reformers upon the lack of variety in, and the unsophisticated nature of, congregational psalmody overlooked the importance of this style of psalm singing to the self-perception of lay Presbyterians. Public singing allowed for the expression of personal piety within the context of the community of believers. Presbyterians engaged in public praise in ways they believed were asserting the biblical principle of simplicity in worship and their own Presbyterian distinctiveness. Even a liberal Presbyterian like John Gamble was able to comment, 'this uncouth jargon, this noisy bawling, as refinement, perhaps, would term it, is delicious to my ears. I am a Presbyterian, and it comes loaded to them, with the sweet associations, and fond recollections of my early years.'[8]

Congregations sang while seated and were led in public praise by the precentor, often from a small platform below the pulpit. The precentor had to 'give out the line' which meant that either one or two lines of the psalm had to be read or sung for the congregation then to follow. This had originally been suggested in the *Directory* as a temporary measure until literacy had improved sufficiently to allow the use of psalm books.[9] However, lining became ingrained in traditional Presbyterian culture, and in Ulster, where literacy rates were high, lining could seriously disrupt the flow of congregational praise. Though the majority of precentors did an adequate job, the surviving evidence, often written from a reformist perspective, is generally disapproving. James Reid Dill of Dromore, County Tyrone, gave out Psalm 100 to a long measure tune but the precentor began with a common measure tune. Before the precentor came to the end of the

---

[7] 'Stereotyped Christianity', *Christian Freeman*, 4 (1836), 96–8; S. L. Orr and A. Haslett, *Historical sketch of Ballyalbany Presbyterian church* (Belfast, n.d.), 127. The names of the twelve tunes are Common, King's, Duke's, English, French, London, Stilt (York), Dunfermline, Dundee, Abbey, Martyrs, and Elgin (Millar Patrick, *Four centuries of Scottish psalmody* (Oxford, 1949), 111).

[8] J. Gamble, *A view of society and manners, in the north of Ireland* (London, 1813), 364.

[9] *Directory*, 393.

first line 'he stopped and called out, "Stap, stap, awee, I've lost the tune". His singing was something I shall never forget, most unnatural and unearthly, a kind of screech.'[10]

Psalm singing was not confined to the meeting-house and psalms were sung in family devotions and often in the workplace.[11] They were popular with the godly as they portrayed a sovereign God in whom his people could find comfort in times of trouble. On his deathbed, John Edgar kept repeating the psalms, especially Psalm 61: 1, 'The rock that is higher than I'.[12] William Orr, on his way to the scaffold in 1797, found solace in Psalm 23 and especially the first verse of Psalm 31:

> In thee, O Lord, I put my trust;
> Shammed let me never be.[13]

Psalms not only provided comfort but also challenged sinful behaviour. Thomas Clark, Burgher minister of Cahans, County Monaghan, neglected to thank God for his freedom on his release from prison. Writing nearly fifty years after the event, in 1792, he still was haunted by Psalm 78: 42:

> They did not call to mind his power,
> Nor yet the day when he
> Delivered them out of the hand
> Of their fierce enemy.[14]

Psalms also provided a focal point and source of comfort at communal events, especially wakes.

> The psalm been read an' grace been said
> He starts them to the singins
> The folk a' roun' raise up the tune

---

[10] J. R. Dill, *Autobiography of a country parson* (Belfast, 1888), 27. Also, W. D. Killen, *Reminiscences of a long life* (London, 1901), 46.

[11] J. Simpson, *Annals of my life, labours and travels* (Belfast, 1895), 4–5; S. Prenter, *The life and labours of the Rev William Johnston, D. D.* (London, 1895), 11. For further details of family worship see Chapter 11.

[12] T. Croskery, 'The Rev. John Edgar, D. D., professor of theology, Belfast', in T. Hamilton (ed.), *Irish worthies; a series of original biographical sketches of eminent ministers and members of the Presbyterian Church in Ireland* (Belfast, 1875), 69.

[13] F. J. Bigger, *William Orr* (Dublin, 1906), 44.

[14] T. Clark, *A pastoral and farewell letter* (Monaghan, 1807), 23.

Till a' their lugs are ringin'
How foxes when dead lay down their head
In quiet peace thegither
An how like grass the human race
Cut down by death do wither
They sing that night.[15]

Given the almost exclusive use of psalms in public and family worship, it is unsurprising that psalm singing had become an important aspect of popular culture in Presbyterian areas where, more generally, singing, dancing, and playing the violin were popular pastimes.[16] The similarity of rhyme and metre with popular ballads may also have made them more generally attractive.[17] One indication of the popularity of psalmody was the many singing schools that dotted Presbyterian Ulster. These schools began to appear with book clubs in the last decades of the eighteenth century, ostensibly to allow the laity to learn or practise psalm tunes. By the 1830s the school at Templepatrick had been running 'for many years' and catered for fifty-seven pupils who paid 3s. per quarter to be taught new tunes.[18] Some pupils created their own illuminated tune books in which they recorded those they were learning.[19] Practice verses were also composed to help them remember the tunes and because some believed that it was inappropriate to sing inspired psalms outside of a meeting-house.[20] Often these were based upon the name of the tune and included information as to how it should be sung. For example, the tune 'French' was sung with the following words.

[15] S. Walker, 'A miscellaneous collection of poetry composed and written by Samuel Walker of Shaneshill near Templepatrick' [n.d.] (BCL, Bigger Collection), 155.
[16] A. Gailey, 'Folk-life study and the Ordnance Survey Memoirs', in idem and D. Ó hÓgáin (eds.), *Gold under furze: studies in folk tradition* (Dublin, 1983), 154–6; J. Hewitt, *Rhyming weavers and other country poets of Antrim and Down* (Belfast, 1974), 27–9.
[17] D. Johnson, *Music and society in lowland Scotland in the eighteenth century* (London, 1972), ch. 9.
[18] *OSMI* (Templepatrick), xxxv. 122.
[19] J. W. Kernohan, *The county of Londonderry in three centuries, with notices of the Ironmongers' estate* (Belfast, 1921), 58; J. Stevenson, *Two centuries of life in Down 1600–1800* (Belfast, 1920), 193–6.
[20] For Scotland, see Johnson, *Music and society*, 181–3 and Patrick, *Scottish psalmody*, ch. 15.

> The first of all begins with French;
> The second measure low;
> The third extended very high;
> The fourth doth downward go.[21]

Some embodied how Presbyterians saw their spiritual lives as pilgrimages in grace towards heaven. A precentor from an unnamed congregation in the north-west composed a long psalm to help children learn to sing psalm tunes, which included the following stanza.

> Singing psalms is the mode,
> With pilgrims on the road,
> While through this dark abode,
>   Sojourners here.[22]

Others were merely silly.

> Newton is a purty place,
>   It stands beside the sea;
> Scrabo is an ugly hill,
>   Three times one are three.[23]

Some other verses were more vindictive in character, as the following example about an ill-tempered teacher suggests.

> When Satan in the days of old
>   The herd of swine destroy,
> He left one surly boar behind.
>   McKinley you're the boy![24]

Singing schools provided an opportunity for social interaction and entertainment alongside religious or musical instruction. Weaver poets honed their poetical gifts and relationships blossomed in the dances or kissing games that sometimes followed the practice.[25] Yet if the other unfavourable comments about public praise are considered alongside such behaviour, it is easy to understand why

---

[21] Stevenson, *Two centuries*, 196.

[22] 'The precentor', *Orthodox Presbyterian*, 4 (1833), 122.

[23] Stevenson, *Two centuries*, 199.

[24] 'Precentors, choirs, and choir stalls', *Irish Presbyterian*, new ser., 16 (1910), 68.

[25] D. Herbison, *The select works of David Herbison* (Belfast, 1883), 113; Stevenson, *Two centuries*, 199–200; *OSMI* (Aghnanloo), xi. 11.

many ministers and other reformers would want to see changes. The Kirk session of Drumbolg Reformed Presbyterian congregation passed a resolution in 1813 that any communicant who attended 'promiscuous' singing events would risk losing their church membership.[26] According to one reformer, the practice verses often of a 'trifling, ludicrous, and even obscene kind' had to be purged or the younger generation would lose all respect for the tunes and devalue the solemnity of public worship.[27] Henry Cooke more broadly condemned the 'vain, and frivolous, and worldly amusements' that characterized many schools; 'No wonder such schools seldom prosper, since nothing can prosper where God is mocked.'[28] Though reformers were appalled at these popular accretions to psalmody, they shared with the laity a conviction that the psalms were a key component of their identity as Presbyterians.

II

From the 1760s, Presbyterians from across the theological spectrum proposed a range of measures to improve the standard of public praise. These included the appointment of singing masters, suitably qualified precentors, increasing the repertoire of tunes, and the publication of collections of psalms and hymns for the use of congregations. The initial impetus for reform came from non-subscribing and liberal Presbyterians, especially those residing in Dublin. In the late seventeenth century the Dublin minister Joseph Boyse, an Englishman of impeccable orthodox credentials, who had nevertheless supported the non-subscribers, produced two collections of hymns and paraphrases especially for use at communion. The influence of a large metropolitan centre promoted such innovations, as did the close connection between southern congregations and English dissenters who were noted innovators in public praise in the early decades of

---

[26] Drumbolg (RP) session book, 15 Dec. 1813 (PRONI, MIC/1C/15C/1).

[27] J. Cochran, *A selection of psalm and hymn tunes* ([Belfast], 1804), 3.

[28] [H. Cooke], *Translations and paraphrases* (Belfast, 1821), p. vi.

the eighteenth century.[29] In 1751 Plunkett Street congregation introduced a 'new collection of psalms and hymns'. This action resulted in a
complaint being sent to the Synod of Ulster from a section of
the congregation, followed by a counter-memorial stating that the
majority was in favour of the new book. The matter seems to have
been resolved after the Synod urged the parties to live in peace.[30]
Later, in 1765, Charles McCollum and Thomas Vance, ministers
respectively of Capel Street and Usher's Quay congregations in the
city, produced a new collection of the psalms that had been approved
by the Synod in the previous year.[31] Usher's Quay was also one of the
first congregations to engage the services of a singing master to teach
psalmody in 1772.[32]

The reform of psalmody did not remain in the south for long. New
Light ministers in Ulster had close links with Dublin Presbyterianism
and were among the first to introduce hymns and reform psalmody.
By the 1780s, new versions of the psalms, a collection of scriptural
paraphrases sanctioned by the Church of Scotland in 1781, and,
more controversially, hymns had already found their way into congregations in Ulster.[33] William Bruce noted in 1784 that Andrew
Craig of Lisburn had 'made great progress in promoting psalmody
in his congregation and excels, in the decent, grave, and deliberate
mode of conducting worship'. Three years later, Craig published
a collection of hymns for the use of his congregation.[34] Bruce himself
produced a volume of psalms and hymns in 1801 and a second
edition in 1818 with the help of the minister of Second Congregation,
the noted poet W. H. Drummond.[35] In 1787 William Steel Dickson's

[29] R. Gillespie, ' "A good and godly exercise": singing the word in Irish dissent',
in K. Herlihy (ed.), *Propagating the word of Irish dissent 1650–1800* (Dublin, 1998),
24–45; M. R. Watts, *The Dissenters*, 2 vols. (Oxford, 1978, 1995), i. 303–15.

[30] *RGSU* ii. (1751), 361–2.

[31] *RGSU* ii. (1764), 481. For details of the authors see, T. Witherow, *Historical and
literary memorials of Presbyterianism in Ireland*, 2 vols. (Belfast, 1879–80), ii. 325.

[32] Usher's Quay (GSU) session book, 2 June 1772 (J. M. Barkley, 'A history of the
ruling eldership in Irish Presbyterianism', 2 vols. (QUB MA, 1952), ii. 204j–k).

[33] [A. G. Malcolm], 'On a new version of psalmody', *Belfast Monthly Magazine*, 7
(1811), 105.

[34] Journal of the Revd William Bruce, 20 June 1784 (PRONI, Bruce papers,
T/3041/3/2); *Hymns for the use of the Presbyterian congregation in Lisburn* (Belfast,
1787).

[35] W. H. McCafferty, 'The psalmody of the Old Congregation in Belfast,
1760–1840', *Transactions of the Unitarian Historical Society*, 7 (1939), 54–5, 60–1.

Portaferry congregation advertised in the local press for a 'man of character, and eminence in his profession, as a teacher of church music' who would 'find encouragement seldom to be met with'.[36] A. G. Malcolm published a collection in 1811, which was used by a number of New Light congregations and included twenty-one tunes composed by the author himself, while another collection was compiled by S. J. Pigott for use in the Presbytery of Antrim and the Synod of Munster.[37] The inclusion in these collections of tunes by well-known composers such as Madan, Purcell, and Haydn indicates a level of musical appreciation on the part of New Light ministers that was not thought necessary by the majority of their conservative opponents. They wanted to make public praise both contemporary and sophisticated. Commenting in 1799 upon Strand Street non-subscribing congregation in Dublin, William Drennan wrote, 'Dr. Moody is organising the meeting-house, and the organists and singers etc. will make it, if possible, a fashionable religion.'[38]

Probably owing to the influence of ministers such as Steel Dickson, these informal measures were given wider purchase by a resolution of the Synod of Ulster in 1789, which lamented the perceptible decline in the standard of psalmody. It recommended that all congregations devote their attention to church music, urging ministers to train those with authority over the young in the principles of music 'that the rising generation may be qualified for joining in the public praises of God with decency, comfort and advantage'.[39] Two years later, the Synod ordered ministers to read this resolution by November, enjoining them 'to use their utmost efforts to have church music cultivated' in their congregations by encouraging the appointment of qualified precentors and 'teachers of psalmody' where possible.[40] With the support of nine presbyteries and numerous ministers, Steel Dickson published an address in 1792 in which he criticized popular notions concerning the divine inspiration and exclusive use of 'the twelve',

---

[36] *Belfast News-Letter*, 25–9 May 1787.
[37] A. G. Malcolm, *A collection of psalms, hymns and spiritual songs* (Newry, 1811); S. J. Pigott, *A collection of psalms and hymns, ancient and modern* (Dublin, n.d.).
[38] J. Agnew (ed.), *The Drennan-McTier letters*, 3 vols. (Dublin, 1998–9), ii. 525.
[39] *RGSU* iii. (1789), 112.
[40] *RGSU* iii. (1791), 133.

pointing out that this had not been the view of the sixteenth-century Protestant Reformers. Indeed, the small number of tunes was an affront to their persecuted Covenanter forefathers, who, he argued, sang no fewer than 140. 'Yet, we are content, not with the *notes* but the *names* of the twelve. In many places, half that number are scarcely known, even by *name*. A majority of the present generation have never learned a single tune; and the rising one seems to be, almost totally, neglected.'[41]

In an effort to improve the standard of public praise and their own social and cultural standing, the New Light congregations of First and Second Belfast in Rosemary Street were at the forefront of musical innovation within Ulster Presbyterianism.[42] From at least 1762, in the case of First Congregation, both had choirs comprised of boys from the local charitable society or poorhouse. They produced their own psalm books, reflecting their New Light theology, and in 1804 the precentor of Second Congregation, Robert Hart, published a musical catechism.[43] The precentors were both well paid; William Hughes of First Congregation received £40 per annum for his services from 1808 to 1827. First Congregation also showed themselves pioneers when they appointed three women to either sing or lead the choir during the period from 1818 to 1840. The most publicly significant innovation, however, was the installation of an organ in Second Congregation. It was first played on 9 September 1806 by their celebrated organist Edward Bunting at a charity service attended by Lord Castlereagh. First Congregation, who had earlier declined the chance to install the organ, expressed concern that it would disrupt their worship and considered changing the time of their service. Although the church organ must have been a source of pride for Second Congregation, worries were expressed about its impact upon the character of public worship. In June 1817, the

---

[41] W. S. Dickson, *Psalmody* (Belfast, 1792), 13.

[42] The following paragraph is based upon, A. Gordon, *Historical memorials of the First Presbyterian Church of Belfast* (Belfast, 1887); McCafferty, 'Psalmody of the Old Congregation'; and D. Steers, '"An admirable finger directed by pure taste": Edward Bunting and Belfast's Second Congregation', *Bulletin of the Presbyterian Historical Society of Ireland*, 25 (1996), 22–9.

[43] *A musical catechism; or, the principles of sacred music laid down in a plain and simple form* (Belfast, 1804).

church committee recommended that the 'symphonies between the verses of the psalms should be discontinued, being of opinion that they break too much upon the solemnity of devotion of that part of our service, by leading the mind to consider the principles of music more than the praise of God'.[44] This conservatism was also expressed when, in 1839, it was resolved that to encourage singing, the congregation would be asked to stand. It was obvious that the congregation was not ready for this and, in an effort to promote singing, the committee directed that only 'plain and simple psalm tunes' would be used.[45] Reflecting the social and financial standing of the congregation, the committee also decided in 1818 to limit spending on praise to £70 per annum, though this figure was surpassed by the £112 spent on singers by First Congregation during the year 1817 to 1818.[46]

The rise to prominence of evangelicalism also provided an impetus for change in both the overall standard of public praise and the type of material employed. One of the most significant collections of psalms produced in the late eighteenth century was for Carrickfergus congregation in 1782 whose minister, John Savage, was a supporter of evangelical missionary societies in the first decades of the nineteenth century.[47] The Burgher Synod in 1801 debated the place of hymns in public worship after one of its members, John Lowry of Upper Clenanees, was disciplined for publishing a pamphlet in favour of their use.[48] The significant aspect of the case was that Lowry was one of the founder members of the Evangelical Society of Ulster. The link between evangelicalism and hymnody is clearly understandable

[44] Second Belfast (PA) committee book, 1 June 1817 (PRONI, CR/4/9/A/1), 126.

[45] S. S. Millin, *History of the Second Congregation of Protestant dissenters in Belfast 1708–1896* (Belfast, 1900), 91.

[46] Second Belfast committee book, 1 Mar. 1818, 141–2; McCafferty, 'Psalmody of the Old Congregation', 59.

[47] [J. Moore], *Psalms carefully suited and applied to the Christian state and worship* (Dublin, 1782). According to a handwritten note, probably by J. S. Reid, in the copy of this work in UTC, the compiler was John Moore, an elder in Carrickfergus. Savage led a prayer meeting in the town for the work of the Irish Evangelical Society (*Hibernian Evangelical Magazine*, 1 (1816), 293).

[48] D. Stewart, *The Seceders in Ireland with annals of their congregations* (Belfast, 1950), 190–2. The full title of Lowry's pamphlet may be found in, E. R. McC. Dix, 'Ulster bibliography. Article VI. Downpatrick, Dungannon, and Hillsborough', *Ulster Journal of Archaeology*, 2nd ser., 8 (1901), 173.

when one considers the centrality of Christ for evangelicals. The metrical psalms could only prefigure Christ whereas paraphrases of New Testament passages, or the hymns of Newton, Watts, and the Wesleys, could explicitly mention Christ and the believers' personal relationship with him.[49] It is clear that a number of Old Light ministers used hymns in public worship and there is evidence to suggest that a handful of their Seceder contemporaries did the same.[50] Again, there was a strong Dublin connection. James Carlile, the non-subscribing evangelical minister of Mary's Abbey, published a book of 119 tunes for congregational use composed by, amongst others, Purcell, Pergolesi, Haydn, Mozart, Beethoven, and Rossini.[51] The range of composers reflected Carlile's love of music as a student at Glasgow where he had taken part in musical entertainments and public concerts. In adult life, he indulged his interest in music by playing his violin during family worship. Henry Cooke published a book of paraphrases in 1821 for his then congregation of Killyleagh, complete with a vigorous defence of the use of hymns and paraphrases in public worship, in the hope that they would be found 'evangelical'.[52] In doing so, Cooke directly challenged the hallowed place of 'the twelve' by pointing out that many lay Presbyterians could not even name them and that fewer than half were used regularly in public praise.[53] The mood of reform also affected the Covenanters, whose Northern Presbytery encouraged their congregations in 1829 to improve singing and to introduce new tunes where necessary.[54]

Unlike its non-subscribing neighbours in Rosemary Street, Third Belfast congregation was the most numerously attended and the ministers of that congregation had always been impeccably orthodox. Samuel Hanna, the noted evangelical, was certainly no exception. When the committee appointed John Cochran precentor in 1801, he was paid £15 per annum with a £5 bonus for running a singing

---

[49] Crawford, *Seasons of grace*, 91–2; [Cooke], *Translations and paraphrases*, pp. iii–iv.

[50] H. Hastings, *Memoir of the life and labours of the late Rev. Josias Wilson, London* (London, 1850), 111.

[51] J. Carlile, *Select sacred melodies* (London and Dublin, n.d.); R. J. Rodgers, 'James Carlile, 1784–1854' (QUB Ph.D., 1973), 10–11.

[52] [Cooke], *Translations and paraphrases*, p. x.

[53] Ibid., pp. vii–ix.

[54] A. Loughridge, *The Covenanters in Ireland* (Belfast, 1984), 124.

school during the summer months.[55] In December 1800, the number of lines given out was increased to two, 'to make harmony more agreeable', and in 1813 lining was ended altogether.[56] Nevertheless, the committee was quick to admonish Cochran in 1802 when he introduced new music, directing him to confine himself in future to 'the old tunes'.[57] In 1821, a selection of hymns was published for the use of the children of the congregation and both Cochran and a successor of his, William Reid, produced selections of psalm and hymn tunes for the use of the Synod of Ulster.[58] Practical problems arose in 1812 when a new precentor was required. Owing to a lack of suitable Irish candidates, David Wilson, a Scot, was appointed 'professor of sacred music' in 1813 and placed in charge of a singing school. However, the school suffered from a lack of numbers (which reduced its financial viability) and misbehaviour by the children, eventually leading to the departure of Wilson in 1815.[59] Two boys from the poorhouse had been drafted in to help with the singing in 1806 and by 1838 it seems that the Third Congregation had a sizeable choir for in November of that year a complaint was submitted to the congregational committee concerning the 'great impropriety' of the boys who assisted in the singing gallery.[60]

Despite growing tensions, both liberal and conservative Presbyterians in the 1820s promoted the reform of psalmody through the Synod. In 1827 a committee was formed to compile a book of tunes 'for the use of such congregations as may choose to adopt it'.[61] Five years previously procedures and expected qualifications for the appointment of suitable precentors were agreed to and subsequently enshrined in the *Code*, which also called for an end to lining where possible.[62] Precentors had to lead congregational singing in a correct

[55] Third Belfast (GSU) committee book, 3 May 1801 (PRONI, MIC/1P/7/5), 99.

[56] J. W. Kernohan, *Rosemary Street Presbyterian Church. A record of the last 200 years* (Belfast, 1923), 41.

[57] Third Belfast (GSU) committee book, 16 May 1802, 104.

[58] Cochran, *Selection of psalm and hymn tunes*; W. Reid, *A selection of sacred tunes for congregational and family worship* (Belfast, [1835]).

[59] Third Belfast (GSU) committee book, 7 June 1813, 11 May, 14 Oct. 1815, 151, 161–2, 164.

[60] Ibid., 5 June 1806, 128; session book, 28 Nov. 1838 (Barkley, 'Eldership', ii. 213).

[61] *RGSU* (1827), 43–4; (1828), 58.

[62] *RGSU* (1822), 29–30; *Code* (1825), 19–20, 88.

manner and to teach the laity new tunes. For instance, those applying
for the post in Carrickfergus congregation had to be competent to
teach 'all the parts in sacred music', practice new tunes in the
committee room before public worship, conduct all public praise,
and teach for free a 'class of twenty children, to be named by the
committee of the congregation, so that they may be able to accom-
pany and assist him in public psalmody'.[63] The nineteenth-century
evidence also makes it clear that the moral character of the precentor
was as important as his musical ability.[64]

After the Remonstrants had been expelled in 1829, the Synod
continued to make the reform of psalmody a priority. An official
tune book was eventually published in 1835 and noted evangelicals
such as James Morgan advocated the use of scriptural paraphrases
and hymns in public worship, though only if expressly permitted by
church courts.[65] Under the influence of evangelicalism, singing
schools were reformed or established for the first time. Founded in
1839, the school at Islandmagee attracted sixty-seven males and
forty-two females, 'its principal object being the introduction of
the more modern psalm tunes instead of the "auld twelve"' that
were still sung by congregations in 'remote and retired districts' and
by the Covenanters.[66] In Ballylinny, lessons were held in a farmer's
house during the winter and were attended by sixty-five pupils, aged
from fourteen to thirty years, who paid one shilling per quarter,
presumably to pay the teacher.[67]

How did these various reforms affect the standard of public praise?
The general impression from visitation presbyteries is one of mixed
success. As indicated by the experiences of Dublin and Belfast, reform

---

[63] Carrickfergus (GSU) minute book, 1 July 1830 (PRONI, MIC/1P/157/1).
[64] *Belfast News-Letter*, 5 and 15 Nov. 1833; Creggan (GSU) session book, 13 Aug.
1837 (Barkley, 'Eldership', ii. 296–7); N. McAllister, 'Contradiction and diversity: the
musical life of Derry in the 1830 decade', in G. O'Brien (ed.), *Derry and Londonderry:
history and society. Interdisciplinary essays on the history of an Irish country* (Dublin,
1999), 476–7.
[65] *A selection of sacred music, designed for the use of the Presbyterian churches in
connexion with the Synod of Ulster*, 2nd edn. (Dromara, 1835); J. Morgan, *Essays in
some of the principal doctrines and duties of the gospel*, 2nd edn. (Belfast, 1837), 151–2;
'Psalmody', *Orthodox Presbyterian*, 1 (1829), 98–102.
[66] *OSMI* (Islandmagee), x. 33.
[67] *OSMI* (Ballylinny), xxxii. 17.

had a greater impact upon congregations located in towns. For instance, First Derry had a small choir, a new precentor, and a book of psalms in 1831, and, by 1836, public worship was reported to be 'very respectable'.[68] Elsewhere, there was a gradual improvement. The New Light minister of Newry reported to the Presbytery of Armagh in 1828 that though some did not join in singing, most of his congregation did, and that 'on the whole ... the psalmody is improving'.[69] Similarly, Robert Gray of Burt, County Donegal, told the Derry Presbytery in 1833 that psalmody in the congregation was 'not altogether so respectable as we would wish' though they did sing the old tunes 'pretty well'.[70] By 1840 Gray was able to report that a 'great proficiency had been made by many therein, and that a great improvement had taken place in the public services by the attention paid to psalmody'.[71] The success of reform would depend to a large degree upon influencing the young. Contemporaries noted that as older members died out new psalm versions and tunes could be more easily introduced. James Reid, minister of Ramelton, County Donegal, found in 1839 that 'psalmody with the aged is in a tolerable state, with the young much improved'.[72] The minister of Newtownards, County Down, considered the 'state of sacred music not so good as it ought to be, owing to a backwardness in sending out the young to receive instruction'.[73]

Any attempt to reform public praise encountered both practical difficulties, such as a lack of books, and the conservatism of the laity. One of the most common observations recorded in presbytery minutes was the attachment of the laity to 'the old tunes'. The consequences could be severe if a minister attempted to foist upon an unwilling congregation an end to lining or introduce new tunes, even those reputedly included amongst 'the twelve'. The following

[68] First Derry (GSU) session book, 8 Oct. 1826, 12 Feb. 1831 (PRONI, T/2711/1/1); *A selection of psalms adopted for public worship* (Londonderry, 1831); Derry Pby (GSU), 3 May 1836 (UTC), 51.

[69] Armagh Pby (GSU), 27 May 1828 (PHS), 24.

[70] Derry Pby (GSU), 7 May 1833.

[71] Burt (GSU) session book, 4 Oct. 1840 (PRONI, MIC/1P/33/2).

[72] Letterkenny Pby (GSU), 14 Aug. 1839 (Church House, strong room), 8. Gamble, *View of society and manners*, 250.

[73] Belfast Pby (GSU), 2 Apr. 1839 (Church House, strong room).

anecdotes published by the *Christian Freeman* in 1836 give an indication of the tenacity of the laity to their traditional practices.

In one [congregation], so soon as an unstereotyped tune was raised, a number of the people snatched up their hats, and were off, one of them exclaiming, 'It is time to be out when the Devil is in'; in another, the clerk having resigned because an elder had threatened, before the assembled congregation, to collar him like a dog; when on the next Sabbath there was a long dead silence on the giving out of the line, another elder rose, and said very sarcastically, 'I think we had better never mind praising God for a while, till we agree about how we are to do it'; while in many other congregations one party with an old stereotyped tune strove, by dint of loud shouting, to sing down the new fangled party with their unstereotyped tune. One venerable old man told me, a short time since, that he sung down the whole congregation of ——; and on my looking into his face somewhat incredulously, as he supposed, he assured me solemnly that he did, and could do it again.[74]

The introduction of a sung hallelujah and the dropping of the line in one congregation led an exasperated member to declare, 'we must make a stand, or there is no telling where he [the minister] may stop—he may be wanting us next to be bowing and kneeling like the high kirk, or to sing in Latin like the papists'.[75]

The success of reform in a given congregation owed much to the desire for self-improvement and social respectability amongst the laity. A study of the Cambuslang revival in the west of Scotland in the eighteenth century noted that the adoption of psalm singing by converts, especially handloom weavers, was part of a 'popular enlightenment' in that area and provided an alternative to bawdy songs and ballads.[76] The same process was occurring in the Ulster countryside in the decades either side of 1800. A writer in 1832 suggested that psalm singing should provide an alternative to the drinking of ardent spirits, jesting, and 'foolish songs'.[77] Religious seriousness and social

[74] 'Stereotyped Christianity', *Christian Freeman*, 4 (1836), 97. Also, 'Psalmody', *Orthodox Presbyterian*, 1 (1829), 99.

[75] Gamble, *View of society and manners*, 251.

[76] N. Landsman, 'Evangelists and their hearers: popular interpretation of revivalist preaching in eighteenth-century Scotland', *Journal of British Studies*, 28 (1989), 144–9.

[77] 'Congregational improvements', *Christian Freeman*, 1 (1832), 25.

respectability were clearly expressed in the practice verse composed
by the unnamed precentor referred to previously.

> Whilst the rude and profane
> Chaunt o'er their songs so vain,
>> Sporting with death;
> Singing psalms is my choice,
> And makes my heart rejoice,
> Thus I'll employ my voice,
>> While I have breath.
> While some unhappy souls
> Doat o'er their setting bowls,
>> Games, balls, and plays,
> I'll to my Bible go,
> My duty there to know,
> That I may wiser grow,
>> In wisdom's ways.[78]

Despite some notable successes, reform would not be achieved over-
night. A survey conducted by the General Assembly in 1858 found
that the standard of psalmody remained at best mixed, though the
reading of the line was 'rapidly becoming obsolete'.[79]

Attempts to reform psalmody brought to the surface theological
and cultural tensions between the various strands of Ulster Presbyterianism. George Mathews observed in 1836 that the Seceders and
Covenanters used only the metrical psalms, the Synod of Ulster sung
psalms and 'a collection of hymns, has of late got partially into use',
while the Unitarians exclusively used hymns and 'in general' had
instrumental accompaniment.[80] There was determined opposition
by conservatives to the use of paraphrases and hymns. Hymns challenged the iconic place of the psalms and, from the time of the
subscription controversy of the 1720s, were believed to be intrinsically
heterodox.[81] Nineteenth-century Presbyterian opponents of hymns
such as Thomas Houston, minister of Knockbracken Reformed
Presbyterian congregation near Belfast, were quick to point out that

---

[78] 'The precentor', *Orthodox Presbyterian*, 4 (1833), 122.
[79] *MGA* ii. (1858), 678–9.
[80] G. Mathews, *An account of the regium donum* (Dublin, 1836), 44.
[81] J. M. Barkley, *The eldership in Irish Presbyterianism* (n.p., 1963), 108.

they had originated in the previous century 'amid declension from the truth'.[82] Conservative Presbyterians, especially Seceders and Covenanters, continued to maintain that God had ordained only the metrical psalms for public praise.[83] The attitude of Irish Seceders is surprising as their co-religionists in Scotland pioneered the use of scriptural paraphrases, which were also sanctioned by their own *Act and Testimony*.[84] Nevertheless, the Union articles of 1840 excluded the use of anything but the psalms in public worship to ensure that it would have the support of all Seceders.[85] Even Cooke withdrew his backing for his 1821 collection of paraphrases, citing as a reason the comfort that psalms brought to him while he was ill. It may also have been an attempt to reassert his Presbyterian credentials in the face of criticism from politically liberal colleagues.[86]

The commitment of the General Assembly in 1840 to unaccompanied psalmody underlines the indebtedness of Presbyterian evangelicalism to previous doctrinal and liturgical traditions. This conservatism is further emphasized by their attitude to the use of instrumental accompaniment. There is evidence that at least three theologically liberal congregations had organs by the 1830s and, if George Mathews is to believed, there may well be other examples.[87] It is no coincidence that when the former New Light congregation of Dundalk returned to the General Assembly in the 1840s their organ fell into disrepair.[88] The debates that periodically rocked the General Assembly in the years between 1868 and 1892 showed the depth of feeling against the use of instruments in public worship and the centrality of unaccompanied singing to the identity of Presbyterians in Ulster. Yet despite the official position of the church, sections of

---

[82] *The true psalmody; or, the Bible psalms the church's only manual of praise*, 3rd edn. (Belfast, 1867), preface.

[83] MASAB (1817), 167; *MPSI* (1839), 32–3; [Thomas Houston], 'Psalmody', *Orthodox Presbyterian*, 1 (1830), 170–5; 'Psalmody', *Covenanter*, new ser., 1 (1834), 241–51; 2 (1835), 1–11; 3 (1836), 97–103, 145–50, 210–16; 4 (1837), 49–57, 123–30.

[84] C. G. McCrie, *The public worship of Presbyterian Scotland historically treated* (Edinburgh, 1892), 297–305, 308–9; MASAB (1817), 167.

[85] W. T. Latimer, *A history of Irish Presbyterians*, 2nd edn. (Belfast, 1902), 469.

[86] *True psalmody*, preface.

[87] The three congregations were Second Belfast, Carlow, and Dundalk (Mathews, *Account*, 26, 44).

[88] Steers, ' "An admirable finger" ', 29 n. 12.

the laity were attracted to hymns and it is little wonder that the revival of 1859 led to the more general use of them.[89]

The deeply ingrained Reformed values of simplicity and intelligibility, when mixed with traditionalism and stubbornness, were formidable barriers to any change in public praise. The Presbyterian laity sincerely loved the metrical psalms and their often monotonous diets of public praise, as these distinguished them from their Anglican and Catholic neighbours. They believed that the psalms they sang and the tunes they used were the same as those used by their Covenanter forefathers who had courageously defended Presbyterianism against its enemies. What is more, God's own people in the Old Testament sang the psalms. For conservative Presbyterians, the psalms were inseparable from the idea of a covenant people that stretched back to the ancient Israelites and through to the Scottish Covenanters. To sing the metrical psalms in eighteenth- and nineteenth-century Ulster was to identify with that history and to declare your identity as the people of God.

[89] Tosh, 'One hundred and fifty years of worship', 140–1, 145.

5

Preaching

The proclamation of God's word through preaching has always been of central importance in the Reformed tradition. For John Calvin and the Scottish and English Puritans who followed him, preaching was not merely the expounding of Scripture, but the declaration of God's will and revelation to his people; a means of grace animated by the Holy Spirit and rooted in the sovereign purposes of God.[1] This was the position of the Westminster divines who, in the *Directory*, declared that preaching was 'the power of God unto salvation, and one of the greatest and most excellent marks belonging to the ministry of the gospel'.[2] The responsibility placed upon those called to be ministers of God's word was consequently great. The *Larger Catechism* stated that ministers of the word were 'to preach sound doctrine, diligently, in season and out of season; plainly, not in enticing words of man's wisdom, but in demonstration of the Spirit, and of power; faithfully, making known the whole counsel of God; wisely, applying themselves to the necessities and capacities of the hearers; zealously, with fervent love to God and the souls of his people; sincerely, aiming at his glory, and their conversion, edification and salvation'.[3] Preachers had to know their congregations, prepare their sermons thoroughly, and proclaim the word faithfully in order to address the needs of their people. There were also

---

[1] J. H. Leith, 'Calvin's doctrine of the proclamation of the word and its significance for today', in T. George (ed.), *John Calvin and the church: a prism of reform* (Louisville, Ky., 1990), 206–29; H. Davies, *The worship of the English Puritans* (London, 1948), ch. 11; G. D. Henderson, *Religious life in seventeenth-century Scotland* (Cambridge, 1937), ch. 9.

[2] *Directory*, 379–81.

[3] *Larger Catechism*, Q. 159.

responsibilities placed upon those who heard the word preached. Those listening had to prepare themselves to receive God's word through prayer, listen attentively for God's voice in the sermon, and apply the lessons prescribed to their own lives.[4] The directions offered in the Westminster formularies acknowledged that good hearing was disciplined and relied upon preparation rooted in the word of God and shaped by the *Shorter Catechism*.[5] The reciprocal duties and responsibilities placed upon the minister and his hearers created a sense of community, formed as the people of God listened to the word of God proclaimed by the servant of God.

The reciprocal nature of preaching was reflected in the ambiguous position of a Presbyterian minister within the local community.[6] On the one hand, by virtue of his ordained status and educational attainments, a minister was a person apart from his congregation. On the other, the fact that the majority of ministers came from a farming background meant they knew well the vicissitudes of farming life. In that context, the act of preaching was an important means of creating and reinforcing a common identity as God's people in a particular locality. For communication to occur, a common set of assumptions, knowledge, and sense of community distinctiveness had to be expressed in the preacher's actions and words.[7] Preaching involved a symbiotic relationship between the preacher and his congregation. As will be seen, many ministers tailored the style and content of their sermons to meet the expectations of their congregations, sometimes deliberately concealing their own theological views. Others often failed to discern the essential expectations of the community they spoke to and so disrupted this delicate relationship.

[4] *Shorter Catechism*, Q. 90.
[5] Leigh Eric Schmidt draws attention to the importance of devotional preparation in shaping how believers heard sermons (*Hearing things: religion, illusion and the American Enlightenment* (Princeton, 2000), 40).
[6] J. M. Barkley, 'The Presbyterian minister in eighteenth-century Ireland', in J. L. M. Haire *et al.*, *Challenge and conflict: essays in Irish Presbyterian history and doctrine* (Belfast, 1981), 46–71; K. D. Brown, 'Life after death? A preliminary survey of the Irish Presbyterian ministry in the nineteenth century', *Irish Economic and Social History*, 22 (1995), 49–63.
[7] R. Gillespie, 'The reformed preacher: Irish Protestant preaching 1660–1700', in A. J. Fletcher and R. Gillespie (eds.), *Irish preaching 700–1700* (Dublin, 2001), 127.

This chapter examines the various traditions and changes within Ulster Presbyterian preaching in the period from 1770 to 1840. It will become clear that to succeed as a preacher a minister had to do more than expound correct doctrine. He had to do so in a way that corresponded with the expectations of his congregation for a certain style of preaching. Over time, the style and content of sermons changed as Puritan themes were modified by the influence of the Enlightenment and Romanticism. While the broader cultural mood determined what was preached and how it was delivered, the idiosyncrasies of individual ministers and congregational expectations also exerted an often less than benign influence upon the proclamation of the word. The chapter will be divided into four sections. The first section provides an overview of Old Light and Seceder preaching, drawing attention to the 'free offer of the gospel' and its importance to the development of evangelicalism within Presbyterianism. Section two begins with some general comments about the influence upon Presbyterian preaching of Enlightenment ideas as mediated through university education and presbytery trials before examining New Light preaching. Section three assesses lay attitudes towards preachers and their sermons. The final section examines the development of an evangelical style of preaching in the nineteenth century that was influenced by the prevailing cultural mood of the time but was also deeply indebted to the Old Light and Seceder preaching of the previous century.

I

Preaching was the focus of public worship in Ulster Presbyterianism in the eighteenth and nineteenth centuries. Such was its importance that the practices of reading the scriptures and singing psalms in public worship were adversely affected, prompting efforts to rectify the imbalance.[8] The preaching of conservatives in the eighteenth

---

[8] MASB (1789), 16; R. S. Tosh, 'An examination of the origin and development of Irish Presbyterian worship' (QUB Ph.D., 1983), 119–26; H. Sefton, 'Revolution to Disruption', in D. Forrester and D. Murray (eds.), *Studies in the history of worship in Scotland* (Edinburgh, 1984), 71–2.

century followed a well-established pattern. The classic Puritan division of the sermon into 'doctrine', 'reason', and 'uses' was intended to help the preacher accurately to expound a text of Scripture, defend the given doctrine, and apply the lessons to those listening by addressing both reason and the affections.[9] This basic structure was used uniformly by orthodox Presbyterians in the eighteenth century in both published and manuscript sermons. Often each heading was further subdivided in order to help those listening to follow the argument of the sermon, though some claimed this hindered genuine understanding of the Bible as a whole.[10] The principal subject matter of weekly sermons was biblical exposition and the explanation of specific doctrines, the latter often in the form of a lecture delivered in the morning and before the sermon in the afternoon. The importance of good sermon preparation was emphasized, though the common problem of stipend arrears meant that some ministers had to curtail preparation in order to provide for his family's material needs.[11] Sermons were usually delivered extemporary. Ministers typically wrote out and then learnt them off before delivery, allowing them during preaching to add new material or topical anecdotes as appropriate. A 'plain simple nervous style' was recommended as the delivery of God's truth included 'plainness, simplicity and perspicuity in declaring it'.[12] The goals of preaching were the conversion of sinners and the edification of believers. Conversion, or more properly in this context regeneration, was firmly embedded in a Reformed framework that emphasized the sovereignty of God in salvation through his predestination of the elect. The preaching of the word was the means of grace by which God called the elect to himself by the Holy Spirit. At their best, orthodox Presbyterian sermons could be biblically sound, doctrinally robust, and pastorally sensitive.

However, individual ministers throughout this period failed to live up to the expected standards of a preacher. As early as 1697 the Synod of Ulster had enjoined all ministers to 'use a sound Form of Words in

[9] Davies, *Puritan worship*, 191; Henderson, *Religious life*, 204.

[10] The Revd John Hutton, sermon notebook (PHS); 'Characteristic sketches—No. II. Rev. Samuel Alexander', *Covenanter*, 1 (1831), 313–14.

[11] H. Hamill, *Ministerial respectability considered* (Strabane, 1788), 21–4.

[12] S. Kelburn, *The duty of preaching the gospel* (Dublin, 1790), 30; F. Pringle, *The gospel ministry, an ordinance of Christ* ([Belfast], 1796), 18.

Preaching, abstaining from all romantick Expressions & hard Words, which the vulgar do not understand, as also from all Sordid Words & Phrases'.[13] The fact that similar advice was repeated in other forms throughout the following century indicates that some ministers did not reach the standards required.[14] Others took the path of least resistance and repeated their sermons. Alexander Carson, a former minister of Tobermore congregation who seceded from the Synod of Ulster in 1803 to become an Independent, claimed that his former colleagues repeated their sermons and used sermon outlines by, amongst others, Hugh Blair and 'the American preacher'.[15] Their lax attitude did not end with the repetition of sermons but also extended to their public prayers. 'One suit of prayers, or two suits of prayers, with perhaps a sacramental suit, when constantly worn for a length of time, will become thread-bare, and though penned by Enfield, must become disgusting.'[16] William McCrea of Donagheady, County Donegal, had a series of fifty-two sermons that he kept in a recess behind his pulpit and repeated year after year, eventually prompting complaints to the Kirk session. The elders decided to place the previous week's sermon on top of the pile in order to catch their minister out. McCrea, however, discovered the plan and reportedly commented, 'Gentlemen I think the old way was the better and we will just go back to it again.'[17]

The style and content of sermons became a source of dispute between Seceders and Synod of Ulster ministers. The propriety of reading sermons became part of the acrimonious exchange between Thomas Clark, Burgher minister of Cahans, and John Semple, minister of Anahilt Synod of Ulster congregation, in the mid-1750s, which comprised charge and counter-charge as to whether read sermons

---

[13] *RGSU* i. (1697), 25.

[14] For example, T. M. Reid, 'The charge', in S. Edgar, *The times, a sermon* (Belfast, 1814), 71–2; J. Rogers, *A sermon preached October 24, 1770, at Newbliss* (Monaghan, n.d.), 32.

[15] A. Carson, *Remarks on a late pastoral address, from the ministers of the Synod of Ulster* (Belfast, 1806), 11. The reference is to a compilation by David Austin entitled, *Select discourses from the American preacher ... By some of the most eminent evangelical ministers in the United States* (Edinburgh, 1798).

[16] Carson, *Remarks*, 10.

[17] J. Rutherford, *Donagheady Presbyterian churches and parish* (Belfast, 1953), 39.

could be used by God or not.[18] In terms of sermon content, the Seceders were shaped by the Marrow controversy that engulfed the Church of Scotland in the early eighteenth century. According to D. C. Lachman, at the heart of the dispute was the issue of the relationship between divine sovereignty and human responsibility in salvation.[19] The Marrowmen 'described the covenant of grace as a testament, containing God's promises of grace in Christ, who was to be freely offered to all. Assurance was founded in Christ and his work and a believer's motives to obedience were said to be love and gratitude.' In part, the large majority of the General Assembly who disagreed with them reflected the legalizing tendencies within Reformed theology that stressed the human element in obtaining both salvation and assurance. In Lachman's judgement, the Marrow-men were on balance more faithful to the Reformed tradition and the teaching of the *Confession*. The doctrines held by the Marrow Brethren formed the doctrinal basis of the Scottish and Irish Secession churches and were summarized in the 'Act of the Associate Presbytery concerning the doctrine of grace' passed in 1742.[20]

Those who opposed the Marrow Brethren believed that the covenant between God and humanity was one of 'mutual obligations'. The offer of the gospel was 'made to the prepared or "sensible" sinner and assurance focused on the good works of the believer'.[21] Contrary to this, both Seceders and Covenanters freely offered the gospel of Christ to everyone, irrespective of their spiritual attainments.[22] In the late eighteenth century, the Covenanter minister William James charged John Holmes of the Synod of Ulster with doctrinal error in not offering freely the gospel to sinners but to only those who had prepared themselves for salvation.[23] Opponents argued that the free

---

[18] T. Clark, *A brief survey of some principles maintained, by the General Synod of Ulster, and practices carried on, by several members thereof* (Armagh, 1751), 37–9; J. Semple, *The survey impartially examined by sacred scripture and sound reason* (Belfast, 1754), 61–5.

[19] D. C. Lachman, 'Marrow controversy', in N. M. de S. Cameron (org. ed.), *Dictionary of Scottish church history and theology* (Edinburgh, 1993), 547.

[20] J. McKerrow, *History of the Secession church*, rev. edn. (Edinburgh, 1847), 177–84.

[21] Lachman, 'Marrow controversy', in Cameron, *Dictionary*, 547.

[22] M. Hutchinson, *The Reformed Presbyterian Church in Scotland: its origin and history 1680–1876* (Paisley, 1893), 205.

[23] W. James, *Homesius Enervatus* (Londonderry, 1772), 75–7.

offer of the gospel repudiated the teaching of the *Confession* by expounding universal salvation and denying that Christ had died only for the elect. According to the Seceders, this did not follow, as God had ordained certain means through which he would call the elect to salvation. Consequently, Seceder sermons invariably ended with an exhortation to 'fly to Christ' or 'close' with him in faith. In January 1778 John Hutton, Antiburgher minister of Ballycopeland, exhorted a congregation, 'Come to Christ then sinner—believe upon and receive him as he is offered to you in the gospel and in this way ye shall be brought in among the blessed people that know etc.'[24] Because of their emphasis upon grace alone, Seceders were charged by their critics with antinomianism, the belief that it was not necessary for Christians to obey God's moral law.[25] This was an unwarranted conclusion as Seceders stressed the importance of personal holiness as an indispensable part of the process of sanctification and upheld strict church discipline.

Before meeting-houses were built, Seceders and Covenanters preached outdoors and continued to do so throughout the eighteenth century as they responded to calls for preaching from across Ulster. The attractiveness of Seceder sermons resulted from a combination of the style of delivery and its theological content. Simplicity of language was held up as a virtue by Seceders who often berated preachers of polished sermons for showing little regard for the souls of the poor. The aged John Rogers admonished his younger ministerial colleagues in 1807 not to rely solely upon 'an excellent pronunciation, emphasis, cadence and delivery' in their sermons.[26] Seceder preaching was fervent, earthy, and often theatrical. As a boy, the great Unitarian leader of the nineteenth century, Henry Montgomery, heard the preaching of Isaac Patton, the first Secession minister in Ireland. Writing in the 1840s, Montgomery recalled that Patton was 'much addicted to the use of quaint and striking, though

---

[24] The Revd John Hutton, sermon on Psalm 89: 15 and 1 Tim. 1: 9 preached at Newtonards 2nd Sabbath in January 1778. See also, W. Laing, *Justification by the faith of Christ, without the deeds of the law* (Newry, 1801), 43.

[25] A. Colville, *The persecuting, disloyal and absurd tenets of those who affect to call themselves Seceders laid open and refuted* (Belfast, 1749), 22–32.

[26] J. Rogers, *The substance of a speech delivered in a synod at Cookstown, July 8, 1808* (Dublin, 1809), 9–10.

often homely and vulgar phraseology. His manner in the pulpit was ardent and excited—sometimes almost wild: and, as he evidently preached extempore, he never hesitated in the middle of his sermon, to attack individuals, or even classes of individuals, who by any look or motion incurred his disapprobation.'[27] Another early Seceder minister was Thomas Clark whose impassioned preaching had a remarkable impact upon his congregation in County Monaghan. One of his hearers recalled, 'I chose to sit in a dark place of the meeting-house, that I might the better conceal the Lord's kindness to me, in hearing the gospel there, for it was so great that I could hardly contain myself.'[28] The style and content of Seceder preaching explains why a number of them were involved in the formation of the Evangelical Society of Ulster (ESU) in 1798. In the inaugural sermon, George Hamilton, minister of Armagh Antiburgher congregation, asked rhetorically, 'O! how incumbent is it upon Gospel ministers, that they be earnest, and importunate in warning stupid sinners, to fly from the wrath to come, and to accept of Christ and his great salvation?'[29]

As will be shown in the next section, the centrality of the doctrines of grace to the Seceders and Covenanters led them to censure Synod of Ulster ministers for preaching legalistic sermons. Though Seceders were evangelical in their preaching, care ought to be taken when assessing both their rhetoric and the charges they made against Synod of Ulster ministers. Their attachment to confessional Presbyterianism and ecclesiology led the earliest Seceders to reject the Cambuslang revival and the ministry of George Whitefield, and later the Irish Secession synods warned their ministers against associating with the ESU and the Independent-dominated Irish Evangelical Society.[30] In addition, Old Light ministers in the Synod of Ulster denounced Deists, Arians, Socinians, Papists, Pelagians, and

---

[27] H. Montgomery, 'Outlines of the history of Presbyterianism in Ireland', *Irish Unitarian Magazine, and Bible Christian*, 2 (1847), 230.

[28] J. S. Reid, *History of the Presbyterian Church in Ireland*, ed. W. D. Killen, 3 vols., 2nd edn. (Belfast, 1867), iii. 314.

[29] G. Hamilton, *The great necessity of itinerant preaching* (Armagh, 1798), 10.

[30] D. Stewart, *The Seceders in Ireland with annals of their congregations* (Belfast, 1950), 104–7, 124–5, 187–90.

Arminians, whether Methodist or otherwise.[31] In both eighteenth-
century New England and Scotland, 'preaching Christ' was the primary means by which evangelical Calvinists sought to counter the
growth of infidelity and theological moderatism with the aim of
promoting a revival of religion.[32] The Old Light ministers who
preached about Christ in their sermons before the Synod of Ulster
demonstrate the same desire to differentiate themselves from less
orthodox opinions. Samuel Delap of Letterkenny declared in 1737,
'It is in Christ God reconciles the world to himself. Election, adoption,
justification, and sanctification, are in Christ. All the promises are yea
and Amen in him.'[33] In a sermon delivered at a particular meeting of
the Synod in 1802, Samuel Dill insisted that the essential mark of a
gospel ministry was a 'crucified Jesus' and the exposure and denunci-
ation of 'the dangerous counterfeits by which pharisaical moralists
and philosophising Christians would impose upon the world'.[34] It is
remarkable how little reference is made to Christ in the sermons of
New Light ministers and it is justifiable to conclude that Christocentr-
ism was the distinguishing mark of Old Light and Seceder preaching.
For theologically conservative Presbyterians, Christ's importance was
soteriological, that is, his death was the divinely appointed means by
which fallen humanity was to be reconciled to God.

For Presbyterian evangelicals in the eighteenth century, the gospel
was formulated within the Reformed tradition that emphasized
God's sovereignty in salvation, the person and work of Christ, and
the decisive influence of the Holy Spirit. The Synod of Ulster's
Presbytery of Tyrone in 1783 drew up a series of questions to be

---

[31] For example, S. Delap, *Synodical sermon at Antrim, June 21st, 1737* (Belfast,
1737), 33–4; T. Croskery, 'The Rev. James Elder, of Finvoy', *Evangelical Witness*, 9
(1870), 62; A. McCreery, *The Presbyterian ministers of Killyleagh: a notice of their lives
and times* (Belfast, 1875), 189–91.

[32] J. R. McIntosh, *Church and theology in enlightenment Scotland: the Popular
Party, 1740–1800* (East Linton, 1998), 63–8; M. J. Crawford, *Seasons of grace: Colonial
New England's revival tradition in its British context* (New York, 1991), 52–80, 82–6.

[33] Delap, *Synodical sermon*, 23. Later examples include, W. Wilson, *The Christian's
consolation in the hope set before him* (Belfast, 1783) and John Thomson, 'To preach
Christ the distinguishing characteristic of a minister of the gospel', 1788 (T. Witherow, *Historical and literary memorials of Presbyterianism in Ireland*, 2 vols. (Belfast,
1879–80), ii. 263–5).

[34] S. Dill, *A sermon on the duty of ministers and their connexion with Christ*
(Londonderry, [1802]), 11–12.

asked at visitation presbyteries that included the following: 'Is the free grace, and love of God the father, the mediatorial appointment and offices of Christ the redeemer, and the gracious operations of the Holy Spirit in his enlightening, sanctifying and comforting influence distinctly explained?'[35] Sinclare Kelburn stated that ministers of the gospel were ministers 'of the word of reconciliation, and an ambassador for Christ'.[36] Kelburn and his fellow Old Light evangelicals called on their hearers to come in faith to Jesus 'for salvation, for pardon, for righteousness, and for sanctification; He is the very saviour you want; in him all fullness dwells; he is able to save even to the uttermost, all that come to the Father by him'.[37] He referred to some ministers, probably his New Light colleagues in the Synod of Ulster, as 'corrupters of the word' who had ignored the doctrines of election, grace, imputed righteousness, and Christ's atonement and divinity.[38] Kelburn maintained that this deliberate withholding of the gospel had an appalling effect upon the spiritual lives of the laity. 'The light is hid from their eyes, the bread of life is withheld from their souls, they are not nourished with the sincere milk of the word.'[39] In language commonly employed in the 1830s, he also asked, 'if the word preached by the apostles was efficacious, under the influences of the Holy Spirit, would not the same word, under the same influences be efficacious now?'[40] The theology of conservative Presbyterians and the fervent style of Seceder preaching would not be submerged by something called evangelicalism in the nineteenth century. Nineteenth-century evangelical preaching was a continuation and adaptation of Reformed principles to meet the exigencies of a new and changing society.

II

Generally speaking, the theological outlook of ministers was shaped both by the education they received at university and by the

[35] Tyrone Pby (GSU), 4 Feb. 1783 (PHS), 33.
[36] Kelburn, *The duty of preaching the gospel*, 9–10. Also, S. Hanna, *A sermon on the qualifications of the ministerial character* (Belfast, 1810), 40.
[37] *The divinity of our Lord Jesus Christ asserted and proved* (Belfast, 1792), 118.
[38] Ibid., 23.
[39] Ibid., 25.
[40] Ibid., 26.

theological outlook of the presbytery to which they were accountable as students and licentiates. Their style of preaching was influenced by instruction at college in homiletics and rhetoric, after graduation through presbytery trials and preaching for vacancies, and, after they were ordained, at visitation presbyteries. From 1690, the Presbyterian authorities in Scotland and Ireland made every effort to ensure they had a graduate ministry with a liberal arts education and sufficient theological training.[41] In 1770 a series of five regulations concerning the licensing and training of ministers was passed by the Synod of Ulster to make sure that candidates remained in university for at least four years. The regulations stipulated that candidates were expected to attend natural and moral philosophy classes and were to be examined at presbytery trials in those subjects as well science, Hebrew, Greek, Latin, logic, metaphysics, theology, and church history. These examinations were spread over three meetings of presbytery, though if the candidate had attended university for four years only one meeting was necessary. During the eighteenth century, the majority of Presbyterian ministers of whatever body received their liberal arts education at Glasgow University.[42] Glasgow was at the forefront of the Scottish Enlightenment and moral philosophy, as taught by Francis Hutcheson, Adam Smith, and Thomas Reid, became the most popular subject taken by Old and New Light students. In addition to a liberal arts degree, the Synod of Ulster decided in 1702 that to enter upon the ministry candidates must have studied divinity for four years after graduation, though this stipulation was relaxed over the following century. From the divinity professors at Glasgow they received a mixture of orthodoxy and Enlightenment, the precise content depending upon the predilections of their lecturer. It has been demonstrated, for example, that John Simson's tenure of the divinity chair (1708–29) provided a

---

[41] The outline given here of ministerial education before 1800 is indebted to R. Allen, *The Presbyterian College Belfast 1853–1953* (Belfast, 1954), 1–36.

[42] I. M. Bishop, 'The education of Ulster students at Glasgow University in the eighteenth century' (QUB MA, 1987); W. I. P. Hazlett, 'Students at Glasgow University from 1747 to 1768 connected with Ireland: an analytical probe', in W. D. Patton (ed.), *Ebb and flow: essays in church history in honour of R. Finlay G. Holmes* (Belfast, 2002), 20–49; A. Loughridge, *The Covenanters in Ireland* (Belfast, 1984), 30; Stewart, *Seceders*, 129.

catalyst for the early spread of New Light opinions in Ulster.[43] This tendency was further developed by a successor of Simson's, William Leechman, Professor of Divinity from 1744 to 1785, who used as the basis of his lectures works by the Swiss theologians Benedict Pictet and Jean Frédéric Ostervald. Both authors reflected Leechman's own liberal attitude to traditional Reformed theology and his gradual move towards Arminianism.[44] The influence of such an education upon potential ministers must have been significant for at least the language they employed, if not for how they formulated the doctrines they preached.

Nevertheless, the undergraduate course at Glasgow comprised three short sessions between May and November and Irish students were often there for even less time as they were known to arrive late and depart early owing to their lack of finances and well-known lackadaisical attitude towards the regulations of the university. Consequently, a more decisive factor in determining the theological outlook of Synod of Ulster ministers was the influence of the presbytery that admitted them to ministerial training in the first place and subsequently supervised their education.[45] Before being licensed to preach, the intending minister was placed on 'first trials' comprising a sermon, lecture, 'exercise and addition' (a critical examination of a text of Scripture and a discussion of its doctrinal implications), 'common head' (a paper on an important theological issue), and a popular sermon. He was also subjected to 'second trials' before ordination, which, again, included an exercise and addition, a common head, a popular sermon, and a lecture. At the end of each college session, the presbytery would examine students in what they had studied in the previous term. During the summer they were prescribed a course of study in civil and church history, Jewish antiquities, biblical criticism, and divinity, and had specimens of 'composition, elocution, and devotional exercises' examined.[46] By 1817, 'candidates for the ministry had a

---

[43] Bishop, 'The education of Ulster students', ch. 4.

[44] J. C. Whytock, 'The history and development of Scottish theological education and training, Kirk and Secession (c. 1560–c. 1850)' (University of Wales Ph.D., 2001), 155–8.

[45] The role of the presbytery is outlined in, J. M. Barkley, *The Westminster formularies in Irish Presbyterianism* (Belfast, 1956), 79–80.

[46] *RGSU* iii. (1807), 321.

minimum academic course of five years, preceded by a presbytery examination on such subjects as Greek, Latin, English and Geography, and including presbytery examinations each summer on the college work of the previous session'.[47] Consequently, the theological tendencies within the presbytery could have a profound influence upon the theology of a young minister eager to please his senior colleagues. In 1825 Cooke identified trials before a non-subscribing or predominantly Arian presbytery as a key factor in predisposing ministers towards Arianism.[48]

Seceder presbyteries followed a similar system, though ever since the breach with the Church of Scotland in 1737, ministerial students obtained their theological education at either the Burgher or the Antiburgher divinity halls.[49] Irish Antiburgher students continued to receive their education at these until 1816, but in 1796 the Burgher synod appointed John Rogers as their own professor of divinity to provide a theological education for their students in Ireland. A home education for all Presbyterian ministerial students in both arts and theology was eventually realized with the formation of the Belfast Academical Institution in 1815, though the issue of the theological complexion of 'Inst' would provide the impetus for Cooke's campaign against Arianism in the late 1820s. In 1815 Samuel Edgar was installed as the Seceders' professor of divinity and two years later the Synod of Ulster appointed Samuel Hanna to a similar chair. As noted in the Introduction, both professors were evangelical Calvinists who helped to shape the outlook of a whole generation of ministers and thus determine the ethos of the church for the rest of the century.

If Old Light ministers and Seceders adhered to confessional orthodoxy, New Light Presbyterians were the embodiment of Enlightenment sensibilities. Historians of the Church of Scotland in the eighteenth century have concluded that, despite receiving the same liberal arts education, Moderates may be distinguished from their Popular Party opponents by their commitment to those studies, a nominal interest in theological matters, and an unwillingness to fan

---

[47] Allen, *The Presbyterian College Belfast*, 10.
[48] *First report of the commission of Irish education inquiry*, HC (1825), xii. 824.
[49] For a list of all Seceder divinity students see, Stewart, *Seceders*, 436–41.

the flames of religious controversy.[50] New Light ministers shared these concerns as well as the pulpit style of Moderate preachers. Moderate homiletics was a mixture of Classical traditions of rhetoric and Enlightenment attitudes to nature and the mind.[51] The sermons of Hugh Blair, the greatest Moderate preacher of the age and whose works were very popular amongst ministers in Ulster, were finely crafted moral treatises addressed to reason in a simple, jargon-free style.[52] In general, Moderate sermons tended 'to be brief in length, clear and simple in diction, unexceptionable in doctrine, and practical rather than abstract in subject matter'.[53] Likewise, New Light ministers avoided doctrinal preaching and instead emphasized a good rhetorical style, practical morality, and the importance of natural religion. In a sermon preached before the Synod of Ulster in 1745, James Carlisle argued that ministers were 'to preach and explain the principles of natural religion, as the basis and foundation of all religion revealed; to enforce the duties of morality, to teach men to govern their appetites and passions by their reason, to bind the rules of virtue on the consciences of men by arguments drawn from reason and the light of nature'.[54] For Carlisle, 'a holy and virtuous life' was of more importance than subscription to man-made creeds.[55] In similar terms, James Bryson, in an ordination sermon delivered in 1772, declared that the prime role of the minister was 'to extend the knowledge, to promote the virtue, and to increase the happiness of the human race'.[56] The same attention to correct

[50] N. Landsman, 'Presbyterians and provincial society: the evangelical enlightenment in the west of Scotland, 1740–1775', in J. Dwyer and R. B. Sher (eds.), *Sociability and society in eighteenth-century Scotland* (Edinburgh, 1991), 194–209; C. Kidd, 'Scotland's invisible Enlightenment: subscription and heterodoxy in the eighteenth-century Kirk', *Records of the Scottish Church History Society*, 30 (2000), 28–59.

[51] T. C. Addington, 'Homiletics', in Cameron, *Dictionary of Scottish church history and theology*, 411–12; T. D. Kennedy, 'William Leechman, pulpit eloquence and the Glasgow Enlightenment', in A. Hook and R. B. Sher (eds.), *The Glasgow Enlightenment* (East Linton, 1995), ch. 3.

[52] For details of Blair's preaching style see, R. B. Sher, *Church and university in the Scottish Enlightenment: the Moderate Literati of Edinburgh* (Edinburgh, 1985), 168–72, 182–6.

[53] Ibid., 171.

[54] J. Carlisle, *The nature of religious zeal* (Belfast, 1745), 26.

[55] Ibid., 31–2.

[56] J. Bryson, *The obtaining of the divine approbation, by dividing the word of truth aright, the supreme object of a Christian minister's pursuit*, 2nd edn. (Belfast, 1773), 13.

pronunciation evident in the homiletics of the Moderates led the committee of overtures of the General Synod to ask presbyteries in 1765 to examine licentiates as to 'whither they read English with propriety, as some, by pronouncing words improperly & ungrammatically, have in their prayers and sermons given offence to men of taste & occasion to speak contemptibly of them'.[57] Similarly, in 1791, the Presbytery of Antrim recommended that their students read Thomas Sheridan, *Lectures on the art of reading* (1775) and *A complete dictionary of the English language* (1789), and Hugh Blair, *Lectures in rhetoric and belles lettres* (1783).[58] Many New Light ministers seem to have lived up to these ideals. According to his panegyrist, Thomas Crawford as a preacher was able to control his imagination and 'exquisite sensibility' by 'good judgement, and elegant taste'. His sermons 'abounded with sentiments of devotion, which were evidently the genuine offspring of his own heart; and all his ministerial performances were remarkably expressive of reverence for the divinity'.[59]

Seceders singled out Carlisle's sermon as a prime example of the New Light rejection of Presbyterian church order and Reformed doctrine. In response, Thomas Clark compiled a list of the distinctive features by which the Presbyterian laity could identify a New Light sermon, which included a focus upon moral philosophy and second-table commandments, the denial of original sin, and the claim that salvation was conditional upon faith, repentance, and obedience, rather than God's grace alone.[60] Orthodox criticisms of New Light sermons were often savage. One anonymous author stated that if anyone entered a New Light meeting-house 'they are all the day entertained with cold lifeless harangues of refined heathenism, or noisy parades of error and delusion, instead of the pure and salutary doctrines of the gospel of Christ!'[61] It was further alleged in 1770 by Benjamin McDowell, then minister at Ballykelly, County Londonderry, that there was 'a greater affinity than the generality are

---

[57] *RGSU* ii. (1765), 489.

[58] Pby of Antrim, 13 Oct. 1791 (PRONI, T/1053/1), 28.

[59] W. Bryson, *The practice of righteousness productive of happiness* (Belfast, 1782), 20, 22.

[60] Clark, *Brief survey*, 103–4.

[61] Pistophilos Philecclesia, *Letters of importance* (Belfast, 1775), 47. Witherow believes that the author may have been Benjamin McDowell (*Memorials*, ii. 149).

aware' between New Light Presbyterianism and popery as 'the former contains the essence of the latter, the merit of works; and naturally leads to it'.[62] Henry Cooke argued that Arian sermons contained none of the distinctive doctrines of the gospel and 'their discussions consist more of essays on ethics'. Cooke attributed this to the sermon models of Blair, which he described as 'miserable dilutions of the doctrines of the Gospel'.[63] Though these critics may have exaggerated their claims, there can be no doubt that New Light sermons were stamped with the values and priorities of their time. These included the exalted place of reason over revelation, the benevolence of God the Father overshadowing the person and work of Christ, the duty of submission to the divine will replacing the need for faith and repentance, and a life of virtue instead of a holiness that came from faith. New Light sermons were often dry, didactic, and unenthusiastic. In 1771 Andrew Alexander warned his Urney congregation (County Tyrone) about the pernicious effects of enthusiasm. According to Thomas Witherow, the sermon reflected Alexander's own lack of evangelical warmth, as it was 'a dry, cold essay, not devoid of literary merit, but deficient in gospel truth'.[64]

The impatience of most New Light ministers with the Reformed tradition resulted in their deliberate repudiation of Calvinism. This drift to Arminianism is not surprising as scholars have identified its presence amongst the non-subscribers of the 1720s.[65] The testimony of nineteenth-century evangelicals such as Alexander Carson and Henry Cooke confirms that cold orthodoxy and Arminianism had crept into the discourses delivered by Old Light ministers.[66] The drift to legalism and formalism that the Marrow Brethren attempted to repel became an important aspect of mainstream Presbyterianism in the eighteenth century and arguably encouraged New Light hegemony within the Synod of Ulster. Examples of the rejection of

---

[62] B. McDowell, *The requiring subscription to well-composed summaries, of the Christian doctrines, as tests of orthodoxy, defended* (Glasgow, 1770), 35.

[63] *First report of the commission of Irish education inquiry*, 824, 827.

[64] Witherow, *Memorials*, ii. 161–2.

[65] A. W. G. Brown, 'A theological interpretation of the first subscription controversy (1719–1728)', in Haire *et al.*, *Challenge and conflict*, 37–8.

[66] Carson, *Remarks*, 16–17 n.; *First report of the commission of Irish education inquiry*, 823.

confessional orthodoxy became more blatant in the period after
1770. In a public resolution printed in 1782, the Presbytery of
Killyleagh referred to the doctrine of original sin as 'blasphemous',
an opinion for which they were subsequently admonished by the
Synod.[67] New Light ministers explicitly taught works righteousness
and in their writings questioned or openly repudiated the Calvinist
doctrines of original sin, vicarious atonement, predestination, and
reprobation.[68] In some cases the exaltation of reason over revelation
within New Light circles led to heterodoxy. In 1772 McDowell
suggested that John Cameron of Dunluce was an Arian, which, on
the evidence of his published work, seems plausible.[69] Arian sentiments became more pronounced in the early nineteenth century and
culminated in the publication of William Bruce's *The study of the
Bible and the doctrines of Christianity* (1824) in which he claimed that
Arian opinions were making 'extensive though silent progress in the
general synod of Ulster'.[70]

III

The Westminster divines insisted that the laity prepare to hear the
word of God preached through personal and family devotions. The
laity also filtered the preached word through their own experiences
and those of the community to which they belonged. Consequently,
it is not just a matter of outlining what the laity heard, but how they
heard it.[71] Indeed, if an adequate understanding of lay religion is to

---

[67] *RGSU* iii. (1782), 45.

[68] J. Cuming, *The apostle Paul's reasoning before Felix* (n.p., 1800); W. Taggart,
Sermons (Strabane, 1788), 209–29; W. Bryson, *The duty of searching the scriptures
recommended and explained* (Belfast, 1786), 18–20; A. Colvill, *Some important queries
humbly and earnestly recommended to the serious consideration of the Protestant
dissenters in the north of Ireland, belonging to the Synodical Association* (Belfast,
1773); A Layman, *Mr McDowel's vindication of the Westminster Confession, examined*
(Dublin, 1774).

[69] B. McDowell, *Observations on Theophilus and Philander* (n.p., 1772), 22; Witherow, *Memorials*, ii. ch. 70.

[70] R. F. G. Holmes, *Henry Cooke* (Belfast, 1981), 33.

[71] N. Landsman, 'Evangelists and their hearers: popular interpretation of revivalist
preaching in eighteenth-century Scotland', *Journal of British Studies*, 28 (1989), 121.

be gained, then it is necessary to examine how the laity responded to preaching, the uses to which they put sermon material, and how sophisticated and disciplined their hearing was. Though lay hearing was shaped by a broader cultural and social context, it is important to appreciate from the outset that many Presbyterians went to meeting on Sunday with a desire to learn from God's word. For instance, Elizabeth Caldwell, writing to her brother Richard in 1772, referred to a sermon preached by her minister, Alexander Marshall of Bally-money, on the duty of submission to the will of God. 'I felt much interested and brought home many of his observations to my own and poor Sibella's lot, and in the words of the Holy Writ considered "it was good for me to be here".[72] Hugh Tynan of Donaghadee, in a poem entitled 'A Sabbath's evening's reflections', underlined the importance of disciplined hearing to many of the Presbyterian laity.

> There, with the ear of faith, the Christian hears
> Salvation's cheering, soul enchanting voice,
> Then Jesus dissipates his doubts and fears,
> And makes his soul with gladness to rejoice.[73]

Like their Scottish forebearers, others recorded sermons in a more permanent way by taking notes. Matthew Bell, for example, noted in his diary the text of the sermon and the application, sometimes with personal remarks about its relevance to his own life.[74]

Many Presbyterians, irrespective of theological opinion, enjoyed discussing the style and content of sermons. In a cantankerous letter written to the Revd John Thomson in 1767, James Macauly observed that the poor never thought of attempting to improve their minds, though on Sundays they did 'lay in a store to dispute upon the following week, whether their preacher taught orthodoxy, or heresy, or whether he prayed well, or was at a loss'.[75] The context of these discussions is well illustrated in the following lines of Francis Boyle, the Seceder weaver poet.

---

[72] J. Caldwell, 'Particulars of history of a north county Irish family' (PRONI, Caldwell papers, T/3541/5/3), 17½ [sic].

[73] H. Tynan, *Poems* (Belfast, 1803), 82.

[74] Diary of Matthew Bell, 1830–70 (PRONI, D/1877/1).

[75] James Macauly to the Revd John Thomson, 29 Nov. 1767 (PHS, Thomson papers).

> Twa or three neebors met thegither,
> To talk a while wi' ane anither:
> The subject o' their conversation,
> Wha preach'd at Grenshaw ordination!
> A man spak' out 'I dinna ken him'.
> Anither said, 'His name is Den__m;
> He in a lasty strain does speak,
> Sometimes in Latin—sometimes, Greek,
> And aye a sentence now and then,
> That we poor sinners dinna ken'.
> Ane says, 'That shews the able scholar'.
> 'Forsooth I wadna gie a dollar
> To hear sic preachin' seven years,
> It pleases men o' itchin' ears;
> I like the truth in laigher strains,
> Sic as the sacred page contains'.[76]

The above poem suggests that the Presbyterian laity favoured simple, biblical sermons. Extempore sermons were especially popular. One old lady boasted that her minister 'just stands up, opens his mouth, and it rins oot o' him like water'.[77] There are two reasons for this preference. First, it was the common view, considerably reinforced by the Seceders, that ministers who read sermons were unorthodox.[78] Second, some lay Presbyterians thought that ministers who read sermons were patronizing them. The use of Greek quotations also suggested a similar attitude on the preacher's part and an unwillingness of the laity to be spoken down to. Samuel Thompson's 'Epigram—To a Reading Preacher' reflects such an opinion.

> With formal pomposity, how you can read,
>   But meddlers scoffingly mock it;
> For sermons, they say, there's no room in your head,
>   So you bear them about you in your pocket.
>
> From your pocket, but the hearer must pay,
>   For the pocket-bred, pitiful jargon;

---

[76] F. Boyle, *County Down poems* (n.p., [*c.*1812]), 10–11.

[77] T. Croskery and T. Witherow, *Life of the Rev. A. P. Goudy, D.D.* (Dublin, 1887), 9.

[78] J. Gamble, *A view of society and manners, in the north of Ireland* (London, 1813), 246–7.

And, grumbling, at close of the year, he will say,
Devil take such a profitless bargain.[79]

On the other hand, liberal Presbyterians resented the lack of learning and refinement displayed by some conservative ministers. Daniel McKissick wrote to his friend John Smith in 1811 about a minister he had recently heard; 'You talk of your preacher being a rigid Calvinist; if it is young Elder you mean *a boy* of his age cannot be supposed capable of forming an opinion on so contested a subject—would I give a fraction for his opinion—I am told he talks well, though his appearance is *vain* and *conceited.*'[80] Other liberal Presbyterians were less condescending in their comments. In his 'Elegy, on the Death of Hugh Blair, D.D.', James Orr praised the famous Scottish preacher for his simple yet godly sermons.

He no strange system built, nor once put forth
A dark enigma to a doating head;
The gloomiest sophist on the captious hearth
Learn'd gentleness and grace from all he said.[81]

If the laity wished to express displeasure, they could do so in a number of ways, including conversing with each other or looking around them during the sermon. A more pronounced demonstration of disapproval was to sleep and snore, though this was often difficult according to one anonymous writer to the *Belfast Monthly Magazine*, as meeting-houses lacked the proper facilities; 'No doubt to sleep with night-caps, blankets, pillows, and such apparatus, would render people still more comfortable, and less liable to take cold.'[82] The writer continued by expressing admiration for 'the politeness and refinement of our college-bred preachers' who aided sleep by a monotonous delivery. At the same time, he castigated the wild, enthusiastic Methodist itinerants, asking whether it was 'either polite or becoming to tell a man to his face, that he will go to hell if he ever shuts his eyes'.[83] It was also believed that Presbyterians were prone to

---

[79] S. Thompson, *New poems on a variety of different subjects* (Belfast, 1799), 210.
[80] Daniel McKissick to John Smith, 13 June 1811 (PRONI, D/2009/4/72).
[81] J. Orr, *Poems, on various subjects* (Belfast, 1804), 93.
[82] 'The investigator. No. II. On sleeping in churches', *Belfast Monthly Magazine*, 13 (1814), 6.
[83] Ibid., 7.

making a more public demonstration of displeasure by denouncing the preacher during his sermon. John Gamble remarked that a 'simple countryman has been known to stand up in the meeting house, and address the preacher, on what he called false doctrine'.[84]

In extreme cases, the laity could report the failings of their minister to the local presbytery. Amongst the six charges that were made against George McEwen of Killinchy before the Presbytery of Belfast in 1791 was that he read out his sermons. In the interests of peace, the presbytery consequently recommended to McEwen 'not to read out his discourses, unless occasioned by trouble or absolute necessity'.[85] Other ministers were reported for repeating old sermons or not exhibiting sufficient variety in their preaching. Mr Wylie, a member of Joseph Lyttle's Letterkenny congregation, stated to a visitation presbytery in 1838 that he was not satisfied with the small number of sermons his minister preached. In fairness, he thought the sermons were good, but he believed that he could now transcribe them all because he had heard them so often. The other commissioners agreed with Wylie and expressed their desire that 'their minister would preach new sermons to them'.[86] Three years previously, Matthew Bell had heard Lyttle preach and had not been impressed. His diary records, 'The application was brief and had very little relation to the subject, the sermon was confused and had very little relation to the text, and all was delivered in so confused, irregular and hasty a manner as to be scarcely intelligible.'[87]

A good example of the depth of feeling that could be generated over unacceptable preaching may be found in a case brought before the Secession Presbytery of Tyrone. On 1 July 1834 a visitation was arranged by the presbytery who had received a request from the elders of Moneymore congregation to remove their minister, the Revd George Thompson. At a visitation held on 4 August, a number of charges were brought against Thompson, including that there was

[84] J. Gamble, *Sketches of history, politics and manners, in Dublin and the north of Ireland, in 1810* (London, 1826), 347.

[85] Belfast Pby (GSU), 25 May 1791 (UTC).

[86] Letterkenny Pby (GSU), 8 Aug. 1835 (Church House, strong room), 261–2. For similar complaints see, Ballymena Pby (GSU), 8 Aug. 1815, 11 Aug. 1818 (PHS), 134, 194–5; Derry Pby (GSU), 1 Nov. 1825 (UTC).

[87] Diary of Matthew Bell, 31 Aug. 1835.

a 'general dissatisfaction among the members of the congregation with regard to the matter and manner' of his preaching. The elders reported that in recent times he had confined himself to the explanation of a few psalms and complained 'that his preaching was ambiguous, formal, and such as to lead them to suspect his soundness in the faith'.[88] Four days later, a special presbytery committee visited the congregation when it was further alleged that Thompson repeated his sermons and on that account some members of the congregation had refused to pay stipend. The session told the committee that they had informed their minister about the concerns of the congregation to which he had promptly responded by rebuking them from the pulpit. Thompson suggested that the ill feeling towards him had originated in the failure of the congregation to liquidate a building debt, but pointed out that thirty-one new seatholders had joined the congregation since he arrived in 1832. The commissioners from the congregation responded by claiming 'that several persons have felt so hurt by the sermons he has preached and the psalms he has sung for some time past as to threaten to leave the place'. In general, the congregation was divided. Some claimed Thompson was well liked, others said that many were secretly disaffected, while one individual claimed Thompson was Arminian.[89] By November, the presbytery had received a petition in favour of Thompson signed by seventy-one members and a contrary petition signed by sixteen. Despite the presbytery's prompting, Thompson refused to resign, so he was suspended and the congregation placed under the care of a committee.[90] Thompson was fully restored in 1836, though trouble was to flare up again in the 1840s. From this case, it is clear that the laity were concerned with not only the content, but also the style and variety of sermons, and that an unacceptable style of preaching could be the point around which other grievances with a minister might crystallize.

The ability of the laity to recognize unorthodox opinions and to respond to them has important implications for our assessment of lay belief. Presbyterianism upheld the fundamental right of the laity

[88] Tyrone Pby (Sec.), 4 Aug. 1834 (Church House, strong room). Further details may be found in Stewart, *Seceders*, 373–5.
[89] Tyrone Pby (Sec.), 8 Aug. 1834.
[90] Ibid., 11 Nov. 1834; Stewart, *Seceders*, 374.

to question what their minister preached and evangelicals repeated this high view of the theological sensitivities of the laity.[91] Nineteenth-century writers claimed that lay attachment to the doctrines of the *Shorter Catechism* had saved Presbyterianism from ruin and accounted for the popularity of the Seceders.[92] At first glance, there is much evidence to support the claim that doctrine was the prime reason for many joining the Seceders, though any consideration of congregational schism must take into consideration broader social and economic factors.[93] The well-known anecdotes, usually related by nineteenth-century evangelical historians, about adverse lay reactions to the preaching of New Light ministers such as Francis Hutcheson and W. D. H. McEwen must also be seen as containing a large element of truth.[94]

A problem remains with these evangelical historians projecting their own partisan views back upon what they saw as the 'lifeless' eighteenth century. How did New Light ministers survive in congregations composed of doctrinally literate and orthodox lay people? Why were these ministers not reported to presbyteries? One answer may lie in the tranquil mood of the Synod of Ulster in the late eighteenth century, especially regarding subscription.[95] In that context, it would have been much harder for the laity to prosecute cases through the church courts, particularly as presbytery visitations in the Synod of Ulster were infrequent. Moreover, both Seceders and Covenanters provided an explicitly orthodox ministry for those who wanted it, yet the majority of lay Presbyterians remained within the Synod of Ulster. Some lay Presbyterians also shared the anti-Calvinist views of New Light ministers, and though these tended to be confined to large, wealthy congregations around Belfast, they included linen weavers.[96] If New Light ministers wanted to preach their views, there

[91] *Code* (1825), 8.

[92] W. T. Latimer, *A history of the Irish Presbyterians*, 2nd edn. (Belfast, 1902), 445; Stewart, *Seceders*, 64; Witherow, *Memorials*, ii. 346–7.

[93] C. G. Brown, *Religion and society in Scotland since 1707* (Edinburgh, 1997), 76–83.

[94] Reid, *History*, iii. 294 n.; McCreery, *Killyleagh*, 224.

[95] I. R. McBride, *Scripture politics: Ulster Presbyterians and Irish radicalism in the late eighteenth century* (Oxford, 1998), 57–9; Barkley, *Westminster formularies*, 13–14.

[96] L. Lunney, 'Attitudes to life and death in the poetry of James Orr, an eighteenth century Ulster weaver', *Ulster Folklife*, 31 (1985), 1–12.

were enough enlightened individuals in congregations to appreciate
their message. For example, although it was clear to the congregation
of Greyabbey and his orthodox opponents that S. M. Stephenson held
unorthodox views and refused to subscribe to the *Confession*, the
congregation still wanted him as their minister in 1774.[97]

Other issues must be addressed in this context. One of the most
important is the nature of the religious vocabulary employed by
ministers. Benjamin McDowell, in a pamphlet defending subscription published in 1770, suggested that 'if everyone is left at liberty to
profess his faith, merely in the words of scripture, it will be absolutely
impossible for bishops, ministers and presbyteries to know the real
sentiments of the persons whom they either admit to communion, or
license to serve in God's vineyard'.[98] If educated churchmen could
not determine the beliefs of ministers, what hope was there for the
unlettered laity? It was hard for them to tell the exact theological
views of their ministers as they all used the same biblical language
and concepts. This was especially true of references to God's providence and the need to treat neighbours with courtesy and respect.
Legalistic preaching may have been incompatible with the doctrines
of grace but it did address issues of common interest such as personal
holiness, and reinforced the code of good neighbourliness that was
an important part of rural Presbyterian communities. The argument
about indefinite terminology could also cut both ways. An anonymous writer charged McDowell with using the phrase '*the truth as it is
in Jesus*', as 'a mere cant phrase, an orthodox finesse of speech, to act
with the deception of jugglery on the vulgar ear, and keep up a
beggarly provincial popularity'.[99] It is obvious that in some cases
the use of orthodox language and ideas was necessary for some Old
and New Light ministers to retain the sympathy of their congregations. William Porter, the Arian minister of Limavady and clerk of
the Synod of Ulster until 1829, had, according to his son, a number
of 'travelling' sermons which he preached when visiting other congregations and which were 'in no respect doctrinal, except, indeed,
in the omission of Calvinistic doctrine'.[100] According to a poem

[97] Bangor Pby (GSU), 31 May and 21 June 1774 (PHS).
[98] McDowell, *Requiring subscription*, 11.
[99] Layman, *McDowel's vindication*, 24.
[100] C. Porter, 'Congregational memoirs: Cairncastle', *Christian Unitarian*, 4
(1865), 335.

ascribed to the Revd William Heron of Ballyclare this was a common occurrence.

> Many there are with travelling phrases flush,
> Fit for all sides, a soft and saintly plush,
> That changes with the *light* in which 'tis seen,
> And like cameleon in the grass is green.[101]

Why would ministers sometimes hide their true opinions? In some cases, it was owing to a desire not to denounce the cherished principles of the majority of a congregation, in others the reasons were more patronizing. William Porter thought it unnecessary 'to perplex and puzzle the minds of a country congregation with abstruse and difficult disquisitions; I generally allow the question respecting the Trinity to remain in a state of abeyance', though the 'respectable part of my hearers' knew he was an Arian.[102] In other cases, the simple reason for veiling their true opinions was to secure their stipends. John Gamble noted in 1813 that the Presbyterian system of choosing ministers ensured a large element of crowd-pleasing. Gamble suggested that in 'manners, modes of living, and doctrine, he [the minister] must often follow, fully as much as he can lead'. This sometimes meant preaching what the minister knew his congregation wanted to hear.[103] In 1791 James Hull of Bangor Presbytery charged James Simpson of Belfast Presbytery for asserting 'that I blindfolded and deceived my hearers by preaching doctrines contrary to my conscience to please them. And that I denied that the son was equal with the father and that I denied the atonement.'[104] It was found that Hull did not deny the divinity of Christ but, according to one witness, he did have an unorthodox view of the atonement 'that he did not wish ... should be made known among his hearers'. The Presbytery of Belfast was unable to act as Hull did not belong to their body, though they did admonish Simpson for acting rashly.

---

[101] [W. Heron], *The Ulster Synod, a poem* (Dublin, 1817), 17.

[102] *Fourth report of the commissioners of Irish education inquiry*, HC (1826–7), xiii.157, 136. See also the views of William Bruce cited in P. Brooke, 'Controversies in Ulster Presbyterianism, 1790–1836' (University of Cambridge Ph.D., 1980), 176.

[103] Gamble, *View of society*, 237; *Fourth report of the commissioners of Irish education inquiry*, 138.

[104] Belfast Pby (GSU), 1 Nov. 1791 (UTC).

If many lay Presbyterians did not have the knowledge or sophistication to determine the precise import of certain phrases and
opinions, there were enough ardent souls who had an inkling that
something was not right. Sometimes this hunch may have been
informed by a simplistic understanding of Reformed doctrine. For
example, there are a number of references in the minutes of Secession
presbyteries about congregations claiming that their ministers did
'not statedly preach catechetic doctrine'.[105] What precisely this meant
is unclear. The fact that presbyteries did not follow up such charges
may indicate an over-scrupulosity or lack of sophistication on behalf
of those complaining. On other occasions, congregations were correct in their assessment of their ministers' unorthodox views. In 1765
the congregation of Ballykelly rightly believed that their minister,
John Nelson, held liberal theological views and, despite his complete
exoneration by the Synod the previous year, forced him to leave.[106]
Once more, the poetry of Francis Boyle gives us an insight into the
mind of the laity. The following poem reveals his opinion that at least
one local New Light minister had hidden his true beliefs.

> The Bible ye can scoff an' scorn,
> 　Whane'er ye get half cockit;
> But ye repent next Sunday morn,
> 　An' slip it in your pocket.
> Unto the Kirk awa' you hie,
> 　A numerous congregation
> Attendin' there, attentively,
> 　To hear your learn'd oration.
> Whan to the sermon you begin,
> 　Ye maun gie them a stretcher,
> Sae monie folk are gather't in'
> 　To hear the auld-light preacher.
> You're but an auld-light in pretence,
> 　The new-light fits you better,
> This is weel ken't by men o' sense,
> 　Wha understand the matter ...[107]

[105] For example, Down Pby (B/Sec.), 10 Dec. 1788 (PHS); S. L. Orr and A. Haslett,
Historical sketches of Ballyalbany Presbyterian church (Belfast, n.d.), 56.
[106] Reid, *History*, iii. 327–9; Witherow, *Memorials*, ii. 325–6.
[107] Boyle, *Poems*, 137.

It seems that the majority of the laity wanted new sermons delivered in a homely, often fervent, style that explained both the Bible and Reformed doctrine. The predilection of the laity towards orthodox belief is confirmed by the growth of the Seceders and the implication that New Light ministers felt the need to hide their beliefs. Yet many were also content with the preaching on moral themes denounced by nineteenth-century evangelicals. This attitude may be linked simply to apathy or to the importance of the local meeting-house to community life and the role moral preaching played in reinforcing good neighbourliness. It may be that it was only with the polarization of views in the late 1820s that Presbyterians saw the true extent of their ministers' views.[108] Furthermore, the faithfulness of the non-subscribing laity in the 1830s should not be gainsaid. Many more could have easily identified with the overwhelming orthodox majority rather than have the courage of their own convictions.

IV

Liberal critics and evangelical biographers gave a prominence to preaching that underlines its importance to the religious and cultural definition of nineteenth-century evangelicalism.[109] During the late eighteenth and early nineteenth centuries, the opportunities for hearing sermons were significantly increased as weekday-evening lectures, Sunday evening services, and various mission events became part and parcel of Presbyterian, and more generally Protestant, religiosity. William McClure, minister of First Derry, informed his presbytery in 1836 that, 'There are three stated services every Sabbath for the congregation, and one in the jail, and I preach, in turn, to seamen and emigrants, and, sometimes, also in the country.'[110] Presbyterian preaching in the nineteenth century became more

---

[108] See the comments of the Revd Samuel Edgar in *Fourth report of the commissioners of Irish education inquiry*, 108.

[109] For an overview of evangelical preaching in nineteenth-century Ulster see, J. N. I. Dickson, 'More than discourse: the sermons of evangelical Protestants in nineteenth-century Ulster' (QUB Ph.D., 2000).

[110] Derry Pby (GSU), 3 May 1836, 51–2.

uniformly evangelical by giving greater prominence to the person and work of Christ and the exhortation of individuals to seek a personal reconciliation with God through Christ. Although Presbyterian ministers would be influenced by developments in America, it is important to emphasize the continuity of nineteenth-century preaching with the earlier traditions outlined in section II. As with eighteenth-century evangelicals in Scotland and America, one of the key aims of Presbyterian preaching in the decades before 1859 was to promote a revival of religion.[111]

At first, the various Presbyterian synods were hostile to itinerant evangelical preachers, though there were significant groups within the Synod of Ulster and Secession synods who were sympathetic to the cause. The Synod of Ulster passed resolutions in 1789 and again in 1804 forbidding ministers to allow unapproved preachers into their pulpits, though significantly Benjamin McDowell dissented from the latter decision.[112] In 1799 McDowell preached a sermon for the General Evangelical Society in Dublin in which he declared that it was the duty of those assembled 'to diffuse the blessings of the gospel of peace, more generally through this benighted land'.[113] As the gospel was for everyone, McDowell argued that preaching should not be confined to church buildings but employed wherever people needed to hear the gospel. Given their early history, it is ironic that both Secession synods were wary about itinerancy and the formation of the Evangelical Society of Ulster in 1798. While expressing guarded support for the aims of the society, both synods held that itinerancy and lay preaching were contrary to Presbyterian ecclesiology and warned ministers who were members of the society to end their involvement.[114] Methodist itinerancy also drew opposition from Presbyterian writers in the early decades of the nineteenth century,

---

[111] Crawford, *Seasons of grace*, ch. 3; H. Hastings, *Memoir of the life and labours of the late Rev. Josias Wilson, London* (London, 1850), 89–90.

[112] *RGSU* iii. (1789), 112; (1804), 279.

[113] B. McDowell, *The standing orders of Christ to the messengers of his grace* (Dublin, 1799), 12.

[114] Stewart, *Seceders*, 104–7, 187–90. Scottish Seceders were also concerned about itinerant preaching and the formation of Sunday schools in the 1790s (McKerrow, *History*, 393–4).

including a pamphlet debate between the minister of Ballywillan, James Huey, and the Methodist preacher Matthew Lanktree.[115]

Until around 1820, individual ministers invited evangelical preachers into their pulpits and became involved in missionary societies that undertook itinerant preaching throughout Ireland. James Morell invited the Methodist preacher Alice Cambridge to Ballybay Synod of Ulster congregation in 1815.[116] David Stuart of Dublin was very involved in the work of the Irish Evangelical Society and this led the Antiburgher Synod to pass a resolution in 1818 urging their members not to support the Society.[117] Despite the initial opposition of the synods, the various Presbyterian bodies formed their own missionary societies and adopted itinerant preaching. As early as 1788/9 the Synod of Ulster had sent ministers, including McDowell and Kelburn, on preaching tours to the south and west of Ireland in an attempt to revive isolated Presbyterian congregations.[118] After the success of re-establishing a congregation in Carlow, the Synod of Ulster and the Synod of Munster formed the Presbyterian Society of Ireland in 1820 'to revive and extend the Presbyterian interest in the south and west of Ireland', and in 1826 the Synod of Ulster Home Mission Society was formed.[119] Those ministers who preached under the auspices of the Dublin Committee of the Presbyterian Society were prominent members of the evangelical party within the Synod of Ulster.[120] These schemes were originally confined to lapsed Presbyterians but, following the lead of the Seceders home mission (1820) whose aim was to spread the 'gospel to those in the south and west of Ireland who have it not', they developed into societies engaged in evangelism amongst Irish Catholics.[121] The onset of population growth and urbanization also

[115] J. Huey, A sermon on the divine appointment of a gospel ministry (Belfast, 1814); M. Lanktree, An apology for what is called lay-preaching (Newry, 1815).

[116] D. Nesbitt, Full circle: a story of Ballybay Presbyterians (Monaghan, 1999), 49–51.

[117] Stewart, Seceders, 124–5.

[118] RGSU iii. (1787), 100; (1789), 111.

[119] First report of the Dublin Presbyterian Committee (Dublin, 1823); RGSU (1826), 33–6.

[120] Minutes of Dublin Presbyterian Committee, 1820–7 (Church House, strong room).

[121] MPSI (1820), 96. Presbyterian missionary activity in Ireland is well surveyed in, R. J. Rodgers, 'Vision unrealised: the Presbyterian mission to Irish Roman Catholics in the nineteenth century', Bulletin of the Presbyterian Historical Society of Ireland, 20 (1991), 12–31.

resulted in Presbyterians using a variety of techniques to reach the unchurched. Ministers increasingly believed that unless they attracted people to their meeting-houses, thousands would perish for want of hearing the gospel. There are many references to ministers preaching 'beyond the bounds' of their charges to people that had little or no contact with the congregation. During his summer preaching in 1827, Robert Magill preached to crowds in excess of one thousand in areas near his Antrim meeting-house.[122] Similarly, David Hamilton, minister of Connor, County Antrim, preached twice each Sunday in the winter and three times during the summer and held services throughout the neighbourhood in various venues, including barns and cottages. Through his efforts, his son claimed that Hamilton gained 190 new communicants for his congregation.[123]

Continuing developments in the late eighteenth century, the first decades of the nineteenth century witnessed a noticeable concentration upon a few key doctrines and a move away from the finer points of covenant or federal theology. This did not mean a rejection of Reformed theology so much as a refocusing of confessional principles to meet the needs of a new age, a process encouraged by the presence of the moderate Calvinists Samuel Hanna and Samuel Edgar as the professors of divinity in the Belfast Academical Institution. The distinctive doctrines that came to dominate Presbyterian evangelicalism were summarised in the 1831 pastoral address of the Synod of Ulster as 'those great doctrines which your fathers held fast, even unto death'. These doctrines were 'still dear to you their children' and comprised those 'of the original sinfulness of human nature—of the supreme deity of the Lord Jesus Christ—of justification by faith alone—and of regeneration and sanctification by the Holy Spirit, the third person in the Godhead'.[124] The similarity between the above list and that compiled by Benjamin McDowell in the midst of New Light dominance in 1772 is striking: 'original sin; the trinity of persons, but unity of essence in the Godhead;

---

[122] J. Kenny, *As the crow flies over rough terrain: incorporating the diary 1827/8 and more of a divine* (Newtownabbey, 1988), 314–16.

[123] T. Hamilton, *'Faithful unto death'. A biographical sketch of the Rev. David Hamilton of Belfast* (Belfast, 1875), 39–40.

[124] *Annual pastoral address of the General Synod of Ulster* (Belfast, 1831), 4.

justification by faith in the righteousness of Christ alone; the absolute necessity of holiness; the necessity of supernatural grace; the resurrection of the body; and eternal judgement'.[125] The important point to notice here is that McDowell wrote these words in the context of fear among orthodox Presbyterians that New Light theology would swamp the Synod. The 1831 pastoral address was also written out of the need for self-definition after the Remonstrants had been expelled. A pared-down list of distinctive doctrines provided a much easier base from which to defend the essentials of the Reformed faith in response to external threats. In addition, it made evangelism much easier and promoted interdenominational co-operation against a common threat. The beauty of evangelical doctrine was its apparent simplicity.

In the previous century, Seceders and Old Light evangelicals had emphasized the person and work of Christ in their sermons. In the nineteenth century evangelicals went a stage further and gave the theme pre-eminence within Ulster Presbyterianism as a whole. Christ was the cornerstone of evangelical theology, and the individual's faith and relationship in Christ meant that they could be assured of their eternal salvation. The traditional reliance upon the Holy Spirit and an appeal to the head and the heart of the hearer through easily understood sermons was ultimately reinforced. John Johnston of Tullylish summed up the view of the majority in 1834 when he declared that 'Christ crucified must be preached, as his atonement is the only foundation of a sinner's hope. But the work of the Spirit is necessary in applying the redemption purchased by Christ, as the death of the saviour was in providing that redemption.'[126] As an expression of thankfulness, believers were to commit themselves to a life of service and devotion to God that was in many respects more demanding than the call to personal holiness in the eighteenth century. Following the Westminster standards, the *Orthodox Presbyterian* made the laity aware of their responsibilities as hearers of the word, especially the application of biblical teaching to their personal lives.[127] In addition, Presbyterians who were exposed to evangelical

[125] McDowell, *Observations*, 7.

[126] *Missionary sermons and speeches delivered at a special meeting of the General Synod of Ulster* (Belfast, 1834), 121.

[127] 'On the hearing of the word', *Orthodox Presbyterian*, 4 (1833), 275–81; 'Bible instruction. No. XIII. Public worship', *Orthodox Presbyterian*, 6 (1834), 53–4, 55–8.

preaching found that greater demands were placed upon them in living an active life of public service as Sunday school teachers, Bible, and tract distributors, or Scripture readers.

Owing to the growing influence of evangelicalism within the Synod of Ulster from the mid-1820s, the church courts tightened the process of ministerial training and increasingly policed the theological opinions of ministers. Most of the examining functions of presbyteries were transferred to four Committees of Examination, identified as Belfast, Aughnacloy, Strabane or Derry, and Ballymoney. The *Code* outlined the structures and functions of these and gave as their rationale the failure of presbyteries in the past to adequately determine the educational attainments of students before they entered both college and theological classes.[128] Cooke knew that if the church was to have an evangelical and Reformed ministry then the personal beliefs of its prospective ministers must be ascertained. To make enquiries into such matters, a Theological Education Committee was established in 1828, which led directly to the Remonstrant exodus.[129] Visitation presbyteries in the 1830s were also directed to address questions to elders on whether their ministers preached key doctrines such as original sin, the Trinity, Christ's atonement, justification by faith, regeneration, sanctification, heaven and hell, the resurrection of the body, and the necessity of personal holiness.[130] The Synod had, in effect, added a theologically correct training in the Reformed and evangelical principles of Presbyterianism to a liberal education. Most ministers were content with the new dispensation as it was articulated within a Reformed theological framework. All orthodox Presbyterians, whether scrupulously confessional or interdenominational evangelicals, were able to subscribe to these key doctrines as they embodied a willingness to remain faithful to the Reformed tradition and to face the challenges of the nineteenth century. More importantly, it appealed to the conservative inclinations of the laity.

---

[128] *Code* (1825), 56–60. The names of the committees in 1841 were Ballymoney, Belfast, Derry, and Monaghan (*Code* (1841), 21–2).

[129] Holmes, *Henry Cooke*, 56–8, 60–2.

[130] 'Questions for visitation presbyteries, adopted by the Presbytery of Raphoe', *Orthodox Presbyterian*, 8 (1837), 166–7.

The preaching of the gospel with conviction was an essential means of promoting religious revival, and whatever their attitude to aspects of 'new measures' revivalism, Ulster Presbyterians were attracted to the style of preaching popularized by Charles Finney in America. For Finney and other revivalists, preaching 'was often more direct, specific, and theatrical'.[131] Though Presbyterians dissented from aspects of the overt emphasis upon human instrumentality, Finney's style of preaching fitted well with traditional forms, especially extempore preaching. The written manuscript was merely an outline for the polished performer and the preacher would add gestures, emphasis and modulation of voice, topical examples and pathetic anecdotes in order to drive home his point. In the mouth of a skilled preacher, the words spoken would have a powerful and lively effect that could be increased by the movement of the body.[132] Whereas the gestures of Cooke and Josias Wilson were described as 'graceful and natural', John Edgar's 'were not infrequently grotesque'.[133] When the seventh edition of Finney's *Lectures on revivals of religion* was published in London in 1838, the *Orthodox Presbyterian* was fulsome in its praise. The reviewer, Samuel Davidson, who would later become a noted proponent of biblical criticism, believed that the primary lesson to be learnt from the lectures was the need to be specific, enthusiastic, and direct in preaching. He admitted that Finney's views smacked of Arminianism and the use of certain means was excessive, yet the lectures were 'a work which every one who desires the conversion of sinners should read, and which all who feel for the danger of those who are living without God in the world will peruse with profit and edification'.[134]

The style of nineteenth-century preaching was designed to achieve the conversion of sinners and to reawaken religiously indifferent

---

[131] R. Carwardine, *Transatlantic revivalism: popular evangelicalism in Britain and America, 1790–1865* (Westport, Conn., 1978), 8.

[132] For a discussion of extempore preaching see H. Stout, *The divine dramatist: George Whitefield and the rise of modern evangelicalism* (Grand Rapids, Mich., 1991), 40–4.

[133] Hastings, *Josias Wilson*, 221; J. L. Porter, *The life and times of Henry Cooke, D.D., LL.D.* (Belfast, 1875), 186; W. D. Killen, *Memoir of John Edgar, D.D., LL.D.* (Belfast, 1867), 17.

[134] *Orthodox Presbyterian*, new ser., 1 (1838), 135–9.

congregations. Consequently, sermon delivery in general tended to display a much greater intensity and earnestness than was the case in the eighteenth century, as sinners were urged to come to Christ. According to W. B. Kirkpatrick, all ministers had to be faithful in declaring the whole counsel of God 'and bringing home the blessing and the curse to every man's conscience with unbending integrity, and, at the same time, with affectionate and fervent desire, that his ministrations may not be in vain'.[135] A writer to the *Christian Freeman* in 1833 lamented that 'it is a melancholic fact, that many heart-stirring sermons are rendered, in their conclusion, worse than powerless, by studied attempts to persuade the audience that they are not expected to do anything but wait'. It was clear to the author that by giving individuals the opportunity to prevaricate on making a decision for Christ the minister had abdicated responsibility for the souls under his care.[136] This sometimes intense style was described by critics as a form of psychological manipulation, as the preacher was pictured searing the imaginations of his hearers with the fires of hell before confronting them with the grace of God.[137] Though some preachers undoubtedly used the imagery of fire and brimstone, recent studies have demostrated that conversion resulted from a variety of considerations, including the guilt of the sinner before God and the concern of some converts with a loss of honour before their neighbours.[138] Moreover, the popularity of Cooke and other evangelical preachers had as much to do with their style and presence as with what they preached. They were not only evangelists but also entertainers.[139] In that regard, evangelical Presbyterian preaching was as much a performance fitted to meet the mood of the age as it was the proclamation of the Good News.

[135] 'On the best mode of seeking a revival of religion in our churches', *Orthodox Presbyterian*, new ser., 2 (1839), 135.

[136] 'Religious revivals', *Christian Freeman*, 1 (1833), 117.

[137] For example, 'Preachers and preaching. No. III. Evangelical preaching', *Bible Christian*, 5 (1834), 232.

[138] D. W. Bebbington, 'Evangelical conversion, c. 1740–1850', *Scottish Bulletin of Evangelical Theology*, 18 (2000), 118; Landsman, 'Evangelists and their hearers', 137–44.

[139] H. Davies, *Worship and theology in England: from Newman to Martineau, 1850–1900* (Princeton, 1962), ch. 10.

Nevertheless, evangelical sermons also did what they aimed to do. James Morgan believed the only criterion by which he could measure the success of his ministry was the number of conversions. As he looked back over his years in Carlow, Lisburn, and Belfast, he hoped God would help him 'call to remembrance examples of the divine blessing in the conversion of sinners'. He could not tell the numbers converted through his ministry, but he did publish the accounts of forty-seven converts in the first six volumes of the *Monthly Messenger*.[140] An excellent example of the impact of evangelical preaching was Alice Spence, an 'exceedingly thoughtless and giddy' girl, who came to Josias Wilson's meeting-house out of curiosity. That day, Wilson 'was warmly urging the sinner to embrace Jesus Christ; and, in one of his most urgent appeals, he threw out his arm, leant over the pulpit, and looked next the gallery, and implored all to fly to the "Lamb of God".' According to his biographer, 'The word went home with power to the heart of this poor girl, and in after-life she became distinguished for piety; and her death, which occurred a few weeks after Mr Wilson's, proved that she was a child of God and an heir of the promises.'[141] The success of Morgan and Wilson as preachers may be attributed to their commitment to pastoral visitation and their awareness of the spiritual and worldly needs of their congregations.[142] The case of Alice Spence also highlights one of the criticisms of evangelical preaching, that it appealed to naturally emotional females, though it is clear that the attraction of evangelicalism for women was its provision of a practical and coherent worldview.[143]

The *Bible Christian* had referred to revivalism as 'the pestilence' in 1833, but despite their obvious dislike of evangelicalism, liberal Presbyterians were influenced by its style of preaching.[144] In the early nineteenth century, some English Unitarians saw the standard prepared sermon as anachronistic in an urban context and so

---

[140] J. Morgan, *Recollections of my life and times* (Belfast, 1874), 157–63.

[141] Hastings, *Josias Wilson*, 234–5.

[142] Ibid., 238–40; Morgan, *Recollections*, 85–6.

[143] For an example of this type of criticism, 'Preachers and preaching. No. XII. Evangelical preaching', *Bible Christian*, 6 (1835), 353–7. The reasons for the appeal of evangelical religion to women are surveyed in D. Hempton, *The religion of the people: Methodism and popular religion in Britain, 1750–1900* (London, 1996), ch. 10.

[144] 'Revival of cant', *Bible Christian*, 4 (1833), 36.

developed a 'more popular style of preaching' in order to propagate their beliefs.[145] Likewise, the Remonstrant Synod decreed in 1832 that all licentiates must learn to preach sermons extemporary so 'that they may deliver them with greater energy and freedom'.[146] One writer declared that 'if the advocates for rational and practical preaching, could acquire the extemporaneous fluency of the evangelicals, and infuse into their sermons greater zeal and tenderness, unction and pathos, we might hope to see pulpit eloquence carried to the summit of perfection'.[147] Others, including George Hill of Ballymoney, pioneer historian of the Ulster plantation, preached beyond the geographical bounds of their congregations.[148] Unitarians knew that evangelical preaching attracted people and this must have been galling given that their previous dominance of Belfast society was crumbling before their eyes. Even then, the orthodox Third Congregation had always been much larger, as the likes of Sinclare Kelburn and Samuel Hanna preached orthodox doctrine with warmth and enthusiasm. In the context of political and religious polarization, direct, emotional preaching appealed to those who wanted their truth in monochrome. The rational discourses of Unitarians changed, but it was too little, too late, and they were consequently drowned out in the din of controversy.

Many of the themes highlighted in this section were important to Old Light and Seceder ministers in the eighteenth century, not least in terms of the free offer of the gospel, which is traditionally seen as a product of the 1859 revival.[149] The major shift in Presbyterian preaching was not so much in terms of the numbers who preached in a certain way but the social prominence and cultural influence of the various groups. In the eighteenth century, New Light preaching was pre-eminent as it accorded with the spirit of the age and New Light Presbyterians had the disproportionate share of social influence within Ulster. During the nineteenth century, direct, emotional

---

[145] D. L. Wykes, ' "A good discourse, well explained in 35 minutes": Unitarians and preaching in the early nineteenth century', *Transactions of the Unitarian Historical Society*, 21 (1997), 173–90.

[146] *MRSU* (1832), 13.

[147] 'The progress of preaching', *Bible Christian*, new ser., 1 (1836), 21.

[148] George Hill, 'Missions to the poor', *Bible Christian*, new ser., 1 (1836), 78–82.

[149] J. E. Davey, *The story of a hundred years* (Belfast, 1940), 45.

preaching fitted well with the cultural mood of the times, increased sectarian tensions, and the growing desire of ministers to confront people with the duties of the gospel and their need of salvation through a personal relationship with Christ. Old Light and Seceder preachers had similar goals in the previous century but did not have the social influence or cultural significance necessary to achieve public prominence. What nineteenth-century evangelicalism did was to energize this tradition by making Presbyterian preaching overwhelmingly Christocentric and directed towards the individual.

Preaching was of central importance to the experience and identity of Presbyterian communities. At one level, preaching defined the group and expressed the differences between them and their neighbours. In the eighteenth century, this usually meant self-definition against other Presbyterians, though it also articulated their difference from Anglicans and Catholics. Concern with group identity was reflected in discussions among the laity about the soundness and style of the sermons they heard. As political and religious polarization increased in the nineteenth century, Presbyterian evangelicals sought conversions and spiritual reawakening through a much more coherent and, in many ways, simpler message. At another level, an examination of preaching highlights the tensions and difficulties between the minister and his congregation. Though the minister was a person apart, he was also the embodiment of community values and identity. If a minister articulated a contradictory view to that of his congregation in an unacceptable style, they could report him to his presbytery or force him to leave. Though doctrinal content was important, orthodoxy was also bound up with how the word was preached, and certain acts such as reading sermons could be seen as patronizing. The style and content of sermons, and the expectations of congregations, reflected social, cultural, and religious changes. In that context preaching provides a unique insight into the symbiotic relationship between high and low culture, and the competing pressures upon preachers to be faithful to the Bible, the expectations of their congregations, and their cultural environment.

6

Communion and Discipline

Communion was one of only two sacraments deemed to have biblical sanction by Protestant Reformers, including the Westminster divines. Baptism and the Lord's Supper were both 'holy signs and seals of the covenant of grace'.[1] The origin of communion was traced back to the Passover of the Old Testament, through to its institution by Christ at the Last Supper, and to the injunctions of the apostle Paul. The *Confession* declared that it was established 'for the perpetual remembrance of the sacrifice of himself [Christ] in his death, the sealing of all benefits thereof unto true believers, their spiritual nourishment and growth in him, their further engagement in and to all duties which they owe unto him, and to be a bond and pledge of their communion with him, and with each other, as members of his mystical body'.[2] Indeed, relationships are central to any understanding of this sacrament, whether relationships conceived of vertically between believers (individual and collective) and God, or horizontally between church members. The Westminster divines and Scottish and Irish Presbyterians regulated these relationships and the purity of communion through a system of church discipline that also upheld biblical values more generally in the local community. Elsewhere in the Westminster standards, the reverential attitude towards communion and the importance of the relationship between sacrament and word were all emphasized and will be highlighted in this chapter.

The *Directory* was accepted by the General Assembly of the Church of Scotland in 1645 with modifications that reflected traditional

---

[1] *Confession*, 27: 1.
[2] *Confession*, 29: 1.

Scottish communion practice as laid out in the *Book of Common Order* (1564).[3] As the ordinance developed amongst Presbyterians in Scotland, Ulster, and America, it did so in two important ways not envisaged by the Westminster divines. First, Calvin had wanted a weekly administration of communion but had to settle for a less frequent service and the *Directory* allowed congregations to determine how often it should be held for the 'comfort and edification' of believers.[4] In Scotland and Ulster communion was held twice a year, around May and October. This was to some degree determined by the difficulties encountered by both groups from the middle decades of the seventeenth century as they attempted to withstand the assaults at various times of Cromwell and Episcopalians. Though it was held infrequently, the importance of communion in the seventeenth century for the self-confidence and identity of the beleaguered Ulster-Scots community ought to be stressed.[5] Second, there developed a weekly series of services of preparation, communion, and thanksgiving known as the communion season. This included a fast day on Thursday, spiritual preparation on Friday, public worship and the examination of communicants on Saturday, communion on Sunday, and services of thanksgiving on Monday. Leigh Eric Schmidt has produced an evocative depiction of how these seasons were experienced by Scottish and American Presbyterians in the seventeenth and eighteenth centuries. During these communions, 'religion and culture, communion and community, piety and sociability combined. Regularly times of renewal and revival, they were the high days of the year.'[6] So central were they to Scots-Irish 'evangelical Presbyterian culture' that they became occasions for revival on both sides of the Atlantic.

Schmidt has uncovered the complex relationships between the sacred and the secular, and between ministers and their

---

[3] J. M. Barkley, *The Westminster formularies in Irish Presbyterianism* (Belfast, 1956), 51–4.

[4] *Directory*, 384.

[5] R. L. Greaves, *God's other children: Protestant nonconformists and the emergence of denominational churches in Ireland, 1660–1700* (Stanford, 1997), 222–7; M. J. Westerkamp, *Triumph of the laity: Scots-Irish piety and the Great Awakening 1625–1760* (New York, 1988), 29–34, 66–7.

[6] L. E. Schmidt, *Holy fairs: Scotland and the making of American revivalism*, 2nd edn. (Grand Rapids, Mich., 2001), 3.

congregations, at communion time. He has outlined the contours of lay belief and the growing embarrassment of social elites with the intemperance of the lower orders, which often blighted these communion seasons and was so memorably satirized by Robert Burns. Schmidt was fortunate in having excellent personal testimonies of converts at the Cambuslang revival in the 1740s. Such first-hand accounts of personal, lay experience simply do not exist for Ulster Presbyterians and nor did the communion season promote revival in Ulster as it did elsewhere. It is also important to note that on three occasions in the early eighteenth century, in 1697, 1700, and 1715, the Synod of Ulster passed overtures regulating the size and moderating the revelry of these events, including the suggestion that communion should be observed more frequently.[7] These overtures did not dismantle the communion season, but owing to the precarious position of Presbyterians in a confessional state in the early eighteenth century, and their own internal problems, it is conceivable that the scale of communions was less in Ulster than in Scotland. In the light of Schmidt's suggestion that the season was central to 'evangelical Presbyterian culture', it is significant that it was Seceders who held communion seasons comparable with those in Scotland.

Despite the lack of first-hand accounts similar to Cambuslang, it is possible to explore the religious and social significance of the communion season in Ulster for those involved. All Presbyterians were agreed as to the importance of the Lord's Supper, but liberals and conservatives differed significantly in their approach to discipline and the theological meaning of communion. The first section of this chapter examines the communal, personal, and practical preparations for communion, including a general discussion of the practice of church discipline. The last two sections explore the organization, structure, and meaning of the communion season while highlighting some of the changes and continuities in the nineteenth century, particularly the impact of the reforms promoted by Presbyterian evangelicals.

---

[7] R. S. Tosh, 'An examination of the origin and development of Irish Presbyterian worship' (QUB Ph.D., 1983), 185–6.

I

According to the Westminster standards, the 'ignorant or scandalous' were to be excluded from communion.[8] Consequently, a system of examination and discipline administered by Kirk sessions was established in order to ensure that communicants possessed sufficient knowledge of the Reformed faith and satisfactory moral character to maintain the purity of the table. Once communicants had passed these prerequisites they were admitted to communion, usually by the giving of a lead communion token either distributed by ministers and elders when visiting church members or in the meeting-house on the fast day.[9] Ministers, and sometimes elders, examined the religious knowledge of first-time communicants in the weeks or months before communion, a practice insisted upon by the Scottish General Assembly when adopting the *Directory*.[10] One of the means of imparting knowledge was through catechizing children in the principles of the tradition of Presbyterianism to which they belonged, a process that will be examined in more detail in Chapter 10. In general, ministers saw the proper instruction of communicants as essential to the prosperity of religion in their congregations, especially amongst the young. James Hunter, Burgher minister of Coleraine, ascribed the success of his congregation to 'the particular care exercised toward young persons admitted to sealing ordinances, by meeting with them 5 or 6 different days and instructing them in doctrinal and experimental religion'.[11]

In addition to basic doctrinal knowledge, the Seceders and Covenanters had other terms of communion. The Seceders in 1744 made the renovation of both Scottish covenants and adherence to their

---

[8] *Larger Catechism*, Q. 173; *Directory*, 384.

[9] J. M. Barkley, 'The evidence of old Irish session books on the sacrament of the Lord's Supper', *Church Service Society Annual*, 22 (May 1952), 30. These communion tokens are catalogued in A. A. Milne, *Communion tokens of the Presbyterian churches in Ireland* (Glasgow, 1920).

[10] *Code* (1825), 94–5; Barkley, *Westminster formularies*, 52.

[11] The Revd James Hunter, 'Narrative of the rise and progress of the Seceding congregation of Coleraine' (PHS).

own principles terms of ministerial and Christian communion.[12] Over time, the obligation of covenanting was laid aside by the Burghers after a debate arose within the Scottish synod about its status as a term of communion. The practice of congregational covenanting does not seem to have been widespread in Ireland and the only surviving example is from an Antiburgher congregation in the 1760s.[13] Indeed, John Semple suspected a decade earlier that Irish Seceders did not examine whether church members agreed to the renovation of the covenants before seeking sealing ordinances.[14] In broader terms, the Synod of Ulster minister Samuel Delap questioned the propriety of making detailed doctrinal and polemical formularies terms of communion when the Westminster standards excluded only the ignorant, scandalous, and ungodly. He also doubted the ability of many sincere believers to understand the content of the various documents.[15] Though the attachment of the Seceders to the covenants weakened considerably, potential members of a Covenanter fellowship were obliged to express adherence to the Old and New Testaments, the various documents of the Westminster Assembly, the Presbyterian system of church government, the perpetual obligation of the National Covenant and Solemn League and Covenant as renewed at Auchinsaugh in 1712, and the various testimonies of the Covenanters. It was usual for Covenanter congregations to renew their commitment to these prior to communion.[16]

Both liberal and conservative Presbyterians in Ulster acknowledged that intending communicants ought to lead a blameless life, though the latter were much more likely to discipline offenders in the interests of a pure table. As communion was about relationships and

[12] J. McKerrow, *History of the Secession church*, rev. edn. (Edinburgh, 1847), 188–96, 530–3.

[13] Roseyards (AB/Sec.) congregational covenant, 18 July 1764 (PRONI, Tennent papers, D/1748/A/2/2).

[14] J. Semple, *The survey impartially examined by sacred Scripture and sound reason* (Belfast, 1754), 103–4.

[15] S. Delap, *Remarks on some articles of the Seceders new covenant, and their act of presbytery* (Belfast, 1749), 36–8.

[16] M. Hutchinson, *The Reformed Presbyterian Church in Scotland: its origin and history 1680–1876* (Paisley, 1893), 212–13; 'On terms of Christian communion', *Covenanter*, 2 (1832), 120–31; A. Loughridge, *The Covenanters in Ireland* (Belfast, 1984), 34–5.

community, it is important to reflect upon the importance of church discipline in maintaining purity of communion. The practice of discipline in Ulster Presbyterianism followed Scottish precedents and procedures. Yet, in many respects, it was easier for Presbyterians in Ulster to develop a coherent and accepted system of discipline than the Church of Scotland, which was hindered from doing so by its status as the Established Church and the overlap of civil and ecclesiastical law.[17] Irish Presbyterians enjoyed a greater degree of disciplinary cohesion as it was easier to regulate a community that submitted willingly to discipline rather than being compelled to do so. Another point of contrast is the persistence of discipline and its decline over time. It has been suggested that, for a variety of reasons, discipline within the Church of Scotland had been almost abandoned by the end of the 1780s.[18] However, new evidence from Scotland and England, and the findings of the present study, suggest a more complex profile of decline as discipline continued in some areas of Ulster into the twentieth century.[19]

Assessing the practice of discipline is difficult as the sources are limited in a number of ways. Fewer than twenty Kirk session books have survived from before 1800 and the greater bulk of material for the early nineteenth century reflects the reorganization of congregations within the Synod of Ulster. In addition, the degree of detail found in the surviving session books is generally slight. Often they record only the names of those who appeared, the offence they were accused of (usually a sexual misdemeanour), and the sentence passed. The fullest details invariably come from Seceder session books. A familiarity with the surviving records reveals the importance of practical considerations, as the degree of discipline experienced in any given area depended on there being a Kirk session in the first place, having a sufficient number and quality of elders to carry out the

[17] Rosalind Mitchison and Leah Leneman have produced a number of important works on Scottish church discipline in the eighteenth century. *Sexuality and social control: Scotland 1660–1780* (Oxford, 1989); *Sin in the city: sexuality and social control in urban Scotland 1660–1780* (Edinburgh, 1998); Leah Leneman and Rosalind Mitchison, 'Acquiescence in and defiance of church discipline in early modern Scotland', *Records of the Scottish Church History Society*, 25 (1993), 19–39.

[18] Leneman and Mitchison, 'Acquiescence and defiance', 20–1.

[19] C. G. Brown, *Religion and society in Scotland since 1707* (Edinburgh, 1997), 69–73; M. R. Watts, *The Dissenters*, 2 vols. (Oxford, 1978, 1995), ii. 198–204.

task of discipline effectively, and the existence of proper Kirk session records. As demonstrated below, the theological outlook of a minister and the Kirk session also had a significant influence upon the character of discipline. An attempt has been made to quantify the number of cases tried by a Kirk session when both necessary and possible, though the poor survival of records and the problem of record-keeping has made a systematic enumeration of cases impracticable.

The procedure followed by Ulster Presbyterians in cases of discipline was based upon the *Form of process* drawn up by the General Assembly of the Church of Scotland in 1707.[20] During the eighteenth century, the Synod of Ulster also passed various regulations regarding discipline that were finally drawn together in a section of the *Code* entitled 'The form of proceeding in cases of scandal, and of inflicting and removing church censures', which sought to ensure that cases were tried in a comprehensive and impartial manner.[21] Church discipline aimed to act as an example to others, to uphold the authority of the laws of Christ and his ministers, and to reclaim and reform the sinner. Reflecting the influence of liberal theological opinion on the drafting committee, it is significant that the *Code* did not include a further aim given in the *Confession* 'for preventing the wrath of God, which might justly fall upon the church, if they should suffer his covenant, and the seals thereof, to be profaned by notorious and obstinate offenders'.[22]

Offences came under the notice of Kirk sessions from public report, rumours, 'complaint, reference, or appeal'.[23] Commentators, both historical and contemporary, have acknowledged that church discipline only functioned effectively if it had the authority of community pressure and upheld accepted values.[24] Indeed, the laity often

[20] *An abridgement of the acts of the General Assemblies of the Church of Scotland* (Edinburgh, 1811), 441–72; J. M. Barkley, *A short history of the Presbyterian Church in Ireland* (Belfast, 1959), 107.

[21] *Code* (1825), 62–83.

[22] *Confession*, 30: 3; *Code* (1825), 63.

[23] *Code* (1825), 64.

[24] For example, 'Religious revivals', *Christian Freeman*, 1 (1833), 116; W. T. Latimer, 'The old session book of Templepatrick Presbyterian church', *Journal of the Royal Society of Antiquarians of Ireland*, 25 (1895), 134; S. J. Connolly, 'Ulster Presbyterians: religion, culture and politics, 1660–1850', in H. T. Blethen and C. W. Wood, Jr (eds.), *Ulster and North America: transatlantic perspectives on the Scotch-Irish* (Tuscaloosa, Ala., 1997), 29.

used Kirk sessions to deal with personal grievances, solve interpersonal conflict, or quash false rumours concerning alleged bad behaviour.[25] The success of church discipline also depended upon people within the community informing elders of wrongdoing. Elders did indeed oversee the congregation and reported offences to their colleagues, but at the most basic level, the social interaction, conversation, and gossip of a community provided the necessary framework for discipline to function effectively.[26] Being the subject of a scandalous rumour damaged the individual's place within small rural communities and it was only through the rituals of confession, rebuke, and restoration, often in public, that a person could be reintegrated into that community. Furthermore, remaining unrepentant also excluded one's children from privileges, which could have serious consequences, given the importance many attached to baptism. Such social pressure explains the small number of fugitives from discipline in the period from around 1660 to 1740, though it is also clear that from then until the end of the century discipline in many Synod of Ulster congregations became lax and in some areas only operated as long as the laity willingly submitted.[27] Seceder presbytery visitations in the late eighteenth century reported that 'some are refractory in respect of discipline and fugitives from it', but, in general, such reports were not usual.[28]

Not every offence brought to the attention of church courts was considered scandalous and neither were all offences treated with equal severity. According to the *Code*, misdemeanours such as swearing, Sabbath breach, drunkenness, or disrespect to parents, could be dealt with in private and without public notice. However, 'fornication, slander, habitual drunkenness, or other such gross offences', were to be immediately reported to the session and not to be set aside until the offender wanted admission to privileges.[29] Though the *Code*

---

[25] For examples see, J. M. Barkley, 'A history of the ruling eldership in Irish Presbyterianism', 2 vols. (QUB MA, 1952), ii. 19, 231–2, 236, 256, 263–4.

[26] C. Parker, 'The moral agency and moral autonomy of church folk in the Dutch Reformed church of Delft, 1580–1620', *Journal of Ecclesiastical History*, 48 (1997), 44–77.

[27] R. M. Browne, 'Kirk and community: Ulster Presbyterian society, 1640–1740' (QUB Ph.D., 1998), 94–8.

[28] Down Pby (B/Sec.), 27 Jan. 1790 (PHS).

[29] *Code* (1825), 68.

was anxious to widen discipline beyond breaches of the seventh commandment, fornication was deemed 'a crime peculiarly injurious to the best interests of society', and owing to its magnitude, offenders ought to appear before the Kirk session or congregation to declare their sorrow and give evidence of repentance.[30] The perception that fornication threatened the cohesion of society explains, in part, why sexual offences were the most frequent cases brought before church courts, though the consequences of a forbidden sexual liaison were obvious in a local community, whether a scandalous rumour, an unmarried pregnant woman, or a broken family.

Before the case was heard, the parties involved and the witnesses, if appropriate, were summoned to attend the session in good time by an elder or the sexton. If those summoned to attend refused to appear, they too would become the subject of disciplinary action. According to the elaborate rules given in the *Code* to ensure the fair treatment of all involved, the session then heard all the evidence and came to a decision that was read to all parties.[31] Those found guilty were rebuked and exhorted either before the session in private or before the congregation on one or more Sabbaths. Offenders could be suspended from communion and baptism until they had repented or, in more serious cases of wilful and continual offending, excommunicated. The sentence passed depended on the notoriety of the case and its impact upon the public testimony of the congregation. If the offence had occurred a long time ago or if it was not public knowledge, Kirk sessions could be lenient, as prosecuting the offender would only bring unwarranted attention and scandal.[32] Specific local circumstances could also influence the level of discipline. Ballybay session recorded that the spate of irregular marriages tried before the Lord's Supper in May 1820 had been the result of a degraded clergyman operating within their bounds. They decided that all couples so married 'shall be rebuked, not for irregular marriage, but fornication; and not in the vestry room, in the presence

[30] Ibid., 69.
[31] Ibid., 66–9.
[32] For sentencing in general, ibid., 65–6, 78–83. Examples of leniency include, Down Pby (B/Sec.), 6 July 1790, 18 Feb. 1823; Ballymoney (GSU) session book, 22 May 1802, 12 May 1804 (UTC); Dromara (GSU) session book, 20 May 1826 (PRONI, T/1447/2).

of the session; but in the meeting-house, and before the congregation at large'.[33] The higher courts of the church were often involved in cases brought before sessions either because the session needed advice owing to the complexity of the case or because those found guilty of an offence had the right to appeal the decision or sentence passed.

This procedural framework was common to all Presbyterians in Ulster, but the volume and character of cases of discipline differed greatly between the various groups. The Kirk session of Ballycarry, a prominent non-subscribing congregation, tried fifty-nine cases between 1740 and 1780. Fornication accounted for no less than forty-nine of those cases, seven were for adultery, and the remaining three were for other offences.[34] The Ballycarry records show a noticeable decline in the number of cases prosecuted by the session after 1750. This trend reflects the influence of Enlightenment humanitarianism upon theologically moderate Presbyterians in general and is in line with other non-subscribing congregations such as First and Second Belfast whose session books do not record a single case of discipline in the whole of the period.[35] As discipline was being tightened in Synod of Ulster congregations in the nineteenth century, Henry Montgomery questioned the right of ministers to exclude anyone from communion at the Lord's Table and criticized the distribution of communion tokens by arguing that the 'only tokens that God requires from sinners are penitence, faith and love'.[36] As early as 1826, at least one non-subscribing congregation had 'laid aside many years ago' the distribution of tokens yet continued to exclude the 'profane and scandalous'.[37] It should be pointed out that the number of adherents to the various non-subscribing bodies in 1834 amounted to fewer than 30,000 and that their membership was predominantly from the upper echelons of Ulster Presbyterian society.[38] The non-subscribing community was in some ways easier

---

[33] Ballybay (GSU) session book, 23 May 1820 (PHS).

[34] Ballycarry (GSU/Rem.) session book, 1740–80 (PRONI, CR/3/31/2).

[35] Mitchison and Leneman, *Sexuality and social control*, 71–2.

[36] R. G. Crawford, 'A critical examination of nineteenth-century non-subscribing Presbyterian theology in Ireland', 2 vols. (QUB Ph.D., 1964), i. 309–10.

[37] C. Porter, 'Congregational memoirs: Cairncastle', *Christian Unitarian*, 4 (1865), 337.

[38] G. Mathews, *An account of the regium donum* (Dublin, 1836), 27.

to discipline because it was small, and it may be that anti-social behaviour was not actually prevalent amongst their adherents. On the other hand, the risk of alienating important benefactors was a deterrent to the disciplining of wealthier members.[39]

The unusually complete session records of Cahans Burgher Secession congregation give us an almost unique insight into church discipline over a long period. From 1752 to 1758, sixty-nine cases were tried, twenty-three for fornication, twenty for irregular marriage, three for adultery, and twenty-three for other offences. Between 1767 and 1836 there were 189 cases; fifty for fornication, twenty-two for premarital fornication, fourteen for adultery, sixty-one irregular marriages, and forty-one others.[40] The example of Cahans highlights the general attitude of the Seceders both in terms of scrupulosity and the sheer volume and variety of cases compared with many Synod of Ulster congregations in the same period. Sexual misdemeanours still comprised the largest proportion of cases heard, but drunkenness, gambling, dancing, profane swearing, Sabbath breach, and other offences were much more likely to be tried. Though the range of discipline was extensive, the number of cases tried was not outrageous, falling between the first and second periods from ten to three per year. Nevertheless, Seceders would continue to uphold high standards of discipline in the nineteenth century as they remained committed to the ideal of a godly community. On the title page of their session books, Secession ministers or clerks of session copied verses from Numbers, Isaiah, and Ezekiel, which identified the congregation with the Children of Israel and urged them to remember their sins and failings in order to maintain purity of communion and bring glory to God.[41]

Covenanters in the late eighteenth and early nineteenth centuries were organized into fellowship societies who reported any cases of misconduct to the Kirk session that supervised them. The surviving records demonstrate that Covenanters prosecuted the same range of

---

[39] Aretin, *An essay on equalisation of bounty* (Belfast, 1811), 7–9; W. H. Oliver, *Pastoral provision* (Belfast, 1856), 70.

[40] Cahans (B/Sec.) session book, 1752–8, 1767–1836 (PRONI, CR/3/25B/1&2).

[41] For example, Down Pby (B/Sec.), title page. The biblical references are, Numbers 33: 2, Isaiah 30: 8, and Ezekiel 43: 11.

cases as the Seceders and that strict discipline continued to be applied in the nineteenth century against non-observance of the Sabbath, intemperance, premarital sex, and insolvency.[42] A unique feature of Covenanter discipline was the number of cases relating to civil matters, a direct result of their political theology and unwillingness to accept the legitimacy of the Erastian state. Consequently, Covenanter session books record cases against those who registered leases, voted in elections, served on juries, took oaths of allegiance, or signed parliamentary petitions.[43]

Seceders accused the Synod of Ulster of allowing unsuitable characters to communicate while they maintained a pure table through church discipline.[44] Synod of Ulster ministers responded by claiming that the ignorant and scandalous were refused admission and it was certainly the case that Old Light and evangelical Synod of Ulster congregations were zealous in 'fencing the table'.[45] For instance, the Kirk session of Carnmoney between 1767 and 1805 tried no fewer than 171 sexual offences.[46] Yet, despite such examples, it is generally the case that Synod of Ulster congregations in the second half of the eighteenth century were not as scrupulous in disciplinary matters as their Seceder counterparts. In the first decade of the nineteenth century, a number of orthodox writers urged the Synod to tighten discipline. One anonymous author observed that attitudes to the maintenance of church discipline had witnessed 'a melancholy change' and recommended that public rebuke should be restored for those who committed public sins.[47] Though formal church

---

[42] Loughridge, *Covenanters*, 111; Drumbolg (RP) session book, 1805–59 (PRONI, MIC/1C/15C/1).

[43] Antrim (RP) session book, 6 June 1805, 5 May 1806, 20–1, 46 (PHS, Stavely papers); Ballenon (RP) session book, 17 Mar. 1830 (PRONI, MIC/1C/16/2); R. L. W. McCollum, 'John Paul and his contribution to the shaping of Presbyterianism in the 19th century' (QUB Ph.D., 1992), 31.

[44] T. Clark, *A brief survey of some principles maintained, by the General Synod of Ulster, and practices carried on, by several members thereof* (Armagh, 1751), 29–31.

[45] Semple, *The survey impartially examined*, 50–4. Anahilt (GSU) session book, 1774–94 (Barkley, 'Eldership', ii. 270–6); Dromara (GSU) session book, 1770–1840.

[46] W. P. Gray, 'A social history of illegitimacy in Ireland from the late eighteenth to the early twentieth century' (QUB Ph.D., 2000), 113–14.

[47] Amicus, *A letter to the ministers of the Synod of Ulster* (n.p., 1807), 11–12. S. Dill, *A sermon on the duty of ministers and their connexion with Christ* (Londonderry, [1802]), 20–2, 34–5, 37–9.

discipline may have varied considerably amongst Presbyterians, they all agreed that the ignorant and scandalous ought to be excluded from taking communion.

In addition to regulating access to communion through discipline, Kirk sessions had also many practical matters to settle, including the date of observance. This was difficult in rural areas where the vicissitudes of farming life often delayed communion. The session of Roseyards had proposed the third Sabbath in October 1803 for their communion but had 'now for many reasons as having moonlight and more time to gather in the remainder of harvest agreed that it be on the 4th Sabbath of October if God permits'.[48] Judging by the numerous communion accounts to have survived, practical preparation for communion was of great importance to the local congregation. Between 1787 and 1791, the treasurer's book of New Row congregation, Coleraine, recorded the following items of expenditure: £3. 15. 0 for thirty bottles of claret; 1s. 1d. for a hundred tokens and 1s. 4d. for 5½ lbs of lead; 9s. 9d. for bread and 5s. 4d. for four yards of diaper cloth; and 1s. 7½d. to 'William McCormick to clean the flagons and buy a brush'.[49] In March 1791, Cullybackey Reformed Presbyterian Kirk session levied three guineas on the congregation 'to purchase basons and plates and to cover communion expenses'.[50] The Kirk session of Magherafelt ordered one of their number in April 1819 to obtain four gallons of port wine and six dozen cakes 'for the approaching solemnity', while in October 1830 the communion accounts included 1s. 3d. for whisky and £1. 11s. 6d. for three and a half gallons of wine.[51] The amount of alcohol bought for these occasions indicates the numbers attending and the social importance of alcohol for Presbyterians before the onset of the temperance movement. It was not merely wine for communion that was purchased, but also bottles of brandy, claret, and whisky for the consumption of the

[48] Roseyards (AB/Sec.) session book, 2 Sept. 1803 (PRONI, Tennent papers, D/1748/A/2/3/1), 36. Dundrod (GSU) session book, 1 Sept. 1833, 4 Oct. 1835 (PRONI, MIC/1P/416/C/1).

[49] New Row (GSU) treasurer's book, 1774–1834 (PRONI, Given papers, D/4164/A/4), 920.

[50] Cited in A. Loughridge, *The Covenanters of Cullybackey 1789–1989* (Rathfriland, 1989), 14.

[51] Magherafelt (GSU) session book, 23 Apr. 1819 and 25 Oct. 1830 (PRONI, CR/3/13/C/1), 8, 57.

Kirk session in the session house. References in other session books to the purchase of mutton and beef may refer to preparations for a communal meal.[52] Such was the importance of the event for congregations that they sometimes got themselves into financial trouble. The Kirk session of Dromara had problems paying for their sacrament in 1817, prompting them to order the treasurer to lay aside half of the congregational collection in order to defray expenses.[53]

Individual believers made their own personal preparations for communion, whether as part of the services of the communion season or in the quietness of their homes. The yearly framework of daily personal and family devotions helped sustain the faith of the individual. Through self-examination, Presbyterians sought to apply the lessons they learnt from reading the Bible, hearing sermons, and observing God's hand at work in the world. They examined their own lives when possible for marks of holiness and assurance of salvation. Special preparation was deemed necessary for the Lord's Table, though non-subscribers were careful not to overemphasize scrupulous preparation or, indeed, the emotional resonance that the ordinance had for conservative Presbyterians.[54] There were important differences in the content of devotional exercises between liberal and conservative believers. Whereas New Light believers wanted to live obedient lives in the presence of an omniscient God, orthodox believers sought a personal relationship with Christ, the marks of true godliness, and personal assurance of salvation.

Some orthodox Presbyterians prepared for communion by making and renewing personal covenants. Personal covenanting was not restricted to the communion season, but these occasions were important times for entering into or renewing such promises to God. In these covenants, individual believers committed to paper their willing submission to God's will and their desire to serve him. A number of such covenants composed by ministers have survived and point to

---

[52] For example, Roseyards (AB/Sec.) session book, 23 June 1784, 208; First Coleraine (GSU) account book, 1 June 1816 (PRONI, Given papers, D/4164/A/17), 3942; J. Brown, *Second Presbyterian Church Newtownards: a history of the congregation 1753–1953* (Newtownards, [1953]), 11.

[53] Dromara (GSU) session book, 7 Sept. 1817.

[54] Remonstrant Synod, *Helps to Christian devotion* (Newry, 1836), 149–55.

a desire to lead holy and devout lives of service to God and his people.[55] Ministers obviously had the language and theological concepts to compose such documents, but lay-folk could also produce covenants of understanding and devotion. The following example is from a collection of covenants written by male and female members of the Holmes family of Coleraine in the 1780s.

I Andrew Holmes according to my baptismal vows do make a solemn dedication of my soul and body to God the Father God the Son and God the Holy Ghost one God in Christ for my portion and my all for time and eternity amen. O my God help me to renounce the thrice enemies of the [glorious] Trinity, the Devil the world and the flesh; and O my God seal me with thy Holy Spirit to the day of Redemption for Christ's sake and in testimony of my desire I subscribe my hand to the Lord. Amen and amen.[56]

Similar sentiments were expressed in a covenant written by the poet and schoolteacher Hugh Tynan, a member of a Seceder congregation near Donaghadee in the late eighteenth century.[57] One of the most notable features of this document is the level of theological understanding exhibited. Of course, Tynan was a teacher and so ought to have known how to express himself, yet he was also able to talk with confidence on topics such as original sin, imputed guilt, the threefold offices of Christ as Prophet, Priest, and King, and of the relationship between his baptismal vows and communion. The other striking feature of the covenant is his clear faith and devotion to God through Christ. At one point he declares, 'I am content to be an eternal debtor to free grace, and that the glory of my salvation be for ever ascribed to Jesus Christ, my Surety, my Saviour, and Redeemer.' Such a commitment did not lead to a mystical introversion but a life of submission and activity, or as Tynan himself put it, a desire to 'forsake sin and continually persevere in thy service'.[58] This new life was to be characterized, in negative terms, by not attending cockfights or horse races, not breaking the Sabbath, avoiding drunkenness, and, positively, by leading a holy life and observing personal

---

[55] For example, J. Mark, *First Dunboe: an historical sketch* (Coleraine, 1915), 12; H. Hastings, *Memoir of the life and labours of the late Rev. Josias Wilson, London* (London, 1850), 92–3.
[56] Holmes papers (PRONI, T/1970/1).
[57] H. Tynan, *Poems* (Belfast, 1803), pp. vii–xiv.
[58] Ibid., pp. x–xi.

and corporate worship. Near the end of his covenant he wrote, 'Heavenly Father, I take thee for my Father—I take Christ for my life—I take the Spirit for my guide—I take thy word for my rule—thy Promises for my encouragement—thy Sabbaths for my delight—thy People for my companions—thy Glory for my end—Holiness for my way—and Heaven for my home.'[59] Not all who took communion could produce such detailed statements of commitment, but it is still important to appreciate that believers took communion seriously and sought to adequately prepare themselves through private prayer and Bible reading.

Both liberal and conservative believers also used works of devotion in preparation for communion. These aids provided information about proper preparation, the nature and symbolism of the sacrament, the qualifications to partake of it, and the dangers of eating and drinking unworthily.[60] Daniel Campbell's *Sacramental meditations* was a best-seller in late seventeenth- and early eighteenth-century Scotland and enjoyed similar success in Ulster where it was advertised for sale as late as 1780.[61] The significant aspect of Campbell's work was its focus upon the person and work of Christ and its emphasis upon 'penitential preparation, not on joyful rebirth'.[62] Robert Craghead of Derry achieved fame as author of *Advice to communicants*, originally published in 1714 in Glasgow and republished in the same city in 1805.[63] Further works on the Lord's Supper by the Puritan writers Thomas Doolittle and Matthew Henry remained steady sellers in Ulster throughout the eighteenth century.[64] The most prominent author was John Willison, whose Christocentric *Sacramental meditations and advices* became the cornerstone of evangelical piety in both Scotland and Ulster during the second half of the eighteenth century.[65] The repeated advertisements and individual editions of

[59] Ibid., p. xiii.
[60] Schmidt, *Holy fairs*, 142.
[61] J. R. R. Adams, *The printed word and the common man: popular culture in Ulster 1700–1900* (Belfast, 1987), 15, 179.
[62] Schmidt, *Holy fairs*, 142–4.
[63] *Advice to communicants for necessary preparation, and profitable improvement of the great and comfortable ordinance of the Lord's Supper* (Glasgow, 1714). The Glasgow edn. of 1805 was published under the same title (Adams, *Printed word and common man*, 45; Schmidt, *Holy fairs*, 46).
[64] Adams, *Printed word and common man*, 44, 189.
[65] Ibid.; Schmidt, *Holy fairs*, 46–7.

these works in Ulster suggest two things about lay Presbyterian piety: the centrality of the cross of Christ and the characterization of the Christian life as one of pilgrimage and penitence, not a preoccupation with a conversion experience. These were key features of Tynan's personal covenant and also of the Presbyterian obituaries and reading material discussed below in Chapters 9 and 10.

In addition to correct preparation, the publication of this type of devotional material aimed to address the spiritual insecurities of intending communicants. The sense of unworthiness experienced by individuals was a common reason for non-attendance and cannot be dismissed lightly as it illustrates the high regard the laity had for the ordinance. Craghead's *Advice to communicants* reflected his own pastoral experience of his congregation, 'some doubting if they should partake, others troubled because they did partake, and some afflicted because they did not partake'.[66] Yet the Christocentric focus of conservative Presbyterian devotions may account for the apparent lack of concern with issues of election and predestination amongst the laity. The fragmentary evidence about how believers thought about their spiritual lives does not allow for broad generalizations though it does suggest that it was the struggle with sin and issues of personal holiness that exercised the consciences of the devout, not election.[67]

Preparation, both corporate and personal, indicates the significance of the Lord's Supper for Ulster Presbyterians. Obviously, not everyone could prepare in either the way they wished, or were required, owing to the pressures of work, the demands of family, and the ability to read or write. Nor were Kirk sessions and ministers uniform in their attitude to the implementation of church discipline or the examination of intending communicants. Nevertheless, the evidence presented demonstrates that Kirk sessions and

[66] Craghead, *Advice to communicants*, 5. For further details about this and other reasons for non-attendance see, 'Antiquity of the frequent observance of the Lord's Supper', *Christian Freeman*, 1 (1833), 311; 'The reformer. No. III. Celebration of the Lord's Supper', *Orthodox Presbyterian*, 2 (1831), 393; Samuel Simpson, 'Second letter to an applicant for admission to the Lord's Table', *Orthodox Presbyterian*, new ser., 2 (1839), 9–13.

[67] A. Holmes, 'Tradition and enlightenment: conversion and assurance of salvation in Ulster Presbyterianism, 1700–1859', in M. Brown, C. I. McGrath, and T. P. Power (eds.), *Converts and conversions in Ireland, 1650–1850* (Dublin, 2005), 140–1.

communicants took seriously proper preparation for communion. The spectacle of the event was sustained by the quiet rhythms of private and corporate devotion, not only in the weeks leading up to communion, but throughout the rest of the year.

II

The communion season, with its various diets of public worship, grew out of seventeenth-century conditions that in turn had been influenced by pre-Reformation practice. The *Directory* stated that a Sabbath's notice should be given before communion was celebrated, but, owing presumably to the infrequency of the event in Ulster, the 1825 revision stipulated four weeks.[68] The season began with the preparation Sabbath when the minister exhorted his congregation to repentance and prayerful preparation. After the faithful had been made formally aware of the sacrament, the next service was the fast day, held on the Thursday of the communion week. As with other ministers, Robert Magill of Antrim examined the new communicants on that day and gave them tokens.[69] Public worship was conducted and usually a neighbouring minister preached a sermon. In Millrow on 10 October 1832, 'Rev. David Hamilton explained Psalm 23 and preached from 1 Peter 2: 7 "To you he is precious"', while, on the same day, Magill disciplined an offender before the session.[70] Once the fast day was over, the final service before the Lord's Supper was a preparation service on the Saturday. Magill's Saturday service in October 1832 again involved visiting preachers, this time the 'Rev. Adam Montgomery preached from Romans 8: 32 Rev. William Wray preached from Romans 5: 18.'[71] These various services were designed to foster an attitude of self-examination and to focus the communicants' minds upon the importance and solemnity of approaching the Lord's Table. In contrast, after the observance of the ordinance on the

---

[68] *Directory*, 384; *Code* (1825), 94.
[69] Diary of the Revd Robert Magill, 28 Sept. 1831 (PHS); Dundrod (GSU) session book, 8 Oct. 1834.
[70] Diary of the Revd Robert Magill, 10 Oct. 1832.
[71] Ibid., 13 Oct. 1832.

Sabbath, the season finished with services of thanksgiving on Monday.[72] The same pattern was repeated in non-subscribing congregations, though, owing to their general wariness about excessive preparation, they probably had fewer services.[73]

Surprisingly perhaps, the number of people who communicated is difficult to determine with any accuracy, as few session books record the total communicants at each sacrament or the number of tokens distributed. While approximate communicant figures were given to visitation presbyteries in the 1830s, there exists no systematic data comparable to that for Sabbath attendance in 1834. It does seem from presbytery reports that all eligible members did not always attend communion, and ministers and Kirk sessions often lamented the neglect of the Lord's Table.[74] Though some Presbyterians did not attend both communion services during the year, in a number of cases the reasons for doing so had as much to do with their high view of the sacrament as with apathy. Anecdotal evidence also distinguishes between those who attended communion services and those actually communicating. For example, Robert Magill preached to over 2,000 people in a tent at Grange in 1823 and to 800 at Newtowncrommelin in 1835. Both congregations were small, according to the 1834 census, and it is impossible that all who heard Magill took communion.[75] Some historians have suggested that attendance was swelled by 'strangers', that is Presbyterians from other areas who would attend and communicate with neighbouring congregations on the basis of a certificate of character from their own minister.[76] While this may have been true for the late seventeenth century, the evidence for the later period is less clear and is complicated by the attempts of the Synod of Ulster to limit the size of communions in the early years of the eighteenth century. There are few surviving transfer certificates and those that do remain usually relate to persons

---

[72] Ibid., 15 Oct. 1832.

[73] See the comments of Henry Montgomery in *Fourth report of the commissioners of Irish education inquiry*, HC (1826–7) xiii. 157, 43.

[74] For example, the Revd Samuel Barber 'An exhortation after the sacrament' (PHS, Barber papers); Ballykelly (GSU) session book, 22 May 1816 (PHS).

[75] Diary of the Revd Robert Magill, 7 Sept. 1823 (PRONI, Young papers, D/2930/9/8) and 29 Mar 1835. A. R. Holmes, 'Ulster Presbyterian belief and practice, 1770–1840' (QUB Ph.D., 2002), 342, 344.

[76] Barkley, 'Lord's Supper', 26–7.

who are permanently moving to another congregation or emigrating overseas.[77] On the other hand, as demonstrated below, communion had an important social function within local communities, attracting those from the surrounding area in search of companionship and alcohol. Also, non-Presbyterian evangelicals were taking communion in the early nineteenth century, suggesting that 'ordinary' Presbyterians could do likewise in neighbouring congregations. Such issues are beyond the nature of the surviving evidence to determine; what is clear is that many people attended the sacrament for other reasons than religious devotion.

The administration of the Lord's Supper on Sunday was the apex of the communion season. For many congregations in the eighteenth century, communion would have often taken place outdoors owing to the numbers attending and the inadequacy of accommodation. For those taking part, the atmosphere was one of solemnity and reverence. Conservative Presbyterians administered communion, they rarely celebrated it, though the non-subscribing minority believed that communion ought to be taken with 'cheerfulness' and 'gladness of heart'.[78] For the Secession laity in particular, attending the Lord's Table was the devotional high point of the year and, consequently, expectations of blessing and emotion were often intense. Responding to censures from Thomas Ledlie Birch, the Revd Thomas Mayne Reid told Thomas Heron at his ordination in 1814 to prepare well for the sacrament, as it was pivotal to the spiritual lives of the laity. Reid was anxious that Heron would 'guard against lukewarmness', but asked him to remember that 'there is, perhaps, no religious exercise in which the devotion of our people tends so strongly to enthusiasm—let there be nothing then, in your address or manner, calculated to encourage it'. Instead, Heron was to direct his best efforts 'against a delusion so fatal to genuine religion; and so diametrically opposed to the design of the sacred institution'.[79] As will be shown, Seceder communion seasons were sometimes scenes of less than godly devotion, and, as such, these admonitions expressed a genuine fear of social

---

[77] Newtownhamilton (AB/Sec.) session book, transfer certificates 1823–34 (MIC/1P/443A/1), 130–52. Roseyards (AB/Sec.) session book, 102–6.

[78] Tosh, 'Irish Presbyterian worship', 180–1; Remonstrant Synod, *Helps to Christian devotion*, 148.

[79] T. M. Reid, 'The charge', in S. Edgar, *The times, a sermon* (Belfast, 1814), 74–5.

and moral disruption that threatened the public testimony of Presbyterianism.

The organization of communion largely followed the pattern laid down in the *Directory*. In adopting this document, the General Assembly of the Church of Scotland did make a number of changes, including the addition of table addresses to be given at each sitting.[80] The form given in the 1825 revision of the *Directory* also differed in some respects from the original, but it does outline how communion was administered in Ulster.[81] The solemnity began with a sermon, the singing of a psalm, usually Psalm 116: 13–14, and a prayer for protection and blessing. The minister would then read and explain the words of institution from First Corinthians or from one of the Gospels. Primarily, the Lord's Table was about defining community. Communion was for the godly, those members of the church who had displayed sufficient knowledge and decency of conduct to receive the elements. A 'solemn warning' not to approach the table, also known as 'fencing the table', was given to the ungodly in case they should demean the ordinance for the godly and place their own souls in eternal jeopardy.[82] James Morell asked before communion in 1811, 'Do your consciences witness against you that hitherto sin hath dominion over you, that you still love its service, and wish to indulge in its forbidden gratifications, then be assured your hearts are not right with God, are not yet the habitations of the spirit and have never yet been sanctified by his grace therefore you cannot without incurring a high degree of guilt partake of this holy ordinance [?]'[83] Once the scandalous and profane had been warned, the minister invited to the table 'such as are sensible of their lost and helpless state by sin, and, depending on the atonement of Christ for pardon and acceptance, are constrained by his love to turn from the evil of their ways, to serve the living God'.[84]

The communicants received the elements from each other whilst seated 'in the aisles, on long forms placed on each side of narrow tables'. In large congregations there 'were often as many as ten tables

---

[80] Barkley, *Westminster formularies*, 54.
[81] *Code* (1825), 95–6.
[82] *Directory*, 384–5.
[83] Nesbitt, *Full circle*, 58.
[84] *Code* (1825), 95.

or ten sets of communicants who succeeded one another'.[85] Communicants left their pews and took their seats at the table where they would visibly identify with other believers by sitting together and handing each other the elements in a show of religious and communal solidarity. A nineteenth-century evangelical believed that when communicants came 'out of our pews from the midst of our companions, and sit down at the sacramental table, we thus distinctly and unequivocally own, before God and men, our desire and determination to devote ourselves, body, soul, and spirit to the service and honour of Him who loved us, and gave himself for us'.[86] The freshly washed white-linen tablecloth visually emphasized that it was a pure table.[87] Before distributing the elements, the minister offered separate prayers asking for God's blessing on the bread and the wine. After the elements had been distributed, the communicants consumed them and when they had finished, the minister or a colleague from a neighbouring congregation gave an address. Once all who wished had communicated, the service was closed with an address, thanksgiving, and prayer.

For a number of writers, communion was a reminder that all believers, irrespective of age, rank, or gender, were equal before God. Thomas McKay declared, 'May we consider ourselves as children of the same great parent; members of the same mystical body, and heirs together of the grace of life.'[88] Similarly, a non-subscriber wrote in 1830 that at the Lord's Table 'all trifling distinctions of sect and party are for the time forgotten; and all ranks of people unite together in one solemn act of harmony and love'.[89] The impression of equality and concern for one another was symbolized at the end of the service by contributing to the poor fund, which had its annual peak at communion times.[90] Whether or not social distinctions were suitably subdued, the symbolism of sharing the same elements, sitting at the

[85] W. Hamilton, *The autobiography of the Rev. William Hamilton of Garvagh, Belfast and North America 1807–1886*, ed. E. Dunlop (Belfast, 1997), 19.

[86] W. B. Kirkpatrick, 'On the best mode of seeking a revival of religion in our churches', *Orthodox Presbyterian*, new ser., 2 (1839), 169.

[87] Schmidt, *Holy fairs*, 82–3.

[88] T. McKay, *Addresses, proper for sacramental occasions* (Belfast, 1786), 8.

[89] 'On the Lord's Supper', *Bible Christian*, 2 (1831), 88.

[90] Barkley, 'Lord's Supper', 29–30.

same table, and worshipping the same God had some social significance for those involved.[91]

For communicants, the bread and the wine symbolized the death of Christ for their sins. A Remonstrant writer acknowledged, 'We have been permitted to see the Redeemer evidently set forth, as crucified before our eyes.'[92] Yet there were profound differences between orthodox Presbyterians and their liberal counterparts regarding the meaning of Christ's death and how Christ was present in the elements. From the late eighteenth century onwards, the majority of non-subscribers, whether New Light or Arian, adopted a moral view of the atonement, that is, they saw the Crucifixion as the supreme example of God's love and Christ's obedience.[93] In general, theologically liberal Presbyterians maintained that Christ's death was exemplary and achieved nothing for the salvation of mankind in itself. The cross demonstrated God's love and led individuals to respond by offering their lives to God in repentance and obedience. Conservative Presbyterians asserted that Christ's death on the cross achieved something tangible, that Christ offered 'up of himself a sacrifice to satisfy divine justice, and reconcile us to God', in accordance with the eternal decrees of God.[94] In writing against the views of the Arian, John Taylor, Samuel Delap argued that the atonement of Christ was propitiatory and substitutionary, consisting of the 'expiation of sin, satisfaction of justice, appeasing of wrath, and reconciliation between God and sinners'.[95] This penal or substitutionary theory of the atonement was central to Reformed theology and to evangelicalism as it came to prominence in the late eighteenth and early nineteenth centuries.[96] Only a fully divine Christ could pay the price for humanity's sin, which explains why Cooke and his supporters were so concerned about the doctrine of the Trinity in the 1820s. A holy life was not the condition of grace but a necessary

---

[91] Schmidt, *Holy fairs*, 99–105.

[92] Remonstrant Synod, *Helps to Christian devotion*, 96.

[93] For example, W. Taggart, *Sermons* (Strabane, 1788), 142–64; A. G. Malcolm, *The communicant's catechism* (Newry, 1812), 15; Crawford, 'Nineteenth-century non-subscribing Presbyterian theology', ii. 514–32.

[94] *Shorter catechism*, Q. 25.

[95] S. Delap, *A dissertation on the important subject of atonement* (Dublin, 1758), 12.

[96] D. W. Bebbington, *Evangelicalism in modern Britain: a history from the 1730s to the 1980s*, rev. edn. (London, 1995), 15–16.

response to it, hence the importance of church discipline in assessing the conduct of potential communicants.

The other major difference between conservative and liberal Presbyterians concerned the presence of Christ in the elements. Following Calvin, conservative Presbyterians held that Christ was spiritually present to those who were of the elect and present in his humanity in heaven to which they were united. The substance of the bread and wine did not change, but 'worthy receivers are, not after a corporal and carnal manner, but by faith, made partakers of his body and blood, with all his benefits, to their spiritual nourishment, and growth in grace'.[97] Reflecting the influence of rationalism, non-subscribers held that the bread and wine were merely symbols or representations of Christ's body and blood upon which the believer was to meditate. S. M. Stephenson dismissed the view that Christ's flesh and blood could be 'spiritually present while it is corporally absent' as 'an absurdity too great for any protestant ... to believe'.[98] For non-subscribers, the elements remained symbolic and powerful motives to moral change; for conservatives, they spiritually conferred the grace of God through Christ to those who partook of them by faith.

These differing understandings of the Lord's Supper and what it symbolized were repeated in the sermons and addresses of Presbyterian ministers. Apart from taking the elements, the central aspect of the service was the preaching of the word and the *Directory* placed the administration of communion immediately after a sermon.[99] There were at least two sermons on each day of preparation before communion. On the sacrament Sabbath, a further two sermons were preached, in addition to various exhortations and table addresses. Robert Magill, a verbose preacher at the best of times, spoke for no less than two-and-a-quarter hours on the words of the institution at Ballycairn; in fact, so long that candles had to be lit in order to serve the last table.[100] At a sacrament in his Armagh charge in 1830,

---

[97] *Shorter Catechism*, Q. 96.
[98] S. M. Stephenson, *The declaration of faith approved by the reverend Presbytery of Bangor* (Belfast, 1774), 7. J. Mears, *A short explanation of the end and design of the Lord's Supper* (Dublin, 1758), 5–7; Remonstrant Synod, *Helps to Christian devotion*, 95, 155–60.
[99] *Directory*, 384; *Code* (1825), 95.
[100] Diary of the Revd Robert Magill, 6 Nov. 1831.

P. S. Henry, later appointed first president of Queen's College, Belfast, spoke at the first table on the honour of taking communion. The Revd Beattie took the second and 'dwelt much upon the love of Christ to man', before proceeding to address the third table. Henry returned and read Colossians chapter 1 and recommended the congregation to study the passage further by themselves at home.[101] There are few remaining non-subscribing communion sermons, though it is reasonably certain that liberals preached the moral nature of the atonement and exhorted communicants to live a renewed life of obedience to God and love to others.

Orthodox sermons tended to follow the motifs outlined earlier. Josias Wilson preached the first communion sermon to the small Seceder congregation of Drogheda in 1823. The discourse he delivered was organized around four themes that helpfully indicate the main preoccupations of orthodox communion sermons. The ordinance was a memorial of the sinfulness of humanity, the redemption accomplished by Christ, the fruits of his death conferred on sinners, and the promise of fellowship with Christ and the saints in heaven.[102] The last theme indicates the eschatological dimension of the Lord's Supper. Communion not only pointed to Christ's death but also his resurrection and the hope of heaven this entailed for true believers.[103] In the immediate context, however, communicants could be assured that they were receiving God's grace, by faith, through the elements. William Dickey declared to his congregation of Seceders at Carnone in July 1810, 'When we eat bread and drink wine in the Kingdom of God, let us feed by faith on Jesus Christ our passover—the true and living bread, which came down from heaven. Let us drink the wine here in full assurance of drinking it new in the kingdom of glory.'[104] For orthodox Presbyterians, salvation history, from the eternal decrees of God to the Second Coming, was recounted around the Lord's table.

The laity undoubtedly understood these different understandings of the Lord's Supper as they were catechized in their respective

---

[101] Diary of Matthew Bell, 14 Nov. 1830 (PRONI, D/1877/1).
[102] J. Wilson, *The death of Christ commemorated* (Dublin, 1823).
[103] Schmidt, *Holy fairs*, 166–8.
[104] W. Dickey, *Sermons* (Strabane, 1819), 36.

doctrines, repeatedly preached to on the same themes, and meditated upon them individually in their personal devotions. This raises the important issue of communion in those Synod of Ulster congregations that had a mixture of conservative and liberal members. Theoretically, the lack of adherence to orthodox doctrines should have meant that liberals were excluded from communion in those congregations with orthodox ministers. Surprisingly perhaps, there is little evidence of anyone being prevented from taking communion because of erroneous belief, which may in part be because the language used by both sides was so similar. A prime example of this is the 1825 revision of the *Directory* that was prepared and approved by both New and Old Light ministers in the Synod of Ulster. The invitation to the table, as noted earlier, was extended to all who were 'sensible of their lost and helpless state by sin, and, depending on the atonement of Christ for pardon and acceptance, are constrained by his love to turn from the evil of their ways, to serve the living God'.[105] It is clear that both moral and penal views of the atonement could be read into this statement. Furthermore, as examination tended to be based on assent to propositions rather than a statement of personal belief (or conversion) it is feasible that many gave assent to doctrinal statements that they conceived of in different ways to the minister. The reminiscences of John Caldwell, a non-subscriber from Ballymoney, concerning the ministry of Alexander Marshall in the late eighteenth century, offers an interesting line of investigation. Commenting upon the good relations between Old and New Light members, he recalled that each group 'would apply to the deacons [elders] of their own choice and partake at the table where their favourite minister officiated in distributing the elements'. This arrangement was 'tacitly understood but not commented upon'. [106] In other words, New Light members applied to New Light elders for admission and took the elements from New Light ministers. Old Light communicants did the same. Caldwell states that this situation soon disappeared with the renewed belligerence of the orthodox party in the 1820s. There is no way of knowing how widespread

---

[105] *Code* (1825), 95.
[106] J. Caldwell, 'Particulars of history of a north county Irish family' (PRONI, Caldwell papers, T/3541/5/3), 80–1.

this practice was, but it is certainly suggestive of the relatively tranquil coexistence between subscribers and non-subscribers in the late eighteenth century.

Though communion was an indispensable part of Presbyterian religiosity, the communion season, as with the Sabbath, did not serve religious needs alone. It was a time of sociability, particularly, though not exclusively, amongst Seceders. The appearance at communion time of stalls selling alcohol was inevitable given the prevalence of such activities at weekly public worship. The scene described by Henry Montgomery in 1847 of the communion held by the Seceders at Lylehill in the late eighteenth century is somewhat embellished but does give an indication of what occurred. 'At Mr Patton's summer sacrament, several thousands usually congregated: the meeting-house was choked up; two ministers were preaching at opposite corners of the green; tents, for all kinds of refreshments, were erected on the sides of the neighbouring highway; and drunkenness and folly profaned the day of rest. Crowds of dissolute or thoughtless persons came from Belfast; and, over a wide circuit of country, "Lyle Fair", was considered a favourite place of amusement.'[107] Presumably as a direct result of this behaviour, Isaac Patton, the minister of Lylehill, refused to administer the sacrament for two years in the late eighteenth century.[108]

In 1796 Thomas Ledlie Birch published an embittered pamphlet against the Seceders after one of their preachers had disturbed his own congregation of Saintfield. Birch saved much of his vitriol for the Seceder communion season, which he characterized as a 'noisy, drunken, idolatrous feast'.[109] According to him, the appearance of large crowds, open air preaching, and stalls selling alcohol, lowered the moral tone of the neighbourhood, encouraged sin, and increased religious discord. The godly indulged in drunken behaviour while the minister preached against intemperance and even the psalm singing was lost in 'the buzz, the murmurs, and laughter of an idle crowd'. With some justification, he argued that the particular

[107] H. Montgomery, 'Outlines of the history of Presbyterianism in Ireland', *Irish Unitarian Magazine, and Bible Christian*, 2 (1847), 231.

[108] D. Stewart, *The Seceders in Ireland with annals of their congregations* (Belfast, 1950), 254–5.

[109] T. L. Birch, *Physicians languishing under disease*, 8th edn. (Belfast, 1796), 33–9.

circumstances of the seventeenth century no longer existed to justify the outdoor celebration of communion. In fairness, there was no meeting-house for the Seceders in that area which meant that they had to meet outdoors, a circumstance repeated in many other areas. Nevertheless, the practical effects of the season were almost apocalyptic in proportions according to Birch:

Hence the profanation of the Lord's day;—the exposing of religion to the scoffs of its enemies;—and encouragement to formality;—a temptation to clandestine marriages;—an inlet to whoredom and bastardy;—an opportunity for the formation of evil plots;—the sowing the seeds of rancour, hatred, breaking out into quarrels, (and those of the worst sort, religious ones) to be decided in neighbouring fairs;—finally, gendering in weak enthusiastic minds, breaking a day's work, defenderism, with a train of consequences, which the reader may easily suggest to himself, to the total depravation of the morals of the people![110]

These political, social, economic, and religious criticisms provided the rationale for the termination of such occasions and echo perfectly those reasons given for the decline of the 'holy fair' in Scotland. Schmidt has argued that by the 1850s the end was assured for these remarkable expressions of popular piety in Scotland and America as the 'sacramental season … yielded to a bourgeois or Victorian Christianity that was more privatised and domesticated, more dignified and decorous than the faith it replaced'.[111] Communions became more frequent, disciplined, sober, and individualistic as Presbyterians adapted their beliefs and practices to a new economic dispensation of thrift and industry that was both a product of, and influence upon, evangelicalism.

III

During the 1820s and 1830s only piecemeal efforts were made to change the traditional patterns and procedures of the Presbyterian

---

[110] Ibid., 38.
[111] Schmidt, *Holy fairs*, 205.

communion season itself. What did change was the religious character of communion through the renewal of church discipline and a more noticeable concern with encouraging individuals to enter into a personal relationship with Christ. The proclamation of large outdoor assemblies before the 1798 rebellion, the temperance movement, the building of more meeting-houses in the 1830s, and deteriorating economic conditions may account for the almost total lack of reference by early nineteenth-century writers to the excesses of the eighteenth-century communion season. The scale of the season was certainly questioned by some ministers, and some congregations did reduce the number of services.[112] Urban congregations took the lead in the reform of communion practice. In 1834 the Kirk session of Third Belfast began a consultation regarding the 'best mode of purifying the admission to the Communion'.[113] Though they reached no immediate conclusion, Samuel Hanna was to intimate their intentions to the congregation on the following Sabbath. The following year elders were asked to make out a list of all communicants in their districts so that an accurate roll could be compiled for the whole congregation. In September 1836 they devised a new means of publicly distributing card tokens in the vestibule on Thursdays and Saturdays and in December 1840 they moved the Saturday service to noon and the Monday morning service to the evening. Both Third Belfast and Ballymoney congregations appointed elders to collect tokens and wait on the tables.[114] One of the most common suggestions was to increase the frequency of communion in order to control popular practice and to return to the ideals of Calvin.[115] Frequent communion initially became widespread in urban congregations and may indicate a desire to regulate the urban laity who were much less under the cognizance of discipline than in rural areas. There is evidence of quarterly communion from the 1820s in Synod of Ulster congregations such as Fisherwick Place, Belfast, Downpatrick, and

---

[112] J. Wilson, *A charge and defence of Presbyterianism* (Drogheda, 1829), 31; J. S. Reid, *The history of the Presbyterian Church in Ireland, briefly reviewed and practically improved* (Belfast, 1828), 18–19.

[113] The following is based on the extracts given in Barkley, 'Eldership', ii. 208–15.

[114] Barkley, *Short history*, 86.

[115] 'Antiquity of the frequent observance of the Lord's Supper', *Christian Freeman*, 1 (1833), 271–7, 305–12; Schmidt, *Holy fairs*, 187–8, 192.

Newry.[116] However, holding quarterly communions could have a negative impact upon the numbers attending any one service. When Portadown changed to four communions in 1837 the number of communicants fell from around fifty to only eighteen.[117] In the longer term, it is clear that any desire for more frequent communion was unrealistic. Figures collected in 1979 showed that in the Presbytery of East Belfast quarterly observance was widespread, whereas in the rural Presbytery of Route communion was held twice a year and united communion between congregations was common.[118]

The reassertion of discipline by Presbyterian evangelicals had a significant impact upon the character of communion. This is an important point as historians of Scottish Presbyterianism have cited evangelical individualism as a key reason for the collapse of discipline by the 1780s.[119] It is obvious that this argument defines evangelicalism in narrowly individualistic terms and does scant justice to the importance Presbyterian evangelicals attached to community, the safeguarding of public morality, and the form of church government laid down in their doctrinal standards. Both the Synod of Ulster and the Secession Synod in the 1830s attempted to exclude the unworthy from the Lord's Table and to increase church discipline across the board. The adherence of conservative Presbyterians to a pure communion table meant that their congregations tended to be more committed to discipline and for longer, even in Belfast.[120] Evidence for the reassertion of discipline during the 1830s is very common. A special visitation committee empowered by the Synod of Ulster to examine congregations in west Ulster recommended in 1834 a 'more rigorous maintenance of discipline'.[121] The following year they reported that they 'have reason to believe that an increased attention to the duties of religion and the discipline of the church

---

[116] J. Morgan, *Recollections of my life and times* (Belfast, 1874), 82; Down Pby (GSU), 2 Oct. 1838 (Church House, strong room); W. G. Strahan, *First Newry (Sandys Street) Presbyterian congregation: its history and relationships* (Newry, 1904), 38.

[117] Armagh Pby (GSU), 7 Feb. 1837 (Church House, strong room).

[118] Tosh, 'Irish Presbyterian worship', 187–8.

[119] Mitchison and Leneman, *Sexuality and social control*, 72.

[120] Alfred Street (B/Sec.) session book, 1824–76 (PRONI, MIC/1P/14/1); Linenhall Street (RP) session book, 1833–62 (PRONI, CR/5/4A/2).

[121] *RGSU* (1834), 22–3, 27–9.

has been excited among them'.[122] Elsewhere, the Kirk session of Portstewart congregation rebuked seventy-seven individuals for fornication between 1829, the year of its foundation, and 1863.[123] The reform agenda also had an impact upon the type of sentence passed in some congregations. In April 1838 the Kirk session of Creggan, County Armagh, agreed to rebuke publicly all those found guilty of cases that came before them from public report 'as in former periods of our church'. The session believed that a rebuke in session was encouraging individuals to relapse into former habits thus injuring the cause of religion.[124]

The more frequent references in presbytery minutes to individuals who refused to submit to discipline and left the congregation as a result suggests that the reassertion of discipline in the 1820s and 1830s was exercised upon a population who had not experienced such regulation before. The Synod of Ulster acknowledged as much in 1833 when it observed that public opinion was often against the exercise of discipline.[125] The minister of Macosquin congregation reported to the Presbytery of Coleraine that in 'several cases, persons do not submit, but go off to other societies, where the discipline is less strict, or where there is no discipline at all—but, generally speaking, they are submissive'.[126] In other cases, ministers and Kirk sessions acted more carefully while advocating higher standards of discipline. The minister of Dunluce reported to the Presbytery of Route in 1831 that his congregation 'will bend to *moderate* discipline, not otherwise'.[127] Likewise, the Presbyterians of Whiteabbey congregation were submissive to discipline 'as far as it is made to bear upon them'.[128]

Public opinion against certain moral failings was also strengthened in the 1830s and 1840s. Though sexual offences continued to dominate the business of church courts, the temperance movement

[122] *RGSU* (1835), 49.
[123] Portstewart (GSU) session book, 1826–77 (PRONI, MIC/1P/83/1).
[124] Creggan (GSU) session book, 29 July 1838 (Barkley, 'Eldership', ii. 297).
[125] *Annual address of the General Synod of Ulster* (Belfast, 1833), 10.
[126] Coleraine Pby (GSU), 28 July 1840 (Church House, strong room). Also, ibid., 25 July 1837; Route Pby (GSU), 28 July 1828 (PHS), 245.
[127] Route Pby (GSU), 10 May 1831, 295.
[128] Belfast Pby (GSU), 1 May 1838 (Church House, strong room).

created a godly public opinion against drunkenness and led to an increase in the number of cases for intemperance brought against ministers and the laity.[129] One of the reasons why this and other movements for social and moral reform made such remarkable progress in Ulster was because it articulated the views of large sections of the working and middle classes who were striving for respectability through sobriety, chastity, and hard work. In doing so, they created precisely the public opinion that would enable discipline in these areas to continue to function. It may be legitimately suggested that the quantitative decline in the number of cases tried over the nineteenth century was in part an outcome of the success of discipline in inculcating the moral and religious standards of both the church and the dominant social groups.[130] Indeed, some ministers reported that they prosecuted few cases of discipline because their church members were well behaved.[131]

Despite notable successes, discipline worked best and for longest in cohesive rural communities that were able to withstand the disruption associated with modern society. In the long term, social and economic change made it almost impossible to uphold discipline amongst a population that increasingly prized individual privacy. Particularly in urban areas from the 1820s onwards, evangelicals realized that inculcating correct behaviour would be better achieved through town missions, Sunday schools, tract distribution, and visitation work. Even the impeccably evangelical congregations of Third Belfast and May Street record no discipline cases for our period. In the countryside, discipline would be increasingly placed within the context of pastoral visitation and not appearance before the Kirk session. More generally, the Reformed understanding of church discipline gradually drifted toward a therapeutic approach to pastoral care in the second half of the nineteenth century that saw sin in social rather than religious terms.[132]

[129] 'Religious revivals', *Christian Freeman*, 1 (1833), 116; Alfred Street (B/Sec.) session book, 1824–76; Linenhall Street (RP) session book, 1833–62; Stewart, *Seceders*, 216–20.

[130] C. D. Cashdollar, *A spiritual home: life in British and American Reformed congregations, 1830–1915* (University Park, Pa., 2000), 139, 148.

[131] For example, Down Pby (Sec.) 14 Aug. 1832, 196–7, 5 Feb. 1833, 204; Letterkenny Pby (GSU), 9 Oct. 1833 (Church House, strong room), 129; Tyrone Pby (GSU), 20 June 1837 (Church House, strong room), 62; *OSMI* (Magherafelt), vi. 98–9.

[132] Cashdollar, *Spiritual Home*, 138–50.

Though the long-term trajectory is clear, the reassertion of discipline in the 1830s and 1840s had an explicit aim by contributing to the growing concern with stimulating a more widespread revival of religion. The 1833 pastoral address of the Synod of Ulster pointed out that the admission of notorious offenders to the Lord's Table had devalued the sacrament, making it no longer 'a privilege peculiar to the true members of the church of Jesus Christ'.[133] The address continued, 'A revival of pure discipline is one of the most important means of revival, and at the same time a most excellent feature of a true revival of religion. Let the children of God earnestly and vigorously set themselves to co-operate with us in raising our church to a holy elevation of discipline.'[134] Seceders also insisted on a link between a pure table and religious revival. John Edgar maintained, 'If we would see religious revivals prospering among us, we must exercise church discipline with more decision and honesty, sparing neither rich nor poor, if they are bringing dishonour on the name of Christ.'[135] Both examples are symptomatic of a general drift within Presbyterianism towards an all-consuming emphasis upon promoting revival. It is ironic that this discussion was linked to the Lord's Supper when in Scotland and America a similar, but by no means identical, connection was becoming less respectable.

The religious character of communion in the nineteenth century was also encouraged by the obvious concern of Presbyterian evangelicals to encourage individuals to come to faith in Christ. After he had seceded from the Synod of Ulster in 1804, the Baptist Alexander Carson wrote that though some congregations had strict admittance procedures, 'in none of them, I believe, is *credible evidence of the new birth* the test of membership'.[136] However, there is evidence that may be interpreted to suggest that, in admitting persons to communion, some ministers accepted evidence of a personal conversion rather than traditional Presbyterian qualifications. One of the reasons why the Burgher Synod in 1801 censured the involvement of some of their members in the Evangelical Society of Ulster was that they would 'not

---

[133] *Annual address of the General Synod of Ulster* (Belfast, 1833), 10.
[134] Ibid., 11.
[135] 'Religious revivals', *Christian Freeman*, 1 (1833), 116.
[136] A. Carson, *Reasons for separating from the General Synod of Ulster* (Belfast, 1805), 93–4.

countenance promiscuous communion, in the ordinance of the Lord's Supper'.[137] The evangelical minister of Ballybay, James Morell, allowed a female Methodist itinerant, Alice Cambridge, to take communion with his congregation in 1815.[138] It seems that personal commitment to Christ and a common evangelical ethos allowed members of different denominations to communicate together when appropriate. Certainly in the nineteenth century, a personal relationship with Christ became a more noticeable priority in Ulster Presbyterianism and there were reports from congregations that communion times were producing conversions.[139] Given the link between communion seasons and revivals, it is significant that some ministers observed that converts in 1859 first had their religious feelings stirred at communions in previous decades.[140]

A number of points need to be made. First, it is unlikely that individuals were allowed to take communion because of the experience of personal conversion and assurance of salvation as opposed to practical evidence of commitment to Christ and a belief in the fundamental doctrines of the gospel. Covenanters expressed their opposition to the view that the consciousness of conversion and the knowledge of a specific time when it occurred were needed for salvation, though they admitted that a public profession of faith was essential for taking communion.[141] Samuel Simpson, minister of Usher's Quay Synod of Ulster congregation in Dublin, also maintained that full assurance of salvation was not needed in order to take communion. 'He is warranted to partake of this ordinance who feels his need of the Saviour, who renounces every dependence except the Saviour, and anxiously desires that the Saviour may reign in the affections of his heart, and by his grace secure the obedience of his life.'[142] However, it would seem that if an Arminian Methodist was receiving the elements, then adherence to Reformed doctrine was not essential for taking communion in Ballybay congregation.

---

[137] MASB (1801), 132.

[138] Nesbitt, *Full circle*, 55–6.

[139] W. Magill, 'The Rev. James Hunter, Coleraine', in T. Hamilton (ed.), *Irish worthies; a series of original biographical sketches of eminent ministers and members of the Presbyterian Church in Ireland* (Belfast, 1875), 78; Morgan, *Recollections*, 82–3.

[140] J. H. Moore, *In memoriam. The Rev. Robert Park, A.M., Ballymoney. Born 15 April 1794. Ordained 18 March 1817. Died 10 May 1876* (Belfast, 1876), 24–5.

[141] 'A religious profession. No. IV', *Covenanter*, 2 (1831), 14–26.

[142] Samuel Simpson, 'Second letter', *Orthodox Presbyterian*, new ser., 2 (1839), 11.

Second, a personal relationship with Christ may have been the hallmark of evangelicalism in the nineteenth century but it was also central to the theology and experiences of Old Light believers and Seceders in the previous century.[143] Eighteenth-century Ulster Presbyterians and Scottish evangelicals conceived of the Christian life as a pilgrimage that began at conversion, the human response to regeneration by the Holy Spirit, but did not consist of that experience alone. Furthermore, the Seceders thought of faith as an active and affectionate commitment to Christ and not merely an intellectual assent to a body of doctrine. David McKee, Secession minister of Anaghlone, distinguished between three types of conversion: 'the violent and the obvious'; 'the ordinary and gradual'; 'the creative and the occult', that is, by the work of the Holy Spirit.[144] He argued that the last two were the norm whereas the first ought to be treated with caution, as it was associated with Methodism. For McKee and Seceders in general, church discipline should continue to focus upon doctrinal knowledge, faith in Christ, and godly conduct as the criteria for admission to communion and not on a stereotypical conversion 'experience'.

This understanding of conversion leads naturally to a third point, namely, the Presbyterian understanding of the church. Presbyterianism, like Anglicanism, is not a gathered church of individuals who demonstrate a conversion experience as proof of membership. For Presbyterians, the church was divided between a visible earthly church and the true invisible church of the elect chosen by God for salvation.[145] Consequently, church membership was through baptism and was confirmed by the individual's personal recognition of his or her baptismal covenant when taking communion. It was impossible for human authorities to determine the secret state of a communicant's soul. Thomas Clark maintained that he was a Presbyterian and not an Independent because he admitted persons to communion with good knowledge and conduct although they could not 'directly give positive signs or marks of their being converted'.[146]

---

[143] Holmes, 'Tradition and enlightenment', 132–41.
[144] D. McKee, *Some remarks on conversion* (Belfast, 1836), 9–16.
[145] *Confession*, ch. 25; *Larger Catechism*, Q. 61–9.
[146] Clark, *A brief survey*, 32–3.

Similarly, James Morgan argued that ministers ought to be satisfied that potential communicants had a scriptural faith and a consistent life, 'Beyond this they have no right to go ... Let them not attempt to judge the heart, not to make their knowledge of regeneration a term of communion; but let them deal faithfully respecting the outward evidences of a renewed heart, even an enlightened mind and an upright life.'[147] Presbyterian congregations were not gathered churches of believers who gave personal testimonies of a conversion experience. The continued concern of ministers with correct doctrine and conduct should act as a corrective to any view of Presbyterianism before 1859 that emphasizes the importance of personal conversion over traditional understandings of faith and church membership.

Communion seasons were central to the religious and social identity of Presbyterian communities in Ulster. As with all areas of public devotion, sacred and secular elements were combined in various ways, and though the drunkenness of 'Lyle Fair' may be a blot on the record of all Presbyterians, the evident piety and devotion of the godly is obvious. During the nineteenth century, the religious character of the communion season became paramount through the renewal of church discipline, the promotion of religious revival, and the attempts to encourage individuals to enter into a personal relationship with Christ. A change in tone was obvious, yet the influence of tradition, in both senses of the word, remained in force. The place of communion in church life, its infrequent observance, and the importance of personal and communal preparations remained. Presbyterian evangelicals may have more openly urged individuals to come to Christ in faith, but this did not entail the jettisoning of the Presbyterian understanding of church membership. The ignorant and scandalous would continue to be excluded and a personal conversion experience would not become a prerequisite for coming to the Lord's Table.

---

[147] J. Morgan, *The foundation, character, and security of the Christian Church* (Belfast, 1832), 19–20. Samuel Simpson, 'Second letter', *Orthodox Presbyterian*, new ser., 2 (1839); [J. Barnett and J. Denham], *A catechism on the government and discipline of the Presbyterian Church* (Belfast, 1835), 8.

Part III

Rites of Passage

The provision of religious ceremonies for births, marriages, and deaths constitutes one of the primary services offered by churches to individuals of varying degrees of religious commitment. Studies of nineteenth-century religious practice see these rites as one of the churches' greatest assets in a period of profound change.[1] These 'rites of passage' are also interpreted by early-modern historians as encapsulating salient differences in society based upon gender and social status, and between the clergy and the laity. Against the views of an older generation of scholars who characterize Protestantism, especially in its Puritan guise, as anti-ritualistic, these scholars also stress that rituals and ritualistic patterns of speech and action existed at the heart of both official and unofficial Protestant beliefs. David Cressy suggests that the 'major episodes of birth, marriage, and death, ... were intensely scripted, marked by customary social performance as well as the regulated routines of religious liturgy'.[2] The interaction between the official standards of the church and the customary beliefs and practices of the laity that this implies forms the basic theme of the following section. A study of these rites of passage in an eighteenth- and nineteenth-century Irish context also highlights new emphases and concepts arising out of the cultural and religious

---

[1] F. Knight, *The nineteenth-century church and English society* (Cambridge, 1995), 86–105; H. McLeod, *Secularisation in western Europe, 1848–1914* (Basingstoke, 2000), 249–51.

[2] D. Cressy, *Birth, marriage, and death: ritual, religion, and the life-cycle in Tudor and Stuart England* (Oxford, 1997), 1. More generally, E. Muir, *Ritual in early modern Europe* (Cambridge, 1997).

changes of the period. As regards death and dying, for instance, seventeenth-century theology and religious practices were revived but developed in new ways by those influenced by evangelicalism and Romanticism. As we attempt to understand Presbyterian attitudes to these important transitional phases in the lives of individuals and communities, another central theme will be the significance of communal customs and church discipline, the latter regulating access to both the ordinances of the church and the life of the community more generally. Furthermore, rites of passage and their theological content were areas of dispute between ministers and their congregations. The practice of these rites also highlights differences of theological opinion between Presbyterians and between Presbyterians and other Christian communities in Ulster. Rites of passage and the way they were administered ultimately embodied the distinctiveness of the Presbyterian community.

The following section is divided into three chapters. Chapter 7 examines the theological understanding, administration, and development of baptism in Ulster Presbyterianism, as well as highlighting popular attitudes and attempts to reform perceived abuses. Chapter 8 looks at marriage and sexual relationships, particularly as they impinged upon relations with the Established Church of Ireland, the exercise of Kirk session discipline, and customary activity in the local community. Chapter 9 examines the place of death within Presbyterianism and the ways in which local communities and individuals tried to deal with the reality of death through wakes and patterned ways of dying well.

7

Baptism

Baptism was the second of only two sacraments recognized by Presbyterians. Their understanding of this sacrament was inseparable from their understanding of the church and the covenant relationship between the community of believers and God. The individual was baptized in the name of the Father, and of the Son, and of the Holy Spirit, 'to be a sign and seal of ingrafting into himself [Christ], of remission of sins by his blood, and regeneration by his Spirit; of adoption, and resurrection unto everlasting life'. The parties baptized were thus admitted into the visible church and engaged 'to be wholly and only the Lord's'.[1] The rite was to be administered only to those who had professed faith in, and obedience to, Christ and who had thus entered the covenant of promise. Furthermore, the children of such believing parents, or parent if only one of them was a self-confessed believer, were also to be baptized into the visible church on the basis of the promises of the covenant. The rite itself did not effect salvation in the one to whom it was administered and nor, obviously, did it depend upon the profession of faith by the infant. The efficacy of the sacrament depended wholly upon the will and grace of God. It was God alone who saved and grace was not only offered 'but really exhibited and conferred by the Holy Ghost, to such (whether of age or infants) as the grace belongeth unto, according to the counsel of God's own will, in his appointed time'.[2] The Presbyterian understanding of baptism sought to challenge both the doctrines of

---

[1] *Larger Catechism*, Q. 165; *Confession*, ch. 28. For an outline of the theory and practice of baptism in Irish Presbyterianism see J. M. Barkley, *The Westminster formularies in Irish Presbyterianism* (Belfast, 1956), ch. 4.

[2] *Confession*, 28: 6.

baptismal regeneration (the view that the act of baptism was itself the
means of the spiritual regeneration of the individual) and believers'
baptism (that the rite was restricted to those who made a profession
of faith and usually involved full immersion).

To the believer, baptism was a sign and seal of Christ and his
benefits. It also provided both comfort and a motive for repentance
and change during a believer's lifetime, and the previous chapter has
shown how individuals renewed their baptismal covenants at communion.[3] Baptism was to be administered by a minister in public
before the congregation, usually after public worship. The *Directory*
stated that the father should present the child for baptism and if he
could not do so a suitable sponsor was to be found.[4] Once notice had
been given that the parents wanted their child baptized, the infant
was presented by the father before the congregation for the ordinance
to be administered. The minister spoke the words of institution and
admonished those present to remember their own baptismal covenant and repent of their sins. He would then exhort the parent to bring
up the child in the knowledge of the doctrines of Christianity and 'in
the nurture and admonition of the Lord', warning him of the dire consequences of not doing so. The minister then said a prayer sanctifying
the water and proceeded to administer the sacrament by sprinkling
the child in the name of the Trinity. The service was concluded with
a prayer of thanksgiving and blessing for the child.

The non-subscribing understanding of baptism was, in many
respects, similar to the orthodox position.[5] A. G. Malcolm of Newry
stated that baptism was 'a religious rite ... in token of our becoming
disciples of Christ, members of his church, and obliged to obey his
laws'.[6] Non-subscribing writers agreed that baptism was a sign of the
new covenant, that children of believers should have the sacrament
administered to them, and that each baptized person should
reflect upon the meaning of their baptism throughout their lives.

---

[3] *Larger Catechism*, Q. 167.

[4] *Directory*, 382–4.

[5] 'Origin and nature of baptism', 'Nature of baptism', and 'Baptism', *Bible Christian*, new ser., 2 (1837), 153–5, 185–90, 278–81; R. G. Crawford, 'A critical examination of nineteenth-century non-subscribing Presbyterian theology in Ireland', 2 vols.
(QUB Ph.D., 1964), ii. 307–9.

[6] A. G. Malcolm, *The communicant's catechism* (Newry, 1812), 12.

Yet theological differences existed between them and orthodox writers over issues such as the basis of salvation and the Trinitarian nature of the sacrament. As noted in the previous chapter, non-subscribers did not hold a penal view of the atonement, and so Malcolm saw water as symbolic of purity and holiness, but did not relate it to the atoning blood of Christ. Furthermore, salvation in non-subscribing theology depended upon human effort as well as upon God's grace. In addition, Old Light Presbyterians such as Sinclare Kelburn saw the Trinitarian rubric in the service as direct evidence of Christ's divinity whereas nineteenth-century non-subscribers focused upon the different roles appointed to Father, Son, and Holy Spirit, not their unity or equality.[7]

As with other aspects of religious practice, the administration of baptism in Ulster Presbyterianism developed in ways not envisaged by the Westminster standards. The practice of private baptism, often in the parental home, became almost universal in the Synod of Ulster during the period under consideration and was given sanction by the 1825 revision of the *Directory*.[8] It is significant that the revision was composed with the aid of non-subscribers who in the 1830s allowed private baptism while orthodox Presbyterians were advocating a return to public administration.[9] The tensions between orthodox and liberal views were also highlighted by the fact that Seceders insisted upon the public baptism of infants in the late eighteenth century.[10] Another area of development was the role of sponsors other than the parent; a role that became almost obsolete and resorted to only in cases of absolute necessity. In this regard, Ulster practice followed a similar development in Scotland where, by an act of the General Assembly in 1712, both parents were allowed to present their child for baptism, a stipulation repeated in the *Code*.[11] It is significant that in this area as well, some Seceders seem to have

---

[7] S. Kelburn, *The divinity of our Lord Jesus Christ asserted and proved* (Belfast, 1792), 81; Malcolm, *Communicant's catechism*, 13; Crawford, 'Nineteenth-century non-subscribing Presbyterian theology', ii. 308.

[8] *Code* (1825), 93.

[9] 'Private baptism and private communion', *Bible Christian*, 4 (1833), 449–50.

[10] For example, Down Pby (B/Sec.), 16 Feb. 1796 (PHS).

[11] *Code* (1825), 93; H. Sefton, 'Revolution to Disruption', in D. Forrester and D. Murray (eds.), *Studies in the history of worship in Scotland* (Edinburgh, 1984), 71.

retained the father's special role into the nineteenth century.[12] Presbyterians were united, however, in their opposition to the regulations of the *Book of Common Prayer* in which godparents were asked to make vows on behalf of the children they were presenting.[13] Finally, it is important to be aware that a number of ministers seceded from the General and Secession Synods and became Independents in the early nineteenth century. The most notable was Alexander Carson who became convinced that neither Presbyterianism nor infant baptism truly reflected the organization and practice of the New Testament church.[14]

According to the Westminster standards, at least one of the parents had to be a believer in order for a child to be baptized. From the evidence of Ulster session books, it is also clear that parents had to be free from church censure, though in the eighteenth century baptismal discipline was more common in Seceder congregations.[15] Beyond the issue of discipline, the laity indulged in a number of practices that were not taught by the standards of the church, including private baptism and the baptism of illegitimate children in parish churches in an attempt to evade Kirk session discipline.[16] As regards beliefs, Presbyterian ministers, especially in the 1830s, voiced concern about the 'superstitious' and popish ideas held by the laity. One writer to the *Christian Freeman* lamented:

Just think of a Protestant mother rolling tape about her child, to get some charm communicated to the tape by the ceremony—think of an unholy struggle between two parents, getting their children baptised at the same time, for who should have his child first sprinkled with water—think of the numberless absurdities prevalent on the subject of having an unbaptised

---

[12] For example, Loughaghery (B/Sec.) session book, 2 Jan. 1818 (PRONI, CR/3/8/1).

[13] [W. D. Killen *et al.*], *The plea of presbytery in behalf of the ordination, government, discipline, and worship of the Christian church, as opposed to the unscriptural claims of prelacy* (Glasgow, 1840), 557–68.

[14] A. Carson, *Reasons for separating from the General Synod of Ulster* (Belfast, 1805). See also, D. M. Thompson, 'The Irish background to Thomas Campbell's "Declaration and Address" ', *Journal of the United Reformed Church History Society*, 5 (1985), 215–25.

[15] *Confession*, 28: 4; Barkley, *Westminster formularies*, 44–5; T. Clark, *New light set in a clear light* ([Dublin], 1755), 50; Boardmills (B/Sec.) session book, Nov. 1826, Apr. 1827, May and July 1828 (PRONI, MIC/1P/72/2); Roseyards (AB/Sec.) session book, 23 Aug. 1801 (PRONI, Tennent papers, D/1748/A/2/3/1).

[16] For example, *OSMI* (Islandmagee), x. 37.

child in the house—bringing a child home without being baptised, who had been taken out for that purpose; think of these, and a hundred other specimens of superstition; and weep over the ignorance and folly of those who, though Protestants in name, are Papists in principle and practice.[17]

Some lay Presbyterians also held baptism in higher esteem than the Lord's Supper, and though the poor would not attend meeting due to lack of suitable clothing, they made an effort to ensure their children were baptized.[18]

The reasons for such behaviour lie in the perceived benefits of the rite and its importance within the wider community. It is clear that the meaning of baptism was linked with the spiritual, and often physical, well-being of the child. Many believed that unless a child was baptized it would not thrive. In some areas baptism was thought necessary to prevent the infant being spirited away by the fairies to be replaced by a 'changeling' and it was supposed in Antrim that if a girl were baptized before a boy she would grow a beard.[19] A recent study of lay attitudes in the nineteenth-century Church of England noted that baptism ensured the place of the child both in the local community, as it gave them a name, and in heaven, as the child would be certain of a Christian burial.[20] The same was also true amongst Reformed believers in seventeenth- and early eighteenth-century New England. There the concept of a 'half-way covenant' developed within Congregationalism to accommodate parents who wanted their infant baptized but who could not take an active role in the church owing to their own lack of a personal conversion experience.[21] Many parents who had lapsed in their observance of their own baptismal obligations deliberately renewed their commitment in order to have their child baptized. The practice underscored the

[17] 'Baptism', *Christian Freeman*, 2 (1833), 16–17.

[18] 'The reformer. No. III. Celebration of the Lord's Supper', *Orthodox Presbyterian*, 2 (1831), 391–2; Derry Pby (GSU), 7 May 1833 (UTC).

[19] [S. McSkimin], 'On fairies', *Belfast Monthly Magazine*, 4 (1810), 171; W. S. Smith, *Historical gleanings in Antrim and neighbourhood* (Belfast, 1888), 149–50.

[20] F. Knight, *The nineteenth-century church and English society* (Cambridge, 1995), 86.

[21] D. D. Hall, *Worlds of wonder, days of judgement: popular religious belief in early New England* (Cambridge, Mass., 1989), 152–6, 164.

importance of the family and gave parents hope in an insecure world that if their child died it would go to heaven.

Without necessarily adopting such categories, it seems reasonable that Ulster Presbyterians were willing to undergo church discipline in order to have these perceived benefits conferred upon their children through baptism. What is more, the actions of Kirk sessions may have helped to perpetuate these popular opinions. It is noteworthy that parents did not necessarily have to be communicant members in order to have their child baptized. For example, the Antiburgher Synod in 1796 declared 'that parents should not be deprived of baptism for their children, simply for their not applying for admission to the Lord's supper'.[22] Congregations such as Ballymoney made special provision for the children of paupers to be baptized without their parents being deemed regular members of the congregation.[23] By not requiring a certain level of commitment from poor and non-communicant members, there was a degree of flexibility that came at the possible price of perpetuating lay misunderstandings of what baptism theoretically did.

The lay interpretation of baptism was, in many respects, a popularized theology of baptismal regeneration. It was believed by some lay Presbyterians that after being baptized the child would be protected from the world, the flesh, and the Devil. The Revd James Denham observed in 1844 that though Presbyterianism taught against the 'monstrous and soul-destroying doctrine of *baptismal regeneration*', many of the laity 'who in words would deny it, have it most strongly rooted in their hearts, as they show when their children are unwell, and they come for the minister, perhaps at midnight, to hasten instantly to baptise them'.[24] Another writer referred to 'the delusion of those who seem to consider baptism as a charm, which in some way, they know not how, may secure their child from some great evil, and who are most anxious to have the rite performed, though themselves living in neglect of all ordinances, and practically heathen in a Christian land'.[25] Baptism was seen as a guarantee of

---

[22] MASAB (1796), 90.

[23] Ballymoney (GSU) session book, 13 July 1823 (UTC), 149.

[24] J. Denham, *Public baptism vindicated by an appeal to Scriptural authority, and the nature and uses of the ordinance* (Derry, 1844), 25.

[25] 'Obligations of parents and churches to promote the instruction of children', *Orthodox Presbyterian*, 2 (1831), 206.

heaven, a belief that may have practically absolved the individual from an onerous commitment to the church in adult life, especially frequent Sabbath attendance or communion. It was not the nurture of the community of faith, the work of the Holy Spirit, or an overt commitment to God through Christ that made the child a believer, but the very act of baptism. As one Seceder put it, 'We are all baptised Christians—Christians by the gross!'[26]

A further aspect of the New England analysis was that baptism gave peace of mind to the parents of infants who faced illness and death in an inhospitable world. This uneasiness about the physical and eternal well-being of the child may also be noted in the customary rituals that followed the safe delivery of the infant. The practice of churching, usually associated with the Roman Catholic and Anglican traditions, seems to have been practised by some Presbyterians in the parish of Islandmagee where it was considered unlucky for the new mother 'to enter a house before she is churched or before thanksgiving'.[27] John Caldwell recalled that the celebratory meal after childbirth in eighteenth-century Ballymoney was 'an offering of gratitude from the faithful husband and is truly the feast of reason and flow of soul to family, friends and neighbours'.[28] This communal aspect was repeated in other Presbyterian areas in the early nineteenth century, especially in south Antrim. There the practice of 'sitting up' involved the friends of the parents coming to the house on the day after the birth where they would spend the night in various forms of amusement.[29] It was reported that the christenings of the infants of wealthy farmers in the parish of Kilbride were 'scenes of festivity and mirth, and are much more so than their weddings'. As many guests as possible were packed into the house for dinner and the evening was spent 'in feasting and dancing, but generally without excess or intemperance'.[30]

---

[26] 'Baptism', *Christian Freeman*, 2 (1833), 19.

[27] *OSMI* (Islandmagee), x. 95.

[28] J. Caldwell, 'Particulars of history of a north county Irish family' (PRONI, Caldwell papers, T/3541/5/3), 29.

[29] A. Gailey, 'Folk-life study and the Ordnance Survey Memoirs', in idem and D. Ó hÓgáin (eds.), *Gold under furze: studies in folk tradition* (Dublin, 1983), 154.

[30] *OSMI* (Kilbride), xxix. 144. Also, (Donegore), xxix. 113, (Ballyeaston), xxxii. 6, (Killead), xxxv. 23.

Baptismal discipline, as noted earlier, was maintained in Secession congregations. The Antiburgher Synod in 1804 set up a working committee to enquire into the propriety of producing a 'formula of confession and obligation' for parents. The Synod decided that parents should engage, according to their ability and opportunity, to fully acquaint themselves with the standards of the church, including the Covenants, under the supervision of Kirk sessions.[31] In 1822 John Lowry made his congregation aware that only communicant members should have their children baptized, as both sacraments were 'seals of the same covenant'. Consequently, he urged parents to examine their conduct and motives before approaching the Kirk session.[32] Inevitably Seceder ministers lamented the 'prostituting of the holy ordinance' of baptism in the Synod of Ulster.[33] While this seems to be broadly the case, not all Kirk sessions in the Synod were lax, though in keeping with general trends, nineteenth-century reformers saw baptism as an area in need of reform. Henry Cooke was one of the first ministers in the Synod of Ulster to question the double standard of having tight discipline for the sacrament of communion while allowing any parent to have their child baptized without enquiry into their conduct.[34] Cooke's concerns were soon addressed as efforts were made to ensure all congregations possessed a well-kept baptismal register, visitation presbyteries enforced correct practice, and Kirk sessions disciplined wayward parents.[35] In accordance with the new mood, the Kirk session of Ballymoney congregation in March 1837 overturned their previous resolution regarding baptism for non-members and agreed to baptize only the children of church members.[36] Reformers attempted to ensure that parents possessed a sufficient degree of religious knowledge to make them fit sponsors for their children. Indeed, it was an almost constant refrain from conservative and liberal Presbyterians in the early nineteenth century that parents were culpable in their failure to teach and

---

[31] MASAB (1804), 179–81.

[32] J. Lowry, *Christian baptism* (Belfast, 1822), 22–3.

[33] 'Baptism', *Christian Freeman*, 2 (1833), 18.

[34] H. Cooke, *A sermon, preached at the opening of the General Synod of Ulster* (Belfast, 1825), 34–6.

[35] *Code* (1825), 43.

[36] Ballymoney (GSU) session book, Mar. 1837 (PRONI CR/3/1/B/4).

encourage their children in the Christian faith.[37] The 1841 Irish revision of the *Directory* sought to deal with this by stipulating that parents should be asked a series of nine doctrinal questions covering issues such as the Trinity, original sin, the work of Christ, sanctification, and the final judgement, along with an exhortation to perform the duties expected of Christian parents.[38]

Public baptism was the final measure of reform advocated in the first half of the nineteenth century. Seceders had endeavoured to uphold public baptism before the 1830s. Loughaghery session, for example, drew up a list of regulations in 1818 stating that private baptism was only to be administered if the family home was more than 2 miles from the meeting-house, if it was winter, if the child or parent was sick, or 'when the sponsor is a female'.[39] Within the Synod of Ulster, the Kirk session of Dunboe as early as 1809 was advocating a return to the practice advocated in the Westminster standards, though it was only in the 1830s that public baptism was more widely championed by James Morgan and Henry Cooke.[40] In 1836 the Synod recommended public baptism to all its congregations, reinforcing what already was the practice in many areas.[41] The 1838 synod was pleased to find that it had been widely adopted, and urged those congregations who had not already done so to do so quickly, though by 1840 a number had still not implemented the reforms.[42] One unintended side-effect of the measure was that some congregations lost members.[43] How far this was a general response is uncertain, though in light of the fact that many Presbyterians did not appreciate the trouble of public baptism it may have been more widespread. Despite all the attention on public baptism, the Remonstrants and

[37] For example, Malcolm, *Communicant's catechism*, 4; 'Infant baptism', *Orthodox Presbyterian*, 6 (1835), 137.

[38] *Code* (1841), 77–8.

[39] Loughaghery (B/Sec.) session book, 2 Jan. 1818. Garvagh (B/Sec.) session book, 24 Oct. 1833 (PRONI, MIC/1P/17), 195–6.

[40] A. A. McCaughan, *Heath, hearth and heart: the story of Dunboe and the meeting-house at Articlave* (Coleraine, 1988), 69; J. Morgan, *Recollections of my life and times* (Belfast, 1874), 83–4.

[41] *RGSU* (1836), 70.

[42] *RGSU* (1838), 41; Barkley, *Westminster formularies*, 42–3.

[43] Barkley, *Westminster formularies*, 43.

the Presbytery of Antrim continued to uphold private baptism as it was 'a domestic ordinance' and also because to enforce public baptism was to infringe the individual's liberty of conscience.[44]

The reform of baptismal practice aimed to make administration more transparent in an effort to promote 'vital godliness'. Private baptism was only allowed in cases of extreme necessity and even then public intimation had to be given from the pulpit.[45] This meant that all who wanted their children baptized had to make a public appearance acknowledging that their child was regularly conceived. In addition, public baptism was a declaration of difference. According to Denham, at both baptism and communion, 'the recipients are declared to be peculiar people, separate from the world, and under covenant engagement to be the Lord's'.[46] One of the main reasons he urged Presbyterians to give up 'superstitious' practices was that 'Puseyism and Popery' were attempting to propagate the doctrine of baptismal regeneration.[47] The desire to reform baptismal practice has therefore to be placed within the context of religious and political polarization in the first half of the nineteenth century. Reform was more than a return to good, scriptural practice. At stake for reformers was their identity as Presbyterians and Protestants.

Baptism was clearly important to the life of communities. At one level, it was the sign of being a member of the local community of believers, a part of the visible church. At another level, it could also have signified membership of the invisible church if God in his grace had predestined the individual to become a true believer. At each service of baptism, the congregation was reminded of their own vows and exhorted again to be true members of God's community on earth. Yet some Presbyterians believed that the act of baptism conferred benefits quite apart from the grace of God, absolving them from a troublesome commitment to the church. The ordinance also had practical functions for it gave the child a name and consequently a place in the local community. What is more, the community shared

---

[44] 'Private baptism and private communion', *Bible Christian*, 4 (1833), 449–51; 'Baptism', *Bible Christian*, new ser., 2 (1837), 281.

[45] *Code* (1841), 76.

[46] Denham, *Public baptism*, 14.

[47] Ibid., 30.

in the joys of a safely delivered infant and in the sorrows of a tragic death. At yet another level, the way baptism was administered distinguished Presbyterians from other Christians, and in the context of increasing sectarian tensions, such a communal identity was critical. Baptism within Ulster Presbyterianism was, therefore, a classic example of the symbiotic relationship between taught orthodoxy and the practice of the laity, who used established motifs and prescribed rituals yet endowed them with a meaning and significance of their own.

8

Marriage and Sexual Relationships

According to the *Confession,* marriage was instituted 'for the mutual help of the husband and wife; for the increase of mankind with a legitimate issue, and of the church with a holy seed; and for prevention of uncleanness'.[1] For these reasons, marriage held an important place not only within society but also within the community of faith. As long as the relationship was not incestuous it was lawful for any to marry who had reached the age of consent or who had obtained the permission of parents if younger. Yet, the *Confession* made it clear that 'such as profess the true reformed religion should not marry with infidels, Papists ... idolaters', or with the immoral. The *Directory* stipulated that before the ceremony the publication of banns had to occur in the couple's respective congregations on the previous three Sabbaths to ensure there were no impediments to the marriage. The ceremony was to take place in the meeting-house before several witnesses and could be held on any day except the Sabbath or a fast day. As couples were to marry in the Lord, a minister of the word was to conduct the service in order 'that he may accordingly counsel them, and pray for a blessing upon them'. An outline of the prayers to be said and the vows to be given were provided in the *Directory* and all congregations were urged to have a marriage register 'for the perusal of all whom it may concern'. Provisions were also made in the *Confession* for divorce in cases of adultery and desertion and it should be pointed out that a distinction was made between a contract of marriage and its solemnization.

The Presbyterians of Ulster developed their marriage customs and attitudes to sexual relationships within the context of these

---

[1] The relevant sections are, *Confession,* ch. 24 and *Directory,* 387–8.

guidelines and in response to the political and social context of the eighteenth and nineteenth centuries. As in other areas of religious practice, not all that called themselves Presbyterian either adhered to official standards or upheld generally assumed moral principles. Marriage was also deeply embedded in the life of local communities and thus surrounded by customary activity, which often oversha- dowed the religious significance of the rite. In order to assess Pres- byterian attitudes to marriage and sexual relationships more generally, this chapter will be divided into two sections. Section one outlines official marriage practices and attitudes with particular reference to the Established Church. Section two examines the com- munal aspect of marriage and sexual relations within the context of church discipline and local community life.

I

In the early decades of the eighteenth century, serious legal questions existed regarding the validity of marriages performed by Presby- terian ministers.[2] Some ministers were prosecuted for performing allegedly illegal ceremonies and, in Anglican ecclesiastical courts, lay Presbyterians were charged with fornication. These legal proceedings depended upon the assumption that only marriages performed by the Established Church were valid. The basic problem was that if the courts recognized the validity of marriages performed by Presbyter- ians they also accepted Presbyterianism as an authentic church and in the ecclesiastical turmoil of the early eighteenth century that was unthinkable. An act of Parliament passed in 1737 provided some relief for Presbyterians by allowing two Presbyterians to marry in accordance with the oaths stipulated in the 1719 Irish Toleration Act. In 1782 the Irish Parliament, in spite of ferocious opposition from the House of Lords, passed an act confirming 'that marriages between protestant dissenters performed by a protestant dissenting minister were as good in law as those of the established church'.[3]

---

[2] The following discussion is based upon, J. C. Beckett, *Protestant dissent in Ireland 1687–1780* (London, 1948), ch. 11.

[3] Ibid., 122.

However, the question of a marriage with an Episcopalian was left begging and it took an act of Parliament passed in 1844 to render marriages performed by Presbyterian ministers legally unassailable.

The Synod of Ulster made strenuous efforts throughout the eighteenth century to ensure that any marriage conducted by their ministers was regular and legal. Early resolutions of the Synod established proclamation on three Sabbaths, ensured that marriage registers were kept, and allowed for the proclamation of banns in the parish church if necessary.[4] In 1712 stiff penalties were introduced for ministers, elders, and lay members who engaged in activity that made a marriage illegal, including suspension from privileges if married by a defrocked clergyman.[5] The situation had degenerated by 1761 when it was reported to the Synod that many ministers celebrated marriages without proclamation. It was decided to reinforce an act of 1755 that handed a six-month suspension to any minister marrying without the proclamation of banns and enjoined Kirk sessions to rebuke publicly any person irregularly married.[6] Between 1720 and 1775 ten ministers were degraded for celebrating marriages irregularly.[7] Inevitably, recently arrived Seceder ministers criticized the Synod of Ulster for laxity in the celebration of marriage.[8] Though they and the Covenanters arrived after the disputes over marriage in the early eighteenth century, the actions of their Kirk sessions and presbyteries testify to their determination to ensure the regular celebration of marriage, especially by ensuring the proclamation of banns.[9] By 1824, however, the Seceder Synod reported that there was a variety of opinion and practice amongst ministers regarding marriage. In an attempt to regulate practice and encourage proclamation, seven resolutions were passed and ministers who violated them were, for the first offence, suspended for two Sabbaths, and, for the second offence, for three months.[10]

---

[4] *RGSU* i. (1701), 53; (1709), 187.

[5] *RGSU* i. (1712), 276.

[6] *RGSU* ii. (1755), 394; (1761), 446.

[7] J. M. Barkley, 'Marriage and the Presbyterian tradition', *Ulster Folklife*, 39 (1993), 35.

[8] T. Clark, *New light set in a clear light* ([Dublin], 1755), 58.

[9] D. Stewart, *The Seceders in Ireland with annals of their congregations* (Belfast, 1950), 410–15.

[10] *MPSI* (1824), 14–17.

By 1784 the Synod of Ulster again expressed concern about irregular marriages and asked all presbyteries to ensure they were not performed within their bounds.[11] An important act passed by the Synod in 1785 stated that a minister marrying a couple not of his congregation or without proper testimonials was to be suspended *ab officio* for three months for a first offence and degraded for a second. Furthermore, if either party belonged to the Established Church, the minister had to obtain the written consent of the local rector or curate.[12] The following year it was reported that eight ministers were suspected of celebrating marriages irregularly and that if they were found guilty they would be immediately degraded and notice would be given in a local newspaper.[13] For this and other misconduct, the Presbytery of Derry in 1786 degraded two of those named, Stephen Brizzle and James Dunn. The presbytery decided to publish a notice in the *Londonderry Journal* informing the public that any marriages performed by these men were invalid.[14] The presbytery in 1789 also decided that the 1782 act of Parliament be read in all their congregations and that any clandestine marriage discovered would result in the couple being suspended from ordinances until they were remarried.[15] Owing to the leniency with which it had been enforced, the 1785 act of the General Synod was repeated in 1787, but by 1803 the sentences for breaching the act were made less onerous and in the following year the proclamation of banns was made optional.[16] The relaxation of proclamation in the early nineteenth century was one of a number of measures enacted by the Synod which were eventually incorporated in the *Code*.[17] This consolidated evolving practice over the previous 128 years and outlined the legal and historical basis for Presbyterian marriages. The *Code* maintained that Church of Scotland ministers had been invited to Ireland by the government in the seventeenth century, granted church livings, and allowed to exercise their right of marrying as in Scotland. Thus the 'right of celebrating

---

[11] *RGSU* iii. (1784), 68.
[12] *RGSU* iii. (1785), 74.
[13] *RGSU* iii. (1786), 81.
[14] Derry Pby (GSU), 7 Feb. 1786 (UTC), 133–4.
[15] Ibid., 4 Aug. 1789, 139–40.
[16] *RGSU* iii. (1787), 90; (1803), 268–9; (1804), 278.
[17] *RGSU* iii. (1805), 297–8; (1806), 308–9; (1819), 511.

marriage comes down to the ministers of the Synod of Ulster, confirmed by the strongest of all human laws, universal custom'. The *Code* made it clear that various laws passed by Parliament had confirmed this principle of custom.[18]

Despite the efforts of the various Presbyterian bodies, the legality of their marriages was to be threatened once more. A marriage bill proposed in the House of Commons in 1832 threatened to imprison Presbyterian ministers who had legally married members of their own congregation to members of the Established Church. The Synod of Ulster ordered that a correspondence be immediately established with the Irish Chief Secretary to ensure that their interests were properly protected.[19] The bill was abandoned, but the issue of Presbyterian ministers marrying either one or both parties who were members of the Established Church was only resolved after an unsettling legal dispute and an act of Parliament in 1844.[20] The Presbyterian sense of grievance over this matter should not be underestimated. In a speech given in Glasgow that year, Richard Dill of Dublin delivered a tirade against the persecution of Presbyterians by Anglicans. Significantly, Dill linked this phenomenon with the spread of 'Puseyism' within the Church of Ireland. Along with other contemporary developments, a considerable number of politically liberal Irish Presbyterians shared Dill's characterization of the Church of Ireland as 'the betrayer, rather than the bulwark, of Protestantism'.[21]

II

In addition to the legal framework outlined above, marriage and sexual relations more generally in Presbyterian areas were regulated by the culture and social mores of the local community as expressed through church discipline and various customary rituals. Breaches of the seventh commandment, whether taken literally as adultery or more broadly as any act of sexual misconduct, were the mainstay of

---

[18] *Code* (1825), 40.
[19] *RGSU* (1832), 35–7.
[20] R. Allen, *James Seaton Reid: a centenary biography* (Belfast, 1951), ch. 11.
[21] R. Dill, *Mixed marriages* (Glasgow, 1844).

Kirk session discipline throughout the eighteenth and into the second half of the nineteenth centuries. Despite the efforts of reformers to increase the range of cases considered, some congregations in the 1830s reported that discipline was usually only brought against fornicators and adulterers.[22] Fornication was the single most prevalent offence tried before Kirk sessions, particularly if it occurred before marriage. In some congregations such as Castledawson those who indulged in premarital sexual activity had to give public evidence of repentance before being readmitted to privileges, which often meant a public rebuke before the congregation.[23] The penalty could be more severe for those who continued in their sin. William Chisick and Janet McKee appeared before the Boardmills session in July 1794 'acknowledging their sin and scandal of antenuptial fornication of long continuance'. The session referred the case to the Presbytery of Down who rebuked the couple before returning them to Boardmills to stand before the congregation on two Sabbaths.[24] William Crimes of Drumbo was sent to the Belfast Presbytery in 1791 for the 'heinous sin of fornication, he having debauched a young woman and afterwards married her sister'. Despite his penitent behaviour since the event, they 'rebuked him most sharply for his sin and exhorted him to humble himself more and more before God and the Church of Christ', before sending him back to the Drumbo session for further examination.[25] In other congregations, the punishment could involve a rebuke before the session, though in Anahilt this occurred only if the couple were subsequently married.[26]

Matters became complicated when an act of passion resulted in an unwanted pregnancy for which the father denied any responsibility. The *Code* stated that it was the duty of the mother to disclose the name of the father on pain of being suspended from privileges.[27] The Secession Presbytery of Down and congregations under its care heard

[22] Down Pby (GSU), 7 May 1839, 2 Feb. and 4 May 1840 (Church House, strong room); Raphoe Pby (GSU), 11 May 1836 (Church House, strong room), 52.

[23] Castledawson (GSU) session book, 12 Mar. 1837 (PRONI, MIC/1P/90/1), 5.

[24] Boardmills (B/Sec.) session book, 9 July 1794 (PRONI, MIC/1P/72/2).

[25] Belfast Pby (GSU), 30 June 1791 (UTC).

[26] Anahilt (GSU) session book, 1774 (J. M. Barkley, 'A history of the ruling eldership in Irish Presbyterianism', 2 vols. (QUB MA, 1952), ii. 270).

[27] *Code* (1825), 68.

a number of such cases and it certainly seems that they were anxious to ensure that fathers took their responsibilities seriously and usually found in favour of the mother when there was sufficient evidence.[28] There may have been other reasons for such a decision apart from natural justice. Scholars of Scottish church discipline in the eighteenth century have suggested a financial motive, namely, that if the presbytery or Kirk session did not determine paternity, the mother and child would have to depend upon the meagre resources of congregational poor relief.[29] Yet when the presbytery of Down did not find in favour of the mother, there were usually good reasons for doing so. For example, Ann Brown accused Thomas Girvin in 1799 of being the father of her child. As she kept changing her story, the presbytery decided to postpone discussion of the case until their next meeting, which proved a wise decision given that Brown neither attended then nor at a subsequent meeting in May 1800.[30]

Even if a couple did not have sex before marriage, their marriage could still be considered irregular for a number of reasons, including elopement, failure to have banns published, or being married by an unauthorized person such as a defrocked minister, a Church of Ireland clergyman, or a Catholic priest.[31] There are many reasons why people chose this course of action, such as bigamy, incest, parental opposition, timing, privacy, a mixed marriage, or mere fashion, which has been identified as a significant factor in Scotland during this period.[32] Bigamy and incest appear very infrequently in church records from Ulster, although those found guilty were roundly condemned and given stiff penalties.[33] Parents often exerted a powerful influence over their children's choice of marriage partner through the granting or otherwise of an inheritance and because both the

---

[28] Down Pby (B/Sec.), 23 Aug. 1786, 3 Jan. 1787, 11 Feb. and 15 Apr. 1794; Boardmills (B/Sec.) session book, 13 Aug. 1784.

[29] L. Leneman and R. Mitchison, 'Acquiescence in and defiance of church discipline in early modern Scotland', *Records of the Scottish Church History Society*, 25 (1993), 27.

[30] Down Pby (B/Sec.), 3 Sept., 5 Nov. 1799, 6 May 1800.

[31] Barkley, 'Marriage', 35.

[32] R. Mitcheson and L. Leneman, *Sexuality and social control: Scotland 1660–1780* (Oxford, 1989), 120–32.

[33] J. M. Barkley, *The eldership in Irish Presbyterianism* (n.p., 1963), 44–5; MASAB (1800), 127–8, 134–5.

Directory and its 1825 Irish revision stipulated that their consent was required for a marriage to be solemnized between those not of a sufficient age. Yet both standards also warned parents against unnecessarily restricting their children's choice of partner and the evidence suggests that church courts ensured that parents did not compel their children into marriage.[34]

The Presbyterian authorities in the eighteenth century constantly endeavoured to ensure the proper proclamation of banns despite the fact that the laity disliked the public fuss involved. This attitude may have contributed to the development, contrary to the *Directory*, of private weddings in the house of either the bride or the minister. Though public weddings did not disappear completely, they only became the norm again in the second half of the nineteenth century.[35] For the Presbyterian couple that did not want the trouble of either a public wedding or asking for their parents' consent, there were two options. The first was elopement. A number of such cases came to the notice of Kirk sessions in this period. For instance, Hanna Cleg, a member of Cahans congregation, ran off 'with one Maginnis a papist', and was subsequently married to him by a priest. As time passed, her husband fell under hard times and left the country. The Kirk session seems to have thought this judgement enough, absolved her of any irregularity, and urged her to 'flee to the blood of Jesus for pardon'.[36] A similar case came before the Synod of Ulster congregation of Dromara in 1835 when Francis McIlroy and his wife Euphemia Bell eloped and were married against their parents' wishes by a degraded clergyman. They eventually returned, submitted themselves to church censure, and had their marriage properly recognized.[37]

The second option for couples was to be married by someone other than their minister. A common person resorted to in these situations was a degraded clergyman or 'bucklebeggar' who offered to marry people for a fee. The status of these marriages was hazy at best. The Antiburgher Synod in 1796 declared that if there was moral

---

[34] *Directory*, 387; *Code* (1825), 98; *MPSI* (1824), 16; Barkley, 'Marriage', 36.

[35] For general developments, L. M. Ballard, *Forgetting frolic: marriage traditions in Ireland* (Belfast, 1998).

[36] Cahans (B/Sec.) session book, 18 Jan. and 4 Feb. 1776, 53.

[37] Dromara (GSU) session book, 12 Apr. 1835 (PRONI, T/1447/2).

certainty that a marriage had been contracted, the marriage was valid, but the couple would have to be disciplined for the irregularity.[38] The Synod of Ulster in 1825 stated that any such marriage was to be declared null and void and the couple were expected to remarry.[39] Examples of bucklebeggar marriages occur frequently in session minutes. The minister of Coronary congregation in 1787 publicly rebuked a couple and a single male after acknowledging their irregular marriage by 'Mr Cookey the bucklebeggar', a degraded curate from the area.[40] William Blakely, who resigned his Carrickfergus charge in 1780 and was *de facto* degraded the same year, returned to his native Ballynahinch and did a brisk trade in irregular marriages. Between 1780 and his death in 1810 three Kirk session books record the names of couples rebuked for being married by him.[41]

In order to bypass formal Presbyterian ceremonies, some of the laity turned to Anglican and Roman Catholic clergymen. The number of cases relating to marriage in the local parish church, especially in the eighteenth century, indicates the depth of hostility Seceders in particular held towards the Established Church. The session book of Cahans, for example, had several of these cases dating from the 1750s. The Kirk session believed that the Anglican rite 'defiled' the ordinance 'by the parties "crossing and cringing at an altar", and by the man stating that he "worshipped a woman in the name of the Trinity" '.[42] A similar attitude was displayed by the Revd Thomas Smith of Ahoghill who wrote a long letter to his friend, William Weir, himself a ruling elder, in 1786 after hearing the decision of Weir to allow his daughter to marry according to the *Book of Common Prayer*. Smith maintained that such a course of action was a breach of Weir's ordination engagements and sacramental vows, a bad example to others, and compromised his position as an elder. Smith became especially flustered when discussing the nature of the marriage oath; 'and is not with my body I do thee worship and with

[38] MASAB (1796), 91; *MPSI* (1824), 16.

[39] *Code* (1825), 42–3.

[40] Coronary (B/Sec.) session book, 20 May 1782 (PRONI, MIC/1P/179/A/1A).

[41] S. McSkimin, *The history and antiquities of the county of the town of Carrickfergus*, ed. E. J. McCrum (Belfast, 1909), 251–2. The sessions were Boardmills, Dromara, and Loughaghery.

[42] W. T. Latimer, *A history of the Irish Presbyterians*, 2nd edn. (Belfast, 1902), 339.

all my worldly goods etc exceptionable if not sinful and sure at least is it broken by all who take it and all this done in the name of the Father etc in the same manner as baptism is dispensed'.[43] Old Light congregations such as Dromara and Carnmoney also rebuked their members for marrying according to the Anglican form.[44] Yet opposition towards Anglican rites was tempered by the need to maintain peaceful relations in a confessional state. The Synod of Ulster's resolution of 1785 reminded ministers that they must have the express permission of the local rector before marrying members of that communion.[45]

Presbyterians were also rebuked if a Catholic priest married them, which raises the important issue of intermarriage between Presbyterians and Roman Catholics.[46] It has already been noted that intermarriage according to the Westminster standards could simply mean not marrying in the Lord and there are examples of sessions taking such matters seriously.[47] There are, of course, examples of Catholics and Presbyterians marrying each other in Ulster during the eighteenth and nineteenth centuries and of Kirk sessions disciplining offenders.[48] Owing to the heightening of religious feelings in the 1830s there was a hardening of attitudes amongst Presbyterians towards intermarriage as it was seen to be reducing the numerical strength of Irish Protestantism. In 1836 Josias Wilson, who had recently moved from Drogheda to Townshend Street, Belfast, wrote a short letter to the *Orthodox Presbyterian* recounting some examples of mixed marriages. He stated that intermarriage was 'supposed to be a Jesuitical plan for the gradual extinction of Protestantism' and referred to a number of incidents in which the Anglican or Presbyterian yielded their faith to their Roman Catholic partner. In one case from Drogheda, the Catholic husband initially allowed his wife to worship at the meeting-house. However, on returning from Sunday

[43] Thomas Smith to William Weir, 17 May 1785 (PRONI, Weir papers, MIC/561/1).

[44] Dromara (GSU) session book, 3 Oct. 1777 (PRONI, T/1447/1); Latimer, *History*, 343.

[45] *RGSU* iii. (1785), 74.

[46] Examples of discipline for marriage by a priest include, Anahilt (GSU) session book, 17 Oct. 1776, 10 Oct. 1779, 20 Oct. 1787 (Barkley, 'Eldership', ii. 272–3); Dromara (GSU) session book, 14 Nov. 1773, 21 Apr. 1775, 22 Oct. 1786.

[47] For example, Alfred Street (B/Sec.) session book, 17 June 1827 (PRONI, MIC/1P/14/1).

[48] Cahans (B/Sec.) session book, 28 Aug. 1768, 8; Dromara (GSU) session book, 14 Nov. 1773.

worship two weeks after her marriage, 'he met her like a tiger, seized her bible, and burned it before her eyes, cut her psalm book and catechism into pieces, and then consigned them to the flames, and forthwith compelled the affrighted creature, at the knee of a priest, to renounce the Protestant faith'.[49] Reflecting the mood of the times, the 1841 *Code* of the General Assembly recommended 'that a minister shall not join in marriage a member of the Presbyterian church with an Infidel or Romanist'.[50] This stipulation, a return to the Westminster ideal, had been omitted from the 1825 *Code* and indicates how far relations between Presbyterians and Catholics had degenerated in fifteen years. Presbyterian fears of being reduced in numbers by intermarriage were unfounded, though in the context of religious and political polarization in the 1830s and 1840s, it is understandable that such anxieties were expressed.

Kirk sessions also dealt with adultery, which was taken very seriously as it threatened the sanctity of marriage and the stability of local communities.[51] It is unsurprising that the church records are replete with examples and it was usually the case that the offender was rebuked before their congregation and then referred to the presbytery for further discipline.[52] Furthermore, cases of desertion and breach of promise were common. Two examples from Cahans are instructive. In January 1773, William Harkness came before the session claiming that Elizabeth Gray had made some kind of consent to marry him but she had subsequently decided to marry someone else. The elders ruled that she was free to marry another, though the Revd John Rogers dissented from the decision.[53] A second notable case lasted for over ten years. In 1777 Thomas Irvine married himself in private, and in accordance with the *Confession*, to Rosanna Lister. They consummated the marriage, but Lister then left Irvine to marry

---

[49] 'Intermarriages with Roman Catholics', *Orthodox Presbyterian*, 7 (1836), 302–5. For similar comments see, A. Montgomery, 'Presbyterian statistics', *Orthodox Presbyterian*, new ser, 1 (1838), 308–10.

[50] *Code* (1841), 38.

[51] *Code* (1825), 18–19; R. M. Browne, 'Kirk and community: Ulster Presbyterian society, 1640–1740' (QUB M.Phil., 1998), 141.

[52] For example: Route Pby (GSU), 25 Jan. 1820, 8 Oct. 1822, 127, 160; Cahans (B/Sec.) session book, 27 May 1787, 20 Sept. and 4 Oct. 1789, 71, 78; Dromara (GSU) session book, 3 May 1776, 27 Jan. 1782, 12 Oct. 1794.

[53] Cahans (B/Sec.) session book, 24 Jan. 1773, 44–7.

another man. The session was unsure how to proceed, so referred the case to the presbytery.[54] Probably owing to a lack of surviving documentation, the next mention of the case is in 1788 when Lister's then husband, David Harshaw, brought the matter before the Burgher Synod after the presbytery had seemingly ruled in favour of Irvine and excluded Lister and Harshaw from privileges. It seems that the Synod rescinded the presbytery's decision.[55] These cases suggest that the laity placed a more liberal interpretation upon what constituted a marriage contract than ministers. In the first case, the elders found in favour of the woman and, in the second, Lister did not see the rituals she performed with Irvine, albeit in private, as constituting a promise to marry.

Both adultery and desertion were identified by the Westminster standards as the only grounds for divorce, though Kirk sessions rarely dealt with such cases, particularly after marriage was made a largely civil matter in 1844.[56] The surviving presbytery records show that both women and men filed for divorce on the grounds laid down in the Westminster standards. At one time the Burgher Presbytery of Upper Tyrone had three petitions for divorce under consideration. In all three cases they freed the woman from the contract on account of their husband's desertion.[57] The lengths to which Kirk sessions went to determine cases may be illustrated by the following example from Ballymoney in 1829. Robert Wray approached the session complaining that he had agreed to separate from his wife, Martha Pinkerton, on certain conditions, but she had subsequently had a child by another man. He wanted the session to dissolve the marriage, but as there were doubts about his church membership, his character, his treatment of Martha, and his motives, a delegation was appointed to converse with Wray. The delegation reported the following month, stating that Wray had never been a church member and expressed doubts about his character. Furthermore, 'he having stated his *only* motive, "his anxiety to get married again" ', his request was dismissed.[58]

---

54 Ibid., 1777, 55–7.
55 MASB (1788), 53; Stewart, *Seceders*, 414.
56 *Confession*, 24: 6.
57 Stewart, *Seceders*, 415.
58 Ballymoney (GSU) session book, 10 May and 14 June 1829.

The exercise of discipline for marital and sexual offences raises the issue of relationships between men and women. From the outset it must be recognized that church courts were solely comprised of men, that Kirk sessions assumed male authority, that more women than men were tried for a relapse into sexual sin or for sexual slander, and that there were instances of what seems to be favouritism towards male defendants.[59] Yet, a number of general points should be made. First, church discipline underlined the fact that individuals, both male and female, were responsible for their own sins and so 'militated against the maintenance of any double standard in the area of sexual ethics'.[60] Consequently, individual men and women as well as couples were held to account whenever a case had to be answered. Sin was sin and had to be dealt with no matter the gender of the accused as the purity of church communion and the soul of the individual were at stake. Second, women were certainly not denied access to church courts, nor the right to appeal to higher courts if a decision went against them in Kirk session. Third, the sources demonstrate that church courts ensured women and mothers were fairly treated and illegitimate children provided for by determining paternity. A representative sample of the sexual offences referred to presbyteries by Kirk sessions in this period show that over 70 per cent of the defendants were males.[61] Finally, the particulars of individual cases and the factors that influenced sentencing must be considered when determining the role of gender in church discipline. However, the majority of existing session books provide only the barest details, thus making it almost impossible to determine the issues at stake in specific cases. The relationship between Presbyterian women and men as reflected in church discipline ought to be placed within a broader context than gender alone and should include the procedural framework, the particularities of individual cases, the prevailing political, social,

[59] For differences in the types of cases brought against men and women see Browne, 'Kirk and community', 116, 170.

[60] M. F. Graham, 'Women and the church courts in Reformation-era Scotland', in E. Ewan and M. M. Meikle (eds.), *Women in Scotland c. 1100–c. 1750* (East Linton, 1999), 196.

[61] W.P. Gray, 'A social history of illegitimacy in Ireland from the late eighteenth to the early twentieth century' (QUB Ph.D., 2000), 105–6, 110–11. For general comments on the treatment of women see Browne, 'Kirk and community', 116, 133–4.

and economic conditions, and the theological outlook of the minister and Kirk session involved.

The prevalence in session records of sexual misconduct in general and fornication in particular also raises questions about Presbyterian attitudes to illegitimacy, sexual intercourse outside of marriage, and the influence of communal pressure. Presbyterians were as prone as anyone else to submit to sexual temptation. As a matter of fact, Irish illegitimacy rates throughout this period were highest in the north-east, and in some staunchly Presbyterian areas premarital sex was not seen as a scandal.[62] Beyond a simple failure to restrain passion, sexual attitudes ought to be related to broader economic and social changes. One possible indicator of sexual mores is the age of marriage, though this is complicated by variations between different regions and different social groups with, for example, better-off farmers and professionals marrying later.[63] The age of marriage also varied in response to the state of the economy and recent research suggests the age was increasing in the 1830s owing to problems experienced by the domestic linen industry.[64] Furthermore, antenuptial fornication was used by some Presbyterians as a means of blackmailing inheritance from parents who did not approve of the match or who refused to subdivide their land. For instance, such action was not seen as disreputable in Carnmoney as it allowed the female to compel her father to grant an attractive dowry while the male could refuse to marry a woman unless her father offered more money.[65] This attitude was reflected in the great number of sexual offences recorded in the Carnmoney session book between 1767 and 1805.[66] According to the *Ordnance Survey Memoirs*, premarital sex was also rife in nearby Islandmagee where the number of Presbyterian children born outside wedlock was significant, though illegitimacy was not common since couples tended to marry subsequently. Yet the age of marriage

---

[62] Gray, 'Illegitimacy', 159–63, 314–5.

[63] V. Morgan and W. Macafee, 'Irish population in the pre-Famine period: evidence from County Antrim', *Economic History Review*, 37 (1984), 182–96.

[64] W. Macafee, 'The demographic history of Ulster, 1750–1841', in H. T. Blethen and C. W. Wood, Jr (eds.), *Ulster and North America: transatlantic perspectives on the Scotch-Irish* (Tuscaloosa, Ala., 1997), 50–5.

[65] *OSMI* (Carnmoney), ii. 59.

[66] Gray, 'Illegitimacy', 115.

remained high due to the unwillingness of farmers to subdivide their land.[67] This example is given an added twist for in 1827 the Revd John Murphy reported to the Presbytery of Templepatrick that the members of his Islandmagee congregation were 'sober, chaste, and temperate'.[68]

Though the above evidence would seem to suggest that Murphy was misguided in his judgement, there are good grounds for asserting that both opinions were equally correct, given that the writer of the *Memoir* was commenting upon all those within the parish who were referred to as Presbyterians whereas Murphy was referring only to his congregation. Church records such as those of the Templepatrick Presbytery undoubtedly provide an invaluable insight into the lives and attitudes of those who were connected with local congregations and who were willing to submit to church discipline. Yet not everyone in Islandmagee or elsewhere who took or was given the name Presbyterian had the same commitment to the church. In addition, marriage within the Presbyterian community was determined by immediate economic and social realities as well as religious concerns. Non-ecclesiastical sources in particular emphasize that marriage was confirmed and regulated within the broader framework of customary and social activity. Studies of popular Catholicism in this period have shown that marriage was subject to various long-established beliefs and rituals and courtship was regulated by economic and cultural constraints.[69] Though the pattern of arranged marriage common in Catholic districts did not exist to anywhere near the same degree in Presbyterian areas, parental advice and economic considerations were still important. Consequently, in order to determine the precise relationship between an individual's belief and subsequent actions, care must be taken to establish the level of attachment to Presbyterianism and to place examples in a broader socio-economic context. For instance, it may be that fornication and early marriage were not frowned upon before the 1830s, but in the context of the economic

[67] *OSMI* (Islandmagee), x. 37. The same was true of the nearby parish of Glynn (*OSMI*, xxvi. 28).

[68] Templepatrick Pby (GSU), 7 Aug. 1827 (PRONI, MIC/1P/85).

[69] S. J. Connolly, 'Marriage in pre-famine Ireland' and C. Ó Danachair, 'Marriage and Irish folk tradition', in A. Cosgrove (ed.), *Marriage in Ireland* (Dublin, 1985), 79–98, 99–115.

and social changes of that decade, late marriage and celibacy made economic sense and corresponded with heightened religious earnestness.

Beyond the choice of marriage partner, local society had other ways of imposing itself upon this important rite of passage for both the couple and the wider community. A parade to and from the ceremony was common in many parts of Presbyterian Ulster. In the parish of Bovevagh, County Londonderry, the 'bridal party march in rank and file to their place of worship and, after the ceremony, solace themselves with bread and butter, tea and whiskey. The Irish always go on foot, the Scotch endeavour to procure a car.'[70] Sometimes, such parades to the wedding resulted in confusion and embarrassment. J. R. Dill, who had also been unhorsed whilst taking part in the 'merry convoy', recalled how, on one occasion, a number of riders had been unceremoniously dumped into a cesspool.[71] The following description of a Presbyterian procession from County Londonderry at the beginning of the nineteenth century well represents the mixture of festivity, danger, and excitement of these occasions:

At the *Scotch* weddings, the groom and his party vie with the other youngsters, who shall gallop first, from the house of the minister to the dwelling of the bride; nor is this feat of gallantry always without danger, for in every village, through which they are expected, they are received with shots of pistols and guns; these discharges, intended to honour the parties, sometimes promote their disgrace; if to be tumbled in the dirt, on such an occasion, can be called a dishonour. At the bride's house is prepared a bowl of *broth*, to be the reward of the victor of the race, which race is therefore called the running of the *brose*.[72]

In both this example and that from Bovevagh there was a clear distinction made between the practices of Presbyterians and the Catholic population around them, whether in terms of the custom itself or the financial ability to procure a carriage. Furthermore, in both examples the friends of the couple brought the bride and groom

[70] *OSMI* (Bovevagh), xxv. 26.

[71] J. R. Dill, *Autobiography of a country parson* (Belfast, 1888), 43–4. W. S. Mason, *A statistical account, or parochial survey of Ireland*, 3 vols. (Dublin, 1814–19), ii. 16.

[72] G. V. Sampson, *A memoir, explanatory of the chart and survey of the county of Londonderry, Ireland* (London, 1814), 191.

to the place of marriage by means that indicate the transition from one sort of relationship to another. It may be, however, that the rationale of those involved was less calculated.

Elsewhere in Ulster, guns were discharged outside the couple's home in order to obtain alcohol in return for leaving them in peace.[73] Similar behaviour in Catholic areas has been interpreted as the reassertion of community authority over the married couple.[74] In some Presbyterian areas, these rituals of reintegration were augmented in ways that drew attention to the community centred upon the meeting-house. On the 'showing Sunday' a week after the marriage ceremony, the bride, bridegroom, and bridal party, often in their wedding clothes, attended the meeting-house seemingly to reintroduce themselves into church life.[75] More tangibly, the Presbyterians of Maghera gave their children a copy of the Bible on their wedding day.[76]

The picture that emerges of marriage and sexual relations within Ulster Presbyterian society is a collage of religious devotion, human frailty, and social mores that often collided with prescribed morality and the standards of the church. What is significant is that many people, male and female, submitted themselves to the discipline of the church in matters of sexual misconduct. Their reasons may be difficult to determine, and though the desire of individuals to be reconciled to God should not be dismissed, other factors ought to be considered. The influence of a powerful commitment to the community centred upon the meeting-house, and the fear of social ostracism if its rules were transgressed, seem to be of great importance. After all, popular pressure made discipline work and being part of a disciplined community set a person apart from society around them. Yet too rigid a barrier should not be erected between religiously committed Presbyterians and those who took the name for different reasons. Devout believers were involved in customary rituals as much as nominal Presbyterians used the services offered by

[73] S. McSkimin, 'A statistical account of Islandmagee', *Newry Magazine*, 3 (1817), 435.

[74] Connolly, 'Marriage in pre-famine Ireland', in Cosgrove, *Marriage in Ireland*, 91–5.

[75] *OSMI* (Cumber), xxviii. 19; Barkley, 'Marriage', 35.

[76] Mason, *Statistical survey*, i. 595.

the church. Furthermore, it is important to place marriage and sexual relationships in the rapidly changing context of nineteenth-century society. This new society would privilege the civil aspect of the marriage contract, question the authority of Kirk sessions to prosecute sexual misconduct, and reduce the opportunities of indulging in raucous activity.

9

Death

Presbyterian attitudes to death and the rituals surrounding the experience of dying changed greatly from the seventeenth to the nineteenth century. The spartan provisions of the *Directory* for managing these experiences and rituals reflected the anti-Catholicism of Puritanism. The practices of praying 'by or towards the corpse' and religious ceremonies both to and at the graveside had been 'grossly abused' and must be laid aside.[1] Eager to divest the rituals of death of any remnants of popish superstition, the Westminster Assembly suggested that the body of the deceased be decently attended to the place of burial without a religious ceremony, though provision was made for civil honours where appropriate. The 'Christian friends' of the deceased ought to improve spiritually the occasion with the aid of a minister if present. During the eighteenth century, the Enlightenment reinforced this desire for simplicity by seeking to divest death of its terrors and traditional religious 'superstitions'.[2] In the following century, death became a more sentimental, familial, and gothic experience owing to the influence of Romanticism and evangelicalism, the latter of which renewed traditional notions of hell and judgement. Class dimensions were also an important component in determining attitudes to death. The gap between the lower classes and the middle and upper classes increased during the nineteenth century, as the art of dying became a virtual obsession with middle-class Victorians. This cultural ambience and the legacy

---

[1] *Directory*, 390–1.

[2] For an overview of changing attitudes to death in the eighteenth and nineteenth centuries see, J. Rugg, 'From reason to regulation: 1760–1850', in P. C. Rupp and C. Gittings (eds.), *Death in England: an illustrated history* (Manchester, 1999), ch. 8.

of the seventeenth-century doctrinal standards shaped Ulster Presbyterian attitudes to dying and death in the decades between 1770 and 1840. The twin themes of community and spiritual improvement are obvious as are the issues of class, sentiment, and judgement, though, as will be shown, the lines of development were blurred. The lack of official guidance as to how death and burial were to be handled meant that this rite of passage was ripe for lay appropriation in a variety of ways. This chapter is primarily concerned with two areas of practice that illustrate how Ulster Presbyterians perceived both life and death. Section one deals with wakes, their social character, the various popular beliefs that surrounded death, and the efforts of the Presbyterian authorities to reform perceived abuses. Section two examines the rituals of the deathbed, specifically the differences and shared experiences of evangelical and liberal Presbyterians as they attempted to 'die well'.

I

Recent anthropological studies have stressed the role of wakes in reaffirming the integrity and cohesion of Roman Catholic communities in the face of death.[3] This interpretation helps make sense of Presbyterian wakes, though there were inevitably significant differences in understanding and practice. John Caldwell described how his Catholic neighbours in Ballymoney would hold wakes for the 'two-fold purpose of praying for the soul of the departed and administering comfort to the afflicted'. Protestants would join with them in the social aspects of the occasion, but instead of offering 'useless' prayers for the deceased, they prayed that the experience would profit the living. Caldwell concluded, 'It is true the rights of hospitality on such occasions are frequently carried too far, but the excess like all the failings of an Irishman proceeds ... from the head and not from the heart; whilst we are amused or horrified at the exaggerated tales of excesses committed at an Irish wake, the extravagances and follies

---

[3] G. Ó Crualaoich, 'The "merry wake"', in J. S. Donnelly and K. A. Miller (eds.), *Irish popular culture 1650–1850* (Dublin, 1998), 191.

of the higher ranks of society are [studiously] kept out of view.'[4] The mixture of religious devotion, excessive festivity, and potential class dimensions will be recurrent themes in this section.

Owing to the symbiotic relationship between weaver poets and the local community to whom they were answerable, the poetry of the rhyming weavers provides a revealing insight into what occurred at Presbyterian wakes in the years between 1770 and around 1825.[5] The wake was usually held on the two nights before the burial. They combined both sacred and secular elements and provided small rural communities with the opportunity for social interaction. The eclectic group of mourners included neighbours, friends, family members disputing the will, the unknown pedant with his list of jokes, stories, and facts, pranksters, and those just there for the eating and drinking. The night was passed in various ways, including discussions, which were often intense and sometimes fuelled by alcohol. George Dugall painted an evocative picture of the content of these discussions in 1824.

> Glass after glass makes ev'ry guest a lord,
> And still fresh bumpers sparkle round the board;
> The madd'ning bliss but few incline to balk—
> Thus fumes of whiskey kindle into talk;
> The topics many—church and state affairs—
> Excisemen, robbers, bulls and breeding mares;
> Manures that suit on soils of diff'rent mould;
> Flax, barley, and potatoes, bought and sold:
> On peace, on war, corn-bill, and townland fine,
> Assert, reply, rejoin, but ne'er decline.
> Now warm debate foments the muddy plea;
> Now cronies differ, and now foes agree;
> So far at length, through knotty points they scan,
> That neither side can tell where they began.[6]

As outlined by the poet Samuel Walker, ghostly tales, accounts of personal bravery, and other stories were repeated, along with more religious and amorous topics.

---

    [4] J. Caldwell, 'Particulars of history of a north county Irish family' (PRONI, Caldwell papers, T/3541/5/3), 28.
    [5] D. H. Akenson and W. H. Crawford, *Local poets and social history: James Orr, bard of Ballycarry* (Belfast, 1977).
    [6] G. Dugall, *The northern cottage* (Londonderry, 1824), 35.

> Here Tam an' Bab, baith glible a' gab
> Are arguin' frae the Scripture
> An' whiles they get sae very hot
> They're like to hae a rupture
> There Meg an' Dick quite back an' thick
> Are in the corner crackin'
> 'Bout love an' sport, an gaine to court
> An' matrimony makin
> Some ither night.[7]

The night was not passed in conversation and worldly pursuits alone. The family of the deceased received comfort from Bible reading and psalm singing. The consolation taken in God's providence and his provision for the family left behind was a source of encouragement for those facing an uncertain future. The following stanza from James Orr's evocative poem, 'The Irish Cottier's Death and Burial', depicts this scene of communal devotion.

> Belyve an auld man lifts the Word o' God,
>   Gies out a line, an' sings o' grief an' pain;
> Reads o'er a chapter, chosen as it should,
>   That maks them sure the dead shall rise again;
> An' prays, that he, wha' hand has gie'n and ta'en,
>   May be the orphan's guide, the widow's stay;
> An' that, rememb'rin' death ere health be gane,
>   They a' may walk in wisdom's Heaven-ward way,
> Like him, the man o' worth, that's now a clod o' clay.[8]

It is noticeable how scripted the rituals of the wake were and Orr emphasises this point by using such phrases as 'chosen as it should' and 'wi' becomin' grace'.[9] On the whole the wake was a potent mixture of communal interaction, social decorum, and religious devotion.

Funerals tended to be humble affairs in the period before 1820, especially those of cottiers.[10] Ballymoney congregation hired out the

---

[7] S. Walker, 'A miscellaneous collection of poetry composed and written by Samuel Walker of Shaneshill near Templepatrick' [n.d.] (BCL, Bigger Collection), 154.

[8] J. Orr, *The posthumous works of James Orr, of Ballycarry* (Belfast, 1817), 74–5.

[9] L. Lunney, 'Attitudes to life and death in the poetry of James Orr, an eighteenth century Ulster weaver', *Ulster Folklife*, 31 (1985), 8.

[10] Ibid.

necessary paraphernalia for funerals, charging two crowns for the pall (three if a non-member), 2s. 8½d. for 'black shag cloth', and cloaks at 1s. each.[11] In Carnmoney funerals were usually held on the Sabbath to allow more people to attend, and a public hearse was available to bear the body of the deceased and alcohol for the mourners.[12] The Westminster injunction regarding graveside services seems to have been adhered to, though funeral services were held in meeting-houses for prominent local people, especially the minister. Graveside addresses and elaborate funerals became a feature of the Presbyterian experience of death in the nineteenth century and the laity came to expect such services. Evangelical ministers used the opportunity of preaching at the graveside for evangelistic purposes, using the experience of death as an occasion to confront people with their own eternal fate.[13] As the century progressed, funerals became grand affairs for prominent personalities, while the sparse funerals of eighteenth-century cottiers became even more modest.[14]

Other popular activities and beliefs surrounded death in Presbyterian areas. In Islandmagee, a man carrying a white rod announced the death of a prominent person and it was usual, as in other parts of Ulster, to stop the clocks in the house of the deceased until after the funeral.[15] Some believed that if a dog or cat passed over the body it should be killed immediately 'as ... the first person it would pass over afterwards would take the *falling sickness*', while in Holywood unexplained deaths were attributed to witchcraft.[16] Both Presbyterians and their Catholic neighbours believed that omens of

---

[11] A. H. Dill et al., *A short history of the Presbyterian churches of Ballymoney, County Antrim* (Bradford, 1898), 25. Antrim (GSU) session book, accounts for cloaks and palls, 1760–6 (J. M. Barkley, 'A history of the ruling eldership in Irish Presbyterianism', 2 vols. (QUB MA, 1952), ii. 62). For a description of a funeral procession see, J. W. Kernohan, *The county of Londonderry in three centuries, with notices of the Ironmongers' estate* (Belfast, 1921), 56.

[12] E. J. McCrum, 'Kirk and other customs of bygone days in Carnmoney', *Irish Presbyterian*, new ser., 12 (1906), 53.

[13] J. L. Porter, *The life and times of Henry Cooke* (Belfast, 1875), 120–1.

[14] Ibid., 461–4; J. Morgan, *Recollections of my life and times* (Belfast, 1874), 211–12; Rugg, 'Reason to regulation', 221–4.

[15] Lunney, 'Life and death', 7; S. McSkimin, 'A statistical account of Islandmagee', *Newry Magazine*, 3 (1817), 435–6; *OSMI* (Islandmagee), x. 95.

[16] S. McSkimin, *The history and antiquities of the county of the town of Carrickfergus*, ed. E. J. McCrum (Belfast, 1909), 350; W. S. Mason, *A statistical account, or parochial survey of Ireland*, 3 vols. (Dublin, 1814–19), iii. 208.

death included a dog howling in the middle of the night, seeing candle wax form certain shapes, or hearing the banshee.[17] The magpie was also the omen for other important phases in life. According to the popular rhyme,

> One is for sorrow, two is mirth
> Three is a wedding and four a birth;
> Five is silver, six is gold,
> Seven's a secret never to be told.[18]

The belief in ghosts and apparitions appears to be common in Presbyterian areas and there is evidence that a Presbyterian minister was involved in an exorcism in the eighteenth century.[19]

Wakes were certainly a mixture of the sacred and the profane, but in light of the criticisms of reformers, the picture painted by the weaver poets is certainly more humane and probably more accurate. Reformers inevitably condemned the immorality associated with wakes and funerals, though, as with other activities, superstitious beliefs were not directly challenged. The disapproval of traditional practice began with Enlightenment-inspired individuals in the early years of the nineteenth century. One correspondent to the *Belfast Monthly Magazine* in 1811 reproduced the dying wishes of the recently departed Joseph Millar of Dromore, County Down, for his funeral.[20] Millar did not wish any alcohol to be served and he desired that all invited should arrive on time, and if the curate of Hillsborough insisted on reading the Anglican burial service at his grave, his body was to be buried elsewhere. Neither did he want a wake as he believed the custom 'tends to introduce irregularity, levity of behaviour, and unprofitable conversation, unbecoming the solemnity of such an occasion'. After praising Millar's sentiments, the correspondent criticized wakes more generally, especially as the lower and

---

[17] Ó Crualaoich, 'Merry wake', in Donnelly and Miller, *Irish popular culture*, 177–80; W. S. Smith, *Historical gleanings in Antrim and neighbourhood* (Belfast, 1888), 147–9; *OSMI* (Desertoghill), xxvii. 18.

[18] Smith, *Historical gleanings*, 148.

[19] *OSMI* (Drumaul), xix. 61, (Ballylinny), xxxii. 19; 'Three supernatural occurrences in Ireland about the year 1760, related by Mr S——', *The Supernatural Magazine* (1809), 99.

[20] 'Observations on the manner of conducting funerals', *Belfast Monthly Magazine*, 7 (1811), 427–30.

middle 'stations' of society spent so much money in an attempt to imitate their social superiors who ought to know better. More important, he alluded to the role of popular opinion in changing practice and acknowledged that many agreed with these sentiments but were unwilling to do anything 'from a fear of being pointed at by their neighbours, and remarked as affecting singularity'.

Though there seems to have been no widespread desire for reform of funeral practices in 1811, the mood of the times was changing. The cult of self-improvement, economic hardships, and the temperance movement would soon provide the moral and numerical influence required. The 1825 *Code* exhibited a mixture of Enlightenment high-mindedness and evangelical zeal by characterizing the practice of assembling at wakes and serving refreshments as 'very inconsistent with the solemnity and seriousness that should reign in the house of mourning' and recommended that they should be discouraged by Kirk sessions.[21] Evangelicalism gave the reform campaign crucial impetus. From the mid-1820s, congregations and presbyteries began to publish resolutions committing themselves to the reform of wakes, which as practised were 'an outrage upon decency and religion, and highly unbecoming such solemn occasions'.[22] The arguments against these practices were a mix of religious, economic, and social concerns. Carntall congregation in County Tyrone produced a resolution in 1831 declaring that whisky drinking at wakes was 'injurious to the temporal and spiritual welfare of society; it tends to harden the mind against all the solemnities of death and eternity; it is distressing to the afflicted feelings of the relatives of the deceased; it is a serious inconvenience to many families by subjecting them to an unnecessary expense; and it cannot possibly by productive of any good to the community'. Moreover, they considered 'the practice of assembling publicly at wakes' to be 'injurious to the morals of the people, and annoying to the relatives of the deceased'.[23]

Surviving presbytery records from the period show that efforts to reform popular practice were widespread though progress was slow.

---

[21] *Code* (1825), 104.

[22] 'Presbytery of Magherafelt', *Orthodox Presbyterian*, 6 (1834), 68. J. Brown, *A sermon on drunkenness* (Belfast, 1825), 26 n.; A. A. McCaughan, *Heath, hearth and heart: the story of Dunboe and the meeting-house at Articlave* (Coleraine, 1988), 71.

[23] Carntall (GSU) committee book, 7 Apr. 1831 (PRONI, MIC/1P/96/2), 223.

The Presbytery of Raphoe, when drawing up its visitation questions in the mid-1830s, included three that related to illicit distilling and drinking at wakes and funerals.[24] As with the neighbouring Presbytery of Derry, some congregations reported a noticeable decline, while others saw mixed progress. A notable example of success was the congregation of Burt whose minister reported in August 1838 that the serving of alcohol at wakes and funerals was fast on the decline.[25] The following July, the Kirk session considered 'the propriety of discouraging throughout the bounds of the congregation burying the dead on the Lord's day, the holding of wakes, and distribution of spirituous liquor at funerals'.[26] By 1841 progress was reported to have been very good and the session resolved to maintain their efforts.[27] Elsewhere, excuses were made for the retention of alcohol in Ballynure where whisky was supposedly required to refresh the pall-bearers.[28] Indeed reform seems to have had a bigger impact upon the mood and decorum of the wake rather than the consumption of alcohol. In the mid-1830s the Presbyterians of Donegore began to issue invitations in order to limit numbers attending wakes. Moreover, their wakes, 'which formerly had been scenes of amusement, are now observed with decorum and propriety'. The Bible was read aloud during the evening and at night refreshments were provided 'consisting of bread and cheese, whiskey, pipe and tobacco'.[29] Alcohol continued to be consumed by ministers also. For his father's funeral in 1828, the evangelical Robert Magill paid John Quin £1. 7. 7. for 2 ½ gallons of spirits and two quarts of wine. His expenses also included 19s. 6d. for cakes, bread, and tobacco, 8d. for candles, and payments to carpenters, the sexton, and the bellman.[30] The presence of alcohol on this occasion was clearly not an

---

[24] 'Questions for visitation presbyteries, adopted by the Presbytery of Raphoe', *Orthodox Presbyterian*, 8 (1837), 168.

[25] Derry Pby (GSU), 7 Aug. 1838 (UTC), 146.

[26] Burt (GSU) session book, 14 July 1839 (PRONI, MIC/1P/33/2).

[27] Ibid., 22 Aug. 1841.

[28] *OSMI* (Ballynure), xxxii. 35.

[29] *OSMI* (Donegore), xxix. 113. See also, (Dundrod), xxi. 138, (Ballycarry), xxvi. 107, and (Ballyeaston), xxxii. 6.

[30] Diary of the Revd Robert Magill, 9 Dec. 1828, reprinted in J. Kenny, *As the crow flies over rough terrain; incorporating the diary 1827/8 and more of a divine* (Newtownabbey, 1988), 357.

aberration for he also purchased a gallon of spirits for his mother's funeral in 1835.[31]

It is important to appreciate the scale of the task facing reformers, as the drinking of spirits was such an important part of popular culture before the onset of the temperance movement. Consequently, individuals risked losing face by declaring adherence to principles that were not generally held by the local community.[32] Many Presbyterian ministers realized that reform would be a long-term undertaking and that a flexible approach was needed to deal with the sensibilities of rural communities. Anaghlone congregation declared against whisky drinking at wakes and funerals in 1829 while stressing that 'we do not rush to discountenance a custom which is established by long use, and founded upon praiseworthy motives'.[33] Another example of this flexible approach was provided by Henry Cooke who outlined his views in a letter to William Campbell, recently installed as minister of Islandmagee in 1829. He began by stating that wakes ought to be discouraged, but argued that if the local custom was for the minister to attend the wake then Campbell should do so. Once there, he should follow Cooke's example and refuse to take alcohol or 'dainties', and seek to preach in the house. Cooke would then bring the corpse to the meeting-house where he would perform a religious service before the committal. He recommended that Campbell 'Introduce no violent departure from old custom, except where it is sinful; but introduce improvement gently and rationally, and God will bless your labours. Substitute for the late hours at wakes something better so soon as you can; but even that do with caution, lest your good be evil spoken of.'[34]

II

The Westminster standards condemned the Catholic rites that had aided the dying, such as confession and absolution, the Eucharist and

---

[31] Diary of the Revd Robert Magill, 28 July 1835 (PHS).
[32] 'Observations on the manner of conducting funerals', 429; Walker, 'Miscellaneous collection', 156.
[33] *Belfast News-Letter*, 4 Dec. 1829.
[34] Porter, *Henry Cooke*, 120–1.

extreme unction. Theoretically, the believer was left confronting eternity without the aid of any comforting ritual. Yet, Protestants, including Puritans, developed their own rituals for the deathbed in order to bring solace to the individual and comfort to family and friends.[35] Dying well remained a meaningful, though less conspicuous goal, in eighteenth-century Protestant piety. The ideal arose to prominence once more in the nineteenth century with the rise to cultural prominence of evangelicalism. It has also been observed that evangelicalism reinforced the role of the family at the deathbed, which was one of the most prominent features of the Victorian experience of death.[36] It is important to recognize from the outset that the published obituaries and funeral sermons, which provide the basic evidence for any study of attitudes to death, were a carefully crafted literary genre in their own right, shaped by the values and mood of the time. As Pat Jalland has observed, 'the good Evangelical death required a rare combination of good luck, convenient illness, and pious character, and was achieved more often in Evangelical tracts than in family life'.[37] The obituaries on which this section is largely based reflect these basic values and the theological priorities of the time. Nevertheless, the representations tell us much about the ideal type of life and death Presbyterians desired to have and, as will be shown, they reflected reality to a remarkable degree. The art of good dying in the nineteenth century, though not confined to the middle and upper classes, was a prominent preoccupation of those groups. The revival of the Puritan deathbed, the impact of evangelicalism, and the growing respectability of the rituals of death are recurrent themes in this section.

An examination of the experience of death illustrates the factors that both united and divided liberal and orthodox Presbyterians in their understanding of some fundamental aspects of the Christian

[35] R. Houlbrooke, 'The Puritan deathbed, c. 1560–c. 1660', in C. Durston and J. Eales (eds.), *The culture of English Puritanism 1560–1700* (Basingstoke, 1996), ch. 4.

[36] P. Jalland, *Death in the Victorian family* (Oxford, 1996); H. D. Rack, 'Evangelical endings: deathbeds in evangelical biography', *Bulletin of the John Rylands University Library of Manchester*, 74 (1992), 39–56.

[37] Jalland, *Death in the Victorian family*, 38. Further information on the use of obituaries may be found in, L. Wilson, *Constrained by zeal: female spirituality amongst Nonconformists 1825–1875* (Carlisle, 2000), 20–40.

faith. Common to both groups were themes such as the ongoing preparation for death throughout life, the correlation between a holy life and a good death, the role of providence and the duty of submission to the divine will, and the hope of eternal life. Though both held an unwavering belief in divine providence, orthodox Presbyterians were more likely than liberals sometimes to see sickness as a judgement from God that should be responded to through repentance. Profound differences were also reflected in the keen polemical edge to their obituaries. After all, if the time of death was an 'honest hour' in which the beliefs of individuals were supposedly vindicated, which theology would better sustain the believer? Would it be Unitarianism or evangelicalism? The issue of deathbed conversions is a good example of this. For liberals who believed that a moral life contributed to salvation, the conversions of notorious sinners at their hour of death seemed not only preposterous but also immoral.[38] Evangelicals, on the other hand, while acknowledging the rarity of such conversions, deemed them neither 'impossible or incredible' for a sinner was saved by God's grace alone and not by his own sinful efforts.[39]

Both groups were convinced that the experience of death was as much about those who were left behind as about the dying individual. The importance of 'improving death', of learning from it and applying the lessons to life, was a central aim of obituaries and other deathbed accounts. J. S. Porter said on the death of William Bruce, senior, that the main reason for preaching on that solemn occasion was 'for awakening feelings and impressing lessons, that may be of everlasting importance'.[40] This process was aided by the constant re-publication in eighteenth- and nineteenth-century Ulster of various mourners' companions by authors such as John Flavel and John Willison.[41] The role of the elder and the minister was also important

---

[38] 'Notice of Wakefield on the punishment of death in the metropolis', *Bible Christian*, 3 (1832), 58–60.
[39] 'Orthodoxy safe and sustaining in the hour of death', *Orthodox Presbyterian*, 2 (1831), 263–5.
[40] J. S. Porter, *The Christian's hope in death* (Belfast, 1841), 5.
[41] J. R. R. Adams, *The printed word and the common man: popular culture in Ulster 1700–1900* (Belfast, 1987), 47, 49, 179; [J. S. Reid], *Catalogue of the Presbyterian congregational library, Carrickfergus* (n.p., [1831]), 2.

in so far as they provided spiritual guidance and exhortation. For example, the elders subjected the sick of Cahans congregation in the eighteenth century to a gruelling interrogation. The first question set the tone; 'If it please God that this disease prove mortal, where do you think your soul will go after death?'[42] Then followed an extensive list of questions designed to explore the soundness of the individual's faith, including, for example, 'Did ever any thought come into your heart that religion was a vanity and the Bible false?' During the 1820s and 1830s elders came under increasing pressure to take seriously their pastoral responsibilities. The 1825 *Code*, for instance, declared that it was the duty of any elder, 'when called upon, or when he thinks advisable, to visit, exhort, and pray for the sick; and also those families that have been visited by death, or other affliction'.[43]

Though a visit from an elder may have been appreciated, it was expected that a minister should attend to the sick or those approaching death. Both the *Directory* and the 1825 *Code* saw the sickbed as a unique God-ordained opportunity 'to minister a word in season to weary souls'.[44] When exhorting the sick, the minister was to demonstrate that their illness came not by chance but by God's providence, 'either for our correction and amendment, for the trial and exercise of our graces, or for other important ends', and that it would end well if 'wise improvement' was made of it.[45] If the person appeared ignorant of the principles of religion, the minister was to instruct them, taking care that the person did not presumptuously depend on his or her own goodness, or, at the same time, to despair of 'the mercy and grace of God in Christ Jesus'.[46] Ministers had to ensure that practical issues such as provision for the family and restitution of wrongs were taken care of before the sick person became 'insensible'.[47]

A minister who proved to be a faithful and effective visitor at the house of mourning was highly thought of amongst his congregation. The assistant and successor to Robert Park of Ballymoney remarked that Park was an assiduous visitor and excelled at presenting the

[42] J. M. Barkley, *The eldership in Irish Presbyterianism* (n.p., 1963), 50–1.
[43] *Code* (1825), 17.
[44] *Directory*, 388–9.
[45] *Code* (1825), 102–3.
[46] *Code* (1825), 103.
[47] *Code* (1825), 103–4; *Directory*, 390.

gospel to the dying, 'which gave him that deep hold on his people that was never relaxed the whole period of his ministry'.[48] Those with medical training were especially valued as they could offer free advice and remedies.[49] Yet, if a minister was not a diligent visitor, congregations had ways of ensuring his future compliance. In some cases they reported their minister to the local presbytery and in others withheld their stipend.[50] In 1811 the congregational committee of Killyleagh presented their minister Joseph Little with a lengthy document outlining their concerns with his organization of the congregation and his ministry. With due caution and respect, they stated that, 'if it is not the duty of the dissenting minister, it would be a Christian charity, at least, for him to take the earliest opportunity of visiting them to request the prayers of the congregation, and affording them such comfortable hopes, and their families such consolation as the case demands'.[51] There is no indication that this request was complied with, though the incident does reveal the importance attached by the laity to ministerial visitation and the need for ministers to cultivate a good relationship with their congregation.

Both evangelicals and Unitarians saw the deathbed as an 'honest hour'. For evangelicals the stark choice was between eternal life and eternal damnation as determined by the individual's attitude to Christ. Enlightenment sensibilities had made the concept and language of hell socially unacceptable in the eighteenth century. In the nineteenth century, there was a debate amongst non-subscribers as to the nature of God's punishment of the wicked, which all agreed was a necessary part of his judgement. Some held that it was remedial, preparing the sinner for heaven, whereas others saw it as punitive and followed by annihilation.[52] Either way, non-subscribers, whether

---

[48] J. H. Moore, *In memoriam. The Rev. Robert Park, A.M., Ballymoney. Born 15 April 1794. Ordained 18 March 1817. Died 10 May 1876* (Belfast, 1876), 24.

[49] A. McCreery, *The Presbyterian ministers of Killyleagh: a notice of their lives and times* (Belfast, 1875), 189; C. Porter, 'Congregational memoirs: Glenarm', *Christian Unitarian*, 5 (1866), 333.

[50] For the well-documented case of the Revd George McEwen of Killinchy see, Belfast Pby (GSU), 25 May 1791, 24 and 30 June 1791 (UTC). Also, Armagh Pby (GSU), 11 Mar. 1812 (PHS), 55–6; Ballymena Pby (GSU), 11 Aug. 1818 (PHS), 196.

[51] McCreery, *Presbyterian ministers of Killyleagh*, 198–200.

[52] R. G. Crawford, 'A critical examination of nineteenth-century non-subscribing Presbyterian theology in Ireland', 2 vols. (QUB Ph.D., 1964), ii. 552–6; Lunney, 'Life and death', 11.

ministers or the laity, did not hold to traditional views of hell. Old Light and Seceder Presbyterians seem to have continued to believe in a literal hell, and with the dawning of the Romantic age and the influence of evangelicalism, hell once more assumed a central place in religious discourse.[53] Beyond the eternal fate of the individual, the death of a believer was to be an example to all, particularly the young, who were seen as too embroiled in the pleasures of life to prepare for death.[54] One orthodox writer, most probably J. S. Reid, described the exemplary deathbed scenes of the pioneers of Irish Presbyterianism, Josias Welsh, Andrew Stewart, and Robert Cunningham. He invited his readers 'to behold them supported by the power of that faith which they had so nobly and consistently maintained, and rejoicing under tribulations that must have otherwise appalled the finest heart'.[55]

From the biographies of the great and the obituaries of the humble believer, a series of fundamental beliefs emerge indicating the core of Presbyterian evangelical beliefs and piety. As with their seventeenth-century forefathers, and evangelicals of other denominations, Presbyterians believed that preparations for death should be made throughout life.[56] According to one writer, 'the true Christian is habitually ready to die—as much so when asleep as awake—whether rejoicing in God, or mourning over sin—when suffering under the fear of death, and triumphing over it'. He continued that it was the believer's duty 'to cultivate the actual readiness of having his loins girt about, his lamps burning, being diligent in business, and waiting till his change come'.[57] The link between the life lived and the type of death experienced was a central theme of obituaries. It vindicated orthodox belief by demonstrating how a person's faith supported them even in death. In a series of articles entitled 'Orthodoxy safe and sustaining in the hour of death', a list of evangelical heroes was compiled showing how their beliefs had led them to live holy lives culminating in a happy death. They included Richard Baxter, Philip

---

[53] Jalland, *Death in the Victorian family,* 21; Rugg, 'Reason to regulation', 215; J. Morgan, *Essays in some of the principal doctrines and duties of the gospel,* 2nd edn. (Belfast, 1837), 226–32.
[54] 'Death', *Orthodox Presbyterian,* 7 (1836), 355–7.
[55] 'Death-bed scenes', *Orthodox Presbyterian,* 1 (1829), 61.
[56] *Directory,* 388; Houlbrooke, 'Puritan deathbed', 129; Rack, 'Evangelical endings', 46.
[57] *Orthodox Presbyterian,* 6 (1835), 381.

Doddridge, Augustus Toplady, John Wesley, Ebenezer Erskine, Bishop Bedell, Samuel Rutherford, and John Knox.[58] By contrast, infidels such as Voltaire were shown to have suffered terrible deaths, stricken by fear and restlessness.[59]

Yet, no matter how spiritually prepared individuals were for death, ministers knew from their pastoral work that there was not a uniform experience of death and allowance had to be made for different temperaments, levels of assurance, and the ravages of mental and physical disease.[60] 'One Christian soldier resigns his spirit in trembling hope—another in calm tranquillity; another, animated and enraptured, musters his dying energies, and shouts, Victory, Victory!'[61] Some believers had doubts about their faith and feared that God would reject them. Despite such difficulties, eighteenth- and nineteenth-century evangelicals maintained that a true Christian died in assurance of salvation as he or she had been saved by grace through the death and resurrection of Christ.[62] Sinclare Kelburn pointed out that it was the 'gospel of Christ alone which comforts us with the assurance, that those who sleep in Jesus shall be raised in glory and their bodies made like to Christ's glorious body, according to the working of his mighty power whereby he is able to subdue all things to himself'.[63] Henry Rack has noted that Calvinist deathbeds in the early nineteenth century were relatively unostentatious scenes, as believers exhibited 'the sense of being sinners dependent solely on the grace and mercy of God'.[64] Different people greeted death in different ways, but obituaries and funeral sermons insisted that the ideal death was to be simple and peaceful. 'Without being depressed by distressing fears on the one hand, or elevated by transporting joys on the other, peace in the hour of their departure, is the attainment of the generality of Christians.'[65]

[58] 'Orthodoxy safe and sustaining', *Orthodox Presbyterian*, 2 (1831), 265–71.

[59] 'A time to die', *Christian Freeman*, 3 (1835), 186–7.

[60] 'Orthodoxy safe and sustaining', 236–7; A. Breakey, *The Christian, the ruling elder, and the philanthropist* (Belfast, 1847), 23–4.

[61] 'Diversities in dying', *Christian Freeman*, 1 (1833), 415.

[62] 'Orthodoxy safe and sustaining', 136–8; Houlbrooke, 'Puritan deathbed', 137; P. G. Ryken, *Thomas Boston as preacher of the fourfold state* (Carlisle, 1999), 230–9.

[63] S. Kelburn, *The duty of preaching the gospel* (Dublin, 1790), 16.

[64] Rack, 'Evangelical endings', 49.

[65] 'Orthodoxy safe and sustaining', 237. See also, 'Diversities in dying', *Christian Freeman*, 1 (1833), 417; 'The death of a believer', *Orthodox Presbyterian*, 7 (1836), 249.

As with Seceders and Old Light evangelicals in the eighteenth century, assurance of salvation for nineteenth-century evangelicals depended upon the person and work of Christ.[66] Obituaries invariably included personal testimony about the sufficiency of Christ for salvation or a desire to depart and be with Christ. They often recorded that those in attendance questioned the dying person about their spiritual condition and interest in Christ.[67] Henry Lynn, a long-time elder in Ballycarry congregation, had always been orthodox but under an evangelical ministry he gained a clearer appreciation of the doctrines of grace. Not long before he died he declared to his minister, 'O, sir ... I am very unworthy; but it is a faithful saying, and worthy of all acceptation, that Jesus Christ came to save sinners, even the chief; and on that faithful saying I rest all my hopes for eternity.'[68] At the beginning of 1835, Miss McCord, who had been suffering from tuberculosis for some time, told her friend that she would soon be dead and then remarked, 'don't grieve for me—I desire to depart. The sting of death is taken away, and the grave shall have no victory. Thanks be to God who giveth us the victory through our Lord Jesus Christ.'[69]

Many obituaries showed how the individual's devotional life had sustained them in death. It was said of Agnes Cuming of Ballymena that she read and prayed regularly on her sickbed. Her favourite authors included John Owen, Thomas Boston, John Flavel, and John Newton, but as death approached, she read nothing but the Bible.[70] It was often recorded that the dying person dispensed practical and religious advice to those attending. On his deathbed in 1782, the New Light minister Thomas Crawford recommended to his family the 'study and practice of virtue and religion, as tending above all things to promote their happiness, both at present and for ever'. Crawford expressed a 'humble confidence in the divine favour, and a

---

[66] A. Holmes, 'Tradition and enlightenment: conversion and assurance of salvation in Ulster Presbyterianism, 1700–1859', in M. Brown, C. I. McGrath, and T. P. Power (eds.), *Converts and conversion in Ireland, 1650–1850* (Dublin, 2005), ch. 6.

[67] *Orthodox Presbyterian*, 6 (1834), 71; new ser., 1 (1838), 219–20.

[68] *Orthodox Presbyterian*, 5 (1833), 110.

[69] *Orthodox Presbyterian*, 6 (1835), 286. For similar sentiments see, *Christian Freeman*, 2 (1834), 180.

[70] *Orthodox Presbyterian*, 3 (1832), 360.

comfortable hope in reaping the blissful fruits of it; and with these pleasing sentiments he calmly expired like one falling asleep'.[71] Similarly, Samuel Steel, a Seceder from Toberkeigh, County Antrim, 'entreated his youngest brother to continue the worship of God, as it had been maintained in his house, morning and evening'.[72] Besides these exhortations, there were the final words of the individual that often echoed biblical passages. Steel declared, 'Into thy hands I commit my spirit, for thou art he, O thou Jehovah, God of truth, that hast redeemed me.' Maria Stewart of Ballycarry was heard to say, 'Lord, lettest thou thy servant depart in peace, *for mine eyes have seen thy salvation.* Lord Jesus, receive my spirit.'[73] In other cases, when the person concerned was unable to speak, signs were often looked for in their countenance that they were at peace or deep in prayer.[74] It was recorded that in his final moments, the Reformed Presbyterian minister Josias Alexander 'when unable to answer a question respecting his prospects ... lifted up his hands and eyes to heaven, in testimony of his assurance of a happy change'.[75]

Though liberal Presbyterians did not feel the need to record the minutiae of death for evidence of commitment to God, distinctive features of their theology and piety are evident in their obituaries.[76] Gawin Orr, an elder in Moneyreagh non-subscribing congregation, died 'believing in one God the Father, and receiving with a grateful heart Jesus Christ his Son, as the messenger of his mercy to an ignorant and guilty world'.[77] A good example of a 'non-enthusiastic' death may be found in the obituary of Mrs Armstrong of Ballynahinch, who died in 1836, aged 86 years. 'Her religious expressions on her deathbed, were consistent with the simple and rational character of her religious convictions—no violent rhapsody—no exaggerated exclamations—no enthusiastic raptures—but the mild, soft, tranquil,

---

[71] W. Bryson, *The practice of righteousness productive of happiness* (Belfast, 1782), 28.

[72] *Christian Freeman,* 3 (1834), 36.

[73] 'The death of a believer', *Orthodox Presbyterian,* 7 (1836), 249.

[74] Jalland, *Death in the Victorian family,* 37–8.

[75] W. Henry, *A funeral sermon, preached on Sabbath evening, November 23, 1823* (Belfast, 1823), 21 n.

[76] 'Erroneous views of death', *Bible Christian,* 6 (1835), 78–9, article reprinted from the *Boston Christian Examiner;* Jalland, *Death in the Victorian family,* 49–51.

[77] *Bible Christian,* 1 (1830), 299.

edifying aspiration of a Christian soul, humbly but steadfastly relying on the boundless mercy and paternal love of the Creator as revealed through the Redeemer of the world.'[78] Liberal Presbyterians believed that the eternal destiny of individuals would be based upon God's assessment of their works. Though they were sinners, believers had confidence in the mercy of God, that he would accept their efforts, forgive them, and grant them eternal life.[79] William Steel Dickson, in his funeral sermon for James Armstrong in 1780, commented that a person's place in heaven was 'according to the rank which they have attained in the scale of virtue'.[80] Furthermore, Dickson sought to improve Armstrong's death for his listeners by exhorting them to live a life similar to their deceased pastor; 'Mark, then, the path of holiness and virtue which he trod before you, and follow him in it with steady pace; for it alone leads to the mansions where he and blessedness dwell together.'[81] As the obituary for John Adams declared, 'If a life distinguished by simplicity, gentleness, benevolence, and an ardent zeal for the promotion of truth and virtue be the pledge of future happiness, his lot must be happy!'[82]

An important theme highlighted in the above examples is the significant amount of autonomy a woman had on her deathbed.[83] It is clear that female deaths were exemplary for both sexes, and women were given the opportunity to exhort and teach those in attendance. The death of Miss G—y, recounted in a two-part article in the *Orthodox Presbyterian*, illustrates this point.[84] Throughout her life, she had been reticent about talking of spiritual things in public, but on her deathbed she talked openly and at length about her spiritual experiences. Near the end, as her relatives, male and female, gathered around her, she was anxious to return them a gift for all their kindness towards her. 'Perhaps, the best way is to show you how to die. To show how little man can do for man in the dying

---

[78] *Bible Christian*, new ser., 1 (1836), 216.
[79] Crawford, 'Nineteenth-century non-subscribing Presbyterian theology', ii. 532–48.
[80] W. S. Dickson, *'Ye shall appear with Christ in glory'* (Belfast, 1780), 14–15.
[81] Ibid., 40.
[82] *Bible Christian*, 5 (1834), 145.
[83] Houlbrooke, 'Puritan deathbed', 139–40.
[84] 'Death of a Christian', *Orthodox Presbyterian*, 1 (1830), 196–9, 233–6.

hour ... Oh! Then seek that friendship, which cheers in life, sup-
ports in death, and blesses through eternity.' Though this account
follows literary conventions, it was designed for male and female
readers. The same applies to other obituaries of pious women. For
evangelicals it was the content of the person's faith and the manner of
their death that mattered rather than the gender of the deceased.

Though the stylized motifs of obituaries may create a somewhat
distorted picture of how evangelicals coped with death, similar
themes and experiences can be seen in the personal papers of Ulster
Presbyterians. There are no surviving manuscript accounts from lay
Presbyterians, but an examination of the papers of three ministers
gives us an insight into how they dealt with the death of a loved one.
John Tennent, minister of Roseyards Antiburgher congregation,
wrote to his son Robert on 2 August 1805 informing him that his
mother had died at midnight according to the providence of God.
John asked that his family would visit him soon and confided, 'And
now I am left alone of worldly company. But I hope God will be my
God and guide.'[85] In a much more detailed letter to his eldest son
William, written seven days later, he reflected upon events. He knew
that his wife was now in a better place while they remained 'here in
the wilderness'. In the light of eternity, the only differences between
individuals that mattered were between the righteous who trusted in
Christ and the wicked that denied him. At the end of his letter he
mentioned that he often thought of the times he and his wife had
together but that such memories 'are like to strike me to the very
heart. This is an affliction and I must bear it.'[86] In January 1807
William's wife Elenor died. The Revd Tennent encouraged his son to
look to God for help and to assure him that Elenor was in a better
place.[87] 'Philosophers may talk of fortitude in adversity and strive to
reason themselves into peace and patience but real religion only
[supplies] us with all we need in a way of betaking ourselves to
God as our own God and father upon the footing of his own word

    [85] The Revd John Tennent to Robert Tennent, 2 Aug. 1805 (PRONI, Tennent
papers, D/1748/C/1/211/49).
    [86] The Revd John Tennent to William Tennent, 9 Aug. 1805 (ibid. D/1748/B/1/
317/57).
    [87] The Revd John Tennent to William Tennent, 27 Jan. 1807 (ibid. D/1748/B/1/
317/63).

and promise and so may say as Ps[alm] 46 God is our refuge and our strength.' The Revd Tennent then compared William's experiences with his own loss a year-and-a-half earlier and wondered 'how shall I speak to calm that turbulent mind of yours like mine once was in a similar situation raging like a wild bull in a net'.

On returning home from meeting on the 30 July 1815, James Morell, minister of the Synod of Ulster congregation of Ballybay, found his youngest daughter, aged fifteen months and who had been ill for some time, near death. The following extract speaks for itself.

Having commended her soul to God by the most fervent prayers I was capable of, she died on my knee at half past twelve on Monday 31st July 1815 aged near 15 months. She breathed her last, without any appearance of pain, with a serene and heavenly smile on her countenance, leaving a confident impression in my mind, that she had tasted the joy of Heaven even before her little heart had ceased to beat upon the earth. May my latter end be as peaceful and as serene as hers.[88]

He continued to reflect upon his tragic loss and reproved himself for having taken life too lightly in the past. 'May God prepare my soul for all the events of the mournful pilgrimage of life. May he sanctify my affliction to my soul, and make all things work together for my good. May the death of my own infant be an awful warning to myself, to prepare to meet my God.' On Tuesday, he buried his daughter in the burial ground beside the meeting-house. It must have been an awful experience, but Morell consoled himself that he and his wife would see their daughter again in heaven. The following Sunday, he recorded the melancholic mood at home; 'My dear wife feels most severely the loss of her infant, but I earnestly hope that God will make it a great blessing to her soul.'

The final example of a personal response to death is that of Robert Magill of Antrim. At ten-to-five on the afternoon of 7 May 1827 Magill's father died after a long illness that had confined him to bed. In his last days his father became 'patient and resigned. He longed for deliverance and put his trust in God his Saviour—retired from the noise, the bustle and confusion of the world. He held converse with

[88] Diary of the Revd James Morell, 30 July 1815, in D. Nesbitt, *Full circle: a story of Ballybay Presbyterians* (Monaghan, 1999), 48. The following quotations are from the same source.

God and through the atoning Blood of our Lord and Saviour Jesus Christ he enjoys I humbly trust the rest enjoyed by those who were once weary and heavy laden.'[89] The diary entries for the following two days recount the funeral and the wake, but, by 10 May, Magill was back at work, visiting and baptizing the members of his congregation. Tragedy struck once more on 14 September 1832 when Magill's wife, Ann Jane, awoke in the morning with cholera and died a mere six hours later.[90] According to his diary, 'she breathed her last with my hand under her head' and 'during the tortures of the disease she never repined but prayed God to look down in pity on her, and frequently her hands were lifted up in silent prayer'. Magill reflected in the same entry upon the fleeting nature of human happiness and expressed his desire to 'put my trust in Him who is the resurrection and the life and may this afflictive and overwhelming dispensation be blessed by God to my salvation'. Magill buried his wife at 5.30 in the evening, kissing her twice before the coffin lid was closed.

All three examples, though written by ministers who knew the correct ways of improving death, are honest and heartfelt attempts to articulate their faith in the midst of tragic circumstances. There is an air of contrived normality in these accounts that indicates both how these men coped with their loss and a familiarity with death that the modern world little appreciates. Despite this tone it is obvious that these individuals and their families were deeply affected by the death of a loved one. What is remarkable is how many of the themes highlighted in printed obituaries appear in these personal accounts. The importance of a good death is underlined and though the dying words are not, or could not be, recorded, the impression of peace and calm is important. In Magill's account his father's death is linked with the life he has lived and his desire to be with Christ in his final days. All submitted to God's will and the centrality of Christ is emphasized with particular clarity in the accounts by Magill and Morell. The most striking feature, however, is the desire of all three men to learn from the deaths, to improve them, to amend their lives, and to renew their commitment to Christ. The personal faith of these

---

[89] Diary of the Revd Robert Magill, 7 May 1827, reprinted in Kenny, *As the crow flies*, 356–7.

[90] Diary of the Revd Robert Magill, 14 Sept. 1832 (PHS).

individuals enabled them to cope with the deaths of their loved ones by placing the events in a broader, providential perspective.

An examination of wakes and of the desire to die well highlights important aspects of Presbyterian belief and practice. The import- ance of the local community, the everyday devotional life of the individual, and differing views of God and his interaction with the world are all present in Presbyterian attitudes towards death. In all these areas differences were being established and identities asserted. However, the constant repetition of words such as peace, humility, simplicity, faith, and trust outline an ideal type of piety that all Presbyterians were to aspire to. Living one's life in the light of death and eternity had implications for the practice of Presbyterian godliness and their attitude to the world. Dignity in the face of death is a difficult thing to achieve, but the presence of family, friends, neighbours, and ministers provided the comfort of community in those final moments. What is more, personal faith sustained the individual and the hope of heaven pointed to a new community of sinless perfection. Though the means of dealing with death became more professionalized as the nineteenth century progressed, the pain and emotion of death remained as tangible as ever.

Part IV

Religious Instruction, Fellowship, and Activity Beyond the Meeting-House

Though the meeting-house provided the focus for formal Presbyterian religious life, the laity continued to learn about and practise their religion outside of that setting. The following section examines the various components of religious instruction and fellowship beyond the meeting-house and assesses the impact of evangelicalism upon religious instruction, pastoral efficiency, and lay involvement in church life. Chapter 10 considers the means of religious education available for Presbyterians by examining catechizing, Sunday and day schools, attitudes towards education, and literacy and reading habits. Chapter 11 outlines the opportunities for fellowship that existed, particularly family worship, prayer meetings, and religious societies, and examines the importance of small groups in sustaining and controlling the beliefs of individual believers. Three important themes run through these chapters: first, the attempts of evangelical reformers in the nineteenth century to regulate the voluntary nature of corporate devotions and lay piety in terms of doctrinal content and the structures involved; second, though evangelical reforms were often imposed from above, the values espoused by reformers were shared more broadly by a significant cross-section of the laity; finally, the activism of evangelicalism provided unprecedented opportunities for lay Presbyterians, especially women, to be involved in church life. Evangelicalism provided a noticeable increase in pastoral efficiency, the availability of knowledge, and created numerous opportunities for the laity to develop the religious and social aspects of their lives.

10

Catechizing, Education, and Reading Practices

The local Kirk session was expected to oversee the life and conduct of the congregation. One important means of doing so was for both ministers and elders to catechize and visit the congregation on a regular basis.[1] Usually the minister did the bulk of the work and, as noted in the previous chapter, ministerial visitation was one of the linchpins of a successful ministry. Regular visitation by the minister imparted religious knowledge and reinforced the relationship between himself and his congregation. By visiting frequently ministers were able to assess the spiritual mood of their people and so tailor their sermons to meet the needs of the laity. As the nineteenth century progressed, the catechizing component of ministerial visitation gradually became less important as Sunday schools provided for the religious education of the laity. This chapter begins by outlining how catechizing and visitation was conducted and the impact evangelicalism had upon pastoral efficiency in the Synod of Ulster. Section two examines the provision of education through Sunday and day schools, noting the symbiotic relationship between the supply of opportunities for education on the part of voluntary societies and the demands of the laity. The chapter will conclude by examining in general terms the reading practices of Presbyterians, what and how they read, and the impact evangelicalism had upon the demand for, and supply of, certain types of reading material.

---

[1] *Code* (1825), 100–2; J. M. Barkley, *A short history of the Presbyterian Church in Ireland* (Belfast, 1959), 98–9.

I

For many ministers in the eighteenth century, the annual round of visitation and catechizing coincided with preparations for the administration of communion. In his visitation of Ballymoney in spring 1775, Alexander Marshall and his elders divided the congregation into districts and examined the young in the *Shorter Catechism* or the *Confession* while the adults were 'called on to state the prevalence of piety and religion and morality in their respective families and vicinage'. The meetings were held in a suitably large building, such as a barn or mill, involved acts of worship, and concluded with suitable hospitality.[2] A number of ministers followed Scottish practice by catechizing in the meeting-house either during or after public worship.[3] In other places ministers chose to visit and catechize their congregations year about due to the large number of families under their care.[4] The expected form of visitations and catechizing was enshrined in the *Code*. Each minister was to visit his congregation annually, or every two years if it was large, while keeping a registry of families visited, the number of Bibles in circulation, the prevalence of family worship, and attendance at communion.[5] Meetings for catechizing were to be publicly appointed for districts of the congregation, and all that resided there, whether adult or child, were to attend. The Westminster catechisms were alone authorized for use and general religious exhortation was to be given to those attending. The prescribed pattern of visitation laid down in the *Code* was followed in most cases, though inevitably there would always be variations. The frequency and success of visitation and catechizing depended upon a number of factors including the size of the congregation and the age, health, and zeal of the minister. The pastorally-minded New Light ministers John Bankhead and

---

[2] J. Caldwell, 'Particulars of history of a north county Irish family' (PRONI, Caldwell papers, T/3541/5/3), 24. Barkley, *Short history*, 98.

[3] Templepatrick Pby (GSU), 3 Aug. 1825 (PRONI, MIC/1P/85/1); J. Agnew (ed.), *The Drennan-McTier letters*, 3 vols. (Dublin, 1998–9), i. 107; T. Croskery, 'Memoir of the Rev. Samuel Dill, of Donoughmore, Co. Donegal', *Evangelical Witness*, 7 (1869), 51.

[4] J. Semple, *The survey impartially examined by sacred Scripture and sound reason* (Belfast, 1754), 54.

[5] *Code* (1825), 100–2.

Nathaniel Alexander both reported high levels of catechetical knowledge amongst their church members.[6] Likewise, the equally committed evangelical minister of Antrim, Robert Magill, recorded in his diary
in 1821 that out of 137 children he had examined, no fewer than eighty-
three were able to repeat the first twenty Psalms and most could repeat
the whole of the *Shorter Catechism*.[7] Catechetical instruction also
involved a dynamic relationship between the catechizer and the catechized. The laity not only filtered the knowledge imparted through
various personal and community values but by their very willingness
to be catechized ensured that the system functioned at all. For example,
Hugh Brooke, minister of Burt congregation, reported to the Presbytery of Derry in 1825 that he was 'not in the habit of catechising owing
to the want of co-operation on the part of the members'.[8]

Evangelical ministers saw pastoral visitation and catechizing as
opportunities to impart religious knowledge and promote the revival
of true religion. District preaching often accompanied visitations and
the establishment of Bible classes aimed to augment the infrequent
routine of catechizing.[9] A good example of the new dispensation was
John Knox Leslie, minister of the newly formed Synod of Ulster
congregation in Cookstown.[10] Knox visited his entire congregation
in 1835, recording the appropriate details and preaching in outlying
areas. In the following year, 'I again visited them inquiring particularly into the state of each family as to copies of the Scriptures, family
worship, capacity to read, attendance at public worship, etc. I selected
one verse, made all the members read it, examined them upon it,
addressed them and prayed.' Over the next two years he visited 499
families within the space of four three-month sessions. After visiting
a number of townlands, Leslie would hold a diet of catechizing for all
the families he had visited, examining them upon the *Shorter
Catechism* and the Bible verses they had learnt.

Catechizing provided the framework in which to assess and understand the doctrinal distinctiveness of the community.[11] The staple

---

[6] Templepatrick Pby (GSU), 1 Aug. 1796, 5 May 1818.

[7] Diary of the Revd Robert Magill, 5 May 1821 (PRONI, Young papers, D/2930/9/6).

[8] Derry Pby (GSU), 1 Nov. 1825 (UTC).

[9] 'Congregational improvement', *Christian Freeman*, 1 (1832), 24–6

[10] Visitation book of the Revd J. K. Leslie, 1837–8 (PHS).

[11] For general comments about the functions of catechizing see, I. Green, *The Christian's ABC: catechisms and catechising in England, c. 1530–1740* (Oxford, 1996), 43.

catechism in the eighteenth and nineteenth centuries was obviously the Westminster *Shorter Catechism*, often known merely as 'the questions' or 'the question beuk'. Evangelicals hailed the influence of the *Shorter Catechism* upon Ulster Presbyterianism, claiming that the laity's immersion in it had saved the eighteenth-century church from wholly succumbing to Arianism.[12] One writer in 1830 declared, 'As a specimen of lucid order, accurate definition, and comprehensive abridgement, it stands amongst the catechisms of the churches, pre-eminent and unrivalled.'[13] Not all shared this view and it was a common complaint that the catechism was beyond the understanding of young children. Samuel Neilson, a United Irishman and son of the Revd Alexander Neilson of Ballyroney, wrote to his wife in 1801 that the 'first part of it is far above the comprehension of children', but in keeping with his commitment to virtuous conduct, 'all the latter part of it, from the preface to the commandments, to the end, is very proper and should be deeply impressed on the memory'.[14] Various authors, both in England and in Scotland, produced catechisms in the seventeenth and eighteenth centuries to improve the explanation of the *Shorter Catechism*.[15] Many were reprinted in Ulster including works by the English authors Joseph Alleine, Thomas Doolittle, and Thomas Vincent. Scottish catechisms were predictably popular in Ulster, especially those produced by John Willison, the Church of Scotland evangelical, and Ebenezer Erskine and John Fisher, two of the founders of the Seceder Associate Presbytery.[16] The nineteenth century saw a resurgence of catechism production amongst evangelicals and orthodox

---

[12] J. S. Reid, *History of the Presbyterian Church in Ireland*, ed. W. D. Killen, 3 vols., 2nd edn. (Belfast, 1867), iii. 460.

[13] 'The reformer. No. II. Reform in the education of youth', *Orthodox Presbyterian*, 2 (1830), 105.

[14] R. R. Madden, *The United Irishmen, their lives and times*, 4 vols., 2nd edn. (Dublin, 1858–60), iv. 121.

[15] Green, *Christian's ABC*, 81–3, 260–2; D. C. Lachman, 'Catechisms', in N. M. de S. Cameron (org. ed.), *Dictionary of Scottish church history and theology* (Edinburgh, 1993), 142–3.

[16] J. R. R. Adams, *The printed word and the common man: popular culture in Ulster 1700–1900* (Belfast, 1987), 44, 179, 183, 184, 189; I. Green, ' "The necessary knowledge of the principles of religion": catechisms and catechising in Ireland, c. 1560–1800', in A. Ford, J. McGuire, and K. Milne (eds.), *As by law established: the Church of Ireland since the Reformation* (Dublin, 1995), 85–6.

Presbyterians in both Ulster and Scotland. Catechisms prepared by the eighteenth-century Seceder John Brown and the nineteenth-century evangelical Andrew Thomson were used extensively by Ulster Presbyterians, especially for communion preparation.[17] Catechisms were also published locally to explain and defend the principles of the orthodox party after 1829 and Presbyterianism more generally. Examples included *A catechism of the government and discipline of the Presbyterian Church*, first published in 1835 and compiled by John Barnett of Moneymore and James Denham then of Brigh, and the reissue of both the Westminster catechisms by Henry Cooke and his mentor Sidney Hamilton Rowan.[18] Evangelicals wished also to improve the effectiveness of catechizing by working with smaller groups and placing less reliance upon rote learning.[19]

While Old Light Presbyterians and the Seceders relied upon the *Shorter Catechism* and Puritan or Scottish works, New Light Presbyterians were producing their own catechisms. Authors included John Bankhead of Ballycarry, Robert Black of Derry, and, the most significant, John Mears of Dublin.[20] The catechisms of Bankhead and Mears were reprinted in the nineteenth century with extensive re-editing that reflected the drift towards Arianism. In 1812 A. G. Malcolm of Newry published a catechism on the principles of the Christian religion and one especially designed for communion preparation, both of which reflected his rational, non-subscribing approach to Christian doctrine.[21] The Presbytery of Antrim recommended another catechism in 1819, which studiously avoided any possibly contentious doctrinal formulations, and Presbyterians more generally promoted the publication of *The Protestant dissenter's*

---

[17] Armagh Pby (GSU), 7 Nov. 1838, 5 May 1840 (Church House, strong room); Belfast Pby (GSU), 7 Mar. and 20 July 1837, 1 May 1838, 4 May 1840 (Church House, strong room).

[18] [J. Barnett and J. Denham], *A catechism on the government and discipline of the Presbyterian church* (Belfast, 1835); H. Cooke (ed.), *The larger catechism* (Belfast, 1835); J. A. McIvor, *Popular education in the Irish Presbyterian Church* (Dublin, 1969), 93.

[19] 'Religious revivals', *Christian Freeman*, 1 (1833), 116; McIvor, *Popular education*, 93.

[20] T. Witherow, *Historical and literary memorials of Presbyterianism in Ireland*, 2 vols. (Belfast, 1879–80), ii. chs. 55, 71, 89.

[21] A. G. Malcolm, *A catechism* (Newry, 1812); idem, *The communicant's catechism* (Newry, 1812).

catechism by Samuel Palmer, an English Independent minister and a non-subscriber.[22] None of these catechisms, however, fulfilled the needs of liberal Presbyterians. A Remonstrant writer in 1836 lamented the lack of a suitable catechism, particularly as the greater efficiency of orthodox catechizing exposed the need to inculcate their principles amongst the young.[23]

The impact of catechizing and visitation upon lay belief varied. As in other areas, Seceders had castigated the Synod of Ulster in the eighteenth century for the standard of their pastoral visitation and the lack of any of the Westminster standards in circulation.[24] These charges were predictably sweeping. John Semple argued that ministers did encourage distribution of the Westminster documents at baptism, during catechizing and visitation, and by distributing them as prizes. Moreover, catechisms, along with Bibles and Psalters, formed the basis of the eighteenth-century book trade.[25] The visitation returns of Templepatrick Presbytery in the late eighteenth century reveal a variety of ministerial experiences. John Bankhead told the presbytery in August 1796 that 'the young people showed great industry in the matter of catechising'.[26] On the other hand, Thomas Read of Glenarm reported in 1780 'that the generality of the people could not be induced to attend catechising', a situation that was repeated in the orthodox Carrickfergus congregation.[27] Presbytery visitations in the 1830s often reported a lack of catechisms and poor attendance at diets of catechizing.[28] However, other sources suggest that conscientious visitation by ministers could lead to better

---

[22] *Abstract of the history of the Bible, in question and answer* (Belfast, 1819); Adams, *Printed word and the common man*, 47.

[23] 'Should we use a catechism of Scripture doctrine in teaching the young?', *Bible Christian*, new ser., 1 (1836), 181–4.

[24] T. Clark, *A brief survey of some principles maintained, by the General Synod of Ulster, and practices carried on, by several members thereof* (Armagh, 1751), 33–7.

[25] Semple, *Survey impartially examined*, 59–61; Adams, *Printed word and the common man*, 43.

[26] Templepatrick Pby (GSU), 1 Aug. 1796.

[27] C. Porter, 'Congregational memoirs. Glenarm', *Christian Unitarian*, 5 (1866), 227; Templepatrick Pby (GSU), Nov. 1796.

[28] Coleraine Pby (GSU), 14 May 1839 (Church House, strong room); Raphoe Pby (GSU), 1834–41 (Church House, strong room); Tyrone Pby (GSU), 1836–41 (Church House, strong room); Belfast Pby (GSU), 7 Mar. 1837 (Church House, strong room).

attendance at public worship and the better observance of family worship.[29]

During the 1820s and 1830s ministers increasingly expressed concern about the infrequency of catechizing and visitation and the consequent lack of influence upon the knowledge of the laity. This reflected increased expectations of what these could achieve and also an awareness that population growth in both rural and urban areas had reduced the effectiveness of the pastoral strategies previously employed. Few Belfast ministers seem to have appreciated the onset of urban growth in the early years of the nineteenth century, prompting one writer to criticize the clergy of the town for their lack of pastoral visitation and their failure to instruct the laity in Presbyterian doctrine.[30] By the 1820s, an awareness of the need to reach the thousands of nominal or unattached people in Belfast led to the formation of voluntary societies such as the Belfast Town Mission and the extension of the Sunday school system. Visitation technique was also adapted to meet the needs of urban society. Josias Wilson, minister of Townsend Street, found it easier to visit from house to house rather than by district as he had done in the countryside around Drogheda.[31] Cooke proposed that the city should be divided into parishes to allow ministers to direct their efforts more easily to specific areas of need, probably borrowing the idea from Thomas Chalmers' efforts in Scotland.[32]

Presbyterians also sought to address the problems raised by population growth through the employment of Scripture readers. The *Code* allowed for the appointment of 'occasional assistants' to preach in the absence of the incumbent minister after proper authorization by the local Kirk session or presbytery.[33] Most readers were Presbyterian licentiates, but some were laymen. Each reader was allotted a certain geographical area to help with visitation, the establishment of

---

[29] Ballymoney (GSU) session book, 'History of the congregation, 1827–66', 24–5 (PRONI, CR/3/1/B/4); Down Pby (B/Sec.), 14 Apr. 1835 (PHS), 249.

[30] A Poor Old Light Presbyterian, *An address to the most reverend the Synod of Ulster on behalf of the poor of the Presbyterian body of the town of Belfast* (Belfast, 1812).

[31] Belfast Pby (GSU), 20 June 1837.

[32] Ibid., 7 Jan. 1840.

[33] *Code* (1825), 43–4.

prayer meetings, catechizing, the circulation of literature, and the promotion of family worship and Sunday schools.[34] A few ministers questioned whether Scripture and Presbyterian procedure warranted the use of untrained and unordained lay people in this role, but supporters of the scheme recognized that the scale of the problem made it unavoidable.[35] Despite the shortage of funds, the statistics are impressive. The number of readers per year in the 1830s fluctuated between seven and twenty. At the peak of effectiveness in 1838, the readers visited 17,979 persons and 4,580 sick people, organized 2,554 meetings for prayer and catechizing, and catechized 3,170 children.[36]

Nineteenth-century evangelicals predictably attributed the problem of nominal Presbyterianism in part to the character of eighteenth-century ministers, many of whom were described as slothful, immoral, and sometimes heterodox.[37] Contrary to this opinion, church courts in the eighteenth century were always concerned about ministers who failed to attain the expected moral and pastoral standards and there continued to be ineffectual pastors in the nineteenth century. Nor did differences in pastoral efficiency necessarily run along theological lines. It is certainly the case that evangelical ministers, such as David Hamiliton, James Morgan, Robert Park, and Josias Wilson, were assiduous visitors and catechizers, but so too were the New Light ministers Nathaniel Alexander, John Bankhead, and George Hill. Still, the tightening of discipline and oversight of ministers in the Synod of Ulster ensured that a higher standard was at least advocated across the board. It is certainly the case that there were increased expectations about a minister's pastoral workload. Eighteenth-century funeral sermons focused upon a minister's eloquence and virtue, rarely that he was a good visitor or catechizer. The new breed of minister was to display intelligence, fidelity, zeal, wisdom,

---

[34] *Report of the Presbyterian Missionary Society of the Synod of Ulster* (Belfast, 1832), 2–4.

[35] For both sides of the argument, see, M. Orr, *Lay preaching in the Synod of Ulster* (Belfast, 1838) and J. Morgan, *Reflections of the death of Mr William Cochrane, one of the agents of the Belfast Town Mission* (Belfast, 1837), 10–11.

[36] *Report of the Presbyterian Missionary Society of the Synod of Ulster* (Belfast, 1839), 7.

[37] 'Synod of Ulster—state of congregations', *Orthodox Presbyterian*, 6 (1835), 240–1.

diligence, and dignity. Most of all, they must have a personal attachment to the person and cause of Christ.[38] To achieve this the Theological Education Committee was established in 1828 to make enquiries into the personal religious character of potential students.[39] The Seceders formed a similar committee four years later to ensure candidates possessed that 'religious knowledge, personal piety, and self-devotedness which are essentially prerequisite' for the ministry after concern was expressed about the lack of attention given to the religious qualifications of students.[40] To help ministers concentrate upon their duties, they were urged to give up any secular employments, which was made easier by an increased *regium donum*.[41]

The new ministry would be helped in the cause of reform by a revived eldership. The common view is that the Presbyterian eldership in the eighteenth and nineteenth century was largely committed, scrupulous, and moral.[42] During the second half of the eighteenth century, Seceders through presbyteries and privy censures had shown themselves to be discerning in their choice of elders and in ensuring they held correct doctrine and did their pastoral duty.[43] Efforts were made in the Synod of Ulster to draw attention to the importance of the eldership, though New Light Presbyterianism may have adversely affected its status.[44] For instance, William Bruce questioned the place of lay elders in church courts and Fletcher Blakely denied that there was any scriptural warrant for the office of lay elder.[45] The need to reform the eldership was perceived to be a priority by Old Light and

[38] For descriptions of the new type of ministers see, S. Hanna, *A sermon on the qualifications of the ministerial character* (Belfast, 1810); H. Cooke, *A sermon, preached at the opening of the General Synod of Ulster* (Belfast, 1825); J. Wilson, *A charge and defence of Presbyterianism* (Drogheda, 1829); J. Brown, *The Christian ambassador* (Belfast, 1833).

[39] R. F. G. Holmes, *Henry Cooke* (Belfast, 1980), 56–8, 60–2.

[40] *MPSI* (1832), 22.

[41] H. Hastings, *Memoir of the life and labours of the late Rev. Josias Wilson* (London, 1850), 39–40, 313–27.

[42] J. M. Barkley, *The eldership in Irish Presbyterianism* (n.p., 1963).

[43] MASB (1788), 54; Barkley, *Eldership*, 26–9; T. Clark, *New light set in a clear light* ([Dublin], 1755), 56.

[44] *RGSU* iii. (1802), 250; (1803), 267.

[45] W. I. Craig, *Presbyterianism in Lisburn from the seventeenth century: First Lisburn Presbyterian church* (Belfast, 1961), 60; R. G. Crawford, 'A critical examination of nineteenth-century non-subscribing Presbyterian theology in Ireland', 2 vols. (QUB Ph.D., 1964), ii. 301–2.

evangelical members of the Synod of Ulster who were committed to the place of the laity in the church. The first resolution of the newly formed orthodox Presbytery of Belfast in 1774 urged ministers 'to have lay elders regularly ordained, in order to represent the Christian people, in our judicatories, and to bring such along with themselves, in order to reason and have voices in our meetings about the affairs belonging to this church'.[46] Elders did not reciprocate the commitment of evangelicals to their office and the records of the Secession and General synods indicate that the attendance of elders was poor throughout this period and that a significant number were charged with a variety of offences, particularly drunkenness. In the nineteenth century, one of the arguments for the appointment of Scripture readers was that the 'eldership of the present day is no efficient help to the ministry—in a large number of instances it is rather a hindrance'.[47] Another writer was moved to ask, 'How often is the session room but a kind of counting house of congregational alms, or a place for the agitation of every question of sordid worldliness? My brethren, ought these things to be so? Surely, surely, no.'[48]

Under their evangelical minister John Johnston, the Kirk session of Tullylish showed signs of a greater attention to the spiritual well-being of their congregation at an early date. In December 1811 the Kirk session adopted six resolutions that represented one of the first attempts to raise the standard of the eldership and displayed the new sense of zeal exhibited by Synod of Ulster elders in the nineteenth century.[49] The first resolution set the tone. The elders were to consecrate their personal and family lives to God, 'being deeply sensible, that to seek the kingdom of God is worthy of our first and uniform attention'. The exercise of church discipline comprised the second resolution, the proper exercise of which, 'through the blessing of God', was seen as a means of 'reviving and establishing the power and practice of vital godliness'. The next two resolutions committed elders to 'watch over those who reside in our respective districts and notice those who walk disorderly or are inattentive to the public

---

[46] Belfast Pby (GSU), 12 July 1774 (UTC), 3.

[47] 'Scripture readers', *Orthodox Presbyterian*, 4 (1833), 302.

[48] A. C. Canning, 'An address to our Presbyterian eldership', *Orthodox Presbyterian*, new ser., 2 (1839), 295.

[49] Tullylish (GSU) session resolutions, 7 Dec. 1811 (PRONI, T/2957/1).

ordinances of God' and to the promotion of the religious education of 'the young and rising generation'. The session was to meet on the first Saturday of every month and, in the final resolution, they requested the advice and help of 'any seriously disposed person in the congregation who may please to meet with us on such occasions'.

In his programmatic sermon before the Synod in 1825, Henry Cooke reflected the resolutions of the Tullylish Kirk session by calling on his colleagues to ensure that the church had a truly spiritual eldership, consisting of men who had led blameless lives and were willing to exercise discipline, visit their districts, and exhort the young.[50] After the *Code* had confirmed the qualifications and duties of elders, a number of Kirk sessions were reorganized and elders were assigned districts for visitation purposes.[51] In 1828 the Synod was presented with a resolution from a number of elders urging Kirk sessions and ministers to carry out all the duties required of them in the *Code*. Their purpose was to further promote 'the revival of religion, which, through the blessing of God we conceive to have already commenced among us'.[52] The Synod in the 1830s continued to call for reform as presbytery visitations uncovered laxity of discipline regarding the appointment, character, and reliability of elders.[53] Elders were to be doctrinally orthodox, active in the establishment of Sunday schools and prayer meetings, and conscientious in visiting their districts. The 1841 revision of the *Code* reinforced these aims and, following the practice of the Seceders, reintroduced full subscription to the *Confession* for all lay elders.[54] The new elders were to be like John Knox of Ballyroney, County Down. In his private life he strictly observed the Sabbath and ensured that his family was instructed in the principles of the gospel. In public life he was 'strict in church discipline, always opposed to the admission of the erroneous, the ignorant, and immoral to sealing ordinances, a steady friend

[50] Cooke, *Sermon preached at the opening of the General Synod of Ulster*, 33–4.

[51] For example, Ballymoney (GSU) session book, 10 and 18 July 1828; Dromara (GSU) session book, 7 Aug. 1833 (PRONI, T/1447/2); Magherafelt (GSU) session book, 1829 (PRONI, CR/3/13/C/1), 50–2.

[52] *RGSU* (1828), 62–3. The duties were enumerated in, *Code* (1825), 15–17.

[53] Brown, *The Christian ambassador*, 27; *Belfast News-Letter*, 16 Aug. 1833; Armagh Pby (GSU), 1 Aug. 1837, 7 Nov. 1838 (PHS); Coleraine Pby (GSU), 10 May 1836.

[54] *Code* (1841), 12–17.

to Bible and Missionary societies, and the superintendent of a Sabbath school in his own congregation'.[55] It was too much to expect that there could be a sudden improvement in the eldership and many ineffectual elders remained in office. In 1844 the General Assembly called on their members to ensure that elders 'be instructed to pay more attention to their duties'.[56] As with ministers, the eldership was never as bad as the laments of Presbyterian reformers suggested. Yet, from 1825, it was clear to Presbyterians that the eldership had to do its job in order for the church to meet the unprecedented demands placed upon it by population growth in both rural and urban areas.

II

The growing mood of self-improvement and respectability amongst the Irish population in general during the nineteenth century was reflected in a desire for knowledge and education. Presbyterians believed that education was essential if the laity, both male and female, were to read the Bible for themselves. However, the Scottish ideal of a school in every parish, as enshrined in John Knox's *First Book of Discipline* (1560), was impracticable for Irish Presbyterians to realize as they existed in a confessional state, the parish structure and endowments of which were in the hands of the Anglican Church of Ireland. Presbyterians, however, remained committed to the importance of education and a number of congregations had established schools in the eighteenth century, though these tended to be few in number and were located in large towns such as Belfast, Derry, or Dublin.[57] Consequently the main providers of education were the 'hedge schools', run in many cases by Presbyterian licentiates or ministers. For a small fee pupils were taught basic reading and writing skills by various materials, from popular chivalric romances

[55] *Orthodox Presbyterian*, 4 (1833), 371. For further examples, A. Breakey, *The Christian, the ruling elder, and the philanthropist* (Belfast, 1847); W. Richey, *Believers inheriting the promises* (Belfast, 1848).

[56] *MGA* i. (1844), 328. See also, *Missionary Herald* (1857), 294, (1855), 3046.

[57] McIvor, *Popular education*, 29–55.

to the Bible and *Shorter Catechism*.[58] Though these schools were sometimes badly organized and brutally supervised, they did provide the opportunity for many to obtain literacy skills.

In the wake of 1798, evangelicals used the opportunity provided by the increased desire for education amongst the population to instil the principles of hard work, temperance, political loyalty, and true religion. More generally, the principles on which many schools were founded reflected an optimistic view of humanity that persons could be improved morally and intellectually through education.[59] According to James Horner of Dublin, the purpose of his congregational schools was to make pupils useful members of society by addressing immoral behaviour, which was the real cause of Irish misery. Education would 'put an end to drunkenness, to profligacy, to idleness and to sloth; and introduce in their room sobriety, industry, frugality and economy, and poverty will in great measure disappear, whilst competence and comfort will prevail'.[60] Similarly, William Carr, a Seceder minister in Belfast, maintained that any individual who opposed the moral education of the poor was 'a traitor to society, an enemy of religion and a rebel to his God'. For Carr the relationship between religious instruction and public peace was inseparable as knowledge of the Bible was 'the security of the throne—the cement of social happiness—the basis of piety—and the beacon-light to heaven'.[61]

Presbyterians took advantage of the facilities and materials offered by the London Hibernian Society (1806) and the Kildare Place Society (1811) to establish schools in Ulster.[62] Despite the misgivings of a few members, the Synod of Ulster affirmed in 1826 that the latter society had 'conferred most important benefits in the great work of education, among the poor in Ireland'.[63] In 1824 Robert Park, the

---

[58] J. R. R. Adams, 'Swine-Tax and Eat-Him-All-Magee: the hedge schools and popular education in Ireland', in J. S. Donnelly and K. A. Miller (eds.), *Irish popular culture 1650–1850* (Dublin, 1998), 97–117; McIvor, *Popular education*, 47–52.

[59] L. Lunney, 'Knowledge and enlightenment: attitudes to education in early nineteenth-century Ulster', in M. Daly and D. Dickson (eds.), *The origins of popular literacy in Ireland: language change and educational development 1700–1920* (Dublin, 1990), 97–112.

[60] J. Horner, *A sermon preached in St Mary's Abbey meeting-house* (Dublin, 1805), 15.

[61] W. Carr, *The importance of religious education* (Belfast, 1822), 5.

[62] McIvor, *Popular education*, 73; D. H. Akenson, *The Irish education experiment: the National System of Education in the nineteenth century* (London, 1970), 85–94.

[63] *RGSU* (1826), 42–3. Also, McIvor, *Popular education*, 64–6.

evangelical minister of Ballymoney congregation, wrote a detailed account of the schools in his parish for the parliamentary commission appointed to determine the state of Irish education.[64] Park was the correspondent for the Kildare Society in the area and gave a positive account of its impact upon the populace. He was at pains to point out that there was no proselytizing and that teachers catechized their pupils in the principles of their respective denominations. Consequently the *Shorter Catechism* was taught to Presbyterian pupils, and local ministers, such as Park and William Minnis of Roseyards, visited the schools on a regular basis. In general the principles of the Society 'are most accordant with the liberal views of the population of this parish respecting their brethren of other denominations'.[65]

These liberal sentiments were soon overshadowed by the obduracy of Cooke and his supporters in the 1830s. In 1831 the annual government grant to the Kildare Place Society was withdrawn owing to the establishment of the National Education system, which aimed to provide a non-sectarian education for all the inhabitants of Ireland. This move had been partly precipitated by Catholic suspicion of the proselytizing implications of the Kildare schools.[66] The National Board was opposed by the majority of Presbyterians who believed that it displaced the Bible as the basis of education.[67] In 1832 the Synod of Ulster passed resolutions against the new system and its exclusion of the Bible during school hours. The following year four propositions were agreed by the Synod and forwarded to the government outlining the basis on which Presbyterians would participate in the scheme. The response to these propositions was unfavourable, precipitating a seven-year standoff between the Synod and the government. Cooke and his conservative followers strongly denounced the system in 1834 though his motion that Presbyterians should withdraw completely from dealings with the

[64] D. Kennedy, 'Robert Park's account of schools in Ballymoney parish, 1825', *Irish Historical Studies*, 6 (1948), 23–43.

[65] Ibid., 42.

[66] Akenson, *Irish education*, 89–94.

[67] The following discussion is based upon Akenson, *Irish education*; T. O'Raifeartaigh, 'Mixed education and the Synod of Ulster, 1831–40', *Irish Historical Studies*, 9 (1955), 280–99; Holmes, *Henry Cooke*, 94–104.

Board was passed by a very small margin with a majority of ministers actually voting against. Consequently a number of ministers dealt with the Board because of the 1833 propositions and by 1836 at least forty ministers were in charge of national schools, though some kept the fact a secret from their congregations for fear of reprisals. The Covenanters supported Cooke, but the Seceders were initially more ambivalent to his hard-line policy. Indeed, the Secession Presbytery of Belfast offered a guarded welcome to the scheme and accused Cooke of being something of a prelate.[68] In 1835 the Synod of Ulster responded to the government scheme by establishing their own schools by means of subscriptions from the Presbyterian laity. The Bible and the Westminster catechisms were the set textbooks. A widely circulated address to the people of the Synod stated, 'All the Presbyterian community will be taught, the poor as well as the rich. They will be taught to know why they are Presbyterians, and be able to give any one who may ask them, a reason for the religious profession to which they are attached.'[69] By 1839, 187,494 pupils attended 151 schools, 118 of which were in the Presbyterian heartland of counties Antrim, Down, and Londonderry.[70] Though the directors' reports confirmed that the schools had prompted an increase in religious seriousness, and a consequent decline in participation in ungodly pursuits, they always suffered from a lack of funds. It was only by generous grants from Scottish Presbyterians, the Hibernian Bible Society, and the London Tract Society that the schools functioned at all. By 1840, however, the government had conceded to the principal demands of the Synod thus allowing Presbyterians to use the funds on offer to equip and run their own schools under the aegis of the board. By doing so the government established a denominational education system that repudiated their original intentions.

---

[68] 'New system of national education', *Covenanter*, 2 (1832), 178–80; 'Signs of the times. No. II. Insensibility', *Covenanter*, new ser., 2 (1835), 192–5; Holmes, *Henry Cooke*, 102–3.

[69] *Address of the Synod of Ulster, to the people under their care, on the subject of education* (Belfast, 1835), 11–12.

[70] *Report of the directors of the schools under the care of the Synod of Ulster* (Belfast, 1839), 4.

Schools were also conceived as a means of evangelism. A system of Irish-language schools, promoted by the Presbytery of Tyrone, was established in 1835.[71] The schools were situated in non-Presbyterian areas and represented a significant effort to win converts to evangelical Christianity. There seems to have been genuine enthusiasm amongst the Catholic population to attend despite increasing opposition from their priests. By 1840 in Tyrone, Monaghan, Fermanagh, and Donegal there were ninety-eight schools containing 3,015 pupils, with 1,171 new pupils enrolled that year. There were also twenty-five schools in the Glens of Antrim attended by 680 pupils.[72]

The most significant development in the provision of education during this period was the appearance of Sunday schools, initially providing education for child labourers who could not attend week-day schools.[73] It was only five years after Robert Raikes founded the first in Gloucester in 1780 that similar schools were established in Ulster at Bangor, Dundonald, Crawfordsburn, Doagh, and Ballyclare, though the movement really took off with the formation of the Hibernian Sunday School Society of Ireland in 1809. The establishment of Sunday schools was not a naked exhibition of social control. The atmosphere of self-improvement affected all levels and sections of society. There was a symbiotic relationship between lay demand for education and the provision of money, materials, and teachers by the middle classes, especially women who were prominent in the organization and running of schools.[74] It is obvious from Park's 1824 report that the existence of Sunday and day schools in his area owed as much to lay demand for education as its provision by education societies. Ballygan School, established over fifty years previously by local initiative, had a committee comprised of 'men rather below the

---

[71] *Report of the Presbyterian Missionary Society of the Synod of Ulster* (Belfast 1835), 9–12; R. J. Rodgers, 'Presbyterian "alternative schools" in the nineteenth century', in R. F. G. Holmes and R. B. Knox (eds.), *The General Assembly of the Presbyterian Church in Ireland 1840–1990: a celebration of Irish Presbyterian witness during a century and a half* (Coleraine, 1990), ch. 6.

[72] *Report of the Presbyterian Missionary Society of the Synod of Ulster* (Belfast, 1840), 11–18.

[73] Adams, *Printed word and the common man*, 15–16, 107–11; D. Hempton and M. Hill, *Evangelical Protestantism in Ulster society 1740–1890* (London, 1992), 59–60.

[74] For examples of female involvement see, *Orthodox Presbyterian*, 8 (1836), 107–8; new ser., 2 (1839), 107–8.

middle rank in life, small farmers and linen manufacturers [handloom weavers], but shrewd and attentive'.[75] Park also noted that there had been 'a decided improvement in the nature and manner of education' since he had become minister of Ballymoney congregation in 1817. By way of explanation he pointed out that a 'taste for something superior for their children than they themselves enjoyed has been generally prevailing amongst parents, and teachers better qualified are receiving encouragement' from educational societies.[76] For example, fourteen Seceder Presbyterians were prompted 'by conscientious feeling' to form Roseyards Sunday school in 1823.[77] The existence of a keen group of benefactors and the desire for education exhibited by ordinary Presbyterians meant that the number of Sunday schools soon increased dramatically in Ulster from 256 in 1816 to 2,010 in 1841, almost two-thirds of the total number in the whole of Ireland.[78] At the second annual meeting of the Rathfriland Sunday School Union held in March 1821 it was reported that the society comprised sixteen schools with around 2,700 scholars and that they had recently established a lending library to counteract the 'corrupting and pernicious' pamphlets in circulation.[79] By 1831 the Belfast Sunday School Union, established in 1823, boasted twenty-three schools, 436 teachers, and 3,917 scholars.[80]

Most of these Sunday schools had been formed by ministers or interested lay people under the auspices of voluntary societies without the assistance of the various Presbyterian synods. During the 1830s these bodies, apart from the Covenanters, attempted to redirect the voluntary enthusiasm of the previous decades towards the establishment of congregational Sunday schools. In 1834 the Synod of Ulster urged all their congregations to establish schools 'as nurseries for the young, in imparting scriptural knowledge, training to habits of docility, respect for the Sabbath and religious ordinances, and attention to all the relative duties of life'.[81] Compared with their conservative co-religionists, liberal Presbyterians were lacklustre in

[75] Kennedy, 'Robert Park's account of schools in Ballymoney parish', 37.
[76] Ibid., 42.
[77] Ibid., 38.
[78] Hempton and Hill, *Evangelical Protestantism*, 60.
[79] *Dublin Christian Instructor*, 4 (1821), 295–6.
[80] 'Sunday-school jubilee', *Orthodox Presbyterian*, 2 (1831), 395.
[81] *RGSU* (1834), 48.

establishing Sunday schools and even struggled to gain recognition from the Sunday School Society on account of their Unitarianism. Consequently the Northern Sunday School Society was established in 1839 to serve the interests of northern Unitarians.[82]

The impact of Sunday schools in terms of those attending is striking, but how far they succeeded in winning new generations to church life is difficult to determine. It is clear from numerous examples that they did encourage a better observance of the Sabbath and a deeper desire for religious knowledge and debate. H. W. Rodgers, the minister of Kilrea Synod of Ulster congregation, reported in 1832 that, since its inception, the Kilrea Sunday School Union had 'elevated the standard of morality and religion, and reclaimed the character of the district'.[83] In Aghadowey, John Brown helped establish eight Sunday schools between 1824 and 1835. The Ordnance Survey Memoir for the parish written in the 1830s commented that the enthusiasm of the pupils and their teachers for reading religious books spread to others and led to the formation of voluntary societies for the discussion of religious topics.[84] In addition to doctrinal knowledge, the laity also received a basic education, access to reading material through prizes or a library attached to the school, clothing, possible admission to an evening school with practical training, and a testimonial of good conduct at the end of their education.[85] The establishment of these various schools demonstrates the desire of Presbyterians to provide opportunities for a basic education and a context for the nurturing of evangelical religion and respectable behaviour.

III

During the decades either side of 1800 Irish literacy increased significantly owing to commercialization, popular involvement in

---

[82] 'Sunday schools', *Bible Christian*, new ser., 2 (1837), 303–8; 'Northern Sunday School Association', *Bible Christian*, 3rd ser., 1 (1839), 352–3.

[83] *Irish Sunday School Magazine*, 1 (1832), 12.

[84] *OSMI* (Aghadowey), xxii. 13. See also, (Ahoghill), xxiii. 15, (Coleraine), xxxiii. 138–40.

[85] Hempton and Hill, *Evangelical Protestantism*, 59.

political and civil affairs, and the efforts of Protestant education and evangelization societies. The last factor was particularly important for it predated the others and increased opportunities for women to obtain literacy skills.[86] The 1841 census recorded that 51 per cent of Ulster females born between 1766 and 1775 could read; for those born between 1816 and 1825, the figure was 68 per cent. General literacy rates for Ulster show that in 1841 over 70 per cent of the inhabitants of the Presbyterian heartland of Antrim, Down, and Londonderry had the ability to read. Evidence suggests, however, that many Presbyterians were content with a minimal level of literacy. In 1841, 73 per cent of school pupils in Ulster were aged between four and ten years, while in the other three provinces pupils were older. Other evidence from the 1830s indicates that while the ability to read and write was widespread, there was little inclination amongst some Presbyterians to know more than the basics.[87] Thus the stereotypical view of Ulster Presbyterians as a literate and intellectually inquisitive group needs to be modified though it remains the case that this was a population who had the ability and, generally, the desire to read books.

It is appropriate before assessing Presbyterian reading habits to offer some comments about why and how people read certain works and not others.[88] The ability to read is an essential prerequisite though the communal nature of reading did not preclude those without the ability to do so from enjoying the printed word. Reader demand for certain titles and types of material has emerged in recent research as a key factor in determining which titles were printed. There was a symbiotic relationship between the types of material available and the mode of distribution. Furthermore, the experience of reading was not uniform and involved various 'communities of interpretation' characterized by differences in wealth, social status,

---

[86] The following paragraph is based upon the analysis and figures provided by N. Ó Cíosáin in *Print and popular culture in Ireland, 1750–1850* (Basingstoke, 1997), 27–49.

[87] *OSMI* (Carnmoney), ii. 54, (Ballynure), xxxii. 36, (Raloo) 97; Tyrone Pby (GSU), 11 Feb. 1840, 159.

[88] The argument of this paragraph is indebted to Bernadette Cunningham, 'Introduction: the experience of reading', in eadem and M. Kennedy (eds.), *The experience of reading: Irish historical perspectives* (Dublin, 1999), 1–10, and I. Green, *Print and Protestantism in early modern England* (Oxford, 2000), 241–7.

religious principle, geographic situation, and whether the individual was a minister or a lay person. Personal factors must also be considered, including a desire for self-improvement, the need to find comfort and encouragement, or the urge to augment personal knowledge of a specific area. In that context, though a book was popular, it does not follow that the reader appropriated the intended meaning of the text. This is a particularly important point in assessing the impact of religious works upon lay belief.

The most suggestive body of research into the reading habits of early modern Protestants is that of the American historian D. D. Hall.[89] For the New England Puritans Hall has studied, reading religious works appears to have been a spiritual exercise involving 'the affective self—the heart, the will'.[90] Due to the relative scarcity of printed material before the nineteenth century, books were treasured items and were often read until they literally fell apart. The laity read these works without clerical supervision, which allowed them to interpret texts in ways that may not have been approved by religious leaders or, for that matter, the author. Furthermore, people read and reread specific works because they embodied the values and beliefs that appealed to them and their community. Certainly through Bible reading, Ulster Presbyterians gained a sense of identity as the people of God and an independence of mind that contributed to the fissiparous nature of the community. A sufficiently detailed account of Presbyterian reading habits cannot be attempted in the space available. This section will focus upon the interaction between the supply of reading materials and the reading habits of Presbyterians. Changes in the character of Ulster Presbyterianism were both reflected in and promoted by developments in these areas.

For Presbyterians the Bible was the foundation of their identity and the final authority in religious matters, though interpretation was conditioned by extra-biblical considerations such as theological traditions, the use of reason, or immediate circumstances. Nevertheless,

---

[89] 'The uses of literacy in New England, 1600–1850', in W. L. Joyce, D. D. Hall, R. D. Brown, and J. R. Hench (eds.), *Printing and society in early America* (Worcester, Mass., 1983), 1–47; *Worlds of wonder, days of judgement: popular religious belief in early New England* (Cambridge, Mass., 1989); 'The literary practices of dissent', in K. Herlihy (ed.), *Propagating the word of Irish dissent 1650–1800* (Dublin, 1998), 11–23.

[90] Hall, *Worlds of wonder*, 40.

the Bible moulded the world-view and language of Ulster Presbyterians and, along with the Psalter and the *Shorter Catechism*, provided the main religious titles of the eighteenth-century book trade.[91] In 1826 John Gamble remarked upon the importance of Bible reading to Presbyterian self-identity; 'It is the first book that is put into their hands, and all their ideas take a tinge from it, and often their phrases; they are accustomed to reflect, and to talk on the doctrines it contains, and are, therefore, great reasoners on theological, as well as other subjects.'[92] Presbyterians took pride in their ownership of a Bible and, for many, the family Bible was of particular importance for it not only told the history of God's people in ancient times but the godly line established and perpetuated within their own family.[93]

The supply of Bibles was given a significant boost in the early nineteenth century as evangelicals marketed its potential to cure the social and political ills of Ireland. Reflecting the growing influence of evangelicalism in the Synod of Ulster, a Bible committee was established in 1807. By 1809, £1,102. 8. 3. had been collected and a grant of £100 had also been received from the British and Foreign Bible Society through Benjamin McDowell. This sum funded the distribution of 3,354 Bibles of various sizes, 2,674 Testaments, and a hundred Psalters to those thirty-eight congregations who had subscribed.[94] Although this committee was short-lived, the Synod urged congregations in 1811 and again in 1826 to support Bible distribution through the Hibernian Bible Society (HBS).[95] Underlining the importance of the Bible to all Presbyterians, these auxiliaries attracted both orthodox and liberal Presbyterians. They became involved for a variety of reasons, including patriotism, social conservatism and respectability, and the desire to civilize and educate the lower orders. The two vice presidents of the Belfast Auxiliary of the HBS were the evangelical Samuel Hanna and the Unitarian William Bruce. The stated

[91] Adams, *Printed word and the common man*, 43.
[92] J. Gamble, *Sketches of history, politics and manners, in Dublin and the north of Ireland, in 1810* (London, 1826), 347.
[93] J. Morgan, *A pastoral address, to the Lisburn Presbyterian congregation* (Belfast, 1824), 51. For the importance of the family Bible in one district see, *OSMI* (Islandmagee), x. 32.
[94] *RGSU* iii. (1807), 322; (1809), 340–2.
[95] *RGSU* iii. (1811), 368; (1826), 45.

aim of the HBS, to encourage the circulation of the Bible in Ireland without note or comment, allowed New Light ministers to be involved without compromising their non-subscribing principles.[96]

Generally speaking, however, Bible societies were evangelical in origin and outlook. It has been demonstrated that only one future Remonstrant minister subscribed to the fund while no fewer than thirteen out of the seventeen ministers who protested against the heterodox views of Josiah Kerr in 1811 did.[97] Individual evangelical ministers like Hanna and James Morrell of Ballybay ensured that the poor were provided with Bibles paid for out of church funds and supplied by the Bible Society.[98] Presbyterians were very involved in the formation of local Bible societies such as the Cookstown Auxiliary Bible Society (1811), which sought to provide the Scriptures at low prices for the destitute in the district. Within a year of its foundation it had distributed from its depository 678 Bibles and 567 testaments.[99] A ladies auxiliary had circulated 314 Bibles and testaments since October 1820, while the Moneymore branch had no fewer than seven different associations in connection with it. The distribution of Bibles came at the price of heightening sectarian feeling throughout Ireland as the Catholic authorities voiced serious concerns about the proselytizing intent of Bible societies and Sunday schools. This was reflected in the reports of the Synod of Ulster's home mission in the 1830s that contained more frequent examples of Catholic opposition to the distribution of Bibles and evangelistic work in general.[100] Tensions were also heightened between orthodox Presbyterians and Remonstrants after 1829. Indeed the formation of the Trinitarian Bible Society in the early 1830s was blamed by the

[96] The nineteenth report of the Belfast Auxiliary Bible Society (Belfast, 1826); A. G. Malcolm, The progress of Christianity (Belfast, 1822), 57–99.

[97] P. Brooke, 'Controversies in Ulster Presbyterianism, 1790–1836' (University of Cambridge Ph.D., 1980), 53–4.

[98] Third Belfast (GSU) committee book, 10 Apr. 1808 and 1809 (PRONI, MIC/1P/7/5), 131–3; Ballybay (GSU) session book, 30 Dec. 1821 (J. M. Barkley, 'A history of the ruling eldership in Irish Presbyterianism', 2 vols. (QUB MA, 1952), ii. 287).

[99] The eleventh report of the Cookstown auxiliary Bible Society (Dungannon, 1823); [T. Millar], To the inhabitants of Cookstown and its vicinity (Cookstown, 1826).

[100] Hempton and Hill, Evangelical Protestantism, ch. 5; Reports of the Presbyterian Missionary Society of the Synod of Ulster, (1835), 11; (1836), 3, 6; (1839), 11.

Bible Christian for introducing sectarian feeling into the distribution of Bibles thus eclipsing the immense good that had been done by the HBS.[101]

Alongside their attachment to the Bible, the Presbyterian laity showed a remarkable appetite for the works of English and Scottish Puritans.[102] In the eighteenth century authors like Thomas Vincent, Matthew Mead, William Guthrie, John Flavel, Matthew Henry, Benjamin Keach, Joseph Alleine, and John Bunyan dominated the best-seller lists. The popularity of other authors such as Henry Scougall (a seventeenth-century Scottish Episcopalian), Isaac Watts, and James Hervey (an English evangelical clergyman) indicates a willingness on the part of Ulster Presbyterians to learn from other Protestant traditions. In general these works either were devotional or sought to explain Reformed doctrine in a simple manner. A variety of devotional manuals, many of them reprinted in Ulster, helped individuals examine their lives for marks of holiness and assurance of salvation. Examples included Matthew Mead's *The almost Christian discovered* or William Guthrie's *The Christian's great interest.* Other popular works were concerned with the person and work of Christ and the individual's relationship with him. Puritan conversion narratives such as Alleine's *Alarm to the unconverted* and Richard Baxter's *Call to the unconverted* proved very popular in Ulster.[103] As authors passed in and out of favour, depending upon demand, it is noteworthy that the works of Scottish evangelicals such as John Willison and the brothers Ebenezer and Ralph Erskine were reprinted many times in Ulster during the second half of the century, the latter especially in the Secession heartland of south Ulster.[104]

Evidence of print runs is given anecdotal colour by contemporary accounts. John Gamble, in his frequent tours of Ulster, made some

[101] 'Trinitarian Bible Society', *Bible Christian*, new ser., 3 (1838), 149–53.

[102] The details below are derived from, Adams, *Printed word and the common man*, 44–9, appendices 1–4.

[103] For a broader discussion of the importance of such conversion narratives in eighteenth-century evangelicalism see, D. B. Hindmarsh, 'Patterns of conversion in early evangelical history and overseas missionary experience', in B. Stanley (ed.), *Christian missions and the Enlightenment* (Grand Rapids, Mich., 2001), ch. 4.

[104] E. R. McC. Dix, 'List of books, pamphlets, newspapers, etc. printed in Newry from 1764 to 1810', *Ulster Journal of Archaeology*, 2nd ser., 13 (1907), 170, 173; 15 (1909), 185.

telling comments about reading habits in the early nineteenth century. On his 1812 tour, Gamble was shown the personal library of a
Presbyterian landlord at Dungiven, County Londonderry. The collection consisted of six dilapidated volumes by conservative Scottish
Presbyterian authors: *The cloud of witnesses, for the royal prerogative
of Jesus Christ*; Alexander Shields, *The hind let loose*; Edward Fisher,
The marrow of modern divinity; and two works by Thomas Boston,
Human nature in its fourfold state and his collected *Sermons*.[105] The
popularity of this material is also indicated by comments in the
Ordnance Survey Memoirs written in the 1830s. The Presbyterians
of Killdolagh parish near Coleraine, for instance, were 'fondest of the
works of old Scottish authors and enjoy with much zest dry theological writings of the divines of that nation'.[106] Another Presbyterian
innkeeper, this time a woman from Crossroads, County Tyrone,
informed Gamble that she could only find the time to read 'a chapter
or two in the Testament, one of Blair's sermons, or a look at Hervey's
meditations'.[107] The references to the sermons of the famous Scottish
Moderate preacher Hugh Blair and the English Anglican James
Hervey make this an intriguing passage. Significantly, Gamble's conversation with the landlady revealed her attachment to the principle
of liberty of conscience and a favourable attitude towards Catholics.
Her reading material may well have reflected her relatively liberal
views towards members of other denominations, though whether
this was a New Light position or an interdenominational evangelical
one is not clear. The continuation of his journey in 1826 led him to a
third inn in Ballygawley, also in Tyrone, where he was given to read
Baxter's *Call to the unconverted* and a work by John Willison on
communion, which comprised the whole of the landlord's library
'except the Bible and the psalm book'.[108]

Presbyterians in the eighteenth century obtained reading material
in hedge schools, through hawkers who travelled the province with a
range of steady sellers, or in grocery shops.[109] From the 1780s onwards

---

[105] J. Gamble, *A view of society and manners, in the north of Ireland* (London,
1813), 264.
[106] *OSMI* (Killdolagh), xxii. 71.
[107] Gamble, *Sketches*, 227–8.
[108] Ibid., 235.
[109] Adams, *Printed word and the common man*, 23–41.

people could also use reading societies, subscription libraries, and book clubs.[110] For a small fee, members were given borrowing rights to the collection that was paid for by their subscriptions. These societies provided the opportunity for members to discuss the works they were reading, which underlines the importance of communal reading to the understanding and appropriation of texts.[111] The first of these societies were founded in east Antrim and included the famous Doagh Book Club, established in 1770 by a schoolmaster, William Gault. Reflecting their social origins and geographical context, these societies 'illustrate the theological, argumentative, and rational strain of the Ulster Presbyterian character'.[112] They also represent the desire for self-improvement and sociability that existed amongst the better-off weavers in the area. James Orr in his poem 'The Reading Society' reflected these characteristics.

> For us in humbler walks, we'll spend our time
> In honest toil, or with a book and friend,
> Still farther up the hill of knowledge climb,
> And bless the hands that help us to ascend.[113]

The books in the library of the Belfast Society for Promoting Knowledge, founded in 1792, were chosen 'to improve the mind and excite a spirit of general enquiry'.[114]

During the 1790s, reading societies were often the hotbeds of republicanism, and the United Irishmen had attempted to place the writings of Tom Paine and other 'infidel' authors into the hands of the Presbyterian laity.[115] Conservative Presbyterians before and after 1798 were understandably alarmed about this type of material and were also troubled by jest books, novels, chivalric romances, and

---

[110] J. R. R. Adams, 'Reading societies in Ulster', *Ulster Folklife*, 26 (1980), 55–64.

[111] Ó Cíosáin, *Print and popular culture*, 186–91.

[112] D. H. Akenson and W. H. Crawford, *Local poets and social history: James Orr, bard of Ballycarry* (Belfast, 1977), 74–8.

[113] J. Orr, *Posthumous works* (Belfast, 1817), 88.

[114] J. Killen, 'The reading habits of a Georgian gentlemen, John Templeton, and the book collections of the Belfast Society for Promoting Knowledge', in Cunningham and Kennedy, *The experience of reading*, 102.

[115] N. J. Curtin discusses the literary activities of the United Irishmen in, *The United Irishmen: popular politics in Ulster and Dublin, 1791–98* (Oxford, 1994), ch. 7.

'lewd' works such as *Moll Flanders* or Ovid's *Art of love*.[116] From the evidence of print runs it is clear that these latter works remained very popular throughout the eighteenth century and beyond. However, those who read serious religious works were less disposed to read 'ungodly' material.[117] In 1803 the Synod of Ulster asked their members to be wary of reading infidel books as they were 'specious, artful and insinuating; but full of deadly poison. You *may* be the worse, you *can* hardly be the better for them.'[118] One of the many charges brought by the members of Ballyblack Secession congregation in 1814 against James Wright their minister was that he had bought and read a jest book of 'immoral tendency'.[119] The Reformed Presbyterian Synod was unhappy about the portrayal of their forefathers in the novels of Sir Walter Scott, while in 1830 they railed against 'lascivious novels, fairy tales, and obscene ballads, the corrupters of the age'.[120] As religious seriousness increased in the early nineteenth century, Presbyterians, along with other sections of Irish society, expressed their desire to replace these works with morally acceptable material.

The first decades of the new century witnessed a marked change in the character of the book clubs. Compared with the rather secular tone of the previous century, the religious atmosphere of these groups was striking. The failure of 1798 had transformed the ethos of the reading societies in a conservative direction both religiously and socially, though clubs in non-subscribing areas retained a broader range of material and eschewed theological works.[121] The impetus to found many of these societies in the 1820s and 1830s came from the less well-off members of society and their desire for self-improvement and information. Much of this mood had been created by evangelicalism and would be reflected in the type of reading

---

[116] For evidence of Presbyterian concern with the spread of infidel works see, H. Tynan, *Poems* (Belfast, 1803), 39, and the opinion of Henry Cooke given in *First report of the commission of Irish education inquiry,* HC (1825), xii, 820.

[117] Adams, *Printed word and the common man,* 49–59.

[118] *A pastoral address from the ministers of the Synod of Ulster* (Dublin, 1803), 4.

[119] Down Pby (B/Sec.), 28 Dec. 1813, 1 Feb. 1814.

[120] *Causes of a fast to be observed by the members of the Reformed Presbyterian Church, in Ireland* (Belfast, 1820), 6; *Causes of thanksgiving, published by appointment of the Reformed Presbyterian Synod of Ireland* (Belfast, 1830), 8.

[121] *OSMI* (Drumbeg), viii. 131–3.

material taken in these clubs. The inhabitants of Billy parish in north Antrim established four book clubs in the late 1820s and early 1830s, stocked with books 'of a religious and useful description'.[122] Of the twenty-nine volumes in the Desertoghill reading society formed in 1832, the overwhelming majority were written by Puritan or evangelical authors such as Philip Doddridge, John Willison, John Newton, John Flavel, and James Hervey.[123]

There was a marked increase in both the range and supply of religious material in the first decades of the nineteenth century as the press was employed in the cause of religious reform. The first religious tracts had been published in Dublin in the 1790s but the republication of works by authors approved by evangelicals reached a new level in the following century.[124] These works were made available through congregational libraries, interdenominational reading rooms, and Scripture readers.[125] The library formed in Ballynahinch Secession congregation, for example, contained over a hundred volumes supplied by the Ulster Religious Tract and Book Society in Belfast. The authors included Baxter, Bunyan, Boston, Doddridge, Erskine, Jonathan Edwards, Flavel, Matthew Henry, Owen, Toplady, Watts, and William Wilberforce.[126] A series of reprinted works by the above writers and others, entitled 'Select Christian Authors', were distributed through the Belfast Depository of the Sunday School Society of Ireland run by William McComb. These works, which were interdenominational in terms of authorship, included introductory essays by the prominent Scottish evangelicals Thomas Chalmers, Andrew Thomson, and Edward Irving.[127] A Unitarian Christian Tract Society, later the Belfast Unitarian Society for the Diffusion of Christian

[122] *OSMI* (Billy), xvi. 48.

[123] *OSMI* (Desertoghill), xxvii. 11.

[124] Ó Cíosáin, *Print and popular culture*, 132–41.

[125] For example, Ramelton (GSU) session book, 1828–1907 (PRONI, MIC/1P/142C/1); Third Congregation (GSU) session book, 8 Oct. 1834 (Barkley, 'Eldership', ii. 209–10); 'Lisburn Religious Lending Library', *OSMI* (Blaris), viii. 56–7; *Report of the Presbyterian Missionary Society of the Synod of Ulster* (Belfast, 1832), 3.

[126] Catalogue of books belonging to the congregation of Seceders in Ballynahinch (PRONI, MIC/1P/110/2). [J. S. Reid], *Catalogue of the Presbyterian congregational library, Carrickfergus* (n.p. [1831]).

[127] See the list on the back cover of, Ministers of the General Synod of Ulster, *Family prayers for every day in the week; with prayers for Sabbath schools* (Belfast, 1829). Copy in Linenhall Library.

Knowledge, was established in Belfast in 1831 and continued to reprint works by the celebrated American Unitarians William Ellery Channing and Henry Ware until its demise in 1837.[128] The visitation returns of the nine Presbytery of Antrim congregations revealed in 1840 that six congregations had libraries with a total of 1,536 volumes with a further 422 in three Sunday School libraries.[129] The establishment of Unitarian libraries was urged to foster a sense of denominational distinctiveness against 'the wildest effusions of pseudo-evangelical Calvinism'.[130]

A significant development in this period was the emergence of a religious periodical press that aimed to encourage a variety of causes including missionary awareness, family and individual devotion, para-church organizations, and factional/denominational interests.[131] Presbyterian evangelicals read indigenous Irish periodicals such as *The Dublin Christian Instructor* and *The Hibernian Evangelical Magazine* alongside Scottish and English publications. With the formation of the Remonstrant Synod in 1829 and the polarization of religious identities in the 1830s, specifically Presbyterian magazines and periodicals appeared. To expound the distinctiveness of their group and to urge their followers to further reform, Synod of Ulster evangelicals had *The Orthodox Presbyterian*, Unitarians *The Bible Christian*, Seceders *The Christian Freeman*, and Reformed Presbyterians *The Covenanter*. Periodicals also appeared that were aimed specifically at lay believers of modest means. *The Monthly Gleaner* first appeared in May 1833 and was produced, in the words of the title, *to promote the moral and religious improvement of Sabbath-school children and Christian youth*. Two years later, *The Presbyterian Penny Magazine; or, Protestant Missionary Revivalist*, sought 'to promote vital godliness, active piety, and a spirit of missionary enterprise amongst professors of religion throughout the province'.[132]

---

[128] 'Unitarian Christian Tract Society', *Bible Christian*, 2 (1831), 95; 3 (1832), 376–8; 'The Belfast Unitarian Tract Society', *Bible Christian*, new ser., 2 (1837), 288.

[129] Pby of Antrim, 1840 (PRONI, T/1053/3), 33.

[130] 'Unitarian libraries', *Bible Christian*, 5 (1834), 518–21.

[131] J. A. H. Dempster, 'Periodicals, religious', in Cameron, *Dictionary of Scottish church history and theology*, 653–4.

[132] *Presbyterian Penny Magazine*, 1 (1835), preface.

During this period Ulster Presbyterianism experienced significant changes in its provision of religious instruction and in its understanding of pastoral ministry. These changes were promoted by a number of interlocking developments. Economic and social change, particularly the growth of Belfast, called into question the strategies employed by Presbyterians in the eighteenth century to provide for the needs of their congregations. Presbyterian evangelicals responded by reforming the ministry and eldership, establishing day and Sunday schools, and providing suitable reading material through reading societies, tract and book depositories, and periodicals. Change was also promoted by a desire for self-improvement amongst the laity who wanted to be educated in general terms and in the principles of true religion. This was in part encouraged through a combination of their long-standing interest in reading and their preference for devotional and practical works of divinity. Ministers and laity were willing to become involved in the various initiatives outlined above for a variety of reasons including, self-respect, the desire to inculcate social and political quietism, and to promote the religious beliefs they sincerely believed would transform their society for the better.

11

Family Worship, Prayer Meetings, and Lay Involvement in Church Life

In previous chapters it has been shown how a sense of community was created through public worship and church discipline. This sense of community can of course exist at various levels as groups of like-minded individuals coalesce for a common end. This chapter describes the opportunities for fellowship and spiritual development that existed alongside public worship. The first section assesses the importance of family worship to the Presbyterian religious experience and how evangelicals in the nineteenth century re-emphasized the importance of the family unit for the future success of the church in similar terms to their seventeenth-century predecessors.[1] Section two charts the development of prayer and fellowship meetings and their importance in diffusing the ethos of evangelicalism amongst the laity. As in the case of discipline, in both these areas evangelicalism promoted a greater sense of community than is sometimes appreciated by scholars who stress the individualistic nature of evangelical religion. The final section offers some general comments on the themes raised in this and the previous chapter concerning the impact of evangelicalism upon lay involvement, especially of women, in religious life more generally and Presbyterian church life in particular.

---

[1] For example, see C. Hambrick-Stowe, *The practice of piety: Puritan devotional disciplines in seventeenth-century New England* (Chapel Hill, N. C., 1982). For the nineteenth century see P. Jalland, *Death in the Victorian family* (Oxford, 1996).

I

The General Assembly of the Church of Scotland adopted *The directory for family worship* in August 1647.[2] In an effort to promote godliness and to ensure that biblical instruction influenced personal and corporate conduct, this document outlined the approved pattern to be observed by all families in daily devotions. The head of the family was to ensure that all members of the household observed family worship, which consisted of prayer, praise, catechizing, and Bible reading. Family worship was deemed an indispensable component of the religious instruction and development of the young and, therefore, the church as a whole. At the baptismal service sponsors were urged to raise their child in 'the nurture and admonition of the Lord'.[3] Nineteenth-century Presbyterians in particular accepted no excuse for the neglect of family worship, insisting that parents take their duties seriously in the religious instruction of their children.[4] As the family was 'the nursery of the church', the context in which children would be taught the principles of the faith and godly living, all Presbyterians agreed that family devotions could not function effectively within a dysfunctional family. Parents were therefore urged to foster a pleasant home that was conducive to the development of piety. It was the father's job to ensure that family worship was observed, though it is clear that mothers did lead devotions in certain circumstances and the eulogies of nineteenth-century male evangelicals indicate the decisive role played by mothers in the spiritual formation of their children.[5]

[2] 'The directory for family worship ... for piety and uniformity in secret and private worship, and mutual edification', in *The Confession of Faith* ... (Inverness, 1976), 417–22.

[3] *Directory*, 383.

[4] For representative views see, 'Religion at home', *Bible Christian*, 3 (1833), 566–76; 'Hints on the causes and cure of popular ignorance', *Orthodox Presbyterian*, 6 (1835), 147–8; A. Loughridge, *The Covenanters in Ireland* (Belfast, 1984), 113–14; S. Butler, *Death and life in many views* (Londonderry, 1826), 287–8.

[5] L. Wilson, *Constrained by zeal: female spirituality amongst Nonconformists 1825–1875* (Carlisle, 2000), 150–2. For a mother's involvement in family worship see *Orthodox Presbyterian*, 8 (1836), 107–8, and *Presbyterian Penny Magazine*, 1 (1834) 30–1. For the influence a mother could have on her children see, J. Simpson, *Annals of my life, labours and travels* (Belfast, 1895), 4–5, and H. Hastings, *Memoir of the life and labours of the late Rev. Josias Wilson, London* (London, 1850), 32.

Family devotions sometimes involved no more than the repetition of biblical texts and prayers and, in the experience of Henry Cooke, parental instruction could indeed be rather cold and formal.[6] At other times, the head of the family, whether through a sense of his own inadequacy or laziness, merely repeated material he had heard during public worship, and it is unsurprising that Sabbath evenings were especially favoured by lay Presbyterians for the instruction of their children.[7] If nothing else, the practice of family worship ensured familiarity with the Bible and the practice of daily prayer. One Remonstrant writer recognized the importance of regular family worship to conservative Presbyterians, 'which has contributed not a little to bind them in the strict bond of Christian fellowship'. He went on to describe the terrible emotional turmoil a Calvinist suffered when tempted to repudiate the doctrines of his or her church; 'Dogmas have to be uprooted which were early planted in his heart, and which grew up and flourished amid all the kindly feelings of his nature. Home and happiness, the family bible, and the five points are so amalgamated, that to separate them becomes impossible.'[8] When done well, family devotions were an indispensable component of Presbyterian self-understanding and religious education.

Though many did observe family worship on a regular basis, ministers from across the theological spectrum lamented its neglect throughout the period. In the eighteenth century New Light ministers were the earliest to recognize that the Presbyterian laity needed help in observing these devotions. Accordingly, John Mears and John Bankhead published works containing prayers and meditations to aid the heads of families in the performance of their duties.[9] Orthodox Presbyterians relied upon Puritan and Scottish works while the Seceders in particular retained a sense that ministers and elders

---

[6] J. L. Porter, *The life and times of Henry Cooke, D.D., LL.D.* (Belfast, 1875), 13.

[7] M. Martin, *Magherally Presbyterian church 1656–1982* (Banbridge, 1982), 42; S. Walker, 'A miscellaneous collection of poetry composed and written by Samuel Walker of Shaneshill near Templepatrick' [n.d.] (BCL, Bigger Collection), 90–5.

[8] 'On the standard of morality and religion', *Bible Christian*, 6 (1836), 544–5.

[9] T. Witherow, *Historical and literary memorials of Presbyterianism in Ireland*, 2 vols. (Belfast, 1879–80), ii. chs. 55, 70.

should provide a model of domestic devotion for the laity to follow.[10] Ministers were therefore not immune from criticism and in 1803 the Synod of Ulster called on its members to observe family devotions.[11] Alexander Carson claimed that a 'lazy Sabbath evening prayer, is generally, I believe, thought sufficient' for Synod of Ulster ministers, whereas prayer on Saturday morning and evening was 'really very extraordinary devotion', and, if in accordance with the standards, 'downright puritanism'.[12]

Nineteenth-century evangelicals and liberals differed in their attitude to the frequency and character of family devotions. For evangelicals in the Synod of Ulster, the resumption of family worship was an important means of reviving the spiritual state of the church.[13] The Synod's pastoral address of 1833 observed both the importance of family worship twice a day in forming the 'character and destinies of the next generation' and the activity of parents 'by which results all important for time and eternity, for the peace of your children and the glory of God, are destined to be effected'.[14] At the same time ministers were sanguine that parents were either capable or inclined to teach their children the principles of religion as the 'great majority' were 'either incompetent to the task, or they think they have not time to attend to it'.[15] To address this problem, a group of evangelical ministers in the Synod published a volume of family prayers for daily use in 1829 and there were further plans mooted by the Presbytery of Derry in 1832 for a similar volume.[16] The preface to the 1829 collection insisted that it aimed to provide forms to encourage those heads of families of low ability and confidence and not to supersede extempore prayer.[17] Liberal Presbyterians continued

[10] Moira and Lisburn Pby (AB), 31 Jan. 1781 (UTC), 144–8; J. M. Barkley, *A short history of the Presbyterian Church in Ireland* (Belfast, 1959), 109–10.

[11] *RGSU* iii. (1803), 268.

[12] A. Carson, *Remarks on a late pastoral address* (Belfast, 1806), 20.

[13] H. Cooke, *A sermon, preached at the opening of the General Synod of Ulster* (Belfast, 1825), 40–1.

[14] *Annual address of the General Synod of Ulster* (Belfast, 1833), 11.

[15] *Address of the General Synod of Ulster, to the people under their care, on the subject of education* (Belfast, 1835), 9.

[16] Ministers of the General Synod of Ulster, *Family prayers for every day in the week; with prayers for Sabbath schools* (Belfast, 1829); Derry Pby (GSU), 14 Nov. 1832 (UTC).

[17] *Family prayers*, pp. v–vi.

their tradition of publishing devotional manuals though the form of
family worship was less onerous than that demanded by evangelicals,
consisting of prayer and reading a chapter of the Bible every evening.
An official volume of prayers from the Remonstrant Synod appeared
in 1836, four years after its inception, and was found to have been
badly printed and too expensive for widespread use.[18] In the mid-
1830s there was an impassioned exchange in the *Bible Christian* over
the necessity of family worship. One writer argued that it should be
laid aside as modern life was not conducive to its observance and
because it led to the neglect of personal devotions.[19] Those who
responded to this charge maintained that such routine and disciplined devotion was a crucial means for establishing religious principles in the minds of the young.[20] Family worship was an
indispensable part of this process and one author urged his fellow
Unitarians to reintroduce the practice into their own homes as it had
been 'sadly, shamefully neglected' among them.[21]

As with attempts to reform other aspects of religious practice,
much depended upon the zeal of the minister and the desire of the
congregation to adopt stricter observance. Some members left
Moneymore Synod of Ulster congregation after John Barnett had
refused to grant them access to privileges unless they practised family
worship on a more regular basis. It seems that a more lax observance
had been the norm under their former minister, William Moore, and
the individuals concerned had been irked by Barnett's demands.[22]
The evidence of presbytery visitations indicates variations in the
observance of family devotions and uneven progress in the cause of
reform. Predictably the situation was worse in recently established
congregations. The minister of Croaghmore (founded, 1828) in
north Antrim told the Route Presbytery in 1839 that many of the
heads of families were 'lamentably defective in keeping up the worship of God in their families. In some families it is observed once

---

[18] N. Alexander, *Family prayers* (Belfast, 1826); *MRSU* (1832), 12; (1836), 18;
Remonstrant Synod of Ulster, *Helps to Christian devotion, a collection of prayers for
general use* (Newry, 1836).

[19] 'Hints for preachers', *Bible Christian*, 6 (1835), 115–17.

[20] 'On the standard of morality and religion', *Bible Christian*, 6 (1836), 541–6.

[21] 'Family worship', *Bible Christian*, new ser., 1 (1836), 145–50.

[22] *OSMI* (Lissan), xxxi. 103–4.

everyday. In others only on the Lord's day. In a considerable class it is not observed.' Nevertheless, he did believe that 'the discharge of the duty is on the increase'.[23] The visitation book of the Revd Leslie of Cookstown indicated the variety of experiences through repeated phrases such as 'regular', 'seldom', 'at nights', 'on Sabbath', 'irregular', 'occasional', 'once a day', or, most rarely, 'twice a day'.[24] Even if these do not indicate a rigid adherence to the standards demanded by the church, they do show that many observed family worship on a regular basis.

As well as family worship, believers were also urged to observe personal devotions every day. As with corporate worship, Bible reading, prayer, and praise were means of grace for individual believers as they sought to develop their spiritual lives. The Holy Spirit worked through these means both to begin spiritual life in regeneration and to develop it in godliness through sanctification. Bible reading and prayer shaped both the character and actions of the believer, whether male or female. George Dugall, in his poem 'The Northern Cottage' published in 1824, alluded to the desire of the laity to adopt the Bible's teachings.

> In God's own book his soul had learn'd to trace
> It's being, hope, and end—all else is vain
> To mortal man; except by heavenly grace
> The mind be guided through art's bright domain,
> And taught at ev'ry step, 'humility is gain'.[25]

The repeated reading and memorizing of certain passages provided a palette of phrases and symbols that coloured everyday language and provided comfort in times of need, especially on the deathbed. Likewise, prayer was an ever-ready means by which an individual could petition God for grace and comfort in the midst of trying circumstances.[26] Prayers could be offered for a variety of ends, such as the recovery of a sick farm animal or imploring revenge upon an enemy. Prayer could also be used to create a sense of solidarity and

---

[23] Route Pby (GSU), 14 May 1839 (Church House, strong room).
[24] Visitation book of the Revd John Knox Leslie, 1837–8 (PHS).
[25] G. Dugall, *The northern cottage* (Londonderry, 1824), 5.
[26] R. Gillespie, ' "Into another intensity": prayer in Irish nonconformity, 1650–1700', in K. Herlihy (ed.), *The religion of Irish dissent* (Blackrock, 1996), 31–47.

ask for divine favour upon both communal and personal activities. Individuals also prayed because they believed that in the process their lives would be changed through communion with God.

II

In addition to weekly public worship, various religious meetings helped to develop corporate and personal devotion through prayer, fellowship, and learning about missionary work overseas. Religious societies for fellowship were prominent features of evangelicalism and had been instrumental in promoting the transatlantic revivals of the 1740s.[27] Within Ulster Presbyterianism, fellowship groups were important for conservative Presbyterians in the eighteenth century, particularly Covenanters.[28] Reformed Presbyterian congregations were comprised of several religious societies that were gathered into district or corresponding societies, which were in turn supervised by a General Meeting for the whole province.[29] These societies provided a significant outlet for the exercise of leadership and organizational gifts amongst the laity. The organization of these groups was regulated by the *Short directory for religious societies in the Covenanting church* published in 1782. The 1815 Irish edition of the rules outlined the importance of prayer, praise, thanksgiving, and fellowship in encouraging members 'in a steady attendance upon all the duties and ordinances of godliness, and adherence to the cause of Christ, his truth, and true religion in the world'.[30] Each group had between eight and twelve members of good character who were to take it in turns to lead devotions. There were to be no gender-specific meetings to

[27] J. Walsh, 'Religious societies: Methodist and evangelical 1738–1800', in W. J. Sheils and D. Wood (eds.), *Voluntary religion*, Studies in Church History, 22 (Oxford, 1986), 279–302; A. Fawcett, *The Cambuslang revival: the Scottish evangelical revival of the eighteenth century* (London, 1971), ch. 4.

[28] For evidence of fellowship groups amongst Seceders see, Moira and Lisburn Pby (AB), 31 Jan. 1781 (UTC), 147; 'Congregational improvement', *Christian Freeman*, 1 (1832), 24.

[29] Loughridge, *Covenanters*, 14, 32–7, 52–4; *A short directory for religious societies, drawn up by appointment of the Reformed Presbytery* (Belfast, 1815).

[30] *A short directory*, 7.

ensure that men were able to control female fancy and frivolousness. By the nineteenth century, the ordination of more ministers and the formation of Kirk sessions and presbyteries reduced the importance of the societies. It is no surprise that when the Reformed Presbytery decided in 1809 to discontinue the district and general correspondence meetings there was significant opposition from the laity.

From the 1790s onwards, informal religious meetings began to appear in Synod of Ulster congregations ministered to by evangelicals such as Benjamin McDowell and Sinclare Kelburn.[31] The formation of these meetings was part of the emergence of a broader evangelical associational culture that aimed to promote temperance, Bible distribution, home and foreign mission, and a host of other philanthropic and educational enterprises. Missionary meetings for prayer and the dissemination of information began to appear in greater numbers during the early years of the nineteenth century to encourage the work of national societies such as the London Missionary Society (LMS).[32] Notable examples include both the Tyrone and Down Missionary Societies formed in 1814 and 1815 to pray for the work of the LMS and to collect subscriptions. Both societies had considerable Presbyterian support and women assumed a prominent role in their affairs.[33] Throughout the first decades of the nineteenth century, voluntarily organized missionary prayer meetings, such as the Ballymoney Association for Religious Purposes and the Belfast Juvenile Society, sprang up across Ulster.[34] The readiness to form these societies indicates the desire of many Presbyterians to promote evangelical ideas and practices outside of the official structures of the church. It is little wonder that the Secession synods and the Synod of Ulster attempted to regulate the establishment and organization of these groups. As early as 1802 the Antiburgher Synod asked all their

---

[31] W. B. Kirkpatrick (ed.), *Memorial services in connexion with the removal of the congregation of Mary's Abbey to Rutland Square, Dublin* (Dublin, 1865), 32–3; G. McCann, *The life of George McCann* (Belfast, n.d.), 18.

[32] D. Hempton and M. Hill, *Evangelical Protestantism in Ulster 1740–1890* (London, 1992), ch. 3.

[33] For the formation of these auxiliaries see, W. P. Addley, 'A study of the birth and development of the overseas missions of the Presbyterian Church in Ireland up to 1910' (QUB Ph.D., 1994), 44–54.

[34] *The regulations of the Ballymoney Association for Religious Purposes* (Belfast, 1827); *First annual report of the Belfast Juvenile Society* (Belfast, 1825).

congregations to establish praying societies in order to draw support from interdenominational groups.[35]

As prayer meetings developed in congregations, rules to regulate those who attended were drawn up by the Synod of Ulster and individual congregations. Only those of good moral character were to be admitted as members and elders were tasked with oversight of the meetings.[36] Long wordy prayers were a particular problem. The Secession Presbytery of Down warned its church members 'to avoid tediousness and all attempts at display' and to refrain from 'occupying the time with vague generalities and set forms of expression'.[37] Reflecting the upsurge of evangelical sentiment, the Synod of Ulster and Secession Synod from the late 1820s formed their own prayer meetings in order to pray for 'the outpouring of the spirit of God on our churches and our country, and for the spread of the gospel among all nations'.[38] A monthly prayer meeting was established in Bovevagh Synod of Ulster congregation in 1830 for the purpose of seeking the 'promised outpouring of the spirit, on our own souls and on the souls of our brethren in gospel lands—and on the exertions of those missionary societies and of those missionaries who are labouring in the cause of the gospel amongst the heathen'.[39] In 1838 the clerk of the Synod received 500 copies of *Thoughts on the importance of special prayer for the general outpouring of the Holy Spirit* by James Haldane Stewart, an evangelical clergyman from London, prompting them to call for a special day of prayer to be observed on the first Monday of the new year.[40]

Prayer meetings and missionary auxiliaries were augmented by religious societies to promote Christian fellowship and vital godliness amongst the laity. It is difficult to tell where a prayer meeting stopped and a religious society began as the terms were often interchangeable.

---

[35] D. Stewart, *The Seceders in Ireland with annals of their congregations* (Belfast, 1950), 106–7.

[36] *Code* (1825), 97–8; Boardmills (B/Sec.) baptismal register, 16 Nov. 1831 (PRONI, MIC/1P/72/2); 'Rules for religious societies', *Orthodox Presbyterian*, 3 (1832), 251.

[37] Down Pby (B/Sec.), 22 Aug. 1837 (PHS), 19. See also, *Presbyterian Penny Magazine*, 1 (1835), 190–1.

[38] *MPSI* (1829), 40; *Annual address* (1833), 9–10.

[39] Bovevagh (GSU) session book, 12 Apr. 1830 (PRONI, MIC/1P/229).

[40] *RGSU* (1838), 42–3.

In distinguishing between the two, it is helpful to emphasize the concern of the religious society with the spiritual development of individuals, as opposed to praying for missionaries and revival. George McCann, a Methodist itinerant and one-time member of a society that met in Kelburn's Third Belfast congregation in the 1790s, described the activities of the group in his memoirs. The meeting was held three times a week and was organized as follows: 'one member opened the meeting with singing a part of a psalm, and then reading a chapter either of the old or new testament, and then prayed; then an hour was allowed to speak on some given subject, and then prayer, etc., concluded our meeting'. The experience had a profound effect upon McCann who believed he had never 'made a greater progress in knowledge, in the same length of time than then'.[41] Societies began to appear in larger numbers across the Ulster countryside from the early nineteenth century. The laity were given the opportunity to exercise talents of leadership and organization that had hitherto been denied them and many may have prayed aloud for the first time at these meetings. The Boveedy Presbyterian Moral or Religious Society read the Bible and religious works together and each member 'in rotation opens and closes the meeting by singing and prayer'.[42] As with prayer meetings, church authorities in the 1830s endeavoured to regulate the membership of these societies, and ministers and elders were encouraged to be actively involved in the establishment and running of societies within their congregations.[43] The tightening of discipline was important for evangelicals if these groups were to influence the spiritual and moral life of the local community. The engagement signed by members of the Kilrea religious society stated 'that the example and exertions of our pious members united together … if steadfastly persevered in, shall remove the present irreligious character of the neighbourhood, fix upon it a better name, and do more—win souls to God'.[44]

[41] McCann, *Life*, 18.

[42] *OSMI* (Boveedy), xviii. 100.

[43] 'The Presbytery of Connor to the people under their charge', *Orthodox Presbyterian*, 7 (1836), 425; W. K. McKay, *Elements of Zion's polity* (Belfast, 1832), 140–2.

[44] H. W. Rodgers, *Scriptural warrant for religious societies and prayer meetings* (Belfast, 1833), 8.

III

Prayer meetings and religious societies were an important means by which the ethos and expectations of evangelicalism were offered to the Presbyterian laity. Their awareness of missionary activity was raised as they prayed for missionaries in far-flung corners of the globe and they were given a central role in promoting the revival of religion. In personal terms, a sense of accountability was encouraged between church members, religious knowledge increased, and confidence was restored through devotional exercises. Through leading groups, and possibly praying and reading aloud for the first time, numerous Presbyterians would have achieved a sense of personal fulfilment. It is true that compared with other forms of church government, particularly Anglicanism, the role of the laity in Presbyterian church affairs had always been marked. They voted for their ministers and were appointed as elders on Kirk sessions. However, in the eighteenth century, the Synod of Ulster placed financial qualifications upon voting rights and in some congregations there were very few elders in post. The Seceders and Covenanters offered the laity a more prominent part in church affairs, but even their public role was still circumscribed. The involvement of ordinary believers in these prayer and fellowship groups was, therefore, a significant development within Ulster Presbyterianism as eighteenth-century church life outside of the Covenanters and a few Seceder congregations had not offered this type of institutional involvement. For every Sunday or day school that was established, teachers were needed. James Morgan urged Presbyterians to ask what they could do in this area. 'All can do something. It needs contribution, and prayer, and labour. He who cannot give one of these may devote to it the other. Let every man have a part in the work.'[45] Organizations like the Belfast Town Mission required tract distributors, home visitors, prayer meeting leaders, and Scripture readers. Clothing societies and poor relief agencies needed administrative staff and volunteers. In this sense at least, evangelicalism emancipated the laity.[46]

---

[45] J. Morgan, *Christian education, the foundation of national prosperity* (Belfast, 1835), 29.

[46] D. W. Lovegrove (ed.), *The emancipation of the laity in evangelical Protestantism* (London, 2002).

Evangelicalism offered new and fulfilling opportunities for the Presbyterian laity to get involved in church life. The greater expectations laid upon the laity, and their enthusiasm to become Sunday school teachers or parochial visitors, is an indication that the ethos of evangelical activism was becoming ingrained in the Ulster Presbyterian mind. The broader commercialization of society, the political mobilization of the 1790s, and the mood of self- and moral-improvement all contributed to this process. Evangelical ministers exhorted church members to become involved in extending God's kingdom and the revival of religion that seemed to be sweeping all the Protestant churches of the day, particularly the Presbyterian churches. On the eve of the great struggle between Cooke and Montgomery at the Synod in June 1828, Cooke and three of his fellow evangelicals published an open letter in a local newspaper stating that 'Reformations have generally begun with what are called the laity, and we trust the Presbyterian people will not be an exception to the general rule.'[47] The importance of the laity was emphasized by Seceders as well. Walter Moffat, minister at Saintfield, told the members of his congregation that they were under duty to spread true religion and to co-operate to effect 'a great work of reformation in the world'. He identified three specific areas, namely, Sunday schools, the congregational missionary society, and the temperance society.[48] Even Covenanters, who were normally wary of interdenominational ventures, co-operated with the spirit of the times by drawing upon their confessional roots. Thomas Houston, minister of Knocbracken congregation, argued that no one could consider having 'the proper character of a member of the Redeemer's Church' unless he had 'assisted in the exertions of the evangelisation of the Heathen—for the in-bringing of the Jews—and for the overthrow of the systems of the Beast and the False Prophet'. This they could do by praying for missionaries, contributing financially, and by getting involved in missionary, Bible, and philanthropic organizations. This they must do according to their Covenanter principles and the dictates of their

---

[47] *Belfast News-Letter*, 17 June 1828.

[48] W. Moffat, *A pastoral address, to the Presbyterian Secession congregation of Saintfield* (Belfast, 1836), 16.

own conscience, though these were not to be used as an excuse for non-participation.[49]

The impact of this expansion of opportunities for lay involvement in church life may be seen as particularly important for women. As noted in the Introduction, some historians have argued that a separate, domestic sphere for women was fostered by evangelicalism and developed along with the formation of the middle class in early nineteenth-century British society. Acknowledging that the majority of churchgoers were women, others argue that religious life was made more feminine during the Victorian period as writers developed a discourse of religion and gender in which the 'fairer sex' was described as more religious and devoted than their uncouth and often godless male counterpart.[50] Particular characteristics such as humility, devotedness, self-sacrifice, and piety were held up as the glory of women and as values needed to be displayed by Christianity more generally. Undoubtedly gender stereotyping existed in Ulster Presbyterianism and women were often expected to know their place in the home.[51] In some cases this could be adopted for sectional purposes. Reflecting upon an address from a number of Unitarian women, the Editor of the *Bible Christian* observed that, 'Many of the best informed, pious, and zealous Unitarians of our acquaintance, are Females, of various ranks in society. Indeed, Unitarianism is peculiarly a religion for the generous, the virtuous, and the humane.'[52] It was generally the case that it was only in times of social and political upheaval that women could adopt a conspicuous role in church life, especially in terms of leadership and preaching. This was certainly true for Presbyterian women before the Restoration who, in a period of hardship and persecution, provided much-needed social, religious, and political support for ministers.[53] In reaction to the 1798

---

[49] T. Houston, *A pastoral address to the members and other individuals connected with the Reformed Presbyterian congregation of Knockbracken* (Belfast, 1829), 30–1.

[50] C. G. Brown, *The death of Christian Britain: understanding secularisation 1800–2000* (London, 2001), chs. 4–5.

[51] A. E. Brozyna, *Labour, love, and prayer: female piety in Ulster religious literature 1850–1914* (Belfast, 1999).

[52] 'Address from the ladies of Warrenpoint congregation, to the Remonstrant Synod', *Bible Christian*, 2 (1831), 531.

[53] M. O'Dowd, *A history of women in Ireland, 1500–1800* (Harlow, 2005), 169–74.

rising, some Presbyterian ministers sought to address the widespread social and political turmoil through evangelical societies. In one case at least, this resulted in the Revd John Morell of Ballybay inviting the Methodist preacher Alice Cambridge to preach at a couple of services in his meeting-house in October 1815.[54] Evangelical imperatives and religious confusion would once more allow women the opportunity to adopt a more public role as preachers during the revival of 1859.[55]

Yet the idea of separate spheres could be used to describe gender relations in any period of early modern history and nor can the emergence of such an ideology in the early nineteenth century be directly related to the development of the middle class.[56] The concept also has an unfortunate tendency to treat women as a single homogenous middle-class group when in fact they 'are no more a cohesive social entity than men and a shared gender does not in itself produce a common experience'.[57] The domestic roles that were applied to women in the Victorian period were also as important in the previous century. For example, the importance of mothers nurturing their children in the faith was almost certainly accepted by all Presbyterians in the previous century and was reinforced by reformers in the nineteenth century who, in the context of baptism, stressed the role of both parents in the religious instruction of their children. The male head of a household was expected to perform family worship, though women also led devotions and were often more influential in the spiritual development of their children on a daily and informal basis. Furthermore, Presbyterians throughout this period and beyond stressed that private prayer and Bible reading were indispensable for all believers. For instance, Joseph Boyse, an early eighteenth-century Presbyterian minister in Dublin, took aim at the Catholic Church who discouraged women from reading the Bible for themselves, stating that it 'is an illusion to persuade oneself, that

---

[54] D. Nesbitt, *Full circle: a story of Ballybay Presbyterians* (Monaghan, 1999), 50–1.

[55] J. Holmes, 'The "world turned upside down": women in the Ulster revival of 1859', in eadem and Diane Urquhart (eds.), *Coming into the light: the work, politics and religion of women in Ulster 1840–1940* (Belfast, 1994), 126–53.

[56] A. Vickery, 'Golden age to separate spheres? A review of the categories and chronology of English women's history', *Historical Journal*, 36 (1993), 383–414.

[57] Hempton and Hill, *Evangelical Protestantism*, 131.

the knowledge of the mysteries of religion must not be imparted to women, by reading of the sacred book. The abuse of Scripture and heresies are not sprung from the simplicity of women, but from the proud knowledge of men.'[58] As noted in Chapter 9, the descriptions of female deaths were exemplary for both sexes, and women were given the opportunity to exhort and teach those in attendance at the deathbed. Obituaries also reveal that middle-class women such as Agnes Cuming were avid readers of the Bible and various religious works and that there was very little difference between the theological beliefs of male and female believers.[59] The importance to these women of reading is underlined by the correspondence of Martha McTier and, more generally, female involvement in book clubs and reading societies.[60]

Women also played a conspicuous role in some of the more public aspects of Presbyterian church life such as church discipline, the choice of a new minister, and as ministers' wives. For example, the greater number of women called before the Kirk session for sexual misdemeanours is often attributed to a latent misogyny amongst exclusively male church leaders, though it is clear from the material presented in Chapter 6 that a broader context than gender must be employed to fully understand the relations between men and women in this matter. Indeed, church discipline stressed that all individuals were responsible for their own sins, and Kirk sessions, in the main, ensured women were treated fairly and given access to church courts. When it came to choosing a minister, it seems that the Synod of Ulster assumed the right of female church members to vote through-out the eighteenth century when the Church of Scotland restricted the right to male church members only. The first Seceders in Scotland and the Antiburghers made a similar restriction, though after 'the Breach' in 1747, the Burgher Synod appears to have allowed women the vote. Certainly in the early nineteenth century, both groups of Seceders in Ireland and Scotland and the Synod of Ulster accepted

---

[58] Cited in O'Dowd, *A history of women in Ireland*, 187–8.
[59] On the latter point see, Wilson, *Constrained by zeal*, ch. 3.
[60] *Orthodox Presbyterian*, 3 (1832), 360; J. Agnew (ed.), *The Drennan-McTier letters*, 3 vols. (Dublin, 1998–9). For the reading habits of middle-class women in early-modern Ireland more generally see, O'Dowd, *A history of women in Ireland*, ch. 7.

the right of all church members, irrespective of gender or financial contributions, to vote for their own minister.[61]

During the seventeenth century, the wives of Presbyterian ministers were clearly identified as 'spiritual companions' for their husbands and given a more exalted place and influence in the life of the church than was the case in Irish Anglicanism.[62] Though the evidence for the eighteenth century is scant, wives continued to give their husbands emotional and spiritual support and, as a consequence of this, funds to provide for the widows and orphans of deceased ministers were established in the Synod of Ulster and Secession synods.[63] The indispensability of a good wife was demonstrated and reinforced by evangelical ministers in the nineteenth century. Mary and Josias Wilson complemented each other well as 'Mrs. Wilson was not only a religious person, but calculating, steady, and economical; qualities in which Mr. Wilson was deficient more than any other.' She provided crucial spiritual and practical support during his challenging pastorates in Drogheda and in Townshend Street, Belfast.[64] In other cases, wives provided a model for others to follow and practical assistance in the work of the congregation. According to W. B. Kirkpatrick, owing to 'Her meekness of temper, her profound humility, her love to Christ, her sympathy with the afflicted, her self-denying efforts to educate and train the young, and to relieve the wants of the poor, her quiet energy in well-doing', the wife of James Carlisle of Dublin had 'left a deep and indelible impression on the memories and hearts of all who knew her'.[65] A fine example of the reciprocal nature of a marriage is that of James and Charlotte Morgan. In a prayer he offered on the day of his marriage in 1823, James asked God that Charlotte would promote holiness in him and that he, in turn, would lead her into numerous

[61] For the situation in Scotland see, L. A. Orr Macdonald, *A unique and glorious mission: women and Presbyterianism in Scotland 1830–1930* (Edinburgh, 2000), 173–4. For Ulster, G. Mathews, *An account of the regium donum* (Dublin, 1836), 38–9; *MPSI* (1834), 39; 'Popular election', *Christian Freeman*, 1 (1833), 393–4.

[62] O'Dowd, *A history of women in Ireland*, 172.

[63] J. S. Reid, *History of the Presbyterian Church in Ireland*, ed. W. D. Killen, 3 vols., 2nd edn. (Belfast, 1867), iii. 289–92; Stewart, *Seceders*, 111–13, 163–6.

[64] Hastings, *Josias Wilson*, 46, 85.

[65] Kirkpatrick, *Memorial services*, 35 n.

areas of Christian activity. It is clear that the Morgans saw their marriage as a united ministry and James prayed that their union would be a blessing to the church and the world. 'Bless our marriage to the best interests of the people over whom Thou hast placed me. May it be the means of making me better acquainted with their wants, more anxious to use every scriptural method of supplying them, and more attentive to my public and private duties among them! May they have reason to bless Thee for our union!'[66]

The idea of separate spheres could refer to women not only as wives and mothers but also in terms of the activities in which they were involved. In the nineteenth century, evangelicalism gave women an opportunity to engage in the public witness of Presbyterianism to an unprecedented degree. Yet, this was an expansion of the activities females could do rather than an alteration of the boundaries between the sexes. New opportunities were presented for women to strengthen family and community life, but these were within a framework that assumed male authority.[67] As demonstrated in a recent history of women in Scottish Presbyterianism during the Victorian period, the feminization of religion involved for women an extension of opportunities for service rather than an increase in status.[68] In some cases, however, the call of God to some form of religious activity beyond the home, or even Ireland, overrode domestic concerns. An address to the Revd Thomas Leslie, missionary to Jamaica, by the students of the Belfast Institution encapsulated the dissonance between the call of God and the expectations of gender roles.

Did we not fear to offend the modesty of the respected lady who is the participator in all your joys and sorrows, we would more fully express the admiration with which we behold the triumph of Christian devotedness over the timidity and sensitiveness of the female character, in relinquishing the peaceful comforts and delights of the home, and all the tender associations connected therewith, for the trials and privations of the missionary life.[69]

---

[66] J. Morgan, *Recollections of my life and times* (Belfast, 1874), 23–6, 25.

[67] See especially, Hempton and Hill, *Evangelical Protestantism*, ch. 7.

[68] Orr Macdonald, *A unique and glorious mission*. For a similar argument see, Wilson, *Constrained by zeal*.

[69] 'Departure of a missionary', *Orthodox Presbyterian*, 6 (1835), 206.

During the nineteenth century, Presbyterians maintained that women were particularly suited to visitation work, running libraries, Sunday school teaching, and various philanthropic acts, including clothing the poor. The Ladies Local Sunday School Association was formed in Belfast in the early 1820s after a number of women in the town had read Thomas Chalmers' *The Christian and civic economy of large towns* (1821).[70] They divided the town into districts and in each a Sunday school was established for thirty females. Both the women teachers and the Ladies Bible Association visited the houses of the poor and acted under the counsel of the Belfast Sunday School Society. Likewise the Ladies Auxiliary of the Cookstown Bible Society distributed Bibles, established a working school in which some of the ladies were teachers, and formed a clothing society to meet the needs of the poor.[71] In obituaries, individual women were held up as exemplars of practical and pious Christianity. Mrs Black of Belfast was a tireless visitor of the sick and ensured that the poor were fed, clothed, and given suitable tracts to read. Her obituary stated that with the poor 'she delighted to have intercourse, and she was their best pastor. She is remembered by them with affectionate tenderness, as a faithful friend and counsellor.'[72] Similarly, Miss McCord undertook 'the charge of a district, where she visited all the families contained in it weekly, reading the Scriptures with them, distributing tracts, and occasionally engaging in prayer'. Later she thought of going as a missionary overseas but a male friend encouraged her to stay in Belfast as there was necessary work to be done as a schoolteacher.[73] Other women were important benefactors of philanthropic and missionary concerns. Agnes Cuming of Ballymena, 'a notable exemplification of practical and unobtrusive piety', was a great patron of good causes who left £100 to the poor and £600 between the Synod of Ulster's Home Mission, the Scottish Missionary Society, and the Jewish Missionary Society.[74]

---

[70] W. Carr, *The importance of religious education* (Belfast, 1822), 30–3.

[71] *The eleventh report of the Cookstown auxiliary Bible Society* (Dungannon, 1823), 25–7.

[72] *Orthodox Presbyterian*, 4 (1833), 399–400.

[73] *Orthodox Presbyterian*, 6 (1835), 281–2.

[74] *Orthodox Presbyterian*, 3 (1832), 360–1.

This interest and involvement in philanthropy continued well beyond 1840. During the Irish famine of the 1840s, and under the guidance of John Edgar, a Belfast Ladies' Relief Association for Connaught was formed to raise funds for famine relief through the organization of female industrial schools in the western province.[75] Though this has been interpreted by D. W. Miller in terms of separate spheres and the need to reconcile Presbyterian women to the new constraints inherent in the ideology, other female activity has been characterized as giving power to women. The Belfast Female Mission, founded in 1859, was a vehicle for female empowerment by allowing women to gain experience in the organization, publicity, and day-to-day toil of the society, thus presenting an avenue for some into wider political and social activity.[76] Foreign missionary activity also provided an outlet for well-educated and well-motivated women in the second half of the nineteenth century. Indeed, between 1873 and 1953, the Women's Missionary Association of the Presbyterian Church in Ireland sent out ninety-eight female missionaries compared with the sixty-eight male missionaries of the Foreign Mission, established thirty-three years earlier, and twenty-one under the auspices of the Jungle Tribes Mission.[77]

The language of separate spheres appears to be more developed within liberal Presbyterianism in the nineteenth century. According to one writer, 'Men may be said to be the head, women the heart of a religious body. Oh, that the Unitarians of Ireland would unite head and heart in the good work!'[78] Many women in the early 1830s were eager to publicly offer their emotional and spiritual support for those men who were leading the Remonstrant struggle against Cooke and the Synod of Ulster, especially in the organization of soirées and tea

---

[75] D. W. Miller, 'Irish Presbyterians and the great famine', in J. Hill and C. Lennon (eds.), *Luxury and austerity*, Historical Studies, 21 (Dublin, 1999), 169–73.

[76] J. N. I. Dickson, 'Evangelical religion and Victorian women: the Belfast Female Mission, 1859–1903', *Journal of Ecclesiastical History*, 55 (2004), 700–25.

[77] These figures are compiled from the list of missionaries given in R. H. Boyd, *The prevailing word* (Belfast, 1953), 9–10. For women more generally in Irish Presbyterian foreign missions, see M. Hill, 'Women in the Irish Protestant foreign missions c. 1873–1914: representations and motivations', in P. N. Holtrop and H. McLeod (eds.), *Missions and missionaries*, Studies in Church History, Subsidia, 13 (Woodbridge, 2000), 170–85.

[78] 'On social meetings', *Bible Christian*, new ser., 2 (1837), 164.

parties.[79] The Revd Henry Montgomery seems to have made a habit of offering toasts to women on these occasions, including one to 'The female sex, the ornament of society, and our faithful help-mates in all the duties of life', and another to 'The ladies, our kind entertainers; may they ever thus cheer us in the path of freedom, truth and virtue.'[80] Liberal Presbyterian women such as Martha McTier could also be found in various philanthropic societies, and at a meeting in Holywood, County Down, for the promotion of religion and general improvement, a toast was given to 'The ladies ... may they continue to mingle in our assemblies, and aid the great cause of social improvement.'[81]

Whether considering the role of women, the eldership, family worship, the establishment of prayer meetings, singing schools, reading societies, Sunday schools, or missionary and philanthropic associations, and much else besides, it is apparent that evangelicalism had a significant impact upon the place of the laity in Presbyterian church life. While centralizing the structures of the church, Presbyterian evangelicals also realized the importance of small groups and local communities in shaping belief and conduct. They attempted to improve the frequency of family worship, the conduct of fellowship meetings, and the supply of suitable reading material. As in other areas of religious practice, there were devout Presbyterians in the eighteenth century as well as those who were indifferent in the nineteenth to these new demands. The main difference, however, was that the expectations of lay conduct had been raised and the provision of opportunities for greater involvement in religious activities increased. Evangelicals also ensured that ministers and elders would oversee these improvements, yet this was not the suppression of one religious culture by a new and more powerful one. Indeed, the impetus for many of these schemes came from the laity. Likewise, the provision of improving literature both reflected and encouraged a desire for self-improvement and education that had already existed within Presbyterianism and the sociability of eighteenth-century

[79] 'Address from the ladies of Warrenpoint congregation', *Bible Christian*, 2 (1831), 531–2.

[80] *Bible Christian*, new ser., 2 (1837), 209, 240.

[81] Agnew, *Drennan-McTier letters*, vol. i, pp. xxxv–vi; *Bible Christian*, new ser, 3 (1838), 144.

book clubs. Once again, there was a symbiotic relationship between the demands of the reformers and the eagerness of sections of the laity, both women and men, to embrace structures that they believed would improve both their social and religious lives. Religious societies provided the context in which the 1859 revival was fostered and it is significant that the laity played a more conspicuous role in the promotion of the revival than the clergy or professional revivalists.[82] In this case, evangelicalism emancipated and empowered the laity. By doing so, Presbyterian evangelicals encouraged religious populism that in the aftermath of 1859 would challenge the official framework of the church and offer an alternative religiosity for those Presbyterians who wanted yet more freedom from the structures of the denomination.[83]

---

[82] W. Gibson, *The year of grace: a history of the Ulster revival of 1859* (Edinburgh, 1860), 20–2; Hempton and Hill, *Evangelical Protestantism*, 149–50.

[83] A. Holmes, 'The experience and understanding of religious revival in Ulster Presbyterianism, c. 1800 to 1930', *Irish Historical Studies* 34 (2005), 361–85.

Conclusion

This book began by posing two questions: how should historians characterize Ulster Presbyterianism, and what made a Presbyterian a Presbyterian? In order to answer those essentially interrelated questions, it has been necessary to examine the provision of religious services, the public and private devotions of the laity, and how belief and practice changed over time. In attempting to characterize the Presbyterian community in Ulster, it is clear that internal and external determinants provided the parameters within which Presbyterians practised their religion. External developments in the early nineteenth century included political and religious polarization and the dislocation caused by population growth, industrialization, and the expansion of Belfast. Presbyterians also shared geographical space with other Christian denominations. Yet Presbyterianism remained a distinct religious culture and Presbyterians were easily distinguished from their Catholic and Anglican neighbours by their Scottish origins, their system of church discipline, their theory and practice of public worship, the observance of their rites of passage, and the Scottish character of their calendrical customs and alternative beliefs. That does not mean that there were not similarities between Presbyterians, Anglicans, and Catholics, but rather that each had unique ways of both conceptualizing and articulating their separate identity.

Presbyterianism was a contested entity both as a system of church organization and as a body of theological ideas. In the eighteenth century, these tensions were in evidence during the acrimonious debate over subscription in the Synod of Ulster in the 1720s and later between the Synod, Seceders, and Covenanters. From the mid-1770s until the end of the century calm descended upon Presbyterianism

only to flare up once more in the late 1820s over the central issue of
the person and work of Christ. Furthermore, there were significant
differences between some lay understandings of what constituted
true Presbyterianism and the pronouncements of ministers and
confessional standards. This traditional Presbyterianism was increasingly challenged by evangelicalism in the nineteenth century. The
contrast should not be overdrawn, however, as ministers upheld lay
understandings either directly or by negotiating with the laity over
calendrical customs, psalmody, the reform of wakes, and the communion season. Preaching pre-eminently embodied this symbiotic
relationship, showing the dynamic interaction between ministerial
and lay perceptions of what constituted orthodoxy. Simultaneously,
in the context of economic, political, and social upheaval, the spread
of the ethos of evangelicalism reflected the needs and aspirations of a
considerable section of Presbyterian opinion, including better-off
farmers, the urban middle classes, especially women, and the upwardly
mobile working classes.

There were also degrees of adherence to both the structures and
beliefs of Presbyterianism. Though community pressure to conform
was often irresistible, both the structural problems associated with
the provision of church accommodation and the lack of suitable
sanction to ensure attendance meant that membership was largely
voluntary. There were individuals who, to the best of their ability, did
all that was required of them by attending meeting regularly, observing family worship, and performing personal devotions. Others used
the provision of rites of passage to excuse themselves from further
onerous commitment to the church and to ensure spiritual and
community blessing upon their decisions. With these various levels
of adherence came a sizeable group, possibly comprising at least one-
fifth of the Presbyterian population, who had no formal link with the
church and whose religious identity was determined by ethnic, cultural, and political factors.

Ulster Presbyterians saw themselves as a separate community and
as a covenanted people. During this period, the language and concept
of covenant was a prominent theme in the administration of the
rites of passage, the Lord's Supper, psalm singing, and the attachment
of sections of the laity to Presbyterian ecclesiology. The important
themes of God's sovereignty and the pilgrimage of both the

community and individuals towards eternity reinforced this sense of separateness, of divine favour, especially as expressed in personal covenants. Though these may have had political implications in certain circumstances and provided a language for political discourse, it is clear that the concept of covenant was normally seen by lay Presbyterians in religious terms as it laid the basis for the Presbyterian understanding of salvation. Consequently, the primary focus upon the cross of Christ and striving for personal holiness and assurance of salvation were prominent in the devotions of those committed to the church and were reflected in the works they read. The religious steady-sellers of the Ulster book trade in this period were devotional works and not works of polemical theology. Furthermore, personal religion and everyday relationships within local communities concerned the laity more often than confessional principles. A commitment to the perpetual obligation of the religio-political convenants of 1638 and 1643, for example, was not universally shared by Presbyterians and, indeed, became less important for conservatives from the 1780s. More important were the Reformed principles that were articulated by covenant theology in general but not confined to it, such as an omnipotent, omniscient, and omnipresent God, original sin, the supreme deity of Christ, justification by faith alone, and of regeneration and sanctification by the Holy Spirit. The dominant character of lay belief was orthodox as nineteenth-century evangelicals argued, though in defining orthodoxy they missed the significance for the laity of the style in which public worship was delivered and of traditional customary activities, which were as important, if not more so, than doctrinal content.

Another significant aspect of Ulster Presbyterianism for much of this period was its embodiment within small rural communities. In some cases this bred an often vehemently conservative or traditional attitude that was intimately connected with the conventions of the local community. Other communities could be forward-looking, especially in east Antrim where book clubs, singing schools, and New Light theological ideas flourished in the late eighteenth century. This sense of place gave local expression and colour to the type of Presbyterianism displayed in any given locality and blurred the boundaries between the sacred and secular, a blend most notably seen in wakes. The rhythm of rural life determined, among other things, seasonal Sabbath attendance, the timing of the Lord's Supper, and the calling of congregational fast days. Within this context, the meeting-house provided the focus for scattered rural communities and the means of expressing a sense of common heritage and faith. Through the administration of the rites of passage and the exercise of church discipline, the mores of the local community were upheld and refined, allowing Presbyterians of varying commitments the opportunity to participate in the beliefs and practices of the church. Evangelicalism reinforced the importance of communities and made the religious content of church practice explicit through the re-establishment of church discipline and the organization of prayer meetings, religious societies, book clubs, and singing schools. Despite the impact of industrialization and urbanization, Ulster Presbyterianism would retain much of its traditional and conservative character, and the persistence of calendrical customs and alternative beliefs bears witness to the continued importance of self-contained rural communities in modern-day Ulster.

Presbyterianism was also experiencing changes as Ulster was transformed by economic developments, political mobilization, and religious polarization. Presbyterian evangelicalism drew upon the Presbyterian theological tradition for its key doctrinal principles and intellectual weight, though it was only after the failure of political radicalism in the 1790s that the movement became socially respectable and provided the primary impetus for religious reform in the following century. The revolutionary changes of that period provided the context in which its ethos of sobriety, hard work, piety, and loyalty was eagerly seized upon to help explain and cope with the momentous times. Initially the Presbyterian authorities struggled to deal with the disruptive implications of interdenominational religious societies and itinerant preaching. As the nineteenth century progressed, however, evangelicals within the synods gained control and the movement more generally became increasingly popular and socially powerful as large numbers of the working, middle, and upper classes were attracted by a mixture of gospel religion and social respectability. Contrary to the stereotypical view, Presbyterian evangelicalism cannot be seen solely in terms of a clichéd conversion experience. Presbyterian evangelicalism was essentially conservative in content and character. It developed from the Presbyterian theological tradition as articulated by certain sections of the Old Light party and the Seceders. As it came to social and cultural prominence in the nineteenth century, it was a religious and social movement that affirmed both religious and social discipline and the importance of correct doctrine. Evangelicalism challenged the traditional understandings of Presbyterianism held by the laity, centralized the structures of the church, instilled the denomination with self-confidence and zeal, increased expectations of what was expected from the laity, and re-emphasized the religious aspect of church life.

This interpretation of the relationship between Presbyterianism, evangelicalism, and social change develops many of the pioneering arguments advanced by David W. Miller. His attempt to understand how Ulster Presbyterianism worked as a religious system, and his extensive statistical and cartographic work, has laid all subsequent historians of Presbyterianism in his debt. As Miller has noted in his most recent articles, the relationship he posited in 1978 between 'prophetic' Calvinism and evangelicalism was much more fluid and continuous in terms of doctrine, personal religion, and ecclesiology than he had originally claimed.[1] This book has confirmed his new understanding and the growing respectability of the denomination in the nineteenth century. It has also challenged and developed some of his other arguments. Presbyterians in the 'modern' nineteenth century continued to believe that God was active in the affairs of the world, applied the interpretation of biblical prophecy to contemporary events, and remained committed to a public role for religion. His argument about 'the transformation of Ulster Presbyterianism from a communal religion whose constituency was the whole community of Scottish settlers to a class-based religion which ... mainly served a middle-class constituency' is also questionable owing to the largely voluntary nature of church adherence in the eighteenth century,

---

[1] Compare 'Presbyterianism and "modernization" in Ulster', *Past and Present*, 80 (1978), 66–90 with 'Did Ulster Presbyterians have a devotional revolution?', in J. H. Murphy (ed.), *Evangelicals and Catholics in nineteenth-century Ireland* (Dublin, 2005), 38–54, and 'Religious commotions in the Scottish diaspora: a transatlantic perspective on "evangelicalism" in a mainline denomination', in M. G. Spencer and D. A. Wilson (eds.), *Ulster Presbyterians in the Atlantic World: religion, politics and identity* (Dublin, 2006), ch. 1.

the significant retention of working-class support in the nineteenth century, and the increasingly global horizons of Presbyterian missionary activity.[2] In addition, Miller argues that the reforms put in place by Presbyterian evangelicals who understood the gospel in doctrinal rather than emotional terms had limited impact upon church life before 1859.[3] Though Miller is correct to stress both the intellectual character of Presbyterian evangelicalism and the impact of religious reforms in a long-term perspective, the preceding chapters have demonstrated that there is considerable evidence for the short-term impact of reforms and that certain structures, such as Sunday schools and prayer meetings, together with an ethos of evangelical activism, had been established and would bear significant fruit in the 1859 revival and beyond. It is a testimony to Professor Miller's pioneering and thought-provoking efforts that all historians who have worked on nineteenth-century Presbyterianism and evangelicalism, including the present author, have had to grapple with his arguments.

Presbyterian evangelicals understood the reformation of church life and a return to the Presbyterian theological tradition as a religious revival. The increasing evangelical character of Presbyterianism led to the union in 1840 of the Synod of Ulster and the Secession synod to form the General Assembly of the Presbyterian Church in Ireland. The union was interpreted as a product of the ongoing revival of religion since the early 1800s and characterized by a concern with missionary activity, doctrinal purity, the enforcement of church discipline, church extension, and the preaching of Christ.[4] In addition, the list of principles underlying the union reflected a desire to return to the doctrines and practices of seventeenth-century Scottish Presbyterianism. Accompanying the shared commitment of the Synod of Ulster and the Seceders to the authority of Scripture, the sole headship of Christ over the church, and the Presbyterian form of church government, these principles also included full subscription to the *Confession* by all office bearers, a simple two-thirds majority

---

[2] 'Irish Presbyterians and the great famine', in Jacqueline Hill and Colm Lennon (eds.), *Luxury and austerity*, Historical Studies, 21 (Dublin, 1999), 168.

[3] Ibid., 176.

[4] *MGA* i. (1840), 22–5.

when voting for a minister, the discipline of ministers and elders, and public baptism. It was agreed that these 'principles claim the admiration of every lover of the "good old way" which was trodden by the Church of Scotland in her days of Covenanted Reformation'. The objects of the union were to encourage discipline and the purity of church membership, the cultivation of personal holiness, the extension of the Presbyterian system of church government, and missionary activity at home and abroad. In 1844 the General Assembly established a committee to consider the best method 'of awakening, under the Divine blessing, a higher spirit of piety in our church'. The accompanying 'Address on the revival of religion' made it clear that revival meant reformation and that no 'new measures' were needed as the Presbyterian system had everything necessary.[5] A State of Religion committee was established and, predictably, the responses they received from presbyteries concerning the means of reviving religion included reform of the eldership, purity of church communion, increased involvement of the laity in church life, Sabbath observance, family prayer, properly conducted prayer meetings, and outdoor preaching.[6]

The union of 1840 was a product of, and stimulus to, a revival of religion. This process would culminate in the remarkable religious awakening of 1859 that mobilized and affected more people than any other event in Ulster in the years between 1798 and 1913.[7] Though the American revival of 1857/8 acted as an accelerator, 1859 was not a spontaneous outburst of religious excitement but a 'planned event'. Yet the Presbyterian character of the revival has been downplayed in order to place the revival within the context of the rise of evangelicalism in Ulster society more generally.[8] Certainly, 1859 witnessed the incidence of Methodist-style practices amongst Presbyterians,

---

[5] *MGA* i. (1844), 327–8; *Missionary Herald* (1844), 146.

[6] *Missionary Herald* (1845), 244–6. *MGA* i. (1845), 405.

[7] The best account of the revival is M. Hill, 'Ulster awakened: the '59 revival reconsidered', *Journal of Ecclesiastical History*, 41 (1990), 443–62. The argument of the following paragraphs is dealt with in more detail in, A. Holmes, 'The experience and understanding of religious revival in Ulster Presbyterianism, c. 1800 to 1930', *Irish Historical Studies* 34 (2005), 361–85.

[8] P. Brooke, *Ulster Presbyterianism: the historical perspective, 1610–1970*, 2nd edn. (Belfast, 1994), 158; D. Hempton and M. Hill, *Evangelical Protestantism in Ulster society 1740–1890* (London, 1992), ch. 8.

including itinerant, lay, and female preaching, protracted revival meetings, and emotionally charged conversions often accompanied by various physical manifestations. However, too many works on Ulster Presbyterianism are based on the mistaken assumption that the basic characteristic of evangelicalism, and indeed revival, is religious enthusiasm as expressed in sudden conversions and physical manifestations. This view limits the understanding of evangelicalism to a certain type of religious experience and does not account for the particular variety of evangelicalism within Presbyterianism. Indeed, the revival originated in the Presbyterian heartland of mid-Antrim in the parish of Connor and reflected the conservative character of Presbyterian evangelicalism. It began eighteen months before the excitement spectacularly overflowed in the summer of 1859, and produced conversions that were gradual and unostentatious. More-over, the various manifestations that caught the imaginations of contemporaries and historians ought to be interpreted as psycho-logical responses to the social and emotional turmoil of the revival. The greater part of these affected those who had little connection with the churches and whose knowledge of Christianity was limited.[9] The Presbyterians who conceived of revival in traditional terms and sought to curb the excesses of the laity were no less evangelical than those who could point to a dramatic religious experience.

The revival of 1859 had such a significant impact on Ulster society precisely because the Presbyterian Church in Ireland, the largest Protestant denomination in Ulster, promoted it. The preceding chapters have demonstrated how the reforms that swept Presbyter-ianism in the 1820s and 1830s were inspired by the desire to promote a revival of religion, which, in that context, meant reformation. It is not surprising, therefore, that the 1859 revival had its greatest influ-ence in those counties with a large Presbyterian population, namely Antrim, Down, Londonderry, and, to a lesser extent, Tyrone and Armagh.[10] Those who were involved in the revival recognized the importance of the preparations that had been made over the previous

---

[9] William Gibson, *The year of grace: a history of the Ulster revival of 1859* (Edin-burgh, 1860), 40; W. Richey, *Connor and Coleraine; or, scenes and sketches of the last Ulster awakening* (Belfast, 1870), 205; F. Wright, *Two lands on one soil: Ulster politics before Home Rule* (Dublin, 1996), 231.

[10] Hill, 'Ulster awakened', 449.

thirty years and more.[11] Moreover, the Presbyterian Church drew back many negligent communicant members and the majority of the converts were already influenced in some way by its structures and programmes. Robert Park of Ballymoney believed that 'a larger proportion of those who have given evidence of a real saving change were connected with our Sabbath schools, either as teachers or receiving instruction, or were the members of families well instructed in divine truth, and more or less regular attendants on the means of grace'.[12] Though the revival caught many by surprise, it was not an unexpected outburst of religious enthusiasm but an eagerly expected and prepared for event. It was the culmination of the campaign officially begun in 1829 to improve church discipline and promote religious revival.

Ulster Presbyterianism between 1770 and 1840 was a distinctive, complex, and changing community. Any attempt to define what a Presbyterian was must take into account the many variables determining the identity of any group, congregation, or individual. Though the complex nature of Presbyterianism has been stressed, it is clear that whether conceived of in terms of religion, ethnicity, or cultural practice, it remained a distinct community within Ireland. Presbyterianism did not suddenly become more religious in the nineteenth century and nor did it reject its Presbyterian principles. In fact, Presbyterian self-confidence and denominational pride became more pronounced under the influence of evangelicalism. It is in that context that the 1859 revival must be placed. Instead of presupposing that the modern nineteenth century saw the death of traditional understandings of religious belief and practice it is surely more constructive to examine the continuities and traditions that were remodelled to meet the needs of a changing society. The placing of religious beliefs and practices in their social and cultural location ought not to necessitate the reduction of religious motives to nothing but social imperatives. Instead, this approach should assert that the religious lives of believers are shaped by the particular contexts in which they exist without at the same time jettisoning the sincerity and integrity of personal religious faith.

---

[11] Gibson, *Year of grace*, chs. 2 and 3; Richey, *Connor and Coleraine*, chs. 9–11.
[12] Gibson, *Year of grace*, 457–8.

Bibliography

Note. This is not an exhaustive bibliography of Ulster Presbyterianism from 1770 to 1840. It records those sources that have been most helpful in writing this book. In the interests of space, I have not included individual essays given in a collection from which more than one essay has been referred to in the footnotes.

1. Primary Sources
A. Manuscript Material
I. Belfast Central Library, Bigger Collection
II. Presbyterian Church House, Belfast
 (1) Presbyterian Historical Society
 (2) Strong Room
III. Public Record Office of Northern Ireland
IV. Queen's University, Belfast—Special Collections
V. Union Theological College, Belfast
B. Printed Material
I. Church Records
 (1) General Synod of Ulster
 (2) General Assembly of the Presbyterian Church in Ireland
 (3) Seceders
 (4) Reformed Presbyterians
 (5) Remonstrant Synod
II. Reports of Religious Societies
III. Parliamentary Reports
IV. Newspapers and Periodicals
V. Contemporary pamphlets and books
2. Secondary Sources and Printed Collections of Documents
A. Published Works
B. Unpublished theses

1. **Primary Sources**

A. **Manuscript Material**

I. **Belfast Central Library, Bigger Collection**

Clarke, James, 'Statistical account of the parish of Billy, County Antrim' (1840)

Walker, Samuel, 'A miscellaneous collection of poetry composed and written by Samuel Walker of Shaneshill near Templepatrick' [n.d.]

II. **Presbyterian Church House, Belfast**

(1) **Presbyterian Historical Society**

Presbytery Minutes

Armagh (GSU) 1797–1816, 1825–32
Armagh (B/Sec.) 1811–20
Armagh (Sec.) 1821–30, 1836–41
Ballymena (GSU) 1808–19
Bangor (GSU) 1739–90
Down (B/Sec.) 1785–1800, 1813–40
Route (GSU) 1811–34
Tyrone (GSU) 1781–1809
Tyrone, Lower (B/Sec.) 1806–9
Tyrone, Upper (B/Sec.) 1802–30

Congregational Records

Antrim (PA) congregational notebook, 1619–1867
Antrim (Millrow) (GSU) volume of seatholders and families, 1820–39
Ballybay (GSU) session book, 1811–34
Ballykelly (GSU) session book, 1803–19
Cahans (B/Sec.) session book, 1824–1911
Carland (GSU) session book, 1754–1801
Carnmoney (GSU) session book, 1767–1821, 1825–59
Second Cookstown (B/Sec.) committee book, 1836–96

Personal Papers

The Revd Samuel Barber, papers, 1781–1810
The Revd Adam Blair, autobiography, 1718–90
The Revd Samuel Edgar, sermon book, 1797–9

The Revd James Hunter, papers, 1796–
The Revd John Hutton, sermon notebook, 1779–1823
The Revd John Knox Leslie, visitation book, 1837–8
The Revd J. McDonnell, sermon diary, 1837–40
The Revd Joseph McKee, sermons, 1826–56
The Revd Robert Magill, diaries, 1831–7
The Revd Thomas Millar, sermons, 1829–30, 1837–8
The Revd Walter Moffat, letters and various papers, 1831–8
The Revd David Moore, notebook, 1808
The Revd James Morell, diary, 1814–22
The Revd William Stavely, various papers
The Revd John Thomson, various papers

(2) **Strong Room**

Presbytery Minutes
Ahoghill (Sec.) 1829–37
Armagh (GSU) 1836–41
Bangor (GSU) 1815–29, 1829–34
Belfast (GSU) 1837–41
Coleraine (GSU) 1834–7 (in volume, 'Minutes of the Presbytery of Route',
    1837–42)
Connaught (GSU) 1825–37, 1838–44
Down (GSU) 1834–41
Letterkenny (GSU) 1819–29, 1829–39, 1839–51
Raphoe (GSU) 1834–41
Route (GSU) 1834–43
Strabane (GSU) 1834–43
Tyrone (GSU) 1836–41
Tyrone, Upper (Sec.) 1823–9
Tyrone (Sec.) 1833–41

Dublin Presbyterian Committee (GSU/Synod of Munster) 1820–7

III. **Public Record Office of Northern Ireland**

CR/3/1/B/4, Ballymoney (GSU) session book, 1827–66
CR/3/2B/1, Antrim (Millrow) (GSU) account and session book, 1821–39
CR/3/8/1, Loughaghery (B/Sec.) session book, 1801–38
CR/3/13/C/1, Magherafelt (GSU) session book, 1818–56
CR/3/13/E/1, Magherafelt (GSU) The Revd James Wilson, visitation book,
    1823–41

CR/3/25B/1 & 2, Cahans (B/Sec.) session book, 1751–8, 1767–1836

CR/3/31/2, Ballycarry (GSU) session book, 1704–80

CR/4/9/A/1, Second Belfast (PA) committee book, 1808–28

CR/5/4A, Linenhall Street (RP) committee minutes and session book, 1825–62

CR/5/5A/1/2A, Minutes of the Reformed Presbytery of Ireland, 1803–11

CR/5/5A/1/3, Minutes of the Reformed Synod of Ireland, 1811–25

CR/5/5A/1/4, Minutes of the Synod of the Reformed Presbyterian Church, 1821–35

CR/5/5B/1/1/1, Northern Reformed Presbytery, 1811–27

CR/5/5B/4/1/1–2, Eastern Reformed Presbytery, 1811–23

D/1748, Tennent papers

D/1877/1, Diary of Matthew Bell, 1830–70

D/2009/4, Daniel McKissick papers

D/2487/1, Magherhamlet (Sec.) session book, 1831–81

D/2930, R. M. Young papers

D/4164 , Maxwell Given papers

MIC/1C/1/3, Western Reformed Presbytery, 1811–28

MIC/1C/15C/1, Drumbolg (RP) session book, 1809–59

MIC/1C/16/2, Ballenon (RP) session book, 1820–48

MIC/1C/19D/1, Cullybackey (RP) session book, 1818–32

MIC/1P/7/5 & 9, Third Belfast (GSU) committee and session books, 1774–1859

MIC/1P/9/3 & 4, Belfast, May Street (GSU) session and committee books, 1834–55

MIC/1P/13, Brigh (GSU) session book, 1826–40

MIC/1P/14/1, Belfast, Alfred Street (Sec.) session book, 1824–76

MIC/1P/17, Garvagh (Sec.) committee and session book, 1827–76

MIC/1P/33/2, Burt (GSU) session book, 1833–69

MIC/1P/53, First Killyleagh (GSU) committee and session books, 1809–60

MIC/1P/72/2, Boardmills (B/Sec.) session book, 1784–1844

MIC/1P/83/1, Portstewart (GSU) session book, 1826–77

MIC/1P/85, Templepatrick Presbytery (GSU), 1795–1841

MIC/1P/87, Kilrea (GSU) session book, 1825–52

MIC/1P/90/1, Castledawson (GSU) session and committee book, 1831–67

MIC/1P/96/2, Carntall (GSU) committee and session books, 1825–48

MIC/1P/110/2, Ballynahinch (Sec.) various records, 1822–37

MIC/1P/114/2, Ballymena (GSU) session book, 1812–27

MIC/1P/142C/1, Ramelton (GSU) session book, 1828–1907

MIC/1P/157/1, Carrickfergus (GSU) committee book, 1824–48

MIC/1P/159/10, Lisburn (GSU) session book, 1779, 1805–26
MIC/1P/167/1, Donaghadee (GSU) committee book, 1783–1826
MIC/1P/179, Coronary (B/Sec.) session book, 1770–89, 1827–40
MIC/1P/215A/1, Magilligan (GSU) session book, 1814–54
MIC/1P/229, Bovevagh (GSU) session book, 1826–37
MIC/1P/299/A/1, Lissara (B/Sec.) session book, 1815–71
MIC/1P/318/A/1, Ballyblack (B/Sec.) session book, 1821–43
MIC/1P/342/A/1, Donacloney (B/Sec.) session book, 1826–78
MIC/1P/385, Tullylish (GSU) session book, 1811–26, 1836–7
MIC/1P/387, Rathfriland (B/Sec.) session book, 1805–49
MIC/1P/416/C/1, Dundrod (GSU) session book, 1829–91
MIC/1P/443A/1, Newtownhamilton (AB/Sec.) session book, 1823–34

MIC/86, McKinney papers
MIC/561, Weir papers
MIC/617, Drapers' Company records
MIC/637, David Stewart papers

T/1013/1, The Revd Samuel Elder, 'Population of Ballyeaston congregation in 1813'
T/1053, Minutes of the Presbytery of Antrim
T/1210, McCracken papers
T/1447, First Dromara (GSU) session book, 1770–1871
T/1970, Holmes papers
T/2523, Clarksbridge (Sec.) session book, 1826–62
T/2711/1/1, First Derry (GSU) committee book, 1810–1949
T/2957/1, Tullylish (GSU) various records, 1811–17
T/3041, Bruce papers
T/3239/1, Samuel Butler, 'A statistical account of the parish of Tamlaght Ard commonly called Magilligan' (1824)
T/3307, Chalmers papers
T/3541, Caldwell papers

IV. Queen's University, Belfast—Special Collections

Robert Allen papers (uncatalogued)

V. Union Theological College, Belfast

Acts and Minutes of the Associate Synod of Ireland (B), 1779–1818
Acts and Proceedings of the Associate Synod of Ireland (AB), 1788–1818
Minutes of the Presbyterian Synod of Ireland (Sec.), 1818–23

Ballymoney (GSU) session book, 1800–23
Belfast Pby (GSU) 1774–1800
Derry Pby (GSU) 1764–96, 1811–39
Derry Sub Synod (GSU) 1744–1802
Moira and Lisburn Pby (AB) 1774–86

B. Printed Material

I. Church Records

(1) General Synod of Ulster

Minutes of the General Synod of Ulster (Belfast, 1821–40).

Records of the General Synod of Ulster from 1691–1820, 3 vols. (Belfast, 1897–8).

Reports of the directors of the schools under the care of the Synod of Ulster (Belfast, 1836–7, 39).

Reports of the Presbyterian Missionary Society of the Synod of Ulster (Belfast, 1832–40).

The constitution and discipline of the Presbyterian Church; with a directory for the celebration of ordinances, and the performance of ministerial duties. Published by authority of the General Synod of Ulster (Belfast, 1825).

A pastoral address from the ministers of the Synod of Ulster to the people under their care. Cookstown, 2nd July, 1803 (Dublin, 1803).

A pastoral address from the ministers of the Synod of Ulster to the people under their care. Cookstown, June 27th, 1804 (n.p., 1804).

A pastoral address from the ministers of the Synod of Ulster to the people under their care. Cookstown, June 26, 1805 (n.p., 1805).

A pastoral address from the ministers of the Synod of Ulster to the people under their care. Cookstown, July 3, 1807 (n.p., 1807).

A pastoral address from the ministers of the Synod of Ulster to the people under their care Cookstown, June 29, 1808 (n.p., 1808).

A pastoral address from the ministers of the Synod of Ulster, assembled at their annual meeting, to the people under their care (n.p., 1809).

First report of the Dublin Presbyterian Committee, appointed to carry into effect the wishes of the Synods of Ulster and Munster, to revive and extend the Presbyterian interest in the south and west of Ireland (Dublin, 1823).

An address to the public, by the committee of the Synod of Ulster Home Mission Society (Belfast, 1827).

Address from the General Synod of Ulster, assigning reasons for a day of public humiliation (n.p., 1831).

Annual pastoral address of the General Synod of Ulster to the congregations under their charge (Belfast, 1831).

Annual address of the General Synod of Ulster to the churches under their care
(Belfast, 1833).

*Missionary sermons and speeches delivered at a special meeting of the General
Synod of Ulster, held in the Scots Church, Mary's Abbey, Dublin, in September, 1833* (Belfast, 1834).

*Address of the General Synod of Ulster, to the people under their care, on the
subject of education* (Belfast, 1835).

(2) General Assembly of the Presbyterian Church in Ireland

*The constitution and discipline of the Presbyterian Church; with a directory for
the celebration of ordinances, and the performance of ministerial duties*
(Belfast, 1841).

Minutes of the General Assembly of the Presbyterian Church in Ireland, vol. i
(1840–50); vol. ii (1851–60).

(3) Seceders

*Minutes and proceedings of the Presbyterian Synod of Ireland, distinguished by
the name Seceders* (1822–40).

*Report of the committee appointed by the Presbyterian Synod of Ireland,
distinguished by the name Seceders; to carry into effect the act of Synod
respecting the extension of the gospel in the destitute parts of Ireland ... July
6th, 1820* (Dublin, 1820).

*Reports of the home mission of the Presbyterian Synod of Ireland, distinguished
by the name Seceders* (1822–5, 1827–9, 1831–2, 1835–9).

Associate Synod (AB), *Testimony, agreed upon by the General Associate
Synod; met at Edinburgh, October, 16, 1801* (Belfast, 1802).

Associate Synod (B), *Reasons for humiliation and thanksgiving, drawn up by
Mr Millar, according to appointment, were read, corrected and approved of
by the Associate Synod of Ireland, extracted by John Rogers, clerk of the
Associate Synod* (n.p., 1811).

—— *The following reasons for humiliation and thanksgiving, were drawn up
by order of the Associate Synod of Ireland. Addressed to the people of their
charge* (Monaghan, 1812).

—— *Act, declaration and testimony, for the doctrine, worship, discipline and
government of the Church of Scotland* (Belfast, 1816).

(4) Reformed Presbyterians

Abstract of the proceedings of the Reformed Presbyterian Synod of Ireland
(Belfast, 1830–40).

Act, declaration, and testimony, for the whole of our covenanted reformation, as attained to, and established in Britain and Ireland; particularly, betwixt the years 1638 and 1649 inclusive: as also, against all the steps of defection from said reformation, whether in former or later times, since the overthrow of that glorious work, down to this present day, 3rd edn. (Edinburgh, 1777).

Address to the people under the inspection of the Reformed Presbytery of Ireland (Belfast, 1809).

The Auchinsaugh covenant, with the acknowledgement of sins and engagement to duties. II. Short account of old dissenters. III. Explanation and defence of the terms of communion of the Reformed Presbyterian Church (Belfast, 1835).

Causes of a fast to be observed by the members of the Reformed Presbyterian Church, in Ireland, on Thursday, 6th January, 1820 (Belfast, 1820).

Causes of thanksgiving, published by appointment of the Reformed Presbyterian Synod of Ireland, met at Coleraine, July 13, 1830 (Belfast, 1830).

A short directory for religious societies, drawn up by appointment of the Reformed Presbytery, for the particular use of the several societies of Christian people under their inspection, at the desire of the said societies and addressed to them (Belfast, 1815).

Statement of the constitution and proceedings of the Reformed Presbyterian Home and Foreign Missionary Society, first established in 1823, and re-modelled, according to appointment of synod, in 1828 (Belfast, 1828).

(5) Remonstrant Synod

Minutes of the Remonstrant Synod of Ulster (Belfast, 1828–40).

Remonstrance of persons connected with the General Synod of Ulster, against certain of the late proceedings of that body; by which measures they conceive that the rights of candidates for the ministry, licenciates, ministers and presbyteries, together with the ecclesiastical privileges of the laity, are directly invaded (Belfast, 1828).

Helps to Christian devotion, a collection of prayers for general use, sanctioned by the Remonstrant Synod of Ulster. Designed principally to promote the practice of family religion. To which is annexed, an explanation of the Lord's Supper (Newry, 1836).

II. Reports of Religious Societies

Ballymoney Association for Religious Purposes, *The regulations of the Ballymoney Association for Religious Purposes, established October, 1826; and the address of the committee* (Belfast, 1827).

Belfast Auxiliary Bible Society, *The nineteenth report of the Belfast Auxiliary Bible Society; adopted at the annual general meeting of the society, held in the Lancasterian school room, Frederick Street, on the 19th of September, MDCCCXXVI* (Belfast, 1826).

Belfast Juvenile Society, *First annual report of the Belfast Juvenile Society, established in September 1824* (Belfast, 1825).

Belfast Town Mission, *Reports* (Belfast, 1828–40).

Cookstown Auxiliary Bible Society, *The eleventh report of the Cookstown auxiliary Bible Society; with a list of subscribers and benefactors for 1822. With an appendix, containing the second report of the Cookstown Ladies Bible Association, and the third report of the Moneymore branch; with a list of subscribers for the year 1823* (Dungannon, 1823).

Irish Evangelical Society, *Reports* (Dublin, 1817–28).

—— *The first report of the northern branch of the Irish Evangelical Society* (Belfast, 1817).

Rosemary Street Congregation, *Presbyterian church, Rosemary Street, in connexion with the General Synod of Ulster. Annual missionary statement, for the year 1839* (Belfast, 1839).

Unitarian Society for the Diffusion of Christian Knowledge, *Report of the Unitarian Society for the Diffusion of Christian knowledge for the year ending 30th Sept 1839; with a list of subscribers, and catalogue of books in the depository* (Belfast, 1839).

III. Parliamentary Reports

First report of the commission of Irish education inquiry, HC (1825), xii.

Fourth report of the commissioners of Irish education inquiry, HC (1826–7), xiii.157.

Report from the select committee on inquiry into drunkenness, with minutes of evidence and appendix, HC (1834), viii.

An account of the application of the sums voted to defray the expense of non-conforming, Seceding, and Protestant dissenting ministers in Ireland, HC (1834), xlii. 523–6.

First report of the commissioners of public instruction, Ireland, HC (1835), xxxiii.

Report from select committee on handloom weavers' petitions, HC (1835), xiii.

IV. Newspapers and Periodicals

Belfast Commercial Chronicle
Belfast Monthly Magazine

Belfast News-Letter
Bible Christian
Christian Enquirer
Christian Freeman
Covenanter
Dublin Christian Instructor
Hibernian Evangelical Magazine
Irish Presbyterian (new ser.)
Missionary Herald
Monthly Gleaner
Monthly Missionary Herald
Northern Whig
Orthodox Presbyterian
Presbyterian Penny Magazine
Religious Advocate, and Christian Monitor
Supernatural Magazine

V. Contemporary Pamphlets and Books

An abridgement of the acts of the General Assemblies of the Church of Scotland, from the year 1638 to 1810 inclusive, alphabetically arranged (Edinburgh, 1811).

Abstract of the history of the Bible, in question and answer. Recommended by the Presbytery of Antrim (Belfast, 1819).

Alexander, Andrew, *The nature, rise and pernicious effects of religious enthusiasm. A sermon preached to the dissenting congregation of Urney, 7 January 1770. And in Londonderry, 25 February 1770* (Belfast, 1771).

Alexander, Nathaniel, *Family prayers* (Belfast, 1826).

Amicus, *A letter to the ministers of the Synod of Ulster* (n.p., 1807).

Aretin, *An essay on equalisation of bounty: being a free and candid enquiry into the causes of the present dissatisfaction among Seceders concerning the royal bounty* (Belfast, 1811).

Bankhead, John, *Faith the spring of holiness: a sermon. Whereunto is annexed, the character of Archibald Edmonstone, late of Red-Hall, Esq.; preached at Broad Island, December 27, 1768* (n.p., 1768).

[Barnett, John and Denham, James], *A catechism on the government and discipline of the Presbyterian church* (Belfast, 1835).

Benn, George, *The history of the town of Belfast* (Belfast, 1823).

Birch, T. L., *The obligations upon Christians, and especially ministers, to be exemplary in their lives; particularly at this important period, when the prophecies are seemingly about to be fulfilled in the fall of Antichrist, as an* introduction to the flowing in of Jew and Gentile into the Christian church. A sermon preached before the very reverend General Synod of Ulster, at Lurgan, June 26th, 1793 (Belfast, 1794).

—— *Physicians languishing under disease. An address to the Seceding, or Associate Synod of Ireland, upon certain tenets and practices alleged to be in enmity with all religious reformation*, 8th edn. (Belfast, 1796).

—— *Seemingly experimental religion, instructors unexperienced—converters unconverted—revivals killing religion—missionaries in need of teaching— or, war against the gospel by its friends. Being the examination of Thomas Ledlie Birch, a foreign ordained minister by the Rev. Presbytery of Ohio, under the very Rev. General Assembly's Alien Act* (Washington, Pa., 1806).

Boyle, Francis, *County Down poems* (n.p., [*c*.1812]).

Breakey, Andrew, *The Christian, the ruling elder, and the philanthropist. A discourse, occasioned by the death of Sidney Hamilton Rowan, Esq. Preached in Killyleagh, Nov. 28, 1847* (Belfast, 1847).

Brown, John, *A sermon on drunkenness* (Belfast, 1825).

—— *The Christian ambassador. A sermon, preached before the General Synod of Ulster, at Cookstown, upon the last Tuesday of June, 1833* (Belfast, 1833).

—— *Meroz: a sermon showing the duty of Scottish Christians to Ireland at the present crisis. Preached in Hope Street Gaelic church, on the 18th November* (Glasgow, 1838).

[Bruce, William], *Psalms, hymns and spiritual songs; selected for the First Congregation of Presbyterians in Belfast* (Belfast, 1801).

—— *A selection of psalms and hymns, for the use of the Presbytery of Antrim, and the congregation of Strand Street, Dublin* (Belfast, 1818).

Bryson, James, *The objections of infidels no sufficient reason for rejecting Christian religion. A discourse delivered before a meeting of dissenting ministers, at Belfast, on Tuesday, November 7th, 1769* (Belfast, 1769).

—— *The obtaining of the divine approbation, by dividing the word of truth aright, the supreme object of a Christian minister's pursuit. A sermon preached at the ordination of the Rev James Caldwell, in the Protestant dissenting congregation of Dundonald, September 1, 1772*, 2nd edn. (Belfast, 1773).

Bryson, William, *The duty of searching the scriptures recommended and explained: a sermon, preached at the ordination of the Revd Futt Marshall, in Ballyclare, February the 9th, 1785* (Belfast, 1786).

—— *The practice of righteousness productive of happiness, both at present and forever. A sermon, preached at Camlin, July 28th, 1782. On occasion of the death of the Reverend Thomas Crawford* (Belfast, 1782).

Butler, Samuel, *Death and life in many views; or, a series of fifty-two discourses* (Londonderry, 1826).

Cairns, William, *On the mutual dependence of mankind for intellectual, moral, and religious improvement. A sermon preached at the anniversary of the British and Foreign School Society, in Great Queen Street Chapel, London, on Wednesday, May 15th, 1822* (London, 1822).

[Cameron, John], *The Catholic Christian; or, the true religion sought and found. By Theophilus Philander* (Belfast, 1769).

—— *The Catholic Christian defended, in a letter to the Rev. Benjamin McDowel* (Belfast, 1771).

—— *Theophilus and Philander: a dialogue. Containing remarks upon the Rev. Mr McDowel's Second Letter to the supposed author of the Catholic Christian* (Belfast, 1773).

Campbell, James, *The poems and songs of James Campbell of Ballynure* (Ballyclare, 1870).

Campbell, William, *The presence of Christ with his church in every age and period of it, explained and improved. A discourse delivered at Antrim, June 28, 1774. At a General Synod of the Protestant dissenting ministers of the Presbyterian communion of Ulster* (Belfast, 1774).

Carlile, James, *The old doctrine of faith asserted in opposition to certain modern innovations, including strictures or reviews of the author's sermons on repentance and faith, published in the Eclectic Review for April, and Edinburgh Christian Monitor for March, 1823; and also an essay on faith, by Thomas Erskine, Esq. Advocate* (London, 1823).

—— *Memorial recommending the establishment of a mission to the Roman Catholics of Ireland* (Dublin, 1825).

—— *The general diffusion of Christianity the duty of the churches. A sermon, preached before the General Synod of Ulster, assembled in Ballymena, June, 1826* (Dublin, 1826).

—— *Select sacred melodies, for all the metres in general use, collected from the works of the most eminent composers, arranged for four voices, with a simple accompaniment for the organ or piano forte, and adapted to a selection of hymns, printed uniformly with the music* (Dublin, n.d.).

Carlisle, James, *The nature of religious zeal. A sermon on Phil. 3.6. Preached at a General Synod held in Antrim, June the eighteenth, 1745* (Belfast, 1745).

Carr, William, *The importance of religious education, and the duty of instructing the children of the ignorant poor, illustrated in a sermon preached in Berry Street meeting-house on Sunday 6th of February, 1822, in aid of the funds of the Belfast Sunday School Society, and the Ladies Sunday Local School Association* (Belfast, 1822).

—— *The conversion of seamen; a sermon: preached in the Berry Street meeting house, Belfast, on Sunday the 16th Nov. 1823, on behalf of the Belfast Seaman's Friend Society and Bethel Union* (Belfast, 1823).

Carson, Alexander, *Reasons for separating from the General Synod of Ulster* (Belfast, 1805).

—— *Remarks on a late pastoral address, from the ministers of the Synod of Ulster, to the people under their care* (Belfast, 1806).

Clark, Thomas, *A brief survey of some principles maintained, by the General Synod of Ulster, and practices carried on, by several members thereof* (Armagh, 1751).

—— *New light set in a clear light* ([Dublin], 1755).

—— *Plain reasons, why neither Dr Watt's imitations of the psalms, nor his other poems, nor any other human composition, ought to be used in the praises of the great God our saviour—but, that metre version of the book of Psalms, examined with wise and critical care, by pious and learned divines, and found by them to be as near the Hebrew meter psalms, as the idiom of the English language would admit, ought to be used. With a short address to ministers and heads of families concerning family government* ([Newry, 1785]).

—— *A pastoral and farewell letter, to the Associate congregation of Presbyterians in Ballybay new erection* (Monaghan, 1807).

Cochran, John, *A selection of psalm and hymn tunes adapted to various metres for the use of the congregations and families to which is prefixed a compendious introduction, with some useful scales and examples* (Belfast, 1804).

A collection of psalms and hymns for Christian worship (Newry, 1783).

Colville, Alexander, *The persecuting, disloyal and absurd tenets of those who affect to call themselves Seceders laid open and refuted, in a letter addressed to the people under the care of the Presbytery of Antrim* (Belfast, 1749).

—— *Some important queries humbly and earnestly recommended to the serious consideration of the Protestant dissenters in the north of Ireland, belonging to the Synodical Association* (Belfast, 1773).

The Confession of Faith; the Larger and Shorter Catechisms, with the Scripture proofs at large ... ([1835] Inverness, 1976).

Cooke, Henry, *A sermon, preached in the meeting-house of the Third Presbyterian Congregation, Belfast, on Sunday, the 18th December, 1814, in aid of the funds of the house of industry* (Belfast, 1815).

—— *Translations and paraphrases, in verse, of several portions of sacred Scripture; collected for the use of the Presbyterian church, Killyleagh* (Belfast, 1821).

—— *A sermon, preached at the opening of the General Synod of Ulster, in Coleraine, on the 28th of June 1825* (Belfast, 1825).

—— *National education. A sermon preached in the Presbyterian church May Street, Belfast, upon, the 15th January, 1832* (Belfast, 1832).

—— (ed.) *The larger catechism, agreed upon by the assembly of divines at Westminster, and approved by the General Assembly of the Kirk of Scotland. With proofs from Scripture* (Belfast, 1835).

—— *Sins of the times. A discourse delivered in the Presbyterian church, May Street, Belfast, on the twentieth of August, 1837* (Belfast, 1837).

Coulter, John, *Ministers addressed on the subject of their own salvation. A sermon, preached at the opening of the Presbyterian Synod of the Secession church in Ireland, assembled in the Berry Street meeting-house, Belfast, July 6, 1830* (Belfast, 1830).

—— *Will the two synods ever unite? The Rev. John Coulter's address to the student's united prayer meeting, Belfast College, on the prospect of union between the General and Secession Synods* (Belfast, 1839).

Craghead, Robert, *Advice to communicants for necessary preparation, and profitable improvement of the great and comfortable ordinance of the Lord's Supper: that therein true spiritual communion with Christ may be obtained, and the eternal enjoyment of God sealed* (Glasgow, 1714). [Another edition, Glasgow, 1805].

Craig, William, *A charge to the minister and congregation of Killinchy, delivered at the ordination of the Rev. D. Anderson, December 6, 1836 ... Also, the speech of the Rev. David Anderson, before the conclusion of the proceedings* (Belfast, 1837).

Cuming, James, *The apostle Paul's reasoning before Felix, explained and applied. A sermon, preached at Ballymoney, November 12th, 1800, on occasion of the ordination of the Revd Benjamin Mitchell, in that place* (n.p., 1800).

Delap, Samuel, *Synodical sermon at Antrim, June 21st, 1737, from Romans xiv. 1, and Titus iii. 10, 11* (Belfast, 1737).

—— *Remarks on some articles of the Seceders new covenant, and their act of presbytery, making it the term of ministerial and Christian communion* (Belfast, 1749).

—— *The scripture doctrine of original sin asserted and explained. A sermon preached the second Lord's Day of July, Anno. Dom. 1740* (Londonderry, 1741).

—— *A dissertation on the important subject of atonement* (Dublin, 1758).

Denham, James, *Revivals of religion and means of obtaining them. A sermon, preached before the General Synod of Ulster, July the 7th, 1840* (Belfast, 1840).

—— *Public baptism vindicated by an appeal to Scriptural authority, and the nature and uses of the ordinance; with an answer to prevailing objections* (Derry, 1844).

Dickey, William, *An essay on the origin and principles of the Seceders* (Strabane, 1793).

—— *Sermons on some of the most remarkable Scripture prophecies; and some of the most illustrious scripture characters.* Part 1 (Strabane, 1819).

—— *The marriage of the lamb; or the joy occasioned by the future conversion of the Jews. A sermon preached in the Seceding meeting-house of Carnone, October 15, 1826, immediately before the dispensation of the Lord's Supper* (Strabane, 1827).

—— *Sermons on important doctrinal and practical subjects* (Derry, 1835).

Dickson, W. S., *Sermons on the following subjects: I. The advantages of national repentance. 1776. II. The ruinous effects of civil war. 1778. III. The coming of the Son of Man. 1777. IV. The hope of meeting, knowing, and rejoicing with virtuous friends in a future world* (Belfast, 1778).

—— *'Ye shall appear with Christ in glory.' A sermon occasioned by the death of the Revd James Armstrong, late dissenting minister of Portaferry: preached, by desire of the congregation of that place, November 14th, 1779* (Belfast, 1780).

—— *Psalmody. An address to the Presbyterian congregations of the Synod of Ulster* (Belfast, 1792).

—— *Three sermons, on the subject of Scripture politics* (Belfast, 1793).

Dill, J. R., *Autobiography of a country parson* (Belfast, 1888).

Dill, Richard, *Mixed marriages; the substance of a speech ... delivered at a public meeting in Glasgow, held on Tuesday, 11th June, on the mixed marriage question* (Glasgow, 1844).

—— *Prelatico Presbyterianism: or, curious chapters in the recent history of the Irish Presbyterian Church* (Dublin, 1856).

Dill, Samuel, *A sermon on the duty of ministers and their connexion with Christ; preached at the meeting of the particular synod in Londonderry, May 18th, 1802* (Londonderry, [1802]).

Dugall, George, *The northern cottage, book 1. And other poems; written partly in the dialect of the north of Ireland* (Londonderry, 1824).

Dunlop, William, *The cultivation of a manly understanding in religion recommended. A sermon, preached before the General Synod of Ulster, at their annual meeting in Cookstown, on Tuesday the 25th June, 1811* (Strabane, 1812).

Edgar, John, *The evils, cause and cure of drunkenness; with an account of the Temperance Societies, of America and Great Britain,* 2nd edn. (Belfast, 1830).

—— *Selected works of John Edgar, D.D., LL.D.,* ed. W. D. Killen (Belfast, 1868).

Edgar, Samuel, *The times, a sermon, preached at the ordination of the Rev. Thomas Heron, Fourtowns, Donoughmore* (Belfast, 1814).

—— *A sermon; preached before the Down Missionary Society, at Rathfriland* (Belfast, 1815).

—— *Improvement of Irish Catholics. A sermon* (Belfast, 1822).

—— 'Recollections of 1798', *Belfast Magazine and Literary Journal*, 1 (1825), 540–8.

Elder, James, *A sermon, preached in the meeting-house of Drumachose, on the Arian controversy, on the 13th January, 1828, in defence of the doctrine of justification, by the imputed righteousness of Christ* (Londonderry, 1828).

Finney, C. G., *Lectures on revivals of religion*, ed. W. G. McLoughlin (Cambridge, Mass., 1960).

Gamble, John, *A view of society and manners, in the north of Ireland, in the summer and autumn of 1812* (London, 1813).

—— *Views of society and manners in the north of Ireland, in a series of letters written in the year 1818* (London, 1819).

—— *Sketches of history, politics and manners, in Dublin and the north of Ireland, in 1810. A new edition* (London, 1826).

Gamble, Samuel, *The sinner ransomed by the death of Christ, a sermon, delivered previous to the celebration of the Lord's Supper in the Associate congregation of Ramelton. November 14, 1814* (Strabane, 1815).

—— *Two discourses: the first, delivered at the ordination of the Rev. James Gamble, A. M. Strabane, September 12, 1816. The second, at the opening of Synod, Cookstown, July 7, 1818: the interesting occasion on which the two synods of Seceders formed a coalition* (Strabane, 1819).

—— *A sermon, delivered at the opening of the Presbyterian Synod of Ireland, in the meeting house of the First congregation, Berry Street, Belfast, July 6, 1824* (Strabane, 1824).

Gibson, William, *The year of grace: a history of the Ulster revival of 1859* (Edinburgh, 1860).

Hall, James, *Tour through Ireland; particularly the interior and least known parts: containing an accurate view of the parties, politics and improvements, in the different provinces*, 2 vols. (London, 1813).

Hamill, Hugh, *Ministerial respectability considered; in a sermon, preached before the reverend Sub Synod of Londonderry at their annual meeting, May 8, 1787* (Strabane, 1788).

Hamilton, David, *A sermon on national education* (Belfast, 1834).

Hamilton, George, *The great necessity of itinerant preaching. A sermon delivered in the new meeting-house of Armagh, at the formation of the Evangelical Society of Ulster, on Wednesday, 10th of October, 1798. With a short introductory memorial respecting the establishment and first attempt of that society* (Armagh, 1798).

Hanna, Samuel, *A sermon on the qualifications of the ministerial character, delivered at the opening of the General Synod of Ulster, in Cookstown, June 26, 1810* (Belfast, 1810).

—— *The utility of the dispensary and fever hospital, of Belfast, pointed out in a discourse, delivered in the meeting-house of the Third Congregation, on Sunday, 14th March, 1813 … With an address from the committee, to the inhabitants of Belfast, and its vicinity* (Belfast, 1813).

—— *Love to Christ: an incitement to ministerial and missionary exertions. A sermon, preached before the London Missionary Society, at Surrey Chapel, on Wednesday morning, May 8, 1822*, 2nd edn. (Belfast, 1822).

[Hart, Robert], *A musical catechism; or, the principles of sacred music laid down in a plain and simple form* (Belfast, 1804).

Hay, George, *A sermon, preached in the meeting-house, Londonderry, for the benefit of the singing boys of the Presbyterian congregation* (Derry, 1814).

[Henry, Henry], *An address to the people of Connor, containing clear and full vindication, of the Synod of Ulster; from the aspersions of the people called Covenanters. By Sanders Donald* (Belfast, 1794).

Henry, William, *A funeral sermon, preached on Sabbath evening, November 23, 1823, after the death of the Rev. Josias Alexander, A. M. late pastor of the Reformed Presbyterian congregation in Belfast* (Belfast, 1823).

Herbison, David, *The select works of David Herbison* (Belfast, 1883).

[Heron, William], *The Ulster Synod, a poem* (Dublin, 1817).

Hogg, Robert, *An attempt to explain the causes and nature of those distinctions in doctrine, which at present exist in the Reformed churches. Being a sermon preached at the opening of the General Synod of Ulster, in Moneymore, on the 29th June, 1824* (Belfast, 1825).

Horner, James, *A sermon preached in St Mary's Abbey meeting-house, on Sunday morning, 3rd March, 1805; for support of the charity schools belonging to said congregation* (Dublin, 1805).

—— *The destination of man after death. A sermon occasioned by the death of the late Benjamin McDowell, D. D., senior minister of the Scots church, Mary's Abbey, Dublin* (Dublin, 1825).

Houston, Thomas, *A pastoral address to the members and other individuals connected with the Reformed Presbyterian congregation of Knockbracken* (Belfast, 1829).

—— *Queries to be proposed to the members in fellowship meetings, at corresponding societies, and at general congregational meetings. Sanctioned by the session of the Reformed Presbyterian congregation of Knockbracken, and recommended to the people under their inspection* (Belfast, 1832).

Huey, James, *A sermon on the divine appointment of a gospel ministry, preached from Hebrews, vth chapter, 4th verse* (Belfast, 1814).

Hull, James, *Religion, founded upon knowledge, and productive of forbearance, moderation and peace. A sermon, preached before a General Synod, of Protestant dissenting ministers; at their annual meeting in Dungannon, June 26th, 1770* (Belfast, 1770).

James, William, *Homesius Enervatus. A letter addressed to Mr John Holmes; containing Ist An essay on church communion. IId The terms of church communion held by the Reformed Presbytery, vindicated. IIId Grounds for separation from the Synod of Ireland. And, IVthly, Animadversions upon a pamphlet, entitled a Testimony, etc written by Mr Holmes, minister of Glendermott* (Londonderry, 1772).

Kelburn, Sinclair, *The morality of the Sabbath defended. A sermon preached in the third meeting-house in Belfast* (Belfast, 1781).

—— *The divinity of our Lord Jesus Christ asserted and proved, and the connection of this doctrine, with practical religion, pointed out, in five sermons* (Belfast, 1792).

—— *The duty of preaching the gospel, explained and recommended. An ordination sermon preached at Newtownards* (Dublin, 1790).

Kennedy, Gilbert, *The character and conduct of St Paul as a teacher of Christianity recommended as a pattern to all who devote themselves to the Christian ministry. A sermon preached at Lurgan, June 26th, 1764 at a General Synod of the Protestant dissenting ministers of the Presbyterian persuasion in Ulster* (Belfast, 1764).

[Killen, W. D., et al.], *The plea of presbytery in behalf of the ordination, government, discipline, and worship of the Christian church, as opposed to the unscriptural claims of prelacy, in a reply to the Rev. Archibald Boyd, A. M., on Episcopacy. Ministers of the General Synod of Ulster* (Glasgow, 1840).

[King, John], *A letter to the Protestant dissenters in the north of Ireland, occasioned by some teachers from Scotland, called Seceders. By a Protestant dissenter* (n.p., 1748).

King, John, *Remarks on the Reverend S. M. Stephenson's declaration of faith. And his reasons for not subscribing the Westminster Confession of Faith. To which are annexed reasons of dissent, of some of the members of the old Presbytery of Bangor, now members of the Presbytery of Belfast, respecting Mr Stephenson's ordination* (Belfast, 1774).

—— *A vindication of the Presbytery of Belfast, against Mr Stephenson's review of Mr King's remarks* (Belfast, 1775).

Kirkpatrick, W. B. (ed.), *Memorial services in connexion with the removal of the congregation of Mary's Abbey to Rutland Square, Dublin* (Dublin, 1865).

Laing, William, *Justification by the faith of Christ, without the deeds of the law: sermon, delivered in the new meeting-house of Newry, on Sabbath, 21st December, 1800* (Newry, 1801).

Lanktree, Matthew, *An apology for what is called lay-preaching; in a series of letters; addressed to the Rev. James Huey, Presbyterian minister of Ballywillan, near Coleraine, occasioned by his sermon on the divine appointment of a gospel ministry* (Newry, 1815).

A Layman, *Mr McDowel's vindication of the Westminster Confession, examined: upon the authority of Jesus Christ, and the human understanding* (Dublin, 1774).

Lisburn congregation, *Hymns for the use of the Presbyterian congregation in Lisburn* (Belfast, 1787).

Lowry, John, *Sermon preached before the Associate Synod of Presbyterians, in Ireland, July 1816* (Belfast, 1816).

—— *Christian baptism: wherein infant baptism is vindicated; baptism by immersion is exploded—that ministers of the gospel ONLY, have a right to administer baptism—fire and water baptism are contrasted and compared. Also, an advice to Christian parents, and all other baptised persons. Being the substance of a sermon preached in Upper-Clennaneese, from Luke iii. 16* (Belfast, 1822).

McAlester, C. J., *Sunday school instruction. The substance of a discourse, preached in the meeting-house of the First Presbyterian Congregation, Holywood* (Belfast, 1840).

McCann, George, *The life of George McCann. Written by himself* (Belfast, n.d.).

McDowell, Benjamin, *The requiring subscription to well-composed summaries, of the Christian doctrines, as tests of orthodoxy, defended* (Glasgow, 1770).

—— *A second letter to the Revd J—n C——n, in answer to his defence of The Catholic Christian* (Belfast, 1771).

—— *Observations on Theophilus and Philander. Addressed to the public* (n.p., 1772).

—— *A vindication of the Westminster Confession of Faith from the attacks of two late writers. Addressed to Presbyterians in general. In which most of the principal doctrines of the gospel are explained and defended* (Belfast, 1774).

—— *The doctrine of salvation by grace, proved; objections against it answered; and, its natural tendency to promote the cause of universal righteousness pointed out* (Belfast, 1777).

—— *The standing orders of Christ to the messengers of his grace, of every church, and in every age; considered, and applied to the present time, in a sermon preached in St Mary's Abbey meeting-house, on Sunday the 21st of*

July, 1799, from Isaiah LXII. 10, at the request of the General Evangelical Society; and now published at their desire (Dublin, 1799).

[McEwen, W. D. H., *et al.*], *The Presbyterian mode of ordaining to the holy ministry; exemplified in the ordination of the Rev. John Baird, in the congregation of Stratford, on Slaney, upon the 24th of September, 1811, by the Presbytery of Dublin* (Dublin, 1812).

MacKay, James, *The character and future reward of the wise and of those who turn many to righteousness. A sermon preached in the new meeting-house in Belfast, May Twenty Third, MDCCVXXII, on occasion of the death of the late Gilbert Kennedy, pastor of that congregation* (Belfast, 1773).

McKay, Thomas, *Addresses, proper for sacramental occasions* (Belfast, 1786).

McKay, W. K., *Elements of Zion's polity* (Belfast, 1832).

McKee, David, *Some remarks on conversion* (Belfast, 1836).

McKinley, John, *Poetic sketches, descriptive of the Giant's Causeway, and the surrounding scenery: with some detached pieces* (Belfast, 1819).

McSkimin, Samuel, 'A statistical account of Islandmagee', *Newry Magazine*, 3 (1817–18).

—— *The history and antiquities of the county of the town of Carrickfergus*, ed. E. J. McCrum, new edn. (Belfast, 1909).

McVity, John, *Select psalm and hymn tunes, adapted to the use of public congregations and private families*, 2nd edn. (Dublin, 1787).

Malcolm, A. G., *A collection of psalms, hymns and spiritual songs, proper for Christian worship; selected and arranged for the use of congregations and families* (Newry, 1811).

—— *A catechism, intended for the instruction of children and young persons, in the principles of the Christian religion. Prepared for the use of the Presbyterian congregation of Newry* (Newry, 1812).

—— *The communicant's catechism; or the nature, design and tendency of baptism and the Lord's Supper explained, in question and answer: to which are added, forms of devotion, proper for communicants* (Newry, 1812).

—— *The progress of Christianity, a sermon, preached at a meeting of the General Synod of Ulster, held at Cookstown, June 26th, 1821. With notes, in which the Bible Society question is particularly considered* (Belfast, 1822).

Mason, W. S., *A statistical account, or parochial survey of Ireland*, 3 vols. (Dublin, 1814–19).

Mathews, George, *An account of the regium donum, issued to the Presbyterian Church in Ireland* Dublin, 1836).

—— *Observations on the parliamentary grant to Presbyterian ministers in Ireland* (Dublin, 1837).

Maxwell, David, *A sermon on the conversion of the heathen. Published, chiefly with a view to promote attention of this important subject* (Belfast, 1815).

Mears, John, *A short explanation of the end and design of the Lord's Supper* (Dublin, 1758).

A Member of the Synod of Ulster, *A sermon. The object of which is to explain and illustrate the conduct Presbyterians ought to pursue, when engaged in choosing a minister* (Belfast, 1824).

[Millar, Thomas], *To the inhabitants of Cookstown and its vicinity, the following observations are addressed, by a friend of the Bible, and a friend of man* (Cookstown, 1826).

Ministers of the General Synod of Ulster, *Family prayers for every day in the week; with prayers for Sabbath schools* (Belfast, 1829).

Moffat, Walter, *A pastoral address, to the Presbyterian Secession Congregation of Saintfield* (Belfast, 1836).

[Moore, John], *Psalms carefully suited and applied to the Christian state and worship; to which are added, hymns and spiritual songs, copied chiefly from those authorised to be sung by the General Assembly of the Church of Scotland. Printed by Joseph Hill, for the use of the Presbyterian dissenting congregation of Carrickfergus* (Dublin, 1782).

Moore, J. H., *In memoriam. The Rev. Robert Park, A. M., Ballymoney. Born 15 April 1794. Ordained 18 March 1817. Died 10 May 1876* (Belfast, 1876).

Morgan, James, *A pastoral address, to the Lisburn Presbyterian congregation* (Belfast, 1824).

—— *A scriptural statement of the nature of the obligations of Christian missions to the heathen world. A sermon preached to the Lisburn Presbyterian congregation, on the 17th September, 1826* (Belfast, 1826).

—— *Growth in grace. A sermon preached in the Presbyterian church, Fisherwick Place, Belfast, on Sunday, the 16th of January, 1831* (Belfast, 1831).

—— *Christian education, the foundation of national prosperity. A sermon, preached to the Belfast Sabbath-School Union, on the 1st of February, 1835* (Belfast, 1835).

—— *Education. A discourse, delivered in the Presbyterian church, Fisherwick Place, upon Sabbath, 6th December, 1835; and particularly addressed to parents and teachers* (Belfast, 1836).

—— *Essays in some of the principal doctrines and duties of the gospel*, 2nd edn. (Belfast, 1837).

—— *Reflections on the death of Mr William Cochrane, one of the agents of the Belfast Town Mission* (Belfast, 1837).

—— *A good man. A discourse on the death of Charles Thomson, Esq. With an appendix containing the official documents connected with the origin and establishment of the congregation of Fisherwick Place* (Belfast, 1855).

—— *Recollections of my life and times* (Belfast, 1874).

Nelson, John, *A letter to the Protestant dissenters in the parish of Ballykelly; occasioned by their objections against their late minister* (Belfast, 1766).

Nelson, Moses, *Whether the light of nature be sufficient to salvation: considered in a discourse delivered at Lurgan, June 26, 1787, at a General Synod of the Protestant dissenting ministers of Ulster* (Belfast, 1788).

Nevin, William, *The nature and evidence of an over-ruling providence considered. A sermon, preached before the Downe Volunteers, and fusiliers, on the 5th of September, 1779, and published at their desire* (Belfast, 1779).

Oliver, William, *Pastoral provision: or, the income of the Irish Presbyterian clergy shown to be insufficient; with the proper means to be adopted for its augmentation* (Belfast, 1856).

Ordnance Survey: memoir of the city and north-western liberties of Londonderry: parish of Templemore (Dublin, 1837).

Orr, James, *Poems, on various subjects* (Belfast, 1804).

—— *The posthumous works of James Orr, of Ballycarry; with a sketch of his life* (Belfast, 1817).

Orr, Malcolm, *Lay preaching in the Synod of Ulster* (Belfast, 1838).

Park, Robert, *Responsibilities and duties of pastor and people. A discourse* (Belfast, 1857).

Paul, John, *The mountain of the Lord's house: a sermon preached at Rathfriland, Sabbath evening, June 16, 1839 ... and published at the request of the committee of the Rathfriland Sabbath School Union* (Belfast, 1839).

Pigott, S. J., *A collection of psalms and hymns, ancient and modern. For the use of the Presbyterian congregations of the Synod of Munster, and the Presbytery of Antrim, selected and arranged for one, two or three voices, with an accompaniment for the organ or piano forte* (Dublin, n.d.).

Pistophilos Philecclesia, *Letters of importance: wherein are contained some serious queries upon several very interesting points; most humbly and respectfully directed to the ensuing venerable Synod of Ulster: craving that they may be read, and seriously considered at their next meeting 1775* (Belfast, 1775).

A Poor Old Light Presbyterian, *An address to the most reverend the Synod of Ulster on behalf of the poor of the Presbyterian body of the town of Belfast: wherein an 'attempt is made' to bring in an old fashion once more into vogue* (Belfast, 1812).

Porter, James, *A sermon, preached to the congregation of Greyabbey, on Thursday the 16th February, the day appointed for a general fast* (Belfast, 1797).

Porter, J. S., *The creed of the many and the faith of the few; a sermon preached in Glasgow, on Sunday afternoon, September 29, 1833* (Belfast, 1833).

Porter, J. S., *A discourse concerning creeds, their origin, authors, and effects; preached in the meeting house of the First Presbyterian congregation, Belfast, on Sunday, May the 8th, 1836* (Belfast, 1836).

—— *The Christian's hope in death: a discourse delivered in the meeting-house of the First Presbyterian Congregation, Belfast, on Sunday, March 7, 1841; on occasion of the death of the Rev. William Bruce, D. D. senior pastor of the congregation* (Belfast, 1841).

Porter, William, *Extracts from the records of the General Synod of Ulster; from the year 1800 till the year 1829* (Belfast, 1822).

A Presbyter of Ireland, *The modes of Presbyterian Church vindicated; in a letter to the blacksmith*, new edn. (Edinburgh, 1826).

Pringle, Francis, *The gospel ministry, an ordinance of Christ; and the duty of ministers and people. A sermon, at the opening of the Associate Synod of Ireland, in Belfast, July 12, 1796* ([Belfast], 1796).

Psalms, paraphrases, and hymns selected for the use of the Presbyterian congregation of Strabane (Strabane, 1822).

Ranken, John, *The exercise and improvement of the understanding recommended, as highly requisite in a minister of the gospel. A sermon preached before the General Synod of the Protestant dissenting ministers in Ulster. The second day of their annual meeting, in Lurgan, July 1st, 1772* (Belfast, 1772).

Rankin, James, *Three sermons, by James Rankin, M. A., minister of the Presbyterian Seceding congregation of Monaghan* (Dublin, 1823).

—— *The trial of the spirits. A sermon, preached at the opening of the Presbyterian Synod of Ireland; distinguished by the name Seceders; in Armagh, July 1, 1818* (Monaghan, 1828).

Reid, J. S., *The history of the Presbyterian Church in Ireland, briefly reviewed and practically improved. A sermon preached at the opening of the General Synod of Ulster, assembled at Cookstown, June 24, 1828* (Belfast, 1828).

—— *Catalogue of the Presbyterian congregational library, Carrickfergus. Established 1831* (n.p., [1831]).

—— *Forty select psalm tunes for the use of the Presbyterian church, Carrickfergus; J. Seaton Reid D. D., minister. Andrew Bruce, precentor* (Belfast, 1837).

Reid, William, *A selection of sacred tunes for congregational and family worship comprising a variety of popular tunes in four parts, adapted to the version of psalms and paraphrases used in the Presbyterian churches in connexion with the Synod of Ulster, with a few additional peculiar measures* (Belfast, [1835]).

Reid, William (ed.), *Authentic records of revival, now in progress in the United Kingdom* (London, 1860).

Rentoul, James, *The angelic anthem, applied to the present times, in two sermons* (Strabane, 1815).

Rentoul, J. B., *Wesleyan Methodism and Calvinism contrasted, in the light of divine truth; especially on the subjects of election and the divine decrees. A sermon* (Belfast, 1836).

Richey, William, *Believers inheriting the promises. A sermon preached in the First Presbyterian church, on the death of Hugh Lyle, Esq., Knockintern* (Belfast, 1848).

——— *Connor and Coleraine; or, scenes and sketches of the last Ulster awakening* (Belfast, 1870).

Rodgers, H. W., *Scriptural warrant for religious societies and prayer meetings, with rules for their management, and arguments in their favour; addressed to the members of the Presbyterian church, Kilrea* (Belfast, 1833).

Rogers, John, *A sermon preached October 24, 1770, at Newbliss; at the ordination of the Rev. Samuel Rutherford. By John Rogers, M. A. of the new erection of Ballybay; being a good way to procure and preserve that respect due to ministers of the gospel* (Monaghan, n.d.).

——— *The substance of a speech delivered in a synod at Cookstown, July 8, 1808, being a vindication of the co-ordinate constitution and formula of the Associate Synod of Ireland* (Dublin, 1809).

Sampson, G. V., *A memoir, explanatory of the chart and survey of the county of Londonderry, Ireland* (London, 1814).

Select melodies for congregational and family worship arranged for two and three voices and adapted to all the measures in ordinary use: with copious elementary instructions in vocal psalmody. Published by a committee representing various sects and denominations of Christians in the town and neighbourhood of Newtownards (Belfast, 1825).

A selection of psalms adapted to public worship (Londonderry, 1831).

A selection of sacred music, designed for the use of the Presbyterian churches, in connexion with the Synod of Ulster, consisting of 100 psalm and hymn tunes adapted to various metres: and comprising nearly all the airs generally used in the churches, chapels, and dissenting congregations throughout the United Kingdom, 2nd edn. (Dromara, 1835).

Semple, John, *The survey impartially examined by sacred Scripture and sound reason. Being an answer to a late pamphlet entitled, A Survey, etc, by Mr Thomas Clark, Seceding minister at Ballybay* (Belfast, 1754).

Sheppard, Samuel, *A select collection of psalm and hymn tunes, in two parts; adapted to the various metres which are used in the Established Church, and the dissenting meeting-houses, and private families in the United Kingdom* (Belfast, n.d.).

Sixty-seven psalm and hymn tunes, with a few anthems selected with the utmost care from the most approved works of the present day, and arranged for 1, 2, or 3 voices; designed for the Presbyterian church at Dromara (Belfast, 1833).

Sloan, E. L., *The bard's offering: a collection of miscellaneous poems* (Belfast, 1854).

Smyth, James, *Calvinism and Arminianism contrasted, in a short explanation of the celebrated five points, viz: predestination, particular redemption, total depravity, conversion, and the perseverance of the saints, with a few observations on sinless perfection* (Belfast, 1832).

Stavely, William, *War proclaimed, and victory ensured; or, the Lamb's conquest illustrated. A sermon, lately delivered, and now published at the earnest request of the auditors* (Belfast, 1795).

Stephenson, S. M., *The declaration of faith approved by the reverend Presbytery of Bangor, and read publicly before the dissenting congregation of Greyabbey, by S. M. Stephenson, at his ordination the 21st Day of June 1774. To which his reasons for not complying with the form of subscription to the Westminster Confession of Faith required of him, are prefixed* (Belfast, 1774).

Stewart, John, *Union in truth and love: a sermon, preached before the Reformed Presbyterian Synod in Ireland, assembled at Moneymore, July 8, 1828* (Belfast, 1828).

Stuart, David, *The call of God to Irish Christians, in behalf of their perishing countrymen, and the guilt and danger of neglecting to hear it: a sermon preached in the new meeting-house, Cookstown, at the opening of the Presbyterian Synod of Ireland, distinguished by the name Seceders; on Tuesday, July 4, 1820* (Dublin, 1820).

—— *The claims of the poor children of Ireland on Christians, stated and enforced: a sermon … preached in the new meeting-house, Mary's Abbey, on Sabbath, the 9th of April, 1820, in aid of the funds of Mary's Abbey Sabbath and weekday evening schools* (Dublin, 1820).

—— *The death of Judas. A discourse, delivered at the Union Monthly lecture for August 1823* (Dublin, 1823).

—— *Christian anniversaries contrasted with Jewish festivals: a sermon, preached on occasion of the annual meetings of the principal national societies of Ireland, for propagating the gospel at home and abroad. On Sabbath, April 11th, 1824* (Dublin, 1824).

Taggart, William, *Sermons* (Strabane, 1788).

Thompson, Samuel, *New poems on a variety of different subjects* (Belfast, 1799).

Thomson, John, *An abstract of the laws and rules of the General Synod of Ulster, from June 15 1694 to June 1800* (Dublin, 1803).

The true psalmody; or, the Bible psalms the church's only manual of praise. With prefaces by the Rev. H. Cooke, D. D., LL. D., Rev. J. Edgar, D. D., LL. D., and Rev. T. Houston, D. D., 3rd edn. (Belfast, 1867).

Tynan, Hugh, *Poems, by the late Hugh Tynan, of Donaghadee* (Belfast, 1803).

A view of Seceders, in some instances of their usage of the General Synod of Ulster, with some of its members. In two letters: viz. a letter from Mr Fisher of Glasgow to Mr King of Drumarragh:—and Mr King's answer to said letter. In which, the Seceders practices in the north of Ireland are, without prejudice, animadverted upon (Belfast, 1748).

Wakefield, Edward, *An Account of Ireland*, 2 vols. (London, 1812).

Walker, Samuel, 'The cotter's Sabbath day', *Belfast Penny Journal*, 1 (1845), 93–4.

Wallace, Henry, *Christ the head over all things to the church. A sermon, preached at the opening of the General Synod of Ulster, at their annual meeting in Belfast, on the 25th June, 1839* (Belfast, 1839).

Warnock, William, *The nature and effect of simplicity and godly sincerity, as opposed to fleshy wisdom, in the character and conversation of a gospel minister, considered. A sermon preached at Lurgan June 30th 1767, before a General Synod of the Protestant dissenting ministers in Ulster* (Belfast, 1769).

Weir, John, *The Ulster awakening: its origins, progress and fruit. With notes of a tour of personal observation and inquiry* (London, 1860).

Wilson, Josias, *The death of Christ commemorated. A sermon, delivered at the celebration of the Lord's Supper in the Associate Presbyterian church, Drogheda* (Dublin, 1823).

—— *A charge and defence of Presbyterianism, delivered at the ordination of the Rev. Matthew McAuley, and the Rev. Samuel Bingham, the former to the pastoral charge of the Associate Presbyterian congregation of Cahans, County Monaghan, the latter, of Lisbellaw, County Fermanagh* (Drogheda, 1829).

Wilson, William, *The Christian's consolation in the hope set before him. A sermon, preached at Lurgan, before the General Synod of Ulster, on the second day of their last meeting* (Belfast, 1783).

2. Secondary Sources and Printed Collections of Documents

A. Published Works

Acheson, A. R., *A history of the Church of Ireland 1691–2001*, 2nd edn. (Dublin, 2002).

Adams, J. R. R., 'Reading societies in Ulster', *Ulster Folklife*, 26 (1980), 55–64.

Adams, J. R. R., *The printed word and the common man: popular culture in Ulster 1700–1900* (Belfast, 1987).

Agnew, Jean (ed.), *The Drennan-McTier letters*, 3 vols. (Dublin, 1998–9).

Akenson, D. H., *The Irish education experiment: the National System of Education in the nineteenth century* (London, 1970).

—— *God's peoples: covenant and land in South Africa, Israel and Ulster* (Ithaca, N. Y., 1992).

Akenson, D. H. and Crawford, W. H., *Local poets and social history: James Orr, bard of Ballycarry* (Belfast, 1977).

Allen, Robert, 'Henry Montgomery, 1788–1865', in H. A. Cronne, T. W. Moody, and D. B. Quinn (eds.), *Essays in British and Irish history* (London, 1949), ch. 14.

—— *James Seaton Reid: a centenary biography* (Belfast, 1951).

—— *The Presbyterian College Belfast 1853–1953* (Belfast, 1954).

—— *Three centuries of Christian witness, being the history of First Randalstown Presbyterian church* (Belfast, 1955).

Anon., 'Fairy annals of Ulster', *Ulster Journal of Archaeology*, 1st ser., 6 &7 (1858–9).

Aston, Nigel, *Christianity and revolutionary Europe c. 1750–1830* (Cambridge, 2002).

Bailie, W. D., *The Six Mile Water revival of 1625* (Belfast, 1976).

—— 'William Steele Dickson, D. D.', comprising *Bulletin of the Presbyterian Historical Society of Ireland*, 6 (1976).

—— (ed.), *History of the congregations of the Presbyterian Church in Ireland, 1610–1982* (Belfast, 1982).

—— 'The Rev. Robert Magill and his journal', *Bulletin of the Presbyterian Historical Society of Ireland*, 23 (1994), 1–8.

Bardon, Jonathan, *A history of Ulster*, new edn. (Belfast, 2001).

Barkley, J. M., 'The evidence of old Irish session books on the sacrament of the Lord's Supper', *Church Service Society Annual*, 22 (May 1952), 24–34.

—— *The Westminster formularies in Irish Presbyterianism* (Belfast, 1956).

—— *A short history of the Presbyterian Church in Ireland* (Belfast, 1959).

—— *The eldership in Irish Presbyterianism* (n.p., 1963).

—— *The worship of the Reformed church*, Ecumenical Studies in Worship, 25 (London, 1966).

—— 'The renaissance of public worship in the Church of Scotland, 1865–1905', in Derek Baker (ed.), *Renaissance and renewal in Christian history*, Studies in Church History, 14 (Oxford, 1977), 339–50.

—— *Blackmouth and dissenter* (Dundonald, 1991).

—— 'Marriage and the Presbyterian tradition', *Ulster Folklife*, 39 (1993), 29–40.

Bebbington, D. W., *Evangelicalism in modern Britain: a history from the 1730s to the 1980s*, rev. edn. (London, 1995).

—— 'Evangelical conversion, c. 1740–1850', *Scottish Bulletin of Evangelical Theology*, 18 (2000), 102–27.

—— *Holiness in nineteenth-century England* (Carlisle, 2000).

—— 'Revival and Enlightenment in eighteenth-century England', in Andrew Walker and Kristin Aune (eds.), *On revival: a critical examination* (Carlisle, 2003), ch. 5.

Beckett, J. C., *Protestant dissent in Ireland 1687–1780* (London, 1948).

Beckett, J. C., et al., *Belfast: the making of a city 1800–1914* (Belfast, 1988).

Bell, J. B. A., *A history of Clarksbridge and First Newtownhamilton Presbyterian churches* (Newry, 1969).

Bell, Muriel, 'Extracts from the diaries of Rev James Wilson, Presbyterian minister of Magherafelt from 1813–54', *Journal of the South Derry Historical Society*, 1 (1981/2), 109–15.

Bigger, F. J., 'Belfast folklore', *Ulster Journal of Archaeology*, 2nd ser., 3 (1897), 136.

—— 'Local folklore', *Proceedings of the Belfast Naturalist's Field Club*, 2nd ser., 3 (1892–3), 545–8.

—— *William Orr* (Dublin, 1906).

—— *Articles and sketches: biographical, historical and topographical*, eds. J. S. Crone and F. C. Bigger (Dublin, 1920).

Blair, S. A., *Kilraughts: a Kirk and people* (n.p., 1973).

—— *The big meeting-house: a history of First Presbyterian church, Ballymoney* (n.p., 1996).

Blethen, H. T. and Wood, Jr, C. W. (eds.), *Ulster and North America: transatlantic perspectives on the Scotch-Irish* (Tuscaloosa, Ala., 1997).

Boyd, R. H., *The prevailing word* (Belfast, 1953).

Bradley, J. E. and Muller, R. E., *Church history: an introduction to research, reference works and methods* (Grand Rapids, Mich., 1995).

Brooke, Christopher, et al., 'What is religious history?', in Juliet Gardiner (ed.), *What is history today?* (Basingstoke, 1988), ch. 5.

Brooke, Peter, *Ulster Presbyterianism: the historical perspective, 1610–1970*, 2nd edn. (Belfast, 1994).

Brown, C. G., 'The Sunday school movement in Scotland, 1780–1914', *Records of the Scottish Church History Society*, 21 (1981), 3–26.

—— 'The costs of pew renting: church management, church-going and social class in nineteenth century Glasgow', *Journal of Ecclesiastical History*, 38 (1987), 347–61.

—— *Religion and society in Scotland since 1707* (Edinburgh, 1997).

—— *The death of Christian Britain: understanding secularisation 1800–2000* (London, 2001)

Brown, John, *Second Presbyterian church Newtownards: a history of the congregation 1753–1953* (Newtownards, [1953]).

Brown, K. D., 'Life after death? A preliminary survey of the Irish Presbyterian ministry in the nineteenth century', *Irish Economic and Social History*, 22 (1995), 49–63.

Brown, S. J., *Thomas Chalmers and the godly commonwealth in Scotland* (Oxford, 1982).

—— 'Presbyterian communities, transatlantic visions and the Ulster revival of 1859', in J. P. Mackey (ed.), *The cultures of Europe: the Irish contribution* (Belfast, 1994), ch. 7.

—— *The national churches of England, Ireland, and Scotland 1801–46* (Oxford, 2001).

Brożyna, A. E., *Labour, love, and prayer: female piety in Ulster religious literature 1850–1914* (Belfast, 1999).

Bruce, Steve, *God save Ulster! The religion and politics of Paisleyism* (Oxford, 1986).

Buchanan, R. H., 'Calendar customs, part one: New Year's Day to Michaelmas', *Ulster Folklife*, 8 (1962), 15–34.

—— 'Calendar customs, part two: harvest to Christmas', *Ulster Folklife*, 9 (1963), 61–79.

Buckley, A. D., 'Beliefs in County Down folklore', in L. Proudfoot (ed.), *Down: history and society. Interdisciplinary essays on the history of an Irish county* (Dublin, 1997), ch. 20

Burke, Peter, *Popular culture in early modern Europe* (London, 1978).

Bushaway, Bob, *By rite: custom, ceremony and community in England 1700–1880* (London, 1982).

Camac, Thomas, 'The parish of Derrykeighan (County Antrim) for three centuries. Part 1', *Ulster Journal of Archaeology*, 2nd ser., 5 (1899), 147–61.

Cameron, N. M. de S., (org. ed.), *Dictionary of Scottish church history and theology* (Edinburgh, 1993).

[Campbell, A. A.], 'An autobiographical sketch of Andrew Craig, 1754–1833. Presbyterian minister of Lisburn', *Ulster Journal of Archaeology*, 2nd ser., 14 (1908), 10–15, 51–5.

Campbell, A. A., *Irish Presbyterian magazines, past and present. A bibliography* (Belfast, 1919).

Carson, J. T., *God's river in spate: the story of the religious awakening of Ulster in 1859*, 2nd edn. (Belfast, 1994).

Carwardine, Richard, *Transatlantic revivalism: popular evangelicalism in Britain and America, 1790–1865* (Westport, Conn., 1978).

Cashdollar, C. D., *A spiritual home: life in British and American Reformed congregations, 1830–1915* (University Park, Pa., 2000).

Connolly, S. J., *Religion and society in nineteenth century Ireland* (Dundalk, 1985).

—— 'Popular culture: patterns of change and adaptation', in idem., R. A. Houston, and R. J. Morris (eds.), *Conflict, identity and economic development: Ireland and Scotland, 1600–1939* (Preston, 1995), ch. 8.

—— (ed.), *The Oxford companion to Irish history* (Oxford, 1998).

—— *Priests and people in pre-Famine Ireland 1780–1845*, 2nd edn. (Dublin, 2001).

—— ' "The moving statue and the turtle dove": approaches to the history of Irish religion', *Irish Economic and Social History*, 31 (2004), 1–22.

Cooper-Foster, Jeanne, 'Ulster folklore', *Proceedings and Reports of the Belfast Natural History and Philosophical Society*, 2nd ser., 2 (1943–4), 148–59.

Cosgrove, Art (ed.), *Marriage in Ireland* (Dublin, 1985).

Craig, W. I., *Presbyterianism in Lisburn from the seventeenth century: First Lisburn Presbyterian church* (Belfast, 1961).

Crawford, M. J., *Seasons of grace: Colonial New England's revival tradition in its British context* (New York, 1991).

Crawford, W. H. and Brooke, Peter (eds.), *Problems of a growing city: Belfast, 1780–1870* (Belfast, 1973).

Crawford, W. H. and Foy, R. H. (eds.), *Townlands in Ulster: local history studies* (Belfast, 1998).

Crawford, W. H. and Trainor, Brian (eds.), *Aspects of Irish social history 1750–1850* (Belfast, 1969).

Cressy, David, *Bonfires and bells: national memory and the Protestant calendar in Elizabethan and Stuart England* (London, 1989).

—— *Birth, marriage and death: ritual, religion, and the life-cycle in Tudor and Stuart England* (Oxford, 1997).

Croskery, Thomas, 'The Rev. James Seaton Reid, D. D.', *Evangelical Witness*, 7 (1868).

—— 'Memoir of the Rev. Samuel Dill, of Donoughmore, Co. Donegal', *Evangelical Witness*, 7 & 8 (1869/70).

—— 'The Rev. James Elder, of Finvoy', *Evangelical Witness*, 9 (1870), 61–4.

Croskery, Thomas and Witherow, Thomas, *Life of the Rev. A. P. Goudy, D. D.* (Dublin, 1887).

Crozier, J. A., *The life of the Rev. Henry Montgomery, LL. D., Dunmurry, Belfast; with selections from his speeches and writings* (London, 1875).

Cunningham, Bernadette, and Kennedy, Maire (eds.), *The experience of reading: Irish historical perspectives* (Dublin, 1999).

Curtin, N. J., *The United Irishmen: popular politics in Ulster and Dublin, 1791–98* (Oxford, 1994).

Danaher, Kevin, *The year in Ireland: Irish calendar customs* (Dublin, 1972).

Davey, J. E., *The story of a hundred years* (Belfast, 1940).

Davies, Horton, *The worship of the English Puritans* (London, 1948).

—— *Worship and theology in England: from Watts and Wesley to Maurice, 1690–1850* (Princeton, 1961).

—— *Worship and theology in England: from Newman to Martineau, 1850–1900* (Princeton, 1962).

Dawson, Jane, 'Calvinism and the Gaidheatachd in Scotland', in A. D. M. Pettegree, Alistair Duke, and Gillian Lewis (eds.), *Calvinism in Europe 1540–1620* (Cambridge, 1994), ch. 12.

Day, Angélique, ' "Habits of the people": traditional life in Ireland, 1830–1840, as recorded in the Ordnance Survey Memoirs', *Ulster Folklife*, 30 (1984), 22–36.

Dickson, David, Keogh, Dáire, and Whelan, Kevin (eds.), *The United Irishmen: republicanism, radicalism and rebellion* (Dublin, 1993).

Dickson, J. N. I., 'Evangelical religion and Victorian women: the Belfast Female Mission, 1859–1903', *Journal of Ecclesiastical History*, 55 (2004), 700–25.

Dill, A. H., *et al.*, *A short history of the Presbyterian churches of Ballymoney, County Antrim* (Bradford, 1898).

Dill, J. R., *The Dill worthies*, 2nd edn. (Belfast, 1892).

Dix, E. R. McC., 'List of books, pamphlets, newspapers, etc. printed in Newry from 1764 to 1810', *Ulster Journal of Archaeology*, 2nd ser., 13 (1907), 170–3; 15 (1909), 184–5.

—— 'Ulster bibliography. Article VI. Downpatrick, Dungannon, and Hillsborough', *Ulster Journal of Archaeology*, 2nd ser., 8 (1901), 172–4.

Donaldson, John, *A historical and statistical account of the barony of Upper Fews in the county of Armagh 1838* (Dundalk, 1923).

Donat, J. G., 'Medicine and religion: on the physical and medical disorders that accompanied the Ulster revival of 1859', in W. F. Bynum, Roy Porter, and Michael Shepherd (eds.), *The anatomy of madness: essays in the history of psychiatry*, 3 vols. (London, 1988), iii. ch. 5.

Donnelly, J. S. and K. A. Miller (eds.), *Irish popular culture 1650–1850* (Dublin, 1998).

Dunlop, Eull (ed.), *The autobiography of the Rev. William Hamilton of Garvagh, Belfast and North America 1807–86* (Belfast, 1997).

—— *Buick's Ahoghill* (Maghera, 1987).

Fawcett, Arthur, *The Cambuslang revival: the Scottish evangelical revival of the eighteenth century* (London, 1971).

Ferguson, Samuel, *Brief biographical sketches of some Irish covenanting ministers who laboured during the latter half of the eighteenth century* (Londonderry, 1897).

Foster, R. F., *Modern Ireland, 1600–1972* (London, 1989).

—— 'Remembering 1798', in I. R. McBride (ed.), *History and memory in modern Ireland* (Cambridge, 2001), ch. 3.

Gailey, Alan, 'Edward L. Sloan's "The Years' Holidays" ', *Ulster Folklife*, 14 (1968), 51–9.

—— 'The Scots element in north Irish popular culture: some problems in the interpretation of an historical acculturation', *Ethnologia Europa*, 8 (1975), 2–22.

—— 'Sources for the historical study of Easter as a popular holiday in Ulster', *Ulster Folklife*, 26 (1980), 68–74.

—— 'Folk-life study and the Ordnance Survey Memoirs', in idem and Dáithí Ó hÓgáin (eds.), *Gold under furze: studies in folk tradition* (Dublin, 1983), 150–64.

Gammon, Vic, ' "Babylonian performances": the rise and suppression of popular church music, 1660–1870', in Eileen Yeo and Stephen Yeo (eds.), *Popular culture and class conflict 1590–1914: explorations in the history of labour and leisure* (Brighton, 1981), ch. 3.

Gibbon, Peter, *The origins of Ulster Unionism: the formation of popular Protestant politics in nineteenth century Ireland* (Manchester, 1975).

Gillespie, Raymond, *A devoted people: belief and religion in early-modern Ireland* (Manchester, 1997).

—— 'The reformed preacher: Irish Protestant preaching 1660–1700', in A. J. Fletcher and Raymond Gillespie (eds.), *Irish preaching 700–1700* (Dublin, 2001), 127–43.

Gordon, A. G., 'Congregational memoirs: Templepatrick', *The Disciple*, 2 & 3 (1882–3).

—— *Historical memorials of the First Presbyterian church of Belfast* (Belfast, 1887).

—— 'Rademon congregation: historical sketch', *The Disciple*, 3 (1883), 136–42.

Gray, John and McCann, Wesley (eds.), *An uncommon bookman: essays in memory of J. R. R. Adams* (Belfast, 1996)

Greaves, R. L., *God's other children: Protestant nonconformists and the emergence of denominational churches in Ireland, 1660–1700* (Stanford, 1997).

Green, I. M., *The Christian's ABC: catechisms and catechising in England, c. 1530–1740* (Oxford, 1996).

—— *Print and Protestantism in early modern England* (Oxford, 2000).

Griffin, Emma, 'Popular culture in industrialising England', *Historical Journal*, 45 (2002), 619–35.

Griffin, Patrick, *The people with no name: Ireland's Ulster Scots, America's Scots Irish, and the creation of the British Atlantic world, 1689–1764* (Princeton, N. J., 2001).

Haire, J. L. M., *et al.*, *Challenge and conflict: essays in Irish Presbyterian history and doctrine* (Belfast, 1981).

Hall, D. D., 'The uses of literacy in New England, 1600–1850', in W. L. Joyce, D. D. Hall, R. D. Brown, and J. R. Hench (eds.), *Printing and society in early America* (Worcester, Mass., 1983), 1–47.

—— *Worlds of wonder, days of judgement: popular religious belief in early New England* (Cambridge, Mass., 1989).

Hambrick-Stowe, Charles, *The practice of piety: Puritan devotional disciplines in seventeenth-century New England* (Chapel Hill, N. C., 1982).

—— *Charles G. Finney and the spirit of American evangelicalism* (Grand Rapids, Mich., 1996).

Hamilton, Thomas, *'Faithful unto death': a biographical sketch of the Rev. David Hamilton, Belfast* (Belfast, 1875).

—— (ed.), *Irish worthies; a series of original biographical sketches of eminent ministers and members of the Presbyterian Church in Ireland* (Belfast, 1875).

—— *History of the Irish Presbyterian Church* (Edinburgh, 1887).

Harris, Tim (ed.), *Popular culture in England, c. 1500–1850* (Basingstoke, 1995).

Harrison, Brian, 'Religion and recreation in Victorian England', *Past and Present*, 38 (1967), 98–125.

Hastings, H., *Memoir of the life and labours of the late Rev. Josias Wilson, London* (London, 1850).

Hazlett, W. I. P., 'Ebbs and flows of theology in Glasgow 1451–1843', in idem. (ed.), *Traditions of theology in Glasgow 1450–1990* (Edinburgh, 1993), ch. 1.

Hempton, David, *Religion and political culture in Great Britain and Ireland from the Glorious Revolution to the decline of empire* (Cambridge, 1996).

—— *The religion of the people: Methodism and popular religion in Britain, 1750–1900* (London, 1996).

Hempton, David, and Hill, Myrtle, 'Godliness and good citizenship: evangelical Protestantism and social control in Ulster, 1790–1850', *Soathar*, 13 (1988), 68–80.

—— *Evangelical Protestantism in Ulster society 1740–1890* (London, 1992).

Henderson, G. D., *Religious life in seventeenth-century Scotland* (Cambridge, 1937).

—— *The burning bush: studies in Scottish church history* (Edinburgh, 1957).

Henderson, Lizanne and Cowan, E. J., *Scottish fairy belief: a history* (East Linton, 2001).

Herbison, Ivan, 'A sense of place: landscape and locality in the work of the rhyming weavers', in Gerald Dawe and J. W. Foster (eds.), *The poet's place: Ulster literature and society. Essays in honour of John Hewitt, 1907–1987* (Belfast, 1991), ch. 5.

—— 'Presbyterianism, politics and poetry in nineteenth-century Ulster: aspects of an Ulster Scots literary tradition', *Bulletin of the Presbyterian Historical Society of Ireland*, 25 (1996), 1–21.

—— ' "The rest is silence": some remarks on the disappearance of Ulster Scots poetry', in John Erskine and Gordon Lucy (eds.), *Cultural traditions in Northern Ireland: varieties of Scottishness—exploring the Ulster-Scottish connection* (Antrim, 1997), ch. 5.

Herlihy, Kevin (ed.), *The Irish dissenting tradition 1650–1750* (Dublin, 1995).

—— *The religion of Irish dissent 1650–1800* (Dublin, 1996).

—— *The politics of Irish dissent 1650–1800* (Dublin, 1997).

—— *Propagating the word of Irish dissent 1650–1800* (Dublin, 1998).

Hewitt, John, *Rhyming weavers and other country poets of Antrim and Down* (Belfast, 1974).

Hill, Myrtle, 'Ulster awakened: the '59 revival reconsidered', *Journal of Ecclesiastical History*, 41 (1990), 443–62.

—— 'Women in the Irish Protestant foreign missions c. 1873–1914: representations and motivations', in P. N. Holtrop and H. McLeod (eds.), *Missions and missionaries*, Studies in Church History, Subsidia, 13 (Woodbridge, 2000), 170–85.

—— *The time of the end: Millenarian beliefs in Ulster* (Belfast, 2001).

Hillis, P. L. M., 'Church and society in Aberdeen and Glasgow, c. 1800–c. 2000', *Journal of Ecclesiastical History*, 53 (2002), 707–34.

Hindmarsh, D. B., *John Newton and the English evangelical tradition between the conversions of Wesley and Wilberforce* (Oxford, 1996).

Hirst, Catherine, *Religion, politics and violence in nineteenth-century Belfast: the Pound and Sandy Row* (Dublin, 2002).

Holmes, A. R., 'Nineteenth-century Ulster Presbyterian perspectives on the 1798 rebellion', in J. Augusteijn, Mary Ann Lyons, and D. McMahon (eds.), *Irish history: a research yearbook, 2* (Dublin, 2003), 43–52.

—— 'Community and discipline in Ulster Presbyterianism, 1770–1840', in Kate Cooper and Jeremy Gregory (eds.), *Retribution, repentance and reconciliation*, Studies in Church History, 40 (Woodbridge, 2004), 266–77.

—— 'Millennialism and the interpretation of prophecy in Ulster Presbyterianism, 1790–1850', in C. Gribben and T. C. F. Stunt (eds.), *Prisoners of hope? Aspects of evangelical millennialism in Scotland and Ireland, 1800–1880* (Carlisle, 2005), ch. 7.

—— 'Tradition and enlightenment: conversion and assurance of salvation in Ulster Presbyterianism, 1700–1859', in M. Brown, C. I. McGrath, and T. P. Power (eds.), *Converts and conversions in Ireland, 1650–1850* (Dublin, 2005), ch. 6.

—— 'The experience and understanding of religious revival in Ulster Presbyterianism, c. 1800 to 1930', *Irish Historical Studies*, 34 (2005), 361–85.

—— 'The uses and interpretation of prophecy in Irish Presbyterianism, 1850–1930', in Crawford Gribben and A. R. Holmes (eds.), *Protestant millennialism, evangelicalism, and Irish society, 1790–2005* (Basingstoke, 2006), ch. 7.

—— 'The shaping of Irish Presbyterian attitudes to mission, 1790–1840', *Journal of Ecclesiastical History* (forthcoming, 2006).

Holmes, Janice, 'The "world turned upside down": women in the Ulster revival of 1859', in eadem and Diane Urquhart (eds.), *Coming into the light: the work, politics and religion of women in Ulster 1840–1940* (Belfast, 1994), 126–53.

Holmes, R. F. G., *Henry Cooke* (Belfast, 1981).

—— 'Ulster Presbyterianism and Irish Nationalism', in Stuart Mews (ed.), *Religion and national identity*, Studies in Church History, 18 (Oxford, 1982), 535–48.

—— *Our Irish Presbyterian heritage* (Belfast, 1985).

—— 'The 1859 revival reconsidered', introduction to J. T. Carson, *God's river in spate: the story of the religious awakening in Ulster in 1859*, 2nd edn. (Belfast, 1994), pp. i–xvii.

—— *The Presbyterian Church in Ireland: a popular history* (Dublin, 2000).

Holmes, R. F. G. and Knox, R. B. (eds.), *The General Assembly of the Presbyterian Church in Ireland 1840–1990: a celebration of Irish Presbyterian witness during a century and a half* (Coleraine, 1990).

Houlbrooke, Ralph, 'The Puritan deathbed, c. 1560–c. 1660', in Christopher Durston and Jacqueline Eales (eds.), *The culture of English Puritanism, 1560–1700* (Basingstoke, 1996), ch. 4.

Hutchinson, Matthew, *The Reformed Presbyterian Church in Scotland: its origin and history 1680–1876* (Paisley, 1893).

Hutton, Ronald, 'The English Reformation and the evidence of folklore', *Past and Present*, 148 (1995), 89–116.

Jalland, Pat, *Death in the Victorian family* (Oxford, 1996).

Jeffrey, K. S., *When the Lord walked the land: the 1858–62 revival in the north east of Scotland* (Carlisle, 2002).

Jenkins, R. P., 'Witches and fairies: supernatural aggression and deviance among the Irish peasantry', *Ulster Folklife*, 23 (1977), 33–56.

Johnson, David, *Music and society in lowland Scotland in the eighteenth century* (London, 1972).

De Jong, J. A., *As the waters cover the sea: millennial expectations and the rise of Anglo-American missions 1640–1810* (Kampen, 1970).

Kennedy, David, 'Robert Park's account of schools in Ballymoney parish, 1825', *Irish Historical Studies*, 6 (1948), 23–43.

Kennedy, Liam and Ollerenshaw, Philip (eds.), *An economic history of Ulster, 1820–1939* (Manchester, 1985).

Kennedy, T. D., 'William Leechman, pulpit eloquence and the Glasgow Enlightenment', in Andrew Hook and R. B. Sher (eds.), *The Glasgow Enlightenment* (East Linton, 1995), ch. 3.

Kenny, James, *As the crow flies over rough terrain; incorporating the diary 1827/8 and more of a divine* (Newtownabbey, 1988).

Kernohan, J. W., *The parishes of Kilrea and Tamlaght O'Crilly. A sketch of their history with an account of Boveedy congregation* (Coleraine, 1912).

—— *The county of Londonderry in three centuries, with notices of the Ironmongers' estate* (Belfast, 1921).

—— *Rosemary Street Presbyterian Church. A record of the last 200 years* (Belfast, 1923).

Kidd, Colin, 'Scotland's invisible Enlightenment: subscription and heterodoxy in the eighteenth century Kirk', *Records of the Scottish Church History Society*, 30 (2000), 28–59.

—— 'Conditional Britons: the Scots covenanting tradition and the eighteenth-century British state', *English Historical Review*, 117 (2002), 1147–76.

Killen, W. D., *Memoir of John Edgar, D. D., LL. D.* (Belfast, 1867).

—— *The ecclesiastical history of Ireland*, 2 vols. (London, 1875).

—— *History of the congregations of the Presbyterian Church in Ireland* (Belfast, 1886).

—— *Reminiscences of a long life* (London, 1901).

Kilpatrick, Thomas, *Millisle and Ballycopeland Presbyterian church: a short history* (Newtownards, 1934).

Kilroy, Phil, *Protestant dissent and controversy in Ireland 1660–1714* (Cork, 1994).

Knight, Frances, *The nineteenth-century church and English society* (Cambridge, 1995).

Knight, R. I., *Tullylish Presbyterian church 1670–1970* (Banbridge, 1970).

Lachman, D. C., *The Marrow controversy 1718–1723: an historical and theological analysis* (Edinburgh, 1988).

Landsman, Ned, 'Evangelists and their hearers: popular interpretation of revivalist preaching in eighteenth-century Scotland', *Journal of British Studies*, 28 (1989), 120–49.

——— 'Presbyterians and provincial society: the evangelical enlightenment in the west of Scotland, 1740–1775', in John Dwyer and R. B. Sher (eds.), *Sociability and society in eighteenth century Scotland* (Edinburgh, 1991), 194–209.

Latimer, W. T., 'The old session book of Templepatrick Presbyterian church', *Journal of the Royal Society of Antiquarians of Ireland*, 25 (1895) and 31 (1901).

——— 'The old session book of the Presbyterian congregation of Dundonald, Co. Down', *Ulster Journal of Archaeology*, 2nd ser., 3 & 4 (1897).

——— *Ulster biographies, relating chiefly to the rebellion of 1798* (Belfast, 1897).

——— *A history of the Irish Presbyterians*, 2nd edn. (Belfast, 1902).

Lecky, A. G., *In the days of the Laggan Presbytery* (Belfast, 1908).

——— *The Laggan and its Presbyterianism* (Belfast, 1905).

Leith, J. H., 'Calvin's doctrine of the proclamation of the word and its significance for today', in Timothy George (ed.), *John Calvin and the church: a prism of reform* (Louisville, Ky., 1990), 206–29.

Leneman, Leah, '"Prophaning" the Lord's Day: Sabbath breach in early modern Scotland', *History*, 74 (1989), 217–31.

Leneman, Leah and Mitchison, Rosalind, 'Acquiescence in and defiance of church discipline in early modern Scotland', *Records of the Scottish Church History Society*, 25 (1993), 19–39.

Loughridge, Adam, *The Covenanters in Ireland* (Belfast, 1984).

——— *The Covenanters in Cullybackey 1789–1989* (Rathfriland, 1989).

Lovegrove, D. W. (ed.), *The emancipation of the laity in evangelical Protestantism* (London, 2002).

Lowry, J. W. S., *Historical account of the Lissara Presbyterian church, Crossgar, containing a biographical sketch of each minister from its origin to the present* (Belfast, 1883).

Lunney, Linde, 'Attitudes to life and death in the poetry of James Orr, an eighteenth century Ulster weaver', *Ulster Folklife*, 31 (1985), 1–12.

——— 'Knowledge and enlightenment: attitudes to education in early nineteenth-century Ulster', in Mary Daly and David Dickson (eds.), *The origins of popular literacy in Ireland: language change and educational development 1700–1920* (Dublin, 1990), 97–112.

McAllister, Nuala, 'Contradiction and diversity: the musical life of Derry in the 1830 decade', in Gerard O'Brien (ed.), *Derry and Londonderry: history and society. Interdisciplinary essays on the history of an Irish county* (Dublin, 1999), ch. 18.

McBride, I. R., ' "The school of virtue": Francis Hutcheson, Irish Presbyterians and the Scottish Enlightenment', in D. G. Boyce, Robert Eccleshall, and Vincent Geoghegan (eds.), *Political thought in Ireland since the seventeenth century* (London, 1993), ch. 3.

—— 'Presbyterians in the penal era', *Bullán*, 1 (1994), 73–86.

—— *Scripture politics: Ulster Presbyterians and Irish radicalism in the late eighteenth century* (Oxford, 1998).

—— 'Reclaiming the rebellion: 1798 in 1998', *Irish Historical Studies*, 31 (1999), 395–410.

McCafferty, W. H., 'The psalmody of the Old Congregation in Belfast, 1760–1840', *Transactions of the Unitarian Historical Society*, 7 (1939), 50–63.

McCaughan, A. A., *Heath, hearth and heart: the story of Dunboe and the meeting-house at Articlave* (Coleraine, 1988).

McClelland, Aiken, 'Thomas Ledlie Birch, United Irishman', *Proceedings and Reports of the Belfast Natural History and Philosophy Society*, 2nd ser., 7 (1965), 24–35.

—— 'The early history of Brown Street primary school', *Ulster Folklife*, 17 (1971), 52–60.

McConnell, James and McConnell, S. J., (eds.), *Fasti of the Irish Presbyterian Church in Ireland* (Belfast, 1951).

McCreery, Alexander, *The Presbyterian ministers of Killyleagh: a notice of their lives and times* (Belfast, 1875).

McCrie, C. G., *The public worship of Presbyterian Scotland historically treated* (Edinburgh, 1892).

McIntosh, J. R., *Church and theology in enlightenment Scotland: the Popular Party, 1740–1800* (East Linton, 1998).

McIvor, J. A., *Popular education in the Irish Presbyterian Church* (Dublin, 1969).

McKean, E. J., 'Blinking or ill-wishing', *Report and Proceeding of the Belfast Natural History and Philosophical Society* (1903–4), 70–3.

McKerrow, John, *History of the Secession church*, rev. edn. (Edinburgh, 1847).

McKinney, C. W., *Killinchy: a brief history of Christianity in the district, with special reference to Presbyterianism* (n.p., n.d.).

McKinney, W. F., 'Old session books of Carnmoney, Co. Antrim', *Ulster Journal of Archaeology*, 2nd ser., 6 (1900), 6–11.

McLeod, Hugh, *Religion and the people of western Europe 1789–1989*, 2nd edn. (Oxford, 1997).

—— *Secularisation in western Europe, 1848–1914* (Basingstoke, 2000).

McMinn, J. R. B., 'Presbyterianism and politics in Ulster, 1871–1906', *Studia Hibernica*, 21 (1981), 127–46.

Madden, R. R., *The United Irishmen, their lives and times*, 4 vols., 2nd edn. (Dublin, 1858–60).

—— *Antrim and Down in 98* (London, n.d.).

Malcolm, Elizabeth, *'Ireland sober, Ireland free': drink and temperance in nineteenth century Ireland* (Dublin, 1986).

Mark, James, *First Dunboe: an historical sketch* (Coleraine, 1915).

Martin, Mary, *Magherally Presbyterian church 1656–1982* (Banbridge, 1982).

Meek, Donald, 'God and Gaelic: the Highland churches and Gaelic cultural identity', in Gordon McCoy and Maolcholaim Scott (eds.), *Gaelic identities: aithne na nGael* (Belfast, 2000), 28–47.

Miller, D. W., 'Presbyterianism and "modernization" in Ulster', *Past and Present*, 80 (1978), 66–90.

—— *Queen's rebels: Ulster Loyalism in historical perspective* (Dublin, 1978).

—— 'Irish Presbyterians and the great famine', in Jacqueline Hill and Colm Lennon (eds.), *Luxury and austerity*, Historical Studies, 21 (Dublin, 1999), ch. 10.

—— 'Irish Christianity and revolution', in Jim Smyth (ed.), *Revolution, counter revolution and Union: Ireland in the 1790s* (Cambridge, 2000), ch. 11.

—— 'Did Ulster Presbyterians have a devotional revolution?', in J. H. Murphy (ed.), *Evangelicals and Catholics in nineteenth-century Ireland* (Dublin, 2005), 38–54.

—— 'Religious commotions in the Scottish diaspora: a transatlantic perspective on "evangelicalism" in a mainline denomination', in M. G. Spencer and D. A. Wilson (eds.), *Ulster Presbyterians in the Atlantic World: religion, politics and identity* (Dublin, 2006), ch. 1.

Millin, S. S., *History of the Second Congregation of Protestant dissenters in Belfast 1708–1896* (Belfast, 1900).

Milne, A. A., *Communion tokens of the Presbyterian churches in Ireland* (Glasgow, 1920).

Mitchison, Rosalind and Leneman, Leah, *Sexuality and social control: Scotland 1660–1780* (Oxford, 1989).

—— *Sin in the city: sexuality and social control in urban Scotland 1660–1780* (Edinburgh, 1998).

Montgomery, Henry, 'Outlines of the history of Presbyterianism in Ireland', *Irish Unitarian Magazine, and Bible Christian*, 1 & 2 (1847).

Morgan, Valerie and Macafee, William, 'Irish population in the pre-Famine period: evidence from County Antrim', *Economic History Review*, 37 (1984), 182–96.

Morrison, R. G. A., 'A household of faith': a historical survey of the First Rathfriland Presbyterian congregation (Rathfriland, 1962).

Muir, Edward, Ritual in early modern Europe (Cambridge, 1997).

Mullin, J. E., The Kirk of Ballywillan since the Scottish settlement (Belfast, 1961).

—— New Row. The history of New Row Presbyterian church, Coleraine, 1727–1977 (Antrim, 1976).

Mullin, T. H., The Kirk and lands of Convoy since the Scottish settlement (Belfast, 1960).

—— Aghadowey. A parish and its linen industry (Belfast, 1972).

Nesbitt, David, Full circle: a story of Ballybay Presbyterians (Monaghan, 1999).

Noll, M. A., 'Revival, Enlightenment, civic humanism, and the evolution of Calvinism in Scotland and America, 1735–1843', in G. A. Rawlyk and M. A. Noll (eds.), Amazing grace: evangelicalism in Australia, Britain, Canada, and the United States (Grand Rapids, Mich., 1993), ch. 3.

—— America's God: from Jonathan Edwards to Abraham Lincoln (New York, 2002).

—— The rise of evangelicalism: the age of Edwards, Whitefield and the Wesleys (Leicester, 2004).

Noll, M. A., Bebbington, D. W., and Rawlyk, G. A. (eds.), Evangelicalism: comparative studies of popular Protestantism in North America, the British Isles, and beyond, 1700–1990 (Oxford, 1994).

O Cíosáin, Niall, Print and popular culture in Ireland, 1750–1850 (Basingstoke, 1997).

O'Dowd, Mary, A history of women in Ireland, 1500–1800 (Harlow, 2005).

O'Raifeartaigh, T., 'Mixed education and the Synod of Ulster, 1831–40', Irish Historical Studies, 9 (1955), 280–99.

Obelkevich, James, Religion and rural society: South Lindsey 1825–1875 (Oxford, 1976).

—— 'Music and religion in the nineteenth century', in idem, Lyndal Roper, and Raphael Samuel (eds.), Disciplines of faith: studies in religion, politics and patriarchy (London, 1987), ch. 35.

Ordnance Survey Memoirs of Ireland, 40 vols., (eds.), Angélique Day, Patrick McWilliams, Nóirín Dobson, Lisa English (Belfast, 1990–8).

Orr, S. L. and Haslett, Alex, Historical sketches of Ballyalbany Presbyterian church (Belfast, n.d.).

Orr Macdonald, L. A., A unique and glorious mission: women and Presbyterianism in Scotland 1830–1930 (Edinburgh, 2000).

Parker, Charles, 'The moral agency and moral autonomy of church folk in the Dutch Reformed church of Delft, 1580–1620', *Journal of Ecclesiastical History*, 48 (1997), 44–70.

Patrick, Millar, *Four centuries of Scottish psalmody* (Oxford, 1949).

Patton, W. D., (ed.), *Ebb and flow: essays in church history in honour of R. Finlay G. Holmes* (Belfast, 2002).

Porter, Classon, 'Congregational memoirs: Ballycarry (or Broadisland) congregation', *Christian Unitarian*, 2 (1863).

—— 'Congregational memoirs: Cairncastle', *Christian Unitarian*, 4 (1865).

—— 'Congregational memoirs: Glenarm', *Christian Unitarian*, 5 (1866/7).

—— *Irish Presbyterian biographical sketches* (Belfast, 1883).

—— *Irish regium donum and ministerial maintenance* (Belfast, 1884).

—— *Congregational memoirs. Old Presbyterian congregation of Larne and Kilwaughter* (Larne, 1929).

Porter, J. L., *The life and times of Henry Cooke, D. D., LL. D.* (Belfast, 1875).

Prenter, Samuel, *Life and labours of the Rev. William Johnston, D. D.* (London, 1895).

PRONI, *Guide to church records: an Irish genealogical resource* (Belfast, 1994).

Rack, H. D., 'Evangelical endings: deathbeds in evangelical biography', *Bulletin of the John Rylands University Library of Manchester*, 74 (1992), 39–56.

Reid, J. S., *History of the Presbyterian Church in Ireland*, ed. W. D. Killen, 3 vols., 2nd edn. (Belfast, 1867).

Robinson, P. S., 'Harvest, Halloween, and Hogmanay: acculturation in some calendar customs of the Ulster Scots', in Jack Santino (ed.), *Halloween and other festivals of death and life* (Knoxville, Tenn., 1994), 3–23.

Rodgers, R. J., 'Vision unrealised: the Presbyterian mission to Irish Roman Catholics in the nineteenth century', *Bulletin of the Presbyterian Historical Society of Ireland*, 20 (1991), 12–31.

Roxborough, K. B. E., *Thomas Gillespie and the origins of the Relief Church in 18th century Scotland* (Berne, 1999).

Rugg, Julie, 'From reason to regulation: 1760–1850', in P. C. Rupp and Clare Gittings (eds.), *Death in England: an illustrated history* (Manchester, 1999), ch. 8.

Rutherford, J. C., *The life and times of the Rev. John Orr, M. A., Portaferry* (Belfast, 1912).

Rutherford, John, *Cumber Presbyterian church and parish* (Londonderry, 1939).

—— *Donagheady Presbyterian churches and parish* (Belfast, 1953).

Rutman, D. B., 'Assessing the little communities of early America', *William and Mary Quarterly*, 3rd ser., 43 (1986), 163–78.

Ryken, P. G., *Thomas Boston as preacher of the fourfold state* (Carlisle, 1999).

Schmidt, L. E., *Hearing things: religion, illusion and the American Enlightenment* (Princeton, 2000).
—— *Holy fairs: Scotland and the making of American revivalism*, 2nd edn. (Grand Rapids, Mich., 2001).
Scott, A. R., *The Ulster revival of 1859* (unpublished Ph. D. thesis, Trinity College Dublin, 1962; reprinted, Belfast, 1994).
Sefton, Henry, 'Revolution to Disruption', in Duncan Forrester and Douglas Murray (eds.), *Studies in the history of worship in Scotland* (Edinburgh, 1984), ch. 5.
Sharpe, James, 'Popular culture in the early modern West', in Michael Bentley (ed.), *Companion to historiography* (London, 1997), ch. 17.
Shaw, William, *Cullybackey: the story of an Ulster village* (Edinburgh, 1913).
Sheils, W. J., and Wood, Diana (eds.), *The churches, Ireland and the Irish*, Studies in Church History, 25 (Oxford, 1989).
Sher, R. B., *Church and university in the Scottish Enlightenment: the Moderate Literati of Edinburgh* (Edinburgh, 1985).
—— 'Witherspoon's *Dominion of providence* and the Scottish jeremiad tradition', in idem and J. R. Smitten (eds.), *Scotland and America in the age of the Enlightenment* (Edinburgh, 1990), ch. 2.
Sibbett, R. M., *For Christ and Crown: the story of a mission* (Belfast, 1926).
Simpson, Jonathan, *Annals of my life, labours and travels* (Belfast, 1895).
Smith, W. S., *Historical gleanings in Antrim and neighbourhood* (Belfast, 1888).
—— 'The hand-bell of Donegore meeting-house', *Ulster Journal of Archaeology*, 2nd ser., 2 (1896), 185–7.
—— 'Presbyterian hand-bells', *Ulster Journal of Archaeology*, 2nd ser., 4 (1898), 133–7.
Spurr, John, *English Puritanism, 1603–1689* (Basingstoke, 1998).
Stanley, Brian, 'The future in the past: eschatological vision in British and American Protestant missionary history', *Tyndale Bulletin*, 51 (2000), 101–20.
—— (ed.), *Christian missions and the Enlightenment* (Grand Rapids, Mich., 2001).
Steers, David, ' "An admirable finger directed by pure taste": Edward Bunting and Belfast's Second Presbyterian congregation', *Bulletin of the Presbyterian Historical Society of Ireland*, 25 (1996), 22–9.
Stevenson, John, *Two centuries of life in Down 1600–1800* (Belfast, 1920).
Stewart, A. T. Q., *The narrow ground: aspects of Ulster 1609–1969* (London, 1977).
Stewart, David, *The history and principles of the Presbyterian Church in Ireland* (Belfast, 1907).

Stewart, David, *The Seceders in Ireland with annals of their congregations* (Belfast, 1950).

Stout, H. S., *The divine dramatist: George Whitefield and the rise of modern evangelicalism* (Grand Rapids, Mich., 1991).

Strahan, W. G., *First Newry (Sandys Street) Presbyterian congregation: its history and relationships* (Newry, 1904).

Thomas, Keith, *Religion and the decline of magic* (London, 1971).

Thompson, D. M., *Denominationalism and dissent, 1795–1835: a question of identity* (London, 1985).

—— 'The Irish background to Thomas Campbell's "Declaration and Address" ', *Journal of the United Reformed Church History Society*, 5 (1985), 215–25.

Thompson, Jack (ed.), *Into all the world: a history of the overseas work of the Presbyterian Church in Ireland 1840–1990* (Belfast, 1990).

Todd, Margo, 'Profane pastimes and Reformed community: the persistence of popular festivities in early modern Scotland', *Journal of British History*, 39 (2000), 123–56.

—— *The culture of Protestantism in early modern Scotland* (New Haven, Conn., 2002).

Vickery, Amanda, 'Golden age to separate spheres? A review of the categories and chronology of English women's history', *Historical Journal*, 36 (1993), 383–414.

Walsh, John, 'Religious societies: Methodist and evangelical 1738–1800', in W. J. Sheils and Diana Wood (eds.), *Voluntary religion*, Studies in Church History, 22 (Oxford, 1986), 279–302.

Walsh, John, Haydon, Colin, and Taylor, Stephen (eds.), *The Church of England c. 1689–c. 1833: from toleration to Tractarianism* (Cambridge, 1993).

Ward, W. R., *The Protestant evangelical awakening* (Cambridge, 1992).

—— *Faith and faction* (London, 1993).

Watts, M. R., *The Dissenters*, 2 vols. (Oxford, 1978, 1995).

Webb, R. K., 'Rational piety', in Knud Haakonssen (ed.), *Enlightenment and religion: rational dissent in eighteenth-century Britain* (Cambridge, 1996), ch. 12.

Westerkamp, M. J., *Triumph of the laity: Scots-Irish piety and the Great Awakening 1625–1760* (New York, 1988).

Whelan, Kevin, *The tree of liberty: radicalism, Catholicism and the construction of Irish identity 1760–1830* (Cork, 1996).

Williams, Gary, 'Was evangelicalism created by the Enlightenment?', *Tyndale Bulletin*, 53 (2002), 283–312.

Williams, S. C., *Religious belief and popular culture in Southwark c. 1880–1939* (Oxford, 1999).

Wilson, D. A., *United Irishmen, United States: immigrant radicals in the early republic* (Dublin, 1998).

Wilson, Linda, *Constrained by zeal: female spirituality amongst Nonconformists 1825–1875* (Carlisle, 2000).

Witherow, Thomas, *Three prophets of our own: a lecture delivered before the Young Men's Christian Association, Maghera, on Wednesday evening, January 3, 1855* (Belfast, 1855).

—— *Historical and literary memorials of Presbyterianism in Ireland*, 2 vols. (Belfast, 1879–80).

Withrington, D. J., 'Non-church-going, c.1750–c.1850: a preliminary survey', *Records of the Scottish Church History Society*, 17 (1970), 99–113.

Woodburn, J. B., *The Ulster Scot: his history and religion* (London, 1914).

Wright, Frank, *Two lands on one soil: Ulster politics before Home Rule* (Dublin, 1996).

Wykes, D. L., ' "A good discourse, well explained in 35 minutes": Unitarians and preaching in the early nineteenth century', *Transactions of the Unitarian Historical Society*, 21 (1997), 173–90.

Young, B. W., 'Religious history and the eighteenth-century historian', *Historical Journal*, 43 (2000), 849–68.

Young, R. M., *Ulster in 98: episodes and anecdotes* (Belfast, 1893).

—— *Historical notices of old Belfast and its vicinity* (Belfast, 1896).

B. Unpublished Theses

Addley, W. P., 'A study of the birth and development of the overseas missions of the Presbyterian Church in Ireland up to 1910' (QUB Ph.D., 1994).

Barkley, J. M., 'A history of the ruling eldership in Irish Presbyterianism', 2 vols. (QUB MA, 1952).

Bishop, I. M., 'The education of Ulster students at Glasgow University during the eighteenth century' (QUB MA, 1987).

Brooke, Peter, 'Controversies in Ulster Presbyterianism, 1790–1836' (University of Cambridge Ph.D., 1980).

Brown, A. W. G., 'Irish Presbyterian theology in the early eighteenth century' (QUB Ph.D., 1977).

Browne, R. M., 'Kirk and community: Ulster Presbyterian society, 1640–1740' (QUB M.Phil., 1998).

Conway, K. P., 'The Presbyterian ministry of Ulster in the eighteenth and nineteenth centuries: a prosopographical study' (QUB Ph.D., 1996).

Crawford, R. G., 'A critical examination of nineteenth-century non-subscribing Presbyterian theology in Ireland', 2 vols. (QUB Ph.D., 1964).

Crawford, W. H., 'Economy and society in eighteenth-century Ulster' (QUB Ph.D., 1982).

Dickson, J. N. I., 'More than discourse: the sermons of evangelical Protestants in nineteenth century Ulster' (QUB Ph.D., 2000).

Gray, W. P., 'A social history of illegitimacy in Ireland from the late eighteenth to the early twentieth century' (QUB Ph.D., 2000).

Holmes, A. R. 'Ulster Presbyterian belief and practice, 1770 to 1840' (QUB Ph.D., 2002).

Huddleston, David, 'Religion and social class: church membership in Belfast, c. 1870–1930' (QUB M.Phil., 1998).

James, K. J., 'Aspects of Protestant culture and society in Mid-Antrim, 1857–67' (University of Edinburgh Ph.D., 2000).

Jennings, R. S., 'The origins of Ulster Presbyterian revivalism in the mid-nineteenth century' (QUB M.Th., 1985).

McCollum, R. L. W., 'John Paul and his contribution to the shaping of Presbyterianism in the 19th century' (QUB Ph.D., 1992).

McKee, W. J. H., 'A critical examination of the doctrine of assurance in revivalism, with particular reference to the revival in Ulster in 1859' (QUB Ph.D., 1988).

Nelson, J. W., 'The Belfast Presbyterians, 1670–1830: an analysis of their political and social interests' (QUB Ph.D., 1985).

Rodgers, R. J., 'James Carlile, 1784–1854' (QUB Ph.D., 1973).

Stewart, A. T. Q., 'The transformation of Presbyterianism radicalism in the north of Ireland, 1792–1825' (QUB MA, 1956).

Tosh, R. S., 'An examination of the origin and development of Irish Presbyterian worship' (QUB Ph.D., 1983).

Whytock, J. C., 'The history and development of Scottish theological education and training, Kirk and Secession (c. 1560–c. 1850)' (University of Wales Ph.D., 2001).

Index

fast days, 53, 54–5, 78–88, 180, 212
  congregational, 86–7
  presbytery, 79, 86
fellowship groups *see* Covenanters;
  religious societies
Fermanagh, County, 270, 312
Finney, Charles G., 49
Fisher, Edward, 36, 278
Fisher, John, 258
Flavel, John, 240, 245, 277, 281
Form of Process (1707), 169
fornication *see* sexual misconduct
free offer of the Gospel, 36–7, 128,
  131–2, 161–2
funerals, 233–4

Gamble, John, 109, 146, 150, 275,
  277–8
gambling, 173
General Assembly of the
  Presbyterian Church in Ireland,
  69, 84, 107, 123,
  124–5
  formation and principles, 2, 31,
  50, 124, 310–11
  State of Religion Committee, 311
  Women's Missionary Association,
  302
  see also Union of the Synods
General Evangelical Society (1787),
  41, 153
Glasgow, 67, 216
Glasgow, University of, 43, 136–7
Glenarm (GSU) Co. Antrim, 260
Glendermott (GSU) Co.
  Londonderry, 61, 71
ghosts, 235
Grange (GSU) Co. Antrim, 181
Gray, Revd Robert, 121
Greyabbey (GSU) Co. Down, 149
Guthrie, William, 277

Hall, D. D., 20–1, 27, 274
Halloween, 54, 55, 91–2, 96, 102
Hamilton, Revd David, 155, 180, 262
Hamilton, Revd George, 133
Hanna, Revd Samuel, 33, 39, 40, 43,
  47, 67, 118, 138, 155, 161, 191,
  275, 276
Hart, Robert, 116
harvest, 55, 79, 80, 89, 91–2, 102,
  175
hell, 159, 230, 242–3
Hempton, David, 38
Hempton, David, and Hill, Myrtle,
  11
Henry, Matthew, 178, 277, 281
Henry, Revd P. S., 186–7
Herdman, John, 100
Heron, Revd Thomas, 182
Heron, Revd William, 150
Hervey, James, 277, 278, 281
Hibernian Bible Society, 41, 42, 269,
  275
Hibernian Sunday School Society of
  Ireland, 270
Hill, Revd George, 161, 262
Hillsborough, Co. Down, 235
Hibernian Evangelical Magazine,
  282
historiography
  of popular religion and culture,
  18–23
  of Ulster Presbyterianism, 7–18
Holmes family, Coleraine, 177
Holmes, Revd John, 131
Holmes, R. F. G., 9–10
holy wells, 96
Holywood, Co. Down, 234, 303
Horner, Revd James, 33, 267
horse racing, 98, 177
Houston, Revd Thomas, 123–4,
  295–6